Research Methods in Personality and Social Psychology

REVIEW OF PERSONALITY AND SOCIAL PSYCHOLOGY

Editor

Margaret S. Clark, *Carnegie Mellon University*

Editorial Board

Research Methods in Personality and Social Psychology

Editors

CLYDE HENDRICK
MARGARET S. CLARK

11

REVIEW of PERSONALITY and SOCIAL PSYCHOLOGY

Published in cooperation with the Society for Personality and Social Psychology, Inc.

SAGE PUBLICATIONS
The International Professional Publishers
Newbury Park   London   New Delhi

For information address:

SAGE Publications, Inc.
2455 Teller Road
Newbury Park, California 91320

SAGE Publications Ltd.
6 Bonhill Street
London EC2A 4PU
United Kingdom

SAGE Publications India Pvt. Ltd.
M-32 Market
Greater Kailash I
New Delhi 110 048 India

Printed in the United States of America

International Standard Book Number: 0-8039-3648-6
0-8039-3649-4 (pbk.)

International Standard Series Number 0270-1987

Library of Congress Card Number 80-649712

SECOND PRINTING, 1991

CONTENTS

Editors' Introduction

RESEARCH METHODS IN
PERSONALITY AND SOCIAL PSYCHOLOGY

CLYDE HENDRICK
MARGARET S. CLARK

Clyde Hendrick is Professor of Psychology and Dean of the Graduate School at Texas Tech University. He was previously Chairperson of Psychology, University of Miami. His scholarly interests include close relationships, sex roles, and philosophy of science. He has served as Editor for *Personality and Social Psychology Bulletin* and as Acting Editor for *Journal of Personality and Social Psychology*.

Margaret S. Clark is Professor of Psychology at Carnegie Mellon University. She has investigated the norms that govern the giving and acceptance of benefits in different types of relationships and the role of emotion in social behavior. She has served as an Associate Editor for *Personality and Social Psychology Bulletin* and as a representative for Division 8 on the Council of Representatives of the American Psychological Association.

Research methods are critical for advances in substantive research in all disciplines. In the social and behavioral sciences, advances in substantive knowledge depend acutely on the quality and sophistication of available research methods. Methods change and evolve in ways similar in many respects to the ways content domains change and evolve. Research methods in personality and social psychology have improved dramatically in the past twenty years. Part of the advance undoubtedly is due to the growth in computing power. Twenty years ago, computer packages for multivariate analyses hardly existed. Today they are routine, and journal articles readily reflect that availability. The possibility of such analyses has broadened the vision of researchers with respect to research designs. It is now possible to gather data in complex, naturalistic settings and in laboratory settings in an abundance and variety undreamed of a generation ago.

EDITORS' NOTE: In addition to members of the Editorial Board who reviewed chapters, we are indebted to the following individuals for their reviews of one or more chapters: Norman H. Anderson, Leonard Bickman, Jasper Brenner, John T. Cacioppo, Harris Cooper, Michael D. Coovert, James H. Davis, Richard L. Gorsuch, Reid Hastie, Larry V. Hedges, Rick H. Hoyle, William Ickes, James Jaccard, David A. Kenny, Ariel Levi, George Levinger, Geoffrey Maruyama, John L. Michela, Richard Moreland, Miles Patterson, Glen Reeder, Norbert Schwarz, William Shadish, David Shapiro, Garold Stasser, and Seymour Sudman.

Despite the growth in methodological sophistication, there are only a few standard books summarizing recent advances. A few years ago, the Publications Committee for the Society for Personality and Social Psychology decided that a volume of the *Review* devoted to research methods would be timely. The present volume is the result of that decision.

The call for chapters for Volume 11 was widely advertised, and 45 proposals for chapters were received. They were evaluated by members of the Editorial Board, and 12 were selected for the volume. The primary criterion for selection was the probability of an outstanding chapter. Considerations for balanced coverage of areas was secondary. Nevertheless, Volume 11 presents a wide range of topics. It represents topics and design issues of current interest quite well. Many of the standard topics are omitted, such as the nuances of the laboratory experiment, survey research, and the like. However, sources describing such general topics are readily available. Instead, this volume is focused primarily on new methodological, procedural, and design techniques, most of which were unavailable to researchers a short time ago. In conjunction with a standard text, the volume should serve well as a methods text in graduate courses in personality and social psychology.

OVERVIEW OF THE CHAPTERS

The chapters divide almost evenly into two types. The first half of the volume describes specific research techniques or strategies, such as design of an interaction laboratory, psychophysiological methods, and use of reaction time as a measure. The second half is concerned with research designs and analyses. Topics include such items as meta-analysis, covariance structure modeling, and dyadic research designs. The last three chapters are concerned in one way or another with the classic distinction between idiographic and nomothetic approaches to research. These three chapters suggest that the field has advanced considerably in the ability to study specific individuals in a rigorous way. Although these chapters thus may be especially useful to students of personality, they also address central topics in social psychology (e.g., attribution theory) and applied problem areas (e.g., health psychology).

William Ickes has been a leader in social interaction research whose work has focused on methodological issues as well as on a range of substantive issues and phenomena. In Chapter 1, Ickes, Bissonnette, Garcia, and Stinson describe a paradigm for research on dyadic interaction that has evolved over the course of the past fifteen years. This paradigm is an observational method that can be used to study both the overt behavior and the covert thoughts and feelings of dyad members during a period of unstructured, naturally occurring interaction. Through its assessment of the actual and inferred thoughts and feelings of interaction partners, the paradigm permits the study of "naturalistic social cognition," including such phenomena as metaperspective taking, intersubjectivity, and empathic accuracy.

At the editors' request, Chapter 1 provides the most detailed description currently available of the methodology, research setting, and equipment used in the dyadic interaction paradigm. The physical layout of the laboratory space, the hardware and software requirements, and the procedures involved in the collection, coding, and analysis of data are carefully explained. In addition, some of the more novel and/or counterintuitive findings from this research program are briefly noted. The primary goal of the chapter is to provide other investigators with the information necessary to create their own laboratories for the study of ongoing dyadic interaction. Because the most recent version of the dyadic interaction paradigm is "state of the art," this chapter should be of interest to all students of social interaction.

Interest in social psychophysiology has grown rapidly during the past few years. Thus Chapter 2, by Blascovich and Kelsey, is timely. Of the several types of physiological measures, they focus on two of the most popular, electrodermal and cardiovascular responses. The chapter is developed around the concept of arousal, primarily as it has been used in social psychology. The approach is practically oriented, beginning with a brief overview of arousal, and followed by a detailed section on the measurement of arousal, as reflected in electrodermal and cardiovascular activity. A fine context for this material is then provided by a thorough discussion of modern psychophysiological theories of arousal. Another section details some of the specifics of making psychophysiological measurements. Appropriate use of such measures is also elaborated through four specific recommendations. Some possible drawbacks (e.g., cost, methodological problems) are given a fair hearing. This chapter provides an excellent introduction to some methods too infrequently used by personality and social psychologists. We hope the chapter will provide the basics for reluctant investigators who would not otherwise have crossed over this "methodological threshold."

Response latency has long been used as a measure by experimental psychologists. Its use by social psychologists to study social processes is of more recent origin. In Chapter 3, Fazio provides an introduction and a "practical guide" to the use of response latency in social psychological experiments. The chapter includes a basic section on research design and procedural issues involved in using response latencies. A variety of apparatus setups are possible, but computer-generated texts as stimuli and button presses for responses are most commonly used. Reaction time tends to be highly variable, and Fazio describes sensible solutions through subject instructions, practice trials, and filler trials. Practical issues such as the number of response options, speed versus accuracy, and differential responses across conditions are given careful attention. A major section is devoted to issues in data analysis, including skewed data, comparison of latency responses across conditions, and use of latencies as an individual difference measure. The concluding section deals with the conceptual uses of latency measures. Latency may be used to assess the spontaneous formation of a construct, as a measure of processing efficiency, and as a measure of associative strength.

This chapter provides the basic tools to allow other researchers to explore the possibility of using response latency in their research. Fazio certainly makes a compelling case for the usefulness of response latencies in answering conceptual questions about social processes.

In an attempt to make verbal reports more objective, researchers sometimes ask respondents for quantitative reports (how often, how much, how many) rather than affective or evaluative reports. However, Schwarz shows in Chapter 4 that frequency reports, especially for mundane behaviors, are prone to bias. His interesting chapter suggests that cognitive psychology may be useful in the practical matters of questionnaire construction. In studying frequency estimates, Schwarz notes that most research assumes that subjects "recall and count." However, much evidence is cited suggesting that subjects use a variety of inference and estimation strategies in answering recall questions, especially open-ended questions. Suppose the researcher provides a precise range of quantitative response alternatives—will that solve the problem? Unfortunately, no. Schwarz cites much work, including his own, that shows that the range of response alternatives provided is used as a frame of reference in estimating behavioral frequencies. If the frequency range is varied, the response varies. Further, respondents may then make different self-attributions based on their differing frequency responses. Schwarz concludes his chapter by noting that judgment principles discovered by cognitive psychology are very useful for design of questionnaire and interview protocols, leading, we hope, to better data in future research.

Computer simulation of physical processes is common in the natural sciences and engineering. Its use has been less frequent in the social sciences, although the situation is changing. Stasser presents a helpful introduction to computer simulations in Chapter 5. He focuses on simulation of interaction, but the principles would apply equally well to simulation of intrapsychic processes and macrosocial processes. In fact, Stasser makes clear that the versatility of simulation lies in the fact that the referent social system is relative to the theorist's interests. One may simulate an individual in some social situation, a dyad, or a larger group. Once the referent system is selected, the theorist must develop a conceptual model of the system. Generally, a conceptual model will consist of several integrated components, for example, a prediscussion information distribution, the group discussion process, individual choice, or collective choice of the group. The computer model is based, in turn, on the conceptual model. Computer models must be precise. In developing the simulation, loose links or inconsistencies in the conceptual model readily become apparent.

Stasser describes the anatomy of a computer model and illustrates modeling through a contrived (but effective) example. Attention is devoted to the interesting methodological controversy of whether a computer model should be construed as a research *method* (comparable to experimentation, survey research, or other methods) or as a *theory* to be tested, revised, and elaborated. Clearly, computer models seem to serve both purposes, depending on the specific problem and the attitude of the investigator. Stasser also includes a useful section on evaluating computer models, including problems of goodness of fit, a Turing test (Can an observer discriminate between computer simulation data and real social data?), and issues such as setting input parameters, program complexity, and sensitivity analysis. Computer simulation is no panacea, but it certainly expands the methodological options of social and personality psychologists. Stasser's contribution should promote wider use of this valuable tool.

Harris Cooper provides an excellent overview of meta-analysis in Chapter 6. He describes the historical context out of which meta-analysis developed and the rapid increase in frequency of literature reviews that use this technique for comparison and combination of results of multiple research reports. A major section describes the current state of meta-analysis procedures, including combining probabilities across studies, estimating effect sizes, and examining variance of effect sizes. Numerous unresolved issues (e.g., whether to use only published studies, identifying whether hypothesis tests are independent) are deftly discussed, as are emerging new issues. The chapter concludes with a more general discussion of issues involved in judging the quality of integrative research reviews. As one might expect from an author expert on issues of integrating research reviews, Cooper does a good job of summarizing, integrating, and presenting the story of meta-analysis for social researchers.

David Kenny has made several important contributions to experimental design. His creativity continues in Chapter 7. His particular concern is with dyadic research. This elegant chapter succinctly considers both single-partner and multiple-partner designs. The focus is on design, not data analysis, although numerous statistical concerns are discussed. The designs are explicated via an example of interruptions in conversations between persons. Four questions to be answered are posed: (a) Do men interrupt conversations more than women? (b) Is there partner reciprocity in interruption? (c) Do people vary in how much they interrupt or are interrupted? and (d) Do people differentially interrupt others (e.g., a disliked other more than a liked other person)? The chapter shows clearly how these and related questions may be answered by the various designs. Three kinds of single-partner designs are described: confederate (all subjects interact with a single confederate), nested (subgroups of subjects interact with different confederates), and standard (each subject interacts with one other subject). Consideration of multiple-partner designs includes ordinary (round-robin, block), special (dyad round-robin, dyad within-block, dyad between-block), and family designs (each subject bears some role relation or occupies some special status relative to each of the other subjects).

This chapter should be exceptionally useful to the student or psychologist who wants to do research on social interaction, but has been stymied by the complexities of the design required for such research. Kenny sorts out many of the complexities in an orderly way, and makes the designs accessible to the relevant audience. The chapter is an outstanding contribution.

Coovert, Penner, and MacCallum provide an introduction to covariance structure modeling (CSM) in Chapter 8. This statistical technique allows a researcher to assess a set of variable relationships, specifically whether an obtained set of relationships matches a hypothesized set of relationships. The hypothesized set of relationships may be called a *model*, and CSM can be used to evaluate relatively complex models. Any useful model has some variables that must make contact in a measurable way with the external world. However, other variables may be internal to the model. That is, some variables may be unobservable (latent), and may mediate relationships with other variables, including both observable and unobservable variables. If the model can be specified well enough in advance, CSM can evaluate both the measured and the latent relationships, something that the more common statistical techniques cannot do.

The authors present their case clearly, beginning with a simple example to explicate basic concepts. Several figures and a data appendix lead the reader through the concepts of CSM step by step. The mathematical representation of CSM is given at a conceptual level. The second half of the chapter deals with a number of practical issues in using CSM, including model identification, parameter estimation, and assessment of fit. Improper solutions, power, and alternatives to LISREL for computing programs are also discussed. This chapter provides a solid introduction to a difficult topic. The chapter deserves careful study; it will repay the effort for those who would like to try CSM.

Tanaka, Panter, Winborne, and Huba approach covariance structure modeling in a different way in Chapter 9. They use a different term, structural equation model (SEM). The basic purpose of their chapter is to motivate personality and social psychologists to consider SEM and perhaps give it a try. The chapter is designed in an interesting way, as a set of 20 questions and answers. The authors begin with a basic question—What is SEM?—and in the answer reveal that the ancient *t*-test is one simple type of SEM. Another item addresses the importance of models for theory building and testing, and further discussion shows how SEM fits this general approach, including both manifest and latent variables. A great variety of conceptual and practical issues are discussed in this delightful chapter. In conjunction with a previous chapter by Coovert et al., this chapter should give the reader a good general introduction to this topic.

During the past several years, several authors have devised methods suitable for research and data analysis on individual subjects. The final three chapters deal with such methods. Chapter 10, by Norman H. Anderson, is a summary of his many years of work. He designates his approach *personal design*. Much of his work has involved cognitive tasks, specifically how people integrate different kinds of information to yield a summary response. He has discovered that people often follow a simple cognitive algebra in integrating information. In the pursuit of this research program over the years, he has learned that research design may often work best at the level of the individual subject, because people differ in terms of values held for specific stimuli, and in the ways they integrate various types of information. The chapter illustrates Anderson's approach to measurement, called *functional measurement*. In this approach, measurement is derivative of the conceptual material with which one is dealing, in this case, cognitive processing of information. The derivation of stimulus values and the integration rule is illustrated in a simple example, followed by other examples from past research. Individual differences as well as similarities across subjects are illustrated quite well with the data. A number of sophisticated research considerations in personal design are discussed including issues of data analysis and presentation, various techniques in experimental procedure, and issues of experimental design. The chapter concludes with a brief consideration of how personal design may be used in the understanding of everyday life.

This substantial chapter makes a contribution to our understanding of how the individual person may be studied in a rigorous experimental situation, from the presentation of initial stimuli to final reduction of the data. It should be of value to researchers who desire to work at the individual level.

The chapter by Anderson focuses primarily on idiographic research within the framework of standard experimental designs. In contrast, Chapter 11, by John Michela, is concerned more with correlational studies, viewing them as essential to the full study of the natural world. The chapter deals with within-person correlational design and associated problems of analysis. The essential basis of within-person studies is the use of two or more variables measured repeatedly for every person in the sample. Given the repetition of measurement, it is possible to compute a correlation for each person separately across variables. In previous years, many social scientists were wary of such statistics. However, given current computing power and enhanced sophistication of multivariate techniques, more researchers are beginning to explore the possibilities of within-person correlations for addressing problems throughout personality and social psychology.

The chapter begins with a very useful orientation to within-person correlation design. The author develops a cube model that illustrates the relations among persons, variables, and occasions. A central section of the chapter deals with the technical issues and practical techniques of using within-person correlations, including topics such as concatenation of data, computer programming techniques, and significance testing and partitioning of variance. This section is detailed, though not excessively difficult. The author relies on SPSS-X, although other programming packages could be adapted and used as well. The last major section of the chapter deals with a variety of additional issues and applications. Topics include within-person factor analysis, empirical generation of taxonomic schemes, issues in interpreting within-person correlations, and the use of within-person correlations as measures. A brief appendix on the use of SPSS-X is provided. This chapter should serve as a useful introduction for researchers who are interested in pursuing within-person correlational design.

Chapter 12, by Jaccard and Dittus, is explicitly concerned with comparison of the idiographic and nomothetic perspectives on research methods. The chapter compares and contrasts three broad approaches, which may be named the strictly idiographic, the aggregate-nomothetic, and the normative-nomothetic approaches to design and data analysis. The chapter is highly informative in terms of some of the problems of inference that can occur at the nomothetic level compared to the stories that the data tell when examined at the idiographic level. Several examples are given, in table or graphic form, that show clearly how different conclusions will be drawn, depending on the level of analysis. Most of these examples are phrased in terms of correlational analysis, although the authors were explicit that the same conclusions would occur for other types of analysis. The authors were careful to point out that no one of the three approaches is necessarily better or worse than the others; it all depends on one's intent. However, many social-personality theorists hope to draw causal conclusions about the relationships among variables. When this desire is translated into the usual nomothetic approach, the conclusions may be erroneous, in that either the conclusions may be false for all specific individuals or, in the case where no relationship is found, there in fact may be relationships of different forms among subsets of the individuals in a sample. Thus the use of idiographic methods may supplement, complement, or supplant the nomothetic approach to research. The authors conclude the chapter with an example that combines the idiographic with the aggregate-nomothetic approach. This example makes clear that the three approaches have considerable value in the arduous task of conducting research and learning the truth about the social world.

In summary, this chapter is an excellent overview of some of the quandaries of data analysis and points toward a growing sophistication in recognizing the problems and developing solutions for them. This chapter should be of considerable use to all researchers who wish to do idiographic research.

CONCLUSION

We believe that the chapters in this volume provide a good overview of recent advances in methods of research in personality and social psychology. As editors, it has been our privilege to work with the authors in developing their chapters. We have learned much and have advanced our own methodological sophistication in the process. We hope the book will similarly benefit those who read it.

1

Implementing and Using
the Dyadic Interaction Paradigm

WILLIAM ICKES
VICTOR BISSONNETTE
STELLA GARCIA
LINDA L. STINSON

William Ickes is Professor of Psychology at the University of Texas at Arlington. He is the editor of *Compatible and Incompatible Relationships*, coeditor (with Eric S. Knowles) of *Personality, Roles, and Social Behavior*, and coeditor (with John H. Harvey and Robert F. Kidd) of the three-volume series *New Directions in Attribution Research*.

Victor Bissonnette is a doctoral candidate in experimental social psychology at the University of Texas at Arlington. His research interests include the social consequences of shyness and physical attractiveness. His interests in statistics and research methodology, coupled with an affinity for computer programming, have led him to develop or refine much of the software used in the dyadic interaction paradigm.

Stella Garcia is a doctoral candidate in experimental social psychology at the University of Texas at Arlington. Her recent theoretical interests have focused on the dynamic interactional approach to the study of personality and social behavior. Her primary research interest involves the application of the dyadic interaction paradigm to the study of empathic accuracy.

Linda L. Stinson holds a Ph.D. from the Institute of Philosophic Studies at the University of Dallas. Her dissertation concerned the topic of human emergence from the perspective of Alfred North Whitehead's process philosophy. She has recently completed a second dissertation, "Empathic Accuracy and Intersubjectivity in the Interactions of Male Friends Versus Male Strangers," for a Ph.D. in experimental social psychology.

Consider the following fictional narrative, something that might be described as a scientific fable:

> A philosopher of science, seeking to broaden his horizons, spent several weeks visiting psychology labs at major universities to learn how experimental social psychologists conduct their research. When one of his colleagues

AUTHORS' NOTE: We would like to thank Clyde Hendrick and the three outside reviewers for their comments on an earlier version of this chapter. Requests for reprints should be sent to William Ickes, Department of Psychology, University of Texas, Arlington, TX 76019.

later asked him what he had learned from the experience, he replied, "There were two things that struck me as being rather curious. First, although the researchers I talked to purported to be studying some aspect of *social* psychology, they typically used research paradigms in which individual subjects were tested alone, one at a time. Even in those cases in which a confederate was present, the subjects' behavior was so constrained by the task instructions or by the demands of the experimental script that they were not allowed to have anything like a genuine interaction with anyone, including the experimenter. Second, despite a lot of noise in their journal articles and grant proposals about the relevance of their research to *behavior*, the use of behavioral measures in studies conducted by social psychologists appears to be the exception rather than the rule. The most commonly-studied "behavior," as far as I can see, is the subjects' placement of pencil marks on research questionnaires."

Are these criticisms shortsighted? Unquestionably. Overly simplistic? Undeniably. Totally without merit? Unfortunately, no. The reason these criticisms are likely to irritate more serious students of social psychology is not that they are completely wrong and misguided, but that they are, to a substantial degree, annoyingly correct and "on target." There is more than a grain of truth in, and more that a little justification for, each of them.

As we all know, however, such criticisms are remarkably easy to make. And, unless they lead the critic to propose some constructive suggestions for solving the problems they identify, they can even be viewed as "cheap shots." The obvious challenge for critics of the admittedly imperfect, status quo methodologies that currently dominate social psychology is to propose better methodological solutions to the research problems that social psychologists commonly encounter. The appropriate goal, in other words, is to learn from the weaknesses of existing research paradigms and then apply this knowledge to the task of building better ones.

If we take seriously the challenge to build better research paradigms for the study of social psychology, what features should be incorporated into such a paradigm? This is a question the first author and his colleagues have been attempting to answer over the course of the last several years (see Ickes, 1982, 1983; Ickes & Robertson, 1984; Ickes, Robertson, Tooke & Teng, 1986; Ickes & Tooke, 1988). Because the list of desirable features continues to grow over time, the following list can in no way be regarded as definitive or complete. Instead, it is only the most recent of our attempts to specify features that we think should be included in a more optimal research paradigm for the study of personality, social cognition, and social behavior.

BUILDING A BETTER RESEARCH PARADIGM

Our "wish list" of the features that would characterize a better research paradigm for social psychology would include the following elements:

First, the paradigm should *not* suffer from either of the frequently encountered problems cited at the beginning of this chapter: (a) the use of single-subject procedures to study what is ostensibly "social" cognition or "social" behavior, and (b) the failure to collect relevant behavioral data. Instead, it should provide a context for the emergence of spontaneous, naturalistic interaction behavior on the part of two or more naive subjects. Such spontaneous, naturally occurring behavior should contrast sharply with the behavior observed in "fixed confederate" paradigms or in paradigms in which subjects are instructed to interact with the prior knowledge that their behavior during the interaction will be recorded and subsequently analyzed.

Second, as a corollary of the first requirement, the paradigm should permit all the behavioral data of interest to be recorded unobtrusively and thus circumvent the common problem of subjects behaving reactively in response to the knowledge that they are being observed. Third, the paradigm should be relatively free from the traditional sources of subject (awareness, self-presentation) bias, experimenter (expectancy) bias, or bias due to other demand characteristics. Fourth, the paradigm should yield results that are both internally and externally valid. Fifth, the paradigm should be ethically defensible and afford protection to the researcher as well as to the subjects.

Sixth, the paradigm should enable researchers to record and analyze a wide range of both (a) individual behaviors (e.g., body orientation, frequency of directed gazes) and (b) dyad- or group-level behaviors (e.g., interpersonal distance, frequency of mutual gazes). In addition, it ideally would enable the collection of data reflecting (c) the dyad or group members' own thoughts and feelings, (d) their inferences about the thoughts and feelings reported by their interaction partners, and (e) their posttest impressions of the interaction. Moreover, to ensure that interrater reliabilities are consistently high and the error of measurement consistently low, the measures in categories (a) through (d) should be multiple-act measures that represent the aggregation of the relevant responses over the entire interaction period.

Seventh, within the framework of the paradigm, researchers should be able to study the effects of independent variables that are either manipulated or systematically varied at two different levels of analysis: within dyads/groups and between dyads/groups. This feature of the paradigm is

important because it would enable the study of *em*
interaction, that is, behavioral and cognitive pheno
level of the dyad or group and that cannot be "reduc
the individual members.

Eighth, the paradigm should permit researchers to
of *naturalistic social cognition*. These aspects sho⟍ ⟋ only
person perception and attribution making, but also such genuinely *social*
cognitive phenomena as metaperspective taking, empathic accuracy, and
intersubjectivity.

Ninth, by permitting both social behavior and social cognition to be studied as they naturally occur, in the same "real-time" frame, the paradigm
should enable researchers to explore their empirical relations in a way that
facilitates a more integrated, holistic view of social interaction.

Tenth, the paradigm should be highly flexible in application. It should be
applicable to studies that are fully experimental, fully correlational, or that
combine the two approaches. Moreover, it should be applicable to both
structural and *external variable* studies of social interaction (Duncan, 1969;
Duncan & Fiske, 1977).

THE DYADIC INTERACTION PARADIGM

Before we are accused of being the unrealistic victims of our own wishful
thinking, we would like to note that a research paradigm currently exists that
incorporates all of the features we have just described. This research paradigm is the topic of the present chapter. Because it was designed for the
study of interaction in dyads rather than in larger groups, it is called the
dyadic interaction paradigm.

The dyadic interaction paradigm is an observational method that can be
used to study both the overt behavior and the covert thoughts and feelings of
dyad members during a period of unstructured interaction (Ickes, 1982,
1983; Ickes & Robertson, 1984; Ickes, Robertson, Tooke, & Teng, 1986;
Ickes & Tooke, 1988). Since its inception in 1975, the paradigm has consistently proved to be an effective method for studying the spontaneous, naturally occurring behavior of dyad members in a reliable and unobtrusive way.
In the most recent version of the paradigm, procedures have been added that
permit the actual thoughts and feelings of the dyad members to be assessed
in a manner that is similarly reliable and nonreactive.

Despite its relatively brief history, the dyadic interaction paradigm has
already been applied to a wide range of research topics. It has been used to

.e effects on social interaction of such personality variables as locus
ntrol (Rajecki, Ickes, & Tanford, 1981), Machiavellianism (Ickes, Reid-
.ead, & Patterson, 1986), self-monitoring (Ickes & Barnes, 1977), shyness
(Garcia, Stinson, Ickes, Bissonnette, & Briggs, 1989), and sex-role orientation (Ickes & Barnes, 1978; Ickes, Schermer, & Steeno, 1979; Lamke &
Bell, 1982). It has been used to study such cultural and role-relevant
phenomena as interracial interactions (Ickes, 1984), differences in the interactions of male friends and male strangers (Stinson, 1989), and in the interaction styles of firstborn versus last-born men and women (Ickes & Turner,
1983). It has been used to study the effect of the larger "social context" in
which initial dyadic interactions can take place (Ickes, 1984), and it has been
used to study how the course of such interactions can be determined by
preinteraction expectancies (Ickes, Patterson, Rajecki, & Tanford, 1982)
and social stereotypes (Ickes, 1984).

In more recent studies, the dyadic interaction paradigm has been
expanded to permit the study of both the overt behavior and the covert
thoughts and feelings of dyad members during a period of unstructured
interaction. With the addition of thought/feeling assessment procedures of
the type developed by researchers at Ohio State University (e.g. Brock,
1967; Cacioppo, Glass, & Merluzzi, 1979; Cacioppo, & Petty, 1981; Greenwald, 1968; Petty & Cacioppo, 1979), the paradigm can now address a wide
range of phenomena that fall under general heading of *naturalistic social
cognition*. The study of naturalistic social cognition is focused on the actual
thoughts and feelings experienced by individuals while they are engaged in
spontaneous, unstructured interaction.

In the first study using the expanded dyadic interaction paradigm, Ickes,
Robertson, Tooke, and Teng (1986) explored several aspects of naturalistic
social cognition. These included (a) thought/feeling correlates of the interactants' perceptions of the quality of the interaction and their liking for each
other, (b) thought/feeling correlates of the interactants' own traits and dispositions, (c) thought/feeling correlates of behavioral measures of interactional involvement, (d) variables moderating the relationship between covert
affect and overt behavior, and (e) individual difference correlates of
metaperspective taking (i.e., adoption of the partner's perspective) during
the interaction.

In two subsequent studies, Ickes, Tooke, Stinson, Baker, and Bissonnette
(1988) used the expanded dyadic interaction paradigm to explore the
phenomenon of *intersubjectivity* in the initial interactions of same-sex
(male-male and female-female) strangers. Defining dyadic intersubjectivity

as "the similarity in the thought-feeling content of two dyad members that develops as a consequence of their interaction," they identified distinctly different patterns of intersubjectivity in the male-male versus the female-female dyads. They also demonstrated that these patterns of intersubjectivity were indeed "emergent" consequences of the unique interactions occurring in the two dyad types.

In the most recent study of this series, Ickes, Stinson, Bissonnette, and Garcia (1989) extended the paradigm still further to explore the phenomenon of *empathic accuracy* in the initial interactions of mixed-sex (male-female) dyads. The results indicated that an important aspect of empathic accuracy—content accuracy—is best characterized as an "emergent" product of dyad-level social interaction processes. Although informational influences on empathic accuracy represented the most frequent and consistent findings, some significant motivational and emotional influences were observed as well. Content accuracy, for example, was affected by the degree to which the perceiver was interested in his or her interaction partner, as indexed by the percentage of partner-relevant thoughts and feelings.

The goal of the present chapter is to provide a detailed description of the expanded dyadic interaction paradigm and offer some practical advice regarding its implementation and use. Following a brief overview of the current version of the paradigm, we examine each aspect of the methodology in some detail. Among the specific issues we consider are (a) the physical setting and equipment required, (b) the measurement of static and dynamic interaction behaviors, (c) the measurement of actual and inferred thought/feeling entries, and (d) the reduction, integration, and analysis of the resulting data. Two custom software packages designed for use in the paradigm, DYAD DYNAMICS and COLLECT YOUR THOUGHTS, are also reviewed.

OVERVIEW OF THE DYADIC INTERACTION PARADIGM

Because the dyadic interaction paradigm is used to study a single short-term interaction in many separate dyads, it is most appropriately applied in what Kenny (1988) has called the *standard dyadic design*. In some of our studies, the subjects are preselected on the basis of relevant personality, sociodemographic, or relationship variables and are recruited by telephone to participate in dyads of predetermined composition (e.g., Ickes & Barnes, 1977, 1978; Ickes et al., 1979; Ickes & Turner, 1983). In other studies, two different sign-up sheets are used to schedule nonpreselected volunteer subjects, who are thus paired on an essentially random basis as the dyad members for a given session (e.g., Ickes, Robertson, Tooke, & Teng, 1986).[1]

Following the directions given on the telephone or on their respective sign-up sheets, the two subjects who are scheduled for a given session report to the appropriate waiting area(s) in the psychology building. After checking the operation of the video equipment, the experimenter collects the two subjects from their waiting area(s) and leads them to the observation room (see Figure 1.1, upper left). This room is furnished with a long couch (1) and an accompanying coffee table (2) that conceals an FM wireless microphone. A video camera focused on the area of the couch and coffee table is concealed in a darkened storage room (15) across a hallway from the observation room. This arrangement permits the dyad members' interaction to be recorded through the open doorways of the storage and observation rooms with minimal likelihood of the camera being detected.

Once they are inside the observation room, the subjects are asked to place any books or other belongings on the table (5), and to be seated on the couch (1). The experimenter then reaches for copies of the informed consent form from a box on one of the bookcases (6), but "discovers" that only one copy of the form is left. Explaining the need to get additional copies of the form, the experimenter leaves the observation room, promising to return "in a few minutes." At this point, a research assistant in the control room activates the video equipment (10) to begin videotaping. Exactly 6 minutes later, at the end of the observation period, the experimenter returns to the observation room and the videotaping is terminated.[2]

After probing for any evidence of suspicion, the experimenter conducts a partial debriefing. The subjects are told that they have been videotaped for the purpose of studying their naturally occurring interaction behavior. The experimenter describes the videotaping procedure, explains the methodological importance of not telling them about the taping in advance, and informs them that their written consent is required for the tape to be used as data. To assure the subjects that their rights to privacy have been protected, the experimenter explains that the videotape has not yet been reviewed or studied in any way. If either or both of the subjects exercise their right to have the tape erased immediately, instead of releasing it for use as data, the content of the interaction will remain their own private concern.

If consent is given, the subjects are seated in separate but identical cubicles (13 and 14), where they are each instructed to view a videotaped copy of the interaction. By stopping the videotape with a remote start/pause control at those points where they remember having had a specific thought or feeling, each subject makes a written time-logged listing of these *actual thought/feeling entries*. The subjects are then instructed to view the videotape a second time, during which the tape is stopped for them at each of those points at which their interaction partner reported a thought or feeling. The subjects' task during this pass through the tape is to infer the content of the partners' thoughts and feelings and provide a written, time-logged listings of these *inferred thought/feeling entries*. When both subjects have completed this task and filled out a short, posttest questionnaire, they are debriefed more completely and then thanked and released.

ESTABLISHING THE SOCIAL INTERACTION LAB

Physical Setting

Although the physical setting for the dyadic interaction paradigm can vary according to the space available, an arrangement that has worked well for us is depicted in Figure 1.1. This figure represents the major features of the UTA Social Interaction Lab, which contains (starting at upper left and moving clockwise) an observation room, a control room, two cubicles for the thought/feeling reporting, and a camera room from which dyad members' interactions are videotaped. Having already discussed the features of the observation room and camera room in our overview of the paradigm, we now consider the arrangement of the control room and the cubicles for the thought/feeling assessment.

The control room is used to house the video and audio equipment operated by the experimenter and a research assistant. Along one wall of the control room is the experimenter's control station. Here the experimenter can sit in front of a single table (10) that supports two identical videocassette recorders that are both connected (by means of a Y-adaptor) to the video camera in the storage room across the hall. Each VCR is also connected respectively to one of two 25-inch color TV monitors (11 and 12) that are oriented to face through one-way mirrors into identical test cubicles. Each test cubicle (13 and 14) is equipped with a "help button" that enables subjects to signal the experimenter (by means of a red light) that they need additional information or assistance of some other type. Each test cubicles also contains (a) a remote start/pause switch connected to the VCR and TV monitor system unique to that cubicle, and (b) a supply of "Thought/Feeling Coding Forms" (to be described below).

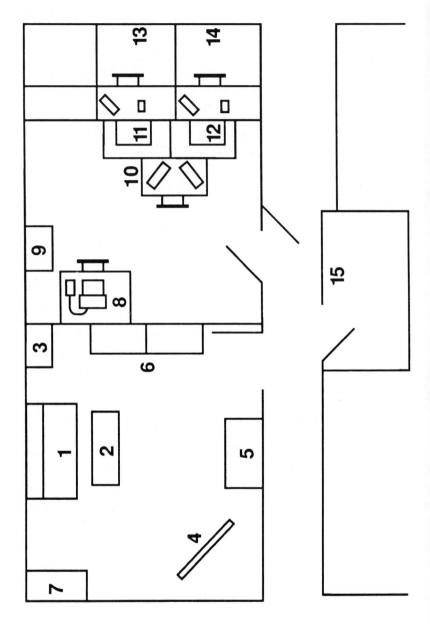

Figure 1.1   Schematic diagram of the laboratory setting.

Equipment

Audiovisual system components. The audiovisual equipment required by the paradigm includes a color television camera, two identical VCRs, two identical large-screen color television monitors, and the necessary cables and adaptors. We recommend a high-resolution color television camera with an 8:1 zoom lens, an ultrasensitive vidicon for taping in low light conditions, and a built-in timer that continuously displays elapsed time on the video-taped record in minutes, seconds, and tenths (or hundredths) of seconds. We recommend 4-head VCRs with high-resolution recording and playback capabilities, low flutter, and excellent freeze-frame image. And we recommend high-resolution, large-screen TV monitors with remote control capability and with headphone jacks installed.

Computer system components. The computer hardware required by the paradigm includes a microcomputer with two disk drives, a printer, and a clock/counter board with programmable I/O ports. Useful optional components include a modem for uploading data to a mainframe computer and a hard disk drive for the local storage of large data files. Although our custom software packages, DYAD DYNAMICS and COLLECT YOUR THOUGHTS, were designed to run on Apple II series microcomputers (Apple II +, IIe, or IIgs), a version of COLLECT YOUR THOUGHTS is available that will run on IBM PCs or their clones. The DYAD DYNAMICS software will currently run only on an Apple II series computer with an ADALAB™ clock/counter board installed in slot 2, but a PC-compatible version of this program may be developed in the future.

MEASURING STATIC AND DYNAMIC BEHAVIORS

Two classes of behavior, static and dynamic, are typically measured in the dyadic interaction paradigm. Static behaviors are defined as those that occur only once or do not vary much over time. Behaviors of this type include interpersonal distance, the degree of body orientation each subject maintains with respect to the other, and the openness of each subject's body posture. Dynamic behaviors, which are defined as more temporally variable, include the frequency and duration of verbalizations, directed gazes, mutual gazes, expressive gestures, and expressions of positive affect. They also include such aspects of the verbal interaction as the number of times each subject initiates a conversation sequence, asks questions, and provides verbal reinforcers or back-channel responses ("uh-huh," "yeah," "right," or the like).

As important as these behaviors are, however, there are obviously many other interesting behaviors that one might choose to investigate, depending on the hypotheses being tested. For example, there are additional nonverbal behaviors such as postural mirroring (LaFrance & Ickes, 1981); there are contingency-based measures of recurring behavior patterns and exchanges (e.g., Gottman, 1979); and there are more specific features of the verbal interaction such as the percentage of first-, second-, and third-person pronouns used by each dyad member (Ickes, Reidhead, & Patterson, 1986). Although our own research has emphasized such primary aspects of interactional involvement as talking, smiling, gazing, and gesturing, the paradigm both allows for and encourages flexibility and innovation in the choice of behaviors to study. With the aid of enhancements in video technology, researchers can now study a wide range of linguistic, paralinguistic, and nonverbal behaviors from videotapes of unstructured dyadic interaction.

Coding the Static Behaviors

The behavioral data of interest are coded from the videotapes by two independent raters who are kept unaware, insofar as possible, of any predictor or independent variables being studied. Because the static behaviors, by definition, occur only once or do not vary much over time, most raters can code these behaviors reliably after only a single short training session. By means of a transparent ruler, interpersonal distance is measured directly from the videotape image as the distance (in millimeters) between the dyad members' proximal shoulders. Body orientation is rated on a scale from 4 to − 4, with each scale point defining a 22.5-degree difference in the estimated angle at which the plane of the subject's body is oriented toward versus away from the interaction partner. In a similar manner, body posture is subjectively estimated on a scale from 0 to 2, where 0 represents a "closed," compacted posture, 1 represents an average, somewhat "open" posture, and 2 represents a very open and expansive posture. Each of these behaviors is coded twice by both raters, once during the first 30 seconds of the interaction and a second time during the last 30 seconds. In previous studies, the interrater reliabilities for these behaviors have ranged from .70 to .90.

Coding the Dynamic Behaviors

Due to the variable nature of the dynamic behaviors and the need for a mechanical means to record them, most raters require 10 to 12 hours of practice training before they can reliably code these data. Using push-button hand panels connected by an interface to a digital I/O board within one of the laboratory microcomputers, each rater tracks the repeated display of a given behavior (e.g. directed gazes) by a given subject by depressing the appropriate button at each onset of the behavior and releasing the button at each offset. Custom software designed to control the operation of the I/O board (see the section on DYAD DYNAMICS, below) automatically records the frequency (number of occurrences) and duration (elapsed time) of the measured behavior. At the end of the observation period, the software computes the minute-by-minute frequencies and durations of the behavior along with the total frequency and duration and then writes these data to a diskette file for subsequent integration and analysis.

Verbalizations are measured in terms of the number (frequency) and length (duration) of speaking turns. All verbalizations are recorded, regardless of their content. Directed gazes are recorded whenever the subject under observation looks directly toward the other person's face. Whenever both dyad members display directed gazes simultaneously, the software controlling the I/O board automatically records the "overlap" behavior as mutual gazes. Expressive gestures are recorded as any instances of gross arm and hand movements that accompany verbalizations and appear to illustrate or supplement their content. Positive affect is operationally defined as any instances of smiling and/or laughing.

In studies conducted to date, the interrater reliabilities for these dynamic behaviors have typically been in the .80 to .99 range, with an average reliability of .90. The four dynamic behaviors just described (talking, gazing, gesturing, and smiling) have consistently proved to be useful in defining the overall level of *interactional involvement* displayed by the dyad members. A factor analysis of these behaviors typically yields a single interactional involvement factor accounting for more than 70% of the total factor variance (see Ickes, Robertson, Tooke, & Teng, 1986).

MEASURING ACTUAL AND INFERRED THOUGHT/FEELING ENTRIES

The second phase of a study using the dyadic interaction paradigm begins when the subjects have provided written consent (a) to release the videotape of their interaction for use as data, and (b) to view a copy of the videotape and make written records of their own thoughts and feelings as well as the inferred thoughts and feelings of their interaction partners.

Procedures and Coding Forms

After the subjects have been seated in their individual cubicles (13 and 14), the experimenter initiates an instructional videotape. This tape is used to give the subjects detailed, standardized instructions regarding the thought/feeling data collection procedure. When the subjects have viewed the tape and have signaled the experimenter that they understand the instructions and are ready to begin, the two identical videotapes of the subjects' interaction are initiated. Using the start/pause controls connected to their VCRs, the subjects are able independently to start and stop their respective copies of the videotape.

Consistent with the instructions they receive, the subjects stop the videotape at each point during the interaction that they recall having had a specific thought or feeling. They record each thought or feeling on a "Thought/Feeling Coding Form" by entering (a) the time the thought or feeling occurred (available as a digital readout on the upper-left part of the videotape), (b) whether the entry was a thought or a feeling (coded "I was thinking:" or "I was feeling:" on the coding sheet), (c) the specific content of the thought/feeling entry (written in sentence form to complete the initial phrase), and (d) whether the entry was presumed to be positive, negative or neutral in its overall affective tone (coded $+$, $-$, or 0 on the coding sheet). A sample coding form, complete with the actual thought/feeling data provided by one of the subjects in a recent study, is reproduced in Figure 1.2.

The instructions the subjects receive explicitly encourage them to report *all* of the thoughts and feelings they remember having had as accurately and honestly as possible. The importance of being completely candid is emphasized, and the subjects are assured that the thoughts and feelings they record will not be seen by their interaction partners. On the other hand, the instructions caution them to report only those thoughts and feelings they distinctly remember having had during the observation period. They are not to report any thoughts and feelings that occur to them for the first time while they are viewing the videotape.

When both subjects have made a complete pass through the videotape and have finished listing all of the thoughts and feelings they recall having had during the 6-minute interaction, the experimenter collects their respective thought/feeling coding forms and tells them that the next phase of the study is about to begin. The experimenter then returns to the station in the control room, and initiates a new set of videotaped instructions that informs the subjects that they will now view the videotape a second time. On this second pass, however, the subjects will not use their remote start/pause controls

TIME	THOUGHT OR FEELING	+, 0, −	
35:33	☐ I was thinking: ☒ I was feeling: apprehensive about what was going to happen	+ 0 (−)	
35:53	☒ I was thinking: he seems real nice and personable ☐ I was feeling:	(+) 0 −	
36:57	☒ I was thinking: now long would it take for the ☐ I was feeling: experimenter to come back	+ 0 (−)	
36:59	☒ I was thinking: I hope I don't run out of things ☐ I was feeling: to say	+ (0) −	
37:05	☐ I was thinking: ☒ I was feeling: that I always forgot when people ask me things	(+) 0 −	
37:23	☒ I was thinking: I hope he doesn't think I always ☐ I was feeling: "play" with my nose	(+) 0 −	
37:50	☐ I was thinking: ☒ I was feeling: like I was being talkative and immature	+ (0) −	
	☐ I was thinking: ☐ I was feeling:	+ 0 −	
	☐ I was thinking: ☐ I was feeling:	+ 0 −	
	☐ I was thinking: ☐ I was feeling:	+ 0 −	

Figure 1.2   Sample "Thought/Feeling Coding Form."

29

to start and stop the tape. Instead, the experimenter (aided by a research assistant) will start and stop each subject's copy of the tape during the second viewing.

Using their own video-synchronized "logs" of the times at which each dyad member's *partner's* thoughts and feelings were reported during the first viewing of the videotapes, the experimenter and the research assistant independently present their copies of the tape to the two dyad members, stopping the tapes at each of those points at which the partner's thoughts and feelings were recorded. The subjects' instructions are in most respects analogous to those of the previous thought-listing task. Each time the tape is stopped for them, the subjects are required to make an inference about the nature of the specific thought or feeling reported by their partners at that point. Then, using the same type of coding form on which they had previously recorded their own thoughts and feelings, the subjects code the inferred content of their partners' thoughts and feelings by entering (a) the time the thought or feeling occurred (available from the digital readout on the videotape), (b) whether the entry was presumed to be a thought or a feeling (coded "he/she was thinking:" or "he/she was feeling:" on the coding sheet), (c) the specific content of the thought or feeling reported in sentence form, and (d) whether the entry was presumed to be positive, neutral, or negative in its overall affective tone (coded as +, 0, or − on the coding sheet).

Coding the Content of the Thought/Feeling Data

Both the actual and the inferred thought/feeling data are later coded by two raters who determine whether each thought/feeling entry represents a direct perspective (subject's own perspective) or a metaperspective (subject's adoption of his or her partner's perspective; see Laing, Phillipson, & Lee, 1966). A summary of the direct perspective and metaperspective categories used by the raters in our research is provided in Table 1.1 The same two raters also determine the target or object of the perception expressed by the entry (self, partner, other person[s], environmental object, event, or circumstance). In previous studies, the rates of interrater agreement for these categorical classifications have ranged from .86 to .99 for perspective and from .87 to .94 for target.

In one of our most recent studies, the raters have also coded the temporal location of the entry (past, present, future, or inclusive/enduring) and the spatial location of the entry (coded as "proximal" to indicate a thought/feeling focused within the immediate room, "local" for a thought/feeling focused elsewhere on campus, "distal" for a thought/feeling directed off-

TABLE 1.1 Direct and Metaperspective Perceptions of Self, Partner, Other(s), and Environment

Direct Perspectives		Metaperspectives	
S > S	S's perception of S	S > P > S	S's perception of P's perception of S
S > P	S's perception of P	S > P > P	S's perception of P's perception of P
S > O	S's perception of O	S > P > O	S's perception of P's perception of O
S > E	S's perception of E	S > P > E	S's perception of P's perception of E

NOTE: S = subject, P = partner, O = other person(s), E = environmental object, event or circumstance.

campus, or "personal" as a thought/feeling about some individual ranging across all spatial locations) (Ickes et al., 1989). The rates of interrater agreement for these categorical classifications were also quite acceptable (.87 for temporal location, .81 for spatial location).

Obtaining Objective Measures of Empathic Accuracy

Two measures of empathic accuracy are derived from comparison of the actual and inferred thought/feeling entries. The first measure, valence accuracy, is an index of the percentage of instances in which a dyad member's inference about the overall emotional tone of his or her partner's entry (positive, neutral, or negative) matches the actual valence label assigned to the entry by the other subject. This measure is computed by one of the programs in the specialized software package called COLLECT YOUR THOUGHTS, the operation of which is described below. The second measure, content accuracy, is an index of the degree to which a dyad member's written description of the inferred content of his or her partner's thought/feeling entry matched the actual content of the sentence that the partner had written to describe the entry.

Because the content accuracy measure requires subjective judgments to be made about the degree of similarity in the written content of the actual and inferred thought/feeling entries, a more elaborate procedure is used to derive this measure. First, a transcript of all the thought/feeling entries reported in the study, both actual and inferred, is created with the aid of a word processor. The printed copy of this transcript is structured such that each dyad member's thought/feeling entries appear on the left side of the page, with the corresponding inferred entries appearing directly beside them on the right. Then separate copies of the transcript are given to six independent raters. Their task is to compare the written content of each actual entry with that of the corresponding inferred entry and rate the degree of similarity (i.e., content accuracy) using a 3-point scale ranging from 0 (essentially different content) through 1 (somewhat similar, but not the same content) to 2 (essentially the same content). In the first two studies in which this scoring procedure was employed (see Table 1.2 for some representative examples), the internal consistency of the six raters' content accuracy was .94.

Once the six raters have provided independent ratings of the degree to which each dyad member has accurately inferred the content of each of his or her partner's actual thought/feeling entries, these data are transformed for subsequent analysis. First, the content accuracy ratings for each inference are averaged across the six raters, as indicated above. Next, these averaged accuracy ratings are aggregated across the entire set of inferences made by a given dyad member and then divided by the total number of inferences made in order to obtain an overall index of content accuracy. Like the valence accuracy measure, this content accuracy measure can vary in its range from a lower bound of .00 (zero accuracy) to a theoretical upper bound of 1.00 (perfect accuracy).

Ideally, these valence and content accuracy measures are relatively pure measures of *differential accuracy* (e.g., Cronbach, 1955; Harackiewicz & DePaulo, 1982; Kenny, 1988) in that they are aggregated measures of how well subjects can discriminate among and differentially infer the specific content of *each* of their partner's reported thoughts and feelings. In fact, however, scores on these measures have been shown to contain a baseline accuracy component that reflects the subjects' "educated" and "uneducated" guesses about what their partners are thinking or feeling. For a description of a procedure to estimate and statistically control for this baseline accuracy component, see Ickes et al. (1989).

DATA REDUCTION, INTEGRATION, AND ANALYSIS

Using the Laboratory Software

Given the preceding discussion of the various forms of data collected in the dyadic interaction paradigm, it should be clear to the reader that a data

TABLE 1.2 Sample Thought/Feeling Entries with Corresponding
Inferences and Mean Content Accuracy Ratings

Dyad Member's Actual Thought/Feeling	Partner's Inference	Mean Content Accuracy Rating (max = 2, min = 0)
I was feeling silly because I couldn't remember my instructor's name.	She was maybe feeling sorta odd for not remembering her teacher's name.	2
I was thinking that I was not missing anything I didn't want to miss. I was thinking that I came to school to learn, not to join organizations.	He was thinking about what he was missing in school.	1
I was thinking about a previous production of the play in another city that a local radio personality was in.	She was thinking if I would ask her out.	0

base of nearly overwhelming size is created during the course of one of these investigations. Among the more recent and important developments of the paradigm are techniques for organizing, transforming, summarizing, and analyzing these data. The microcomputer has proved to be an invaluable research tool in this regard. To date, two custom software packages have been developed: one that aids in the coding of the dynamic behaviors and one that organizes, transforms, and summarizes the thought/feeling data. These packages, DYAD DYNAMICS and COLLECT YOUR THOUGHTS, are the products of hundreds of hours of software development, testing, and revision.[3]

DYAD DYNAMICS. DYAD DYNAMICS is an Applesoft BASIC program written for Apple II series microcomputers by Ickes and Trued (1985). This program is used to collect, summarize, and store the various dynamic behaviors that are recorded from the videotapes created in the dyadic interaction paradigm. It is designed to work in conjunction with Interactive Microware's ADALAB™ clock/counter board and the accompanying QUICKI/O™ software, which are available for all Apple II series computers. Data are input to the system by means of two push-button hand panels that are connected to the digital inputs of the ADALAB™ board.[4]

When the DYAD DYNAMICS software is booted up, it prompts the users (two data coders) to input relevant identifier information that includes the date, the dyad number, a condition code, the names and sex of the dyad members, and the labels of the behavior(s) to be coded. The users are then prompted to (a) start the videotape for the interaction they plan to code, and (b) initiate the data coding interval by depressing one of the top buttons on either of their respective hand panels. As soon as this button is released, the clocks and counters on the ADALAB™ board are activated and the data collection interval begins. During this interval, each data coder monitors the videotaped behavior of one of the dyad members, depressing the appropriate button at the onset of each occurrence of a given behavior and releasing the button at its offset. For example, when coding verbalizations, a data coder presses the appropriate button on the hand panel whenever the subject being monitored begins to talk and continues to hold the button down until the subject stops talking.

By means of this hardware/software system, the behaviors displayed by each of two interactants (dyad members) can be collected and stored in the form of minute-by-minute summaries of the behavior(s)' frequency and duration. This feature of the data collection system allows the user to code social interaction data in a form suitable for time-based trend analysis. A subroutine in DYAD DYNAMICS collects the simultaneous expressions of a behavior by both dyad members (e.g., mutual gaze or "eye contact," simultaneous or interrupted speech) and stores minute-by-minute summaries of the frequency and duration of this "overlap behavior" as well. If a more fine-grained recording of the behavior is desired, another (optional) subroutine enables the real-time clocks on the ADALAB™ board to record the exact times when each button is depressed and released during each minute of the interaction.

At the end of the data collection interval, DYAD DYNAMICS stores the resulting summary data in a disk file. This file is written in standard ASCII text format and can be uploaded directly to a mainframe computer for analysis. Because each dyad's data are identified with a unique dyad number, the data created by DYAD DYNAMICS can later be merged with the data created by our other software package, COLLECT YOUR THOUGHTS.

COLLECT YOUR THOUGHTS. The COLLECT YOUR THOUGHTS software package, developed by Ickes and Bissonnette, consists of five integrated programs. These programs (a) organize and store the thought/feeling data, (b) transform the data to create a number of aggregated thought/feeling variables, and (c) create a data input file, complete with data labels, that can be uploaded to a mainframe computer for subsequent data analyses. All of these programs are written in Pascal and can be compiled and executed on most microcomputers, including Apple II and IBM-compatible PCs.

The first of the COLLECT YOUR THOUGHTS programs "sets up" the data collection for a given study by requesting the user to define certain parameters of the research project. The user is asked to specify the name of the study, the number of individual difference (e.g., personality) variables to be collected (from 0 to 8), the number of posttest variables to be collected (from 0 to 8), and the disk drive to which the data files will be written. The user is prompted to provide a label for each of the variables to be coded. A small disk file is then created that, when accessed, passes this information to any of the other programs in the COLLECT YOUR THOUGHTS package.

The second program in the package is a collection program that organizes and stores the thought/feeling data. This program presents a series of screens, each of which prompts the user for information. The first screen prompts the user to enter the dyad number, the date on which the data were collected, the dyad's condition code (if used), and the name, sex, ID number, and number of thought/feeling entries for each of the two dyad members. The second screen collects all of the individual difference variables for each dyad member. The labels of these variables that were previously written to the "setup" program appear on this screen.

The program then requests information relevant to each of the dyad members' thought/feeling entries. For each individual thought/feeling entry, a screen is presented that first prompts the user to input the entry's unique identification number. The user is then prompted to input the dyad member's self-reported classification of the entry as a thought or a feeling (T or F) and as positive, neutral, or negative (+, 0, or −) in its overall emotional valence. Finally, the user is prompted to input the perspective and target of the entry, the temporal and spatial location of the entry (optional), and the partner's empathic inference of the valence of the entry (also optional). When all of the entries for each dyad member have been coded, the last screen of this program prompts entry of the data from the posttest questionnaire items. Following completion of the data entry, the user receives instructions for writing all of the data for that dyad to diskette. The user can then either exit the program or repeat the process and begin entering the data for the next dyad.

The program just described may process several thousand data points for a single research project. Because at least a few data-entry errors are inevitable in such large data sets, the next two COLLECT YOUR THOUGHTS programs were designed to help users find and correct such errors. The third program permits the user to print part or all of the dyadic data files created by the data collection program. This printout can be checked against the original data to locate any data-entry errors. When errors are discovered, the fourth program allows the user to modify any of the data points within a given dyad's file and then resave the corrected data. The format of this program is identical to that of the collection program. The user can specify which screen should be modified, and then correct any data point on that screen and resave the corrected data.

The fifth and final COLLECT YOUR THOUGHTS program epitomizes the virtues of speed and accuracy. It makes impressively short work of what is otherwise the painfully long and tedious work of aggregating and transforming the thought/feeling data. Up to this point, the software has collected and stored data representing ratings on various dimensions of each of the thought/feeling entries reported by the dyad members. The last program begins by accessing these untransformed data. It then aggregates the data within each dyad member's file to create summary measures of the percentage of entries in specific content categories. These summary measures include the percentage of each dyad member's entries that are coded as thoughts, feelings, positive entries, neutral entries, negative entries, self (relevant) entries, partner entries, other-person entries, environment entries, direct perspective entries, and metaperspective entries.

Several cross-classified summary measures (e.g., percentage of negative self entries, positive partner entries) are also computed. Among these is a measure of the percentage of partner attribution entries. The category of partner attribution entries is defined as all entries for which (a) the interaction partner was coded as the target of the thought or feeling, (b) the temporal perspective of the entry was coded as inclusive/enduring, and (c) the "spatial location" of the entry was coded as personal. These entries represent the dyad members' attributions about the relatively stable and enduring characteristics of their interaction partners (e.g., "this guy is pretty creative," "she is snobbish," "what a weirdo!"). For an example of research employing the partner attribution measure, see Ickes et al. (1989).

Valence accuracy is also computed by the fifth COLLECT YOUR THOUGHTS program. A subroutine in this program accesses the appropriate untransformed data and then counts the number of times that the valence inferred by a subject (i.e., perceiver) matches the actual valence assigned to the entry by the partner (i.e., target) who reported it. When this count is divided by the total number of entries for which such inferences were made, the result is an overall measure of valence accuracy that represents the percentage of correct inferences.

The data integration/transformation program just described computes nearly 40 summary measures for each subject (i.e., dyad member). These variables, along with the demographic, personality, and posttest data also collected by the second program, are written to a new, master data file that is the final product of COLLECT YOUR THOUGHTS. This file is written in standard ASCII format and can be uploaded directly to a mainframe computer for analysis. It is created by COLLECT YOUR THOUGHTS in less than 10 minutes and transmitted to a mainframe computer in about 30, with virtually perfect accuracy. The same master data file, created by hand and manually entered into a mainframe, would require months of patient work by a team of research assistants, and would be prone to error at every stage of the process.

Micro-Mainframe Interfacing

The final products of the DYAD DYNAMICS and COLLECT YOUR THOUGHTS software systems are several large data files stored on floppy diskettes. Our assumption is that most of the data analyses will be conducted by means of a mainframe statistical package such as SAS, SPSSX, or BMDP. The master data files created by DYAD DYNAMICS and COLLECT YOUR THOUGHTS can be transmitted via modem from the microcomputer to the mainframe computer. Once the data files have been uploaded to the mainframe, they can be merged and saved as a single permanent data set that is ready for analysis.

Data Analysis

As Kenny (1988) has noted, special statistical problems apply whenever researchers analyze data collected from subjects interacting in dyads (or in larger groups). These problems include (a) the interdependence of behavior in dyadic relationships and the resulting nondependence of the dyad members' responses, (b) the difficulty of establishing causal priority in such interdependent exchanges, (c) the problem of testing statistical relationships and establishing their generality at both the individual and dyad levels of analysis, and (d) the problem that it is often arbitrary which dyad member's response is used as the X or Y variable when correlating paired responses from heterogeneous ("similar partners") dyads.

According to Kenny (1988), all but the second of these problems can be addressed through the application of special statistical techniques. For at least a decade, Kenny has been the major proponent and originator of a "family" of such techniques. Two of the most useful for researchers studying dyadic interaction are (a) the social relations model (e.g., Kenny & LaVoie,

1984; Malloy & Kenny, 1986) and (b) a procedure for separating correlational effects at the individual and dyad (i.e., group) levels of analysis (Kenny & LaVoie, 1985).

The first of these techniques is not applicable to the dyadic interaction paradigm because it requires data sets in which each subject participates in more than one dyad with different partners. For designs meeting this requirement, however, the social relations model is an elegant and innovative technique for partitioning the variance in the dyad members' behavior into components reflecting the independent contributions of actors, partners, and actor × partner interactions. The second of these techniques *is* applicable to the dyadic interaction paradigm, and can be used to determine whether a relationship between two variables exists (a) at the individual level only, (b) at the dyad level only, or (c) at both levels simultaneously. For more information about these and other related techniques, see the informative review by Kenny (1988) as well as the chapters by Jaccard and Dittus and by Kenny in the present volume.

A data-analytic problem that is somewhat unique to the dyadic interaction paradigm is the enormous number of individual-level and dyad-level correlations that can be computed from the massive data sets generated whenever the paradigm is fully implemented. Because roughly 5% of these correlations can be expected to attain conventional levels of significance due to chance (i.e., Type I error) alone, it is important to take precautions against reporting spuriously significant effects. Obviously, the most effective of these precautions is to test only relationships that were predicted a priori. However, because one of the major strengths of the paradigm is its serendipitous capacity to reveal unexpected relationships as well, other precautions should be taken when the paradigm is used for inductive exploration rather than for deductive hypothesis testing.

Although space does not permit an extended discussion of these other precautions, we should mention at least two that are used in our own research. The first precaution is to obtain the standard descriptive statistics (mean, variance, skewness, kurtosis) for each of the variables measured in the study and then use this information to identify any variables with distributions that do not satisfy the assumptions of "normality." Statisticians have warned that such variables are particularly likely to contribute to spurious correlations. Consistent with this warning, we have found that most of the seemingly anomalous effects in our preliminary analyses vanish into statistical oblivion when those variables with nonnormal distributions are either "normalized" through an appropriate transformation or, failing that, are deleted completely from the data set. The second precaution is to require that any remaining significant effects in the data be supported by the "multiple corroboration" of other findings (Lykken, 1968). In general, we are considerably more reluctant to report effects that appear to stand alone, in isolation, than to report effects that appear to be part of a larger, conceptually meaningful *pattern* of results.

ON THE HEURISTIC VALUE OF THE PARADIGM

Before concluding this chapter, we would like to call attention to one of the greatest strengths of the dyadic interaction paradigm: its heuristic value as a method for revealing new phenomena and suggesting new theoretical insights.

The following are only a few selected examples of the novel and/or counterintuitive findings that have emerged in studies employing the dyadic interaction paradigm. In one of the earliest of these studies, Ickes and Barnes (1978) found that mixed-sex dyads composed of a stereotypically "masculine" man and a stereotypically "feminine" woman had initial interactions that were characterized by significantly less liking and interactional involvement (talking, smiling, gesturing, and so on) than dyads in which either or both of the members were androgynous. This study was the first to reveal the finding—later replicated in at least three subsequent studies of the relationships of married or cohabiting couples (Antill, 1983; Shaver, Pullis, & Olds, 1980; Zammichieli, Gilroy, & Sherman, 1988)—that the "traditional" pairing of a masculine man and a feminine woman is far from optimal in terms of the quality of the resulting relationship.

In another study of mixed-sex dyads, Ickes and Turner (1982) systematically paired men who had either older or younger sisters with women who had either older or younger brothers. Their findings clearly revealed that interactions involving last-borns who had opposite-sex siblings were more active and rewarding than those involving firstborns who had opposite-sex siblings. Moreover, the effects due to the men's birth order were more directly evident than those due to the women's birth order. Last-born men not only talked twice as long as firstborn men, but also got a much better reception from their women partners, who looked at them longer, engaged them in more mutual gazes (i.e., eye contact), and expressed more liking for them than did the partners of the firstborn men.

In a study of the initial interactions of interracial (Black-White) dyads, Ickes (1984) found that the White members' general attitude toward Blacks (i.e., their measured disposition to "approach" versus "avoid" Blacks) was clearly expressed in their behavior only when the White members had *solo minority status* in the social context of the experiment. In other words, when *both* the experimenter and the other subject (the interaction partner) were Black, the White subjects were particularly likely to "act out" their latent dispositions, with White "avoider" subjects looking and smiling at their Black partners significantly less than White "approachers."

In a study of the influences of shyness and physical attractiveness on the initial interactions of mixed-sex dyads, Garcia et al. (1989) found some novel (though not counterintuitive) effects for both of the predictor variables. With respect to the first variable, shy men were found actively to control and limit the amount of eye contact they had with their women partners by looking away when they sensed that their partners were about to "meet" their own gaze and establish eye contact. With respect to the second variable, the physical attractiveness of the male dyad members elicited a range of reactions in their female partners that included (a) a cognitive disposition to view both partners as the members of a "we" relationship and (b) a corresponding behavioral disposition to create a more "exclusive" conversational context by limiting references to any third-party individuals outside of the interaction.

Perhaps the largest number of novel, serendipitous effects have emerged in our most recent studies of *naturalistic social cognition*. The first study in this series indicated, among other things, that men symbolically adopt their interaction partners' perspective as an instrumental means to achieve some (other) end, whereas women engage in *metaperspective taking* as an end in itself (Ickes, Robertson, Tooke, & Teng, 1986). The next two studies revealed that the initial interactions of male-male versus female-female strangers give rise to characteristically different patterns of *intersubjective* thought/feeling content (Ickes et al., 1988). And the fourth study revealed that, in mixed-sex dyads, the accuracy of the dyad members' inferences about the content of their partners' thoughts and feelings was affected by their own degree of interest in their partners, as indexed by the percentage of partner-relevant thoughts and feelings they reported (Ickes et al., 1989).

As a consequence of its ability to reveal unexpected empirical relationships, the dyadic interaction paradigm also has heuristic value as a method for inductive theory construction. Its value in this regard is perhaps best illustrated by the theoretical model of sex-role influences on dyadic interaction proposed by Ickes (1981, 1985). This model, which was derived *inductively* from the data reported by Ickes and Barnes (1978) and by Ickes et al. (1979), has been supported by subsequent findings (Antill, 1983; Lamke & Bell, 1982; Shaver et al., 1980; Zammichieli et al., 1988) that are generally quite consistent with the theory's *deductive* implications.

CONCLUSION

By means of the newest version of the dyadic interaction paradigm, the scope of observational research can be expanded to include the study of subjective thoughts and feelings in addition to the study of objectively rated behavior. Our procedures for assessing the actual and inferred thoughts and feelings of interaction partners have already opened up several novel lines of inquiry for future research. By permitting the study of "naturalistic social cognition," they enable researchers to explore such genuinely *social-*cognitive phenomena as metaperspective taking, intersubjectivity, and empathic accuracy. Moreover, because social behavior and social cognition are both studied as they naturally occur, and in the same "real-time" frame, researchers can explore their empirical relations in a way that facilitates a more integrated, holistic view of social interaction. Although the costs of using the technique are substantial, they have consistently been outweighed by the value of the findings obtained with this procedure.

NOTES

1. The separate sign-up sheets, which not only bear the names of different experiments and experimenters but also direct subjects to report to different waiting areas, are used to help ensure (a) that two friends or previously acquainted individuals will not sign up for the same session, and (b) that each scheduled pair of subjects will be unlikely to meet and interact before their session begins. Obviously, in studies of the interactions of dyads whose members already have an established relationship (e.g., friends, roommates, dating or married couples), the precautions just described are unnecessary and can be dispensed with.

2. The cover story that the experimenter has to leave the room in order to obtain more copies of the consent form is only one possible scenario that can be used to justify the experimenter's temporary absence. We have had equivalent success with a scenario in which the experimenter "tests" a slide projector set up in the observation room to see that it is working properly. In fact, the projector is rigged with an electronic flash that convincingly simulates a projector lamp burning out. This event also provides an appropriate errand (obtaining a new projector lamp) that justifies the experimenter's temporary absence.

3. Researchers interested in using DYAD DYNAMICS or COLLECT YOUR THOUGHTS in their own research should contact William Ickes, Department of Psychology, University of Texas, Arlington, TX 76019.

4. ADALAB™ and QUICKI/0™ are registered trademarks of Interactive Microware, Inc., P.O. Box 139, State College, PA 16804-0139.

REFERENCES

Antill, J. K. (1983). Sex role complementarity versus similarity in married couples. *Journal of Personality and Social Psychology, 45*, 145–155.

Brock, T. C. (1967). Communication discrepancy and intent to persuade as determinants of counterargument production. *Journal of Experimental Social Psychology, 3*, 269–309.

Cacioppo, J. T., Glass, C. R., & Merluzzi, T. V. (1979). Self-statements and self-evaluations: A cognitive response analysis of heterosexual anxiety. *Cognitive Therapy and Research, 3*, 249–262.

Cacioppo, J. T., & Petty, R. E. (1981). Social psychological procedures for cognitive response assessment: The thought-listing technique. In T. Merluzzi, C. Glass, & M. Genest (Eds.), *Cognitive assessment* (pp. 309–342). New York: Guilford.

Cronbach, L. J. (1955). Processes affecting scores on "understanding of" others and "assumed similarity." *Psychological Bulletin, 52*, 177–193.

Duncan, S. D., Jr. (1969). Nonverbal communication. *Psychological Bulletin, 72*, 118–137.

Duncan, S. D., Jr., & Fiske, D. W. (1977). *Face-to-face interaction: Research, methods, and theory.* Hillsdale, NJ: Erlbaum.

Garcia, S., Stinson, L., Ickes, W., Bissonette, V., & Briggs, S. (1989). Correlates of shyness and physical attractiveness in mixed-sex dyads. Manuscript submitted for publication.

Gottman, J. M. (1979). *Marital interaction: Experimental investigations.* New York: Academic Press.

Greenwald, A. G. (1968). Cognitive learning, cognitive response to persuasion, and attitude change. In A. G. Greenwald, T. C. Brock, & T. M. Ostrom (Eds.), *Psychological foundations of attitudes* (pp. 147–170). New York: Academic Press.

Harackiewicz, J. M., & DePaulo, B. M. (1982). Accuracy of person perception: A component analysis according to Cronbach. *Personality and Social Psychology Bulletin, 8*, 247–256.

Ickes, W. (1981). Sex-role influences in dyadic interaction: A theoretical model. In C. Mayo & N. Henley (Eds.), *Gender and nonverbal behavior* (pp. 95–128). New York: Springer-Verlag.

Ickes, W. (1982). A basic paradigm for the study of personality, roles, and social behavior. In W. Ickes & E. S. Knowles (Eds.), *Personality, roles, and social behavior* (pp. 305–341). New York: Springer-Verlag.

Ickes, W. (1983). A basic paradigm for the study of unstructured dyadic interaction. In H. Reis (Ed.), *New directions for methodology of social and behavioral science* (pp. 5–21). San Francisco: Jossey-Bass.

Ickes, W. (1984). Compositions in black and white: Determinants of interaction in interracial dyads. *Journal of Personality and Social Psychology, 47*, 330–341.

Ickes, W. (1985). Sex-role influences on compatibility in relationships. In W. Ickes (Ed.), *Compatible and incompatible relationships* (pp. 187–207). New York: Springer-Verlag

Ickes, W., & Barnes, R. D. (1977). The role of sex and self-monitoring in unstructured dyadic interactions. *Journal of Personality and Social Psychology, 35*, 315–330.

Ickes, W., & Barnes, R. D. (1978). Boys and girls together—and alienated: On enacting stereotyped sex roles in mixed-sex dyads. *Journal of Personality and Social Psychology, 36*, 669–683.

Ickes, W., Patterson, M. L., Rajecki, D. W., & Tanford, S. (1982). Behavioral and cognitive consequences of reciprocal versus compensatory responses to preinteraction expectancies. *Social Cognition, 1,* 160–190.

Ickes, W., Reidhead, S., & Patterson, M. L. (1986). Machiavellianism and self-monitoring: As different as "me" and "you." *Social Cognition, 4,* 58–74.

Ickes, W., & Robertson, E. (1984). A new paradigm for the study of personality. In O. Neumaier (Ed.), *Mind, language and society* (pp. 31–41). Vienna: vwgo-verlag.

Ickes, W., Robertson, E., Tooke, W., & Teng, G. (1986). Naturalistic social cognition: Methodology, assessment, and validation. *Journal of Personality and Social Psychology, 51,* 66–82.

Ickes, W., Schermer, B., & Steeno, J. (1979). Sex and sex-role influences in same-sex dyads. *Social Psychology Quarterly, 42,* 373–385.

Ickes, W., Stinson, L., Bissonnette, V., & Garcia, S. (1989). *Naturalistic social cognition: Empathic accuracy in mixed-sex dyads.* Manuscript submitted for publication.

Ickes, W., & Tooke, W. (1988). The observational method: Studying the interaction of minds and bodies. In S. Duck, D. Hay, S. Hobfoll, W. Ickes, & B. Montgomery (Eds.), *The handbook of personal relationships: Theory, research, and interventions* (pp. 79–97). Chichester: John Wiley.

Ickes, W., Tooke, W., Stinson, L., Baker, V. L., & Bissonnette, V. (1988). Naturalistic social cognition: Intersubjectivity in same-sex dyads. *Journal of Nonverbal Behavior, 12,* 58–84.

Ickes, W., & Trued, S. (1985). A system for collecting dyadic interaction data on the Apple II. *Electronic Social Psychology, 1,* Article #8501012.

Ickes, W., & Turner, M. (1983). On the social advantages of having an older, opposite-sex sibling: Birth-order influences in mixed-sex dyads. *Journal of Personality and Social Psychology, 45,* 210–222.

Kenny, D. A. (1988). The analysis of data from two-person relationships. In S. Duck, D. Hay, S. Hobfoll, W. Ickes, & B. Montgomery (Eds.), *The handbook of personal relationships: Theory, research, and interventions* (pp. 57–77). Chichester: John Wiley.

Kenny, D. A., & La Voie, L. (1984). The social relations model. In L. Berkowitz (Ed.), *Advances in experimental social psychology* (Vol. 18, pp. 141–182). New York: Academic Press.

Kenny, D. A., & La Voie, L. (1985). Separating individual and group effects. *Journal of Personality and Social Psychology, 48,* 339–348.

LaFrance, M., & Ickes, W. (1981). Postural mirroring and interactional involvement: Sex and sex-typing effects. *Journal of Nonverbal Behavior, 5,* 139–154.

Laing, R. D., Phillipson, H., & Lee, A. R. (1966). *Interpersonal perception: A theory and method of research.* New York: Harper & Row.

Lamke, L. K., & Bell, N. J. (1982). Sex-role orientation and relationship development in same-sex dyads. *Journal of Research in Personality, 16,* 343–354.

Lykken, D. T. (1968). Statistical significance in psychological research. *Psychological Bulletin, 70,* 151–159.

Malloy, T. E., & Kenny, D. A. (1986). The social relations model: An integrative method for personality research. *Journal of Personality, 54,* 101–127.

Petty, R. E., & Cacioppo, J. T. (1979). Effects of forewarning and persuasive intent and involvement on cognitive responses and persuasion. *Personality and Social Psychology Bulletin, 5,* 173–176.

Rajecki, D. W., Ickes, W., & Tanford, S. (1981). Locus of control and reactions to a stranger. *Personality and Social Psychology Bulletin, 7,* 282–289.

Shaver, P., Pullis, C., & Olds, D. (1980). *Report on the LHJ "Intimacy Today" Survey.* Private research report to the *Ladies' Home Journal.*

Stinson, L. (1989). *Intersubjectivity and empathic accuracy in the interactions of male friends and male strangers.* Unpublished doctoral disseration, University of Texas at Arlington.

Stinson, L., Ickes, W., Garcia, S., Bissoneete, V., & Briggs, S. (1989). Correlates of shyness and physical attractiveness in mixed-sex dyads. Manuscript submitted for publication.

Zammichieli, M. E., Gilroy, F. D., & Sherman, M. F. (1988). Relation between sex-role orientation and marital satisfaction. *Personality and Social Psychology Bulletin, 14,* 747–754.

2

Using Electrodermal and Cardiovascular Measures of Arousal in Social Psychological Research

JIM BLASCOVICH
ROBERT M. KELSEY

Jim Blascovich is Director of the Center for the Study of Behavioral and Social Aspects of Health and Associate Professor of Psychology at the State University of New York at Buffalo. In addition to his interest in social psychophysiological methods, he has published research articles and reviews on visceral perception. He is currently the Secretary-Treasurer of the Society for Personality and Social Psychology, Inc., and Division 8 of the American Psychological Association.

Robert M. Kelsey is a Postdoctoral Fellow at the Center for the Study of Behavioral and Social Aspects of Health at the State University of New York at Buffalo. His research interests include cardiovascular psychophysiology and the correlates of individual differences in psychophysiological reactivity to stress. He is a coauthor of the impedance cardiography guidelines of the Society for Psychophysiological Research to be published in *Psychophysiology*.

The use of psychophysiological measures in social psychological research is the exception to the rule of self-report and behavioral measures. This circumstance persists despite publications over the past 30 years delineating improvements in physiological measurement techniques and proclaiming the promise of "social psychophysiology" (see Cacioppo & Petty, 1983a, 1986; Kaplan & Bloom, 1960; Shapiro & Crider, 1969; Waid, 1984). It also persists despite the appeal of the objective and unbiased nature of psychophysiological responses as measures of intraindividual processes central to social psychological theory, particularly processes involving arousal or activation.

A psychINFO™ data base search for the past 20 years of the *Journal of Personality and Social Psychology,* the *Journal of Experimental Social Psychology,* and *Personality and Social Psychology Bulletin* revealed that

AUTHORS' NOTE: Support for the research reported in this chapter was provided in part by a postdoctoral fellowship to the second author by the Center for the Study of Behavioral and Social Aspects of Health at the State University of New York at Buffalo. We gratefully acknowledge comments on earlier versions of this manuscript by John T. Cacioppo and an anonymous reviewer.

despite substantial increases in articles published, a small but steady decline over consecutive 5-year periods occurred in the number of articles that reported physiological measures. Overall, less than 3% of the articles fit in this category. Although many such studies appear in journals such as *Psychophysiology* and in edited volumes (see Cacioppo & Petty, 1983a; Waid, 1984), their scarcity in the field's major journals is notable.

Various reasons for this paucity have been suggested: (a) relatively little knowledge about psychophysiological theory and measurement on the part of social psychologists, (b) the lack of physiological measurement instrumentation in their laboratories, (c) difficulty in interpreting physiological data, and (d) a bias toward acceptance of self-report measures when they conflict with results based on psychophysiological measures (Cacioppo & Petty, 1986). To these we add (e) the perceived lack of an unambiguous physiological measure of arousal—the lack of a sort of "magic litmus test" of arousal.

In our view, the last four reasons follow from the first. Consequently, our goal is to provide information about psychophysiological theory and measurement to help researchers weigh the value of using psychophysiological measures of arousal. Our aim is to provide *practical information*. Comprehensive information regarding psychophysiological theories and measurement techniques is available in the references cited here and elsewhere (see Coles, Donchin, & Porges, 1986; Martin & Venables, 1980). Specifically, our purposes are (a) to discuss specific theoretical and methodological issues related to the use of psychophysiological measures of arousal, (b) to describe state-of-the-art electrodermal and cardiovascular measurement techniques, and (c) to emphasize the use of patterns of electrodermal and cardiovascular responses as indexes of arousal.

THE NATURE OF AROUSAL
IN SOCIAL PSYCHOLOGICAL RESEARCH

"Arousal" is ubiquitous in social psychological theory, extending across a broad spectrum of social psychological phenomena, including theories of emotion, attitudes and attitude change, aggression, helping behavior, social facilitation, social justice, interpersonal attraction, and social ecology (Blascovich & Katkin, 1982). In social psychological experiments "arousal" can be identified as an independent, intervening, or dependent variable. Although psychophysiological measures have provided manipulation checks of arousal as an independent variable (e.g., Cantor, Zillmann, & Bryant,

1975; Wegner & Giulani, 1980), as an intervening variable (e.g., Croyle & Cooper, 1983; Gleason & Katkin, 1978), and as a dependent measure (e.g., Austin & Walster, 1974; Cline, Croft, & Courrier, 1973), in general, psychophysiological measures have been used only rarely to measure arousal variables.

The major role of arousal in social psychological theory has been as a mediating (i.e., intervening) variable. Prototypically, arousal-based theories of social behavior postulate conditions (antecedents) causing changes in arousal (mediator) that affect social behavior (consequents). For example, according to dissonance theory, opposing cognitions generate psychic tension, leading to behavioral or attitudinal changes (Festinger, 1957).

Given the usual implicit use of its referents (tension, stress, dissonance, inconsistency, and so on), it is not surprising that arousal serves often as a symbolic rather than psychophysiological construct (Averill, 1974). The arousal basis of a theory of social behavior is demonstrable physiologically only if arousal is specified in biological terms. Arousal need not remain a hypothetical construct or an empirical variable assessed indirectly through self-report and behavioral responses. Rather, it can be assessed empirically, serving as a tool in delineating fundamental stages of social processes.

THE NATURE OF AROUSAL
AS MEASURED PSYCHOPHYSIOLOGICALLY

Galen and Erasistratos are the ancients credited with the first systematic social psychophysiological observations of arousal (Mesulam & Perry, 1972). Apparently, Galen diagnosed a woman's "lovesickness" on the basis of pulse rate irregularities that he observed consistently across several examinations whenever he mentioned a certain male's name. Erasistratos made the same diagnosis about a young man who exhibited a syndrome of peripheral physiological responses, including not only pulse variability but also increased sweating and pallor, in the presence of his young stepmother.

Interestingly, Galen based his conclusion on repeated observations of a single psychophysiological response to a stimulus, while Erasistratos based his on the observation of a pattern of psychophysiological responses. As we will argue, social psychologists can increase the utility of psychophysiological measures of arousal by following both Galen's model of continuous or repeated measurement and Erasistratos's model of observing response patterns.

Most modern psychophysiological research on arousal has concentrated on autonomic nervous system activity, particularly electordermal and cardiovascular responses. Since interpretation of psychophysiological data requires a firm grounding in basic physiological principles, we begin with a necessarily brief and simplified review of the nervous system and electrodermal and cardiovascular physiology. Researchers are urged to read more detailed reviews (see Fowles, 1986; Larsen, Schneiderman, & Pasin, 1986; Van Toller, 1979).

The Nervous System

The nervous system is categorized into the central nervous system (CNS), consisting of all neural tissue contained within the skull and the spine (i.e., brain, brain stem, and spinal cord), and the peripheral nervous system, consisting of all remaining neural tissue. The peripheral nervous system is categorized into the somatic nervous system, consisting of the nerves serving skeletal muscles, and the autonomic nervous system (ANS), consisting of the nerves serving the smooth muscles of the heart, visceral organs, and endocrine glands. Although these classifications are based on anatomical and functional characteristics, they are somewhat arbitrary and are meant to serve primarily as aids to conceptualization. *It is important to remember that all behavior reflects the activity of a single, integrated nervous system, and that the various subsystems do not operate independently.*

The autonomic nervous system. The ANS consists of two interacting divisions, the parasympathetic nervous system (PNS) and the sympathetic nervous system (SNS), which differ anatomically and functionally. The SNS serves to mobilize and expend bodily resources (catabolism), whereas the PNS serves to conserve and restore bodily resources (anabolism).

Parasympathetic nerves emerge from the cranial and sacral regions of the CNS, and project to isolated ganglia situated in or near target organs, accounting for the *discrete* effects of the PNS. Sympathetic nerves emerge from the thoracic and lumbar spinal regions and travel a short distance to chains of interconnected ganglia located parallel to the spinal cord. The interconnections of these ganglia permit extensive communication so that activity in one ganglion may trigger "sympathetic" activity in nearby ganglia, accounting for the *diffuse* effects of the SNS. However, recent studies using microneurographic recordings indicate that sympathetic neural discharges to the skin are not necessarily coincident with those to skeletal muscles, suggesting that SNS activity may not be as unitary as generally assumed (Wallin, 1981).

The PNS and SNS can generally be distinguished by the type of neurotransmitter released at the target organ. Postganglionic parasympathetic stimulation involves cholinergic transmission, with acetylcholine as the neurotransmitter, whereas postganglionic sympathetic stimulation usually involves adrenergic transmission, with norepinephrine (noradrenaline) as the neurotransmitter. However, different types of postsynaptic receptors are involved in adrenergic transmission at different target organs. For example, sympathetic transmission to the heart involves beta-adrenergic receptors, while sympathetic transmission to the vasculature involves both beta- and alpha-adrenergic receptors. It is important to note that while SNS transmission is predominantly adrenergic, sympathetic stimulation of certain target organs, such as the sweat glands and certain limb muscles, is cholinergic. Thus SNS effects on various target organs may vary as a function of differences in neurotransmitter and receptors.

Electrodermal Activity

Electrodermal responses, historically termed "galvanic skin responses," are among the most used psychophysiological measures. This popularity stems from the relative ease and low cost of such measurement, and the lawful relations of electrodermal responses to certain stimuli.

Electrodermal activity (i.e., the electrical activity of the skin) is due primarily to eccrine sweat gland activity. The SNS is the common pathway to the eccrine sweat glands from CNS areas controlling motor activity, emotional behavior, homeostatic functions, arousal, and attention (Fowles, 1986). When the sympathetic nerves that innervate eccrine sweat glands are stimulated, they release acetylcholine, which stimulates cholinergic receptors on the sweat glands, causing them to secrete sweat into coiled sweat ducts. This sympathetically mediated secretion of sweat is detected at the skin surface as an electrodermal response, with response size depending primarily on the level of duct-filling. Some sweat is absorbed by the skin (corneal hydration), thereby contributing to variations in electrodermal level and response size (Fowles, 1986).

The concentration of eccrine sweat glands is greatest on the palms and soles, so electrodermal activity (EDA) is recorded typically from either surface, with palmar sites being more popular. Although eccrine sweat gland activity at the palms and soles is involved in thermoregulation under some circumstances, its primary function is apparently to maintain proper moisture levels in the outer layer of the skin (corneum) on the hands and feet (Fowles, 1986). This results in improved abrasion resistance and gripping, and enhanced tactile sensitivity. Since these effects are adaptive in situations requiring fight or flight, it is not surprising that increased EDA is a prominent feature of the sympathetically mediated defense reaction (fight-flight response). In addition, electrodermal responses are an integral part of the orienting reaction to novel or significant stimuli (Graham & Clifton, 1966).

Unlike most autonomic measures, electrodermal activity is influenced by SNS but not PNS activity; thus electrodermal measures hold considerable promise as indexes of SNS activity. However, this promise is tempered somewhat by the fact that sympathetic influences on electrodermal activity are mediated by cholinergic rather than adrenergic transmission. Since there are differences between cholinergic and adrenergic transmitter systems in neurotransmitter metabolism and in susceptibility to circulating catecholamines (i.e., epinephrine and norepinephrine), electrodermal measures may not reflect general SNS activity across physiological systems and target organs.

Cardiovascular Activity

As with EDA, central control of cardiovascular activity can be traced to CNS pathways involved in a variety of activities, including motor activity, emotional reactions, homeostatic functions, arousal, and attention. The ANS provides the common pathway from these central systems to the heart and the vasculature (Larsen et al., 1986). The heart and the vasculature form a closed *system* that supplies blood to the body. This system consists of a pump (heart), a series of distributing and collecting tubes (arteries and veins), and a network of thin vessels (capillaries) allowing substance exchange between the blood and body tissues (Larsen et al., 1986).

The heart consists of two dual-chambered pumps, each with an atrium and a ventricle. The right atrium receives oxygen-depleted blood (venous blood) from the body, passing it to the right ventricle, which pumps it to the lungs via the pulmonary artery. The left atrium receives oxygen-rich blood from the lungs via the pulmonary vein, passing it to the left ventricle, which pumps it to the rest of the body via the aorta.

The *cardiac cycle* begins with depolarization ("firing") of the sinoatrial node, the cardiac pacemaker. Depolarization and contraction of both atria and depolarization of the atrioventricular node follow. Depolarization then spreads through conduction tissue (the Purkinje network) to the ventricles, where ventricular contraction is initiated, generating the force required to eject blood from the ventricles into the pulmonary and systemic (aorta) arteries. A rest period follows, allowing for repolarization before the next cycle. The phase of the cycle in which depolarization, contraction, and ejection occur is termed *systole*, while the rest phase is termed *diastole*.

After leaving the heart, the blood flows as a pulse wave through a series of arteries of diminishing diameter, with resistance to flow increasing as the diameter decreases. The blood passes from the arteries through the capillaries, where it exchanges nutrients for local metabolic wastes. The blood then proceeds through a series of veins of gradually increasing diameter as it returns to the heart.

Cardiac activity. The activity of the heart can be described in terms of the *rate* at which it beats, *chronotropic* performance, and the *force* with which it beats, *inotropic* performance (Larsen et al., 1986). Both are influenced by a variety of neural, hormonal, and intrinsic regulatory mechanisms. Contractile force and venous return determine the volume of blood pumped by the heart on each beat, the stroke volume. Stroke volume and heart rate, in turn, interact to determine the volume of blood pumped by the heart over time, the cardiac output.

Neural control of the heart is accomplished by complex SNS and PNS interaction (Larsen et al., 1986; Obrist, 1981). Although there is much overlap, the PNS and SNS differ in the extent to which they control chronotropic and inotropic performance, with the PNS predominating over the former (i.e., rate) and the SNS predominating over the latter (i.e., contractile force). Parasympathetic effects on the heart are mediated by cholinergic transmission involving acetylcholine released by the vagus nerve, while sympathetic effects are mediated by beta-adrenergic transmission involving norepinephrine released by the cardiac sympathetic nerves. Myocardial beta-adrenergic receptors also are sensitive to circulating epinephrine released by the adrenal medulla upon SNS activation.

In the absence of neural control, intrinsic heart rate exceeds 100 beats per minute (bpm), the spontaneous firing rate of the SA node. However, adult resting heart rate (HR) is closer to 70 bpm due to the restraining influence exerted by the vagus nerve of the PNS (Larsen et al., 1986). Consequently, increases in HR may be accomplished efficiently by the simple withdrawal of vagal (PNS) restraint. Conversely, decreases in HR may be accomplished by an increase in vagal restraint. Increases or decreases in HR mediated respectively by increases or decreases in SNS activation appear to be of secondary importance under most circumstances, although SNS influences may trigger or modulate variations in PNS restraint (Larsen et al., 1986; Obrist, 1981). Heart rate also varies with the respiratory cycle, increasing during inspiration and decreasing during expiration. This cyclical pattern of respiratory-related HR fluctuations is termed *respiratory sinus arrhythmia* (RSA). The extent of RSA appears to be related directly to the degree of cardiac vagal tone (Grossman & Wientjes, 1986).

In contrast to rate, variations in contractile force are more closely related to variations in SNS influences, with PNS and intrinsic influences playing a secondary role under most conditions encountered in psychophysiological research (Larsen et al., 1986; Newlin & Levenson, 1979; Obrist, 1981). Thus increases in contractile force usually reflect increased beta-adrenergic SNS effects on the heart.

Vascular activity. Resistance encountered by the blood as it passes through the arteries is a key factor in the regulation of blood pressure and flow (Larsen et al., 1986). Since vascular resistance to blood flow is inversely related to vessel diameter, blood flow can be regulated by altering vessel diameter. Blood flow distribution is coordinated by increasing *vasoconstriction* (decreasing vessel diameter) in relatively inactive regions of the body while increasing *vasodilation* (increasing vessel diameter) in more active regions.

In contrast to the heart, neural regulation of vascular tone is accomplished exclusively by the SNS (Larsen et al., 1986). Norepinephrine released by sympathetic nerves and circulating epinephrine released by the adrenal medulla stimulate alpha-adrenergic receptors on vascular smooth muscle, inducing vasoconstriction. Conversely, vasodilation may be accomplished in a variety of ways: (a) A decrease in alpha-adrenergic stimulation results in relaxation of vascular smooth muscle; (b) stimulation of peripheral beta-adrenergic receptors by circulating epinephrine produces vasodilation in certain vascular beds; (c) stimulation of cholinergic receptors by sympathetic nerves produces rapid vasodilation of the arteries in certain limb muscles. Also, local metabolic processes alter vascular tone in certain arteries, including those serving the heart and active muscles. Thus, although cardiac output determines total flow, the vasculature determines how that flow is distributed.

Cardiac output and arterial resistance, along with blood volume, interact to determine mean arterial blood pressure, the average blood pressure over the entire cardiac cycle (Larsen et al., 1986; Obrist, 1981). Blood pressure varies throughout the cardiac cycle, reaching its highest level during the systolic phase and its lowest level during the diastolic phase. Systolic blood pressure (SBP) is influenced by vascular resistance and by the volume of blood pumped into the arterial system, which is, in turn, influenced by contractile force (Obrist, 1981; Steptoe, 1980). Diastolic blood pressure (DBP) is influenced by vascular resistance and HR (Obrist, 1981; Steptoe, 1980). Heart rate affects DBP by limiting the proportion of time spent in diastole; at higher rates, the heart spends less time in diastole, which allows less time for peripheral runoff of blood from the arterial side to the venous side. Under these conditions, a greater volume of blood remains in the arteries during diastole, thereby elevating DBP.

PSYCHOPHYSIOLOGICAL THEORIES OF AROUSAL

Relationships among electrodermal, cardiac, and vascular measures have played a crucial role in the development of psychophysiological theories of arousal. Traditional arousal theories attempted to provide a physiological basis for the Hullian drive concept by extending Cannon's emergency reaction, consisting of SNS activation and energy mobilization during strong emotion (i.e., the fight-flight response), to the *intensity* aspect of all behavior (for example, see Duffy, 1957; Malmo, 1959). The intensity aspect was distinguished from the directional aspect of behavior (e.g., approach versus avoidance), and was described in terms of a unidimensional continuum of arousal ranging from states of deep sleep to states of extreme stress. Arousal was related theoretically to behavioral performance by an inverted U-shaped function, with maximal performance occurring at moderate levels of arousal. Visceral manifestations of arousal were presumably mediated by the SNS, and substantial covariation among measures of electrodermal, cardiac, and vascular activity was generally expected. Unfortunately, this notion of covariation among autonomic measures has fostered the use of electrodermal, cardiac, and vascular measures as interchangeable, unidimensional indexes of arousal.

Although covariation among autonomic measures in often apparent, Lacey (1967) demonstrated that "directional fractionation" of autonomic responses occurs under certain conditions, a phenomenon known as *situational stereotypy* or *stimulus-response specificity.* He noted that conditions involving the *rejection* of environmental stimulation are characterized by increases in both EDA and HR, whereas conditions involving the *intake* of environmental stimulation are characterized by increases in EDA but decreases in HR. Directional fractionation may even appear *within* the cardiovascular system, such that increases in sympathetically mediated vasoconstriction may be accompanied by either increases *or* decreases in HR, depending upon the situation. Based on observations such as these, Lacey (1967) proposed his intake-rejection theory, suggesting that ANS response patterns reflect directional as well as intensity aspects of behavior, and that electrodermal, cardiac, and vascular measures of arousal are *not* interchangeable. Moreover, Lacey suggested that variations in HR and blood pressure under different environmental conditions are instrumental in modulating cortical arousal, with HR deceleration triggering an increase in cortical processing of environmental information, and HR acceleration triggering a decrease in such processing.

Graham and Clifton (1966) integrated Lacey's intake-rejection concept with work on the orienting and defense reflexes, drawing parallels between the orienting response to novel stimuli and sensory intake on the one hand, and the defensive response to threatening stimuli and sensory rejection on the other. They summarized evidence indicating that the orienting response is associated with an increase in EDA but a decrease in HR, whereas the defensive response is associated with increases in both EDA and HR. Thus it is theorized that directional fractionation of HR and EDA appears during sensory intake and orienting behavior, and that covariation between HR and EDA appears during sensory rejection and defensive behavior.

Directional fractionation usually involves unexpected variations in HR with concurrent increases in EDA. As discussed, however, EDA is controlled exclusively by the SNS, while HR is under both SNS and PNS control. Since the PNS predominates in the control of HR, instances of directional fractionation of HR responses may be due to masking of SNS influences on the heart by more powerful PNS influences, an effect that cannot occur at the sweat glands. If this is the case, then cardiac measures that are influenced predominantly by the SNS, such as inotropic indexes, should covary more closely with EDA. Preliminary evidence in support of this hypothesis has been obtained in our laboratory (Kelsey, 1988).

An alternative to Lacey's intake-rejection theory is Obrist's cardiac-somatic theory. Obrist (1981) proposed that cardiovascular and somatomotor activity are integrated by the CNS under most conditions, and that such cardiac-somatic coupling is apparent when the heart is under vagal (PNS) control. *Cardiac-somatic coupling* and vagal control of the heart predominate during rest and exercise, as well as during conditions that involve the passive receipt of environmental stimulation (i.e., passive coping). *Cardiac-somatic uncoupling* and sympathetic influences on the heart are hypothesized to emerge during conditions that require active efforts to cope with the environment (i.e., active coping). More recently, Brener (1987) has suggested that SNS influences on the heart tend to emerge under novel or unpredictable environmental conditions. Thus variations in SNS and PNS influences on the heart are theoretically related to dimensions of active-passive coping and novelty-familiarity.

Obrist's active coping concept shares some features with Lacey's sensory rejection concept and the defensive response, while his passive coping concept shares certain features with Lacey's sensory intake concept and the orienting response; however, these dimensions are not completely congruent. For example, both the cold pressor task and a mental arithmetic task qualify as sensory rejection tasks according to Lacey, since both of them elicit substantial increases in HR. However, the increase in HR evoked by mental arithmetic is mediated by both beta-adrenergic activation and vagal (i.e., PNS) withdrawal, whereas the increase in HR evoked by the cold pressor is mediated almost entirely by the withdrawal of vagal restraint. Thus, according to Obrist, mental arithmetic qualifies as an active coping task, while the cold pressor qualifies as a passive coping task. The theories of Obrist and Lacey also lead to different interpretations of the functional significance of the HR deceleration that accompanies the orienting response. According to Lacey's theory, this HR deceleration is instrumental in increasing cortical activation, but according to Obrist it is a peripheral manifestation of CNS processes involved in the integration of somatic and cardiac activity, such that the HR deceleration accompanies a reduction in somatic activity that serves to minimize somatosensory interference during orienting.

More recent theories have attempted to differentiate a general arousal concept into two or more regulatory systems. For example, Fowles (1980) has proposed a psychophysiological theory that deals specifically with the relationship between EDA and HR. According to this theory, variations in HR reflect the activity of a *behavioral activation system* (BAS), whereas variations in electrodermal activity reflect the activity of a *behavioral inhibition system* (BIS). The BAS represents an appetitive motivational system that initiates behavior in response to conditioned stimuli for reward, approach, or active avoidance. Such stimuli elicit increases in HR, but have little or no effect on EDA. In contrast, the BIS represents an aversive motivational system that inhibits behavior in response to conditioned stimuli for punishment, extinction, or passive avoidance. Such aversive stimuli elicit increases in EDA, but have no consistent effects on HR.

Others have differentiated between an arousal system and an activation system (see, e.g., Pribram & McGuinness, 1975; Tucker & Williamson, 1984). According to these theorists, the arousal system responds phasically to environmental input and is involved in perceptual processes, whereas the activation system maintains a tonic readiness to respond and is involved in motor processes. Although these theories do not make specific predictions about cardiovascular and electrodermal responses, it follows that the arousal system may subserve orienting and sensory intake processes, while the activation system may subserve defensive and sensory rejection processes.

These psychophysiological perspectives may be useful for delineating and assessing arousal in social psychological research (see below). However, additional factors must be considered, including phenomena related to adaptation (habituation) effects and individual differences in autonomic responsiveness. Although theoretically interesting themselves, these phenomena may confound the interpretation of physiological responses in arousal studies.

Adaptation effects. Whereas arousal is associated usually with increases in ANS activity in response to stimuli, adaptation is associated with decreases in ANS activity over time. Several psychophysiological phenomena reflecting various aspects of adaptation include habituation effects, homeostatic processes, orienting and defensive responses, and initial values effects (see Cacioppo & Petty, 1983b; Stern, Ray, & Davis, 1980, for overviews). Under most conditions, psychophysiological responses diminish with repetition of the same or similar stimuli, a phenomenon known as *adaptation* or *habituation*. Such effects may reflect aspects of information processing or learning, or homeostatic processes (Brener, 1987; Graham & Clifton, 1966; Kelsey, 1988). The rate of habituation varies with the type of stimulation: innocuous, novel stimuli tend to elicit an orienting response that habituates quickly, whereas noxious, threatening stimuli tend to elicit a defensive response that habituates slowly (Graham & Clifton, 1966). The response to a stimulus also may be restrained by initial prestimulus values, such that higher prestimulus levels may be associated with smaller responses to stimulation (Wilder, 1967). Such ceiling effects are more likely to occur with some measures (e.g., skin resistance, HR) than others (e.g., skin conductance, preejection period). In general, the presence of adaptation effects increases the risk of Type I error for manipulations designed to *decrease* arousal, but increases the risk of Type II error for manipulations designed to *increase* arousal.

Individual response stereotypy. Although different tasks may elicit different patterns of ANS responding (i.e., stimulus-response specificity), there also are consistent individual differences in patterns of ANS responding across situations, a phenomenon known as *individual response stereotypy* (Lacey & Lacey, 1958). Some people may show large increases in EDA but little change in cardiovascular activity, while others may show the reverse pattern. Thus subjects may be classified as HR reactors or nonreactors (see Obrist, 1981) or as EDA responders or nonresponders (see Venables &

Christie, 1980), and so forth. Attempts have been made to relate different patterns of individual differences in autonomic reactivity (i.e., responsiveness) to different personality dimensions and disease states (Obrist, 1981; Venables & Christie, 1980). Although in many cases individual differences in autonomic responding reflect interesting differences in patterns of neural influences and arousal, there are probably some cases in which individual response stereotypy is associated with peripheral factors unrelated to arousal and neural control.

PSYCHOPHYSIOLOGICAL MEASUREMENT

Electrodermal Measures

Electrodermal activity is recorded using one of two techniques. *Exosomatic* recording involves a small external electrical current or voltage applied to the skin. Variations in the resistance to or the conductance of current flow are measured from two electrodes placed on the palmar surface, usually at the thenar and hypothenar eminences or the medial phalanges of the first two fingers. Skin resistance is measured if a constant current is applied to the skin, whereas skin conductance is measured if a constant voltage is applied. *Endosomatic* recording involves the measurement of the endogenous potential difference, or skin potential, between an active electrode placed on the palm and a reference electrode placed at an inactive site (e.g., the elbow). Thus an electrodermal response may be recorded exosomatically as a decrease in resistance or an increase in conductance, or endosomatically as a change in potential.

Exosomatic measurement (conductance or resistance) is generally preferred because skin conductance responses and skin resistance responses are unidirectional, whereas skin potential responses can be bidirectional, and hence difficult to interpret (Fowles, 1986). Skin conductance is more meaningful physiologically than skin resistance because the electrical properties of sweat glands resemble those of a circuit composed of variable resistors connected in parallel. The effective resistance of such a circuit is equal to the sum of the reciprocals of the resistances, which is the sum of the conductances (Fowles, 1986). In addition, skin conductance changes are influenced less by initial levels than are skin resistance changes, and skin conductance data are distributed more normally than skin resistance data (Venables & Christie, 1980). Consequently, skin conductance measurement is preferred over either skin resistance or skin potential measurement (see Fowles, 1986; Fowles et al., 1981; Venables & Christie, 1980).

Three types of electrodermal activity are typically distinguished: level, specific or elicited responses, and nonspecific or spontaneous responses (Fowles, 1986; Venables & Christie, 1980).[1] Electrodermal level reflects the average amount of activity (e.g., average conductance) recorded during a given time period. A specific electrodermal response is a fluctuation in activity elicited by a specific, known stimulus, while a nonspecific electrodermal response is a fluctuation occurring in the absence of any known stimulus. Typically, specific electrodermal responses are measured in terms of amplitude, and nonspecific responses are measured in terms of frequency.

Electrodermal level is a widely accepted measure of arousal, with increases in arousal indicated by decreases in skin resistance, or by increases in skin conductance or potential; similarly, the amplitude of specific electrodermal responses may serve as an arousal index (Venables & Christie, 1980). However, the most sensitive electrodermal measure of arousal appears to be the frequency of nonspecific electrodermal responses during a given time period (Bundy & Mangan, 1979; Fowles, 1986). Evidence indicates that electrodermal response frequency is influenced almost exclusively by SNS activation, whereas electrodermal level and response amplitude are influenced by prior electrodermal activity and skin hydration as well (Bundy & Mangan, 1979; Fowles, 1986).

Cardiovascular Measures

Chronotropic measurement. Heart rate, the most popular psychophysiological measure, can be assessed indirectly by sensing pulse wave frequency at a peripheral site. However, such measures are susceptible to considerable error unless long measurement periods are employed (Jennings et al., 1981). More accurate determinations are obtained by recording the electrocardiogram (EKG) and measuring the *interbeat interval* (IBI) in milliseconds. The IBI can be used as a chronotropic measure or can be converted to heart rate in beats per minute (60,000/IBI).

EKG recording requires two or more electrodes to detect the bioelectric potentials generated by events in the cardiac cycle (see Jennings et al., 1981.) Since IBI is usually measured as the time between successive EKG R-waves, most psychophysiologists use an electrode configuration that yields the largest R-waves, placing active electrodes on the right arm and left leg, with a ground electrode on the right leg. This configuration is susceptible to artifacts from arm or leg movements in certain experimental situations. In such cases, the active electrodes may be placed on the upper right collarbone and the lower left ribcage.

Since the amount of respiratory-related heart rate variability appears to reflect the degree of cardiac vagal tone, the quantification of respiratory sinus arrythmia may provide a valid index of parasympathetic effects on the heart (Grossman & Wientjes, 1986). Although various methods for quantifying RSA have been proposed, including computerized spectral analysis and digital filtering techniques, the simple peak-to-trough method appears to be appropriate for most applications (Grossman & Wientjes, 1986). This method involves calculating the difference between the minimum heart rate (maximum IBI) during expiration and the maximum heart rate (minimum IBI) during inspiration for each respiratory cycle, and then averaging these differences over all of the respiratory cycles contained within a given measurement period. Thus only an EKG and a respiratory transducer are required.

Inotropic measurement. Contractile force is not as easy to measure as HR. Such measures are important, however, because they complement HR data to provide a more complete description of myocardial performance, and they provide a better index of SNS influences on the heart than HR does. Although several measures of inotropic activity have been suggested, *preejection period*, a systolic time interval, appears to be the best noninvasive measure at present (Newlin & Levenson, 1979; Obrist, 1981).

The principal systolic time intervals are preejection period, left ventricular ejection time, and electromechanical systole, all of which tend to decrease as myocardial performance increases (Larsen et al., 1986). Preejection period (PEP) extends from the onset of ventricular depolarization to the onset of ventricular ejection. Left ventricular ejection time (LVET) spans the interval between the onset and the end of ventricular ejection. Combining PEP and LVET yields electromechanical systole (EMS), which incorporates all of the events between the onset of ventricular depolarization and the end of ventricular ejection. Since PEP includes the time period in which contractile force is generated, changes in PEP tend to reflect changes in contractile force, with decreases reflecting increased contractility. Given that alterations in contractile force are largely mediated by beta-adrenergic influences, PEP provides an excellent index of SNS effects on the heart (Newlin & Levenson, 1979; Obrist, 1981). Since EMS includes PEP, it also provides some indication of SNS influences on the heart (Larsen et al., 1986).

The traditional method for measuring systolic time intervals requires an EKG, a heart sounds microphone (phonocardiogram), and a peripheral pulse transducer at the ear or the carotid artery. Left ventricular ejection time is estimated from the peripheral pulse wave, and EMS is calculated as the interval between the EKG Q-wave and the second heart sound. Preejection period is determined indirectly as the difference between EMS and LVET, with the disadvantage that measurement errors in LVET and EMS are compounded in PEP. Also, the heart sounds and pulse transducers are sensitive to noise and movement artifacts.

Impedance cardiography provides a more powerful noninvasive technique for assessing myocardial performance (Sherwood et al., in press). With this technique a small-amplitude, radio frequency, alternating current is passed through an outer pair of electrodes at the upper neck and abdomen. Resulting variations in impedance (i.e., opposition) to the current flow occurring within each cardiac cycle are recorded from an inner pair of electrodes at the base of the neck and sternum. By recording basal transthoracic impedance (Z_0) and the first derivative of the pulsatile change in impedance (dZ/dt) in conjunction with an EKG, a variety of cardiac measures can be derived, including stroke volume, cardiac output, and direct measures of the systolic time intervals. Since inflections corresponding to the onset and end of left ventricular ejection are apparent in the dZ/dt waveform, PEP can be measured directly as the interval between the EKG Q-wave and the dZ/dt B-wave, which indicate, respectively, the onset of ventricular depolarization and the onset of ventricular ejection. Thus this technique has the distinct advantage of providing a direct measure of PEP.

The interval between the EKG R-wave and the arrival of the pulse wave at a peripheral site, termed *R-wave to pulse interval* (RPI) or *pulse transit time* (PTT), also provides a useful measure of inotropic performance. Since it includes most of the cardiac preejection period, PTT is sensitive to variations in contractile force and cardiac sympathetic effects, as well as variations in systolic blood pressure (Obrist, 1981). Only an EKG and a peripheral pulse transducer are required. The chief disadvantage involves interpretation problems arising from the large arterial transit time component incorporated in PTT. It is possible, for example, that a decrease in PTT associated with a beta-adrenergically mediated decrease in PEP may be counteracted by an increase in PTT associated with a beta-adrenergically mediated increase in vasodilation, resulting in little or no change in PTT despite a generalized increase in beta-adrenergic activation. This problem can be minimized somewhat by choosing a pulse site close to the heart, such as the ear or the carotid artery.

Blood pressure. Blood pressure is recorded typically by placing a cuff over an artery (e.g., brachial), inflating it until the artery occludes (blood flow ceases), and then slowly deflating it. When blood flow resumes, certain pulsatile sounds (i.e., Korotkoff sounds) can be detected via a stethoscope or microphone, and a pulse will appear distal to the cuff. Systolic blood pressure (SBP) is defined as the cuff pressure at which these sounds, or the distal pulse, appear. Diastolic blood pressure (DBP) is the cuff pressure at the cessation of the Korotkoff sounds. The chief disadvantage of occlusion methods is that they can yield only a limited amount of data over time before unacceptable subject discomfort occurs. Continuous estimates of blood pressure changes, particularly SBP changes, may be obtained by measuring pulse transit time or its reciprocal, pulse wave velocity; however, the accuracy of such estimates may vary considerably across individuals and conditions (Obrist, 1981; Steptoe, 1980).

Peripheral blood flow. Since neural influences on vascular tone are mediated exclusively by the SNS (see above), vascular measures should be good indicators of SNS activity. Unfortunately, there are no readily available direct, noninvasive measures of vascular tone. Since regional blood flow is inversely related to vascular resistance, measures of peripheral blood flow can be used to assess peripheral vascular activity (Jennings, Tahmoush, & Redmond, 1980). Peripheral blood flow is not an unambiguous index of vascular tone, however, since blood flow is influenced by cardiac output as well as vascular resistance. Decreases in blood flow may reflect increases in vasoconstriction, decreases in cardiac output, or both, while increases in blood flow may reflect enhanced vasodilatory effects or increased myocardial performance. To rule out such cardiac effects, measures of myocardial performance (e.g., cardiac output or stroke volume) and peripheral blood flow should be assessed concurrently. If myocardial performance remains constant, then regional blood flow changes are most likely vascular in origin.

Photoplethysmography has evolved as the most practical method of measuring blood flow, particularly in the skin. A small light source is concentrated on the skin surface, and changes in the amount of light transmitted through or reflected from the skin are recorded. The amount of light transmitted is related inversely to the red blood cell concentration in the recording area, while the amount of light reflected from the area is related directly to the red cell concentration. Since the concentration of red cells varies directly with blood flow, photoplethysmography provides a measure of relative blood flow through an area.

APPROPRIATE USE OF
PSYCHOPHYSIOLOGICAL MEASURES OF AROUSAL

To this point, we have reviewed psychologically relevant neural influences and irrelevant intrinsic influences on electrodermal and cardiovascular measures of arousal. These are summarized in Table 2.1. Further,

TABLE 2.1   Influences on Electrodermal and Cardiovascular Measures

Measure[a]	Neural Influences		Other Influences
	Primary	Secondary	
Nonspecific skin conductance response	SNS	–	–
Skin conductance level	SNS	–	hydration
Skin conductance response amplitude	SNS	–	hydration
Heart rate	PNS	SNS	respiration, reflexes (e.g., baroreflex)
Respiratory sinus arrhythmia	PNS	–	respiration
Preejection period	SNS	PNS	diastolic filling and pressure
Pulse transit time	SNS	PNS	arterial length and rigidity
Systolic blood pressure	SNS	PNS	arterial rigidity, blood volume
Diastolic blood pressure	SNS	PNS	arterial rigidity, blood volume
Peripheral blood flow	SNS	–	peripheral vascular disease

NOTE: Influences shown here have been simplified for the sake of clarity. They represent some of the important empirically demonstrated influences that may contribute to variations in psychophysiological measures. SNS = sympathetic nervous system; PNS = parasympathetic nervous system.

a. Each of these measures may be influenced by individual differences in responsiveness (i.e., individual response stereotypy).

major psychophysiological theories of arousal, which have evolved with increasing sophistication and behavioral specificity, have been described. Here we make four recommendations, based on implications from the discussions above, for the use of psychophysiological measures of arousal in social psychological research:

1. Specify an arousal construct tied explicitly to psychophysiological theory.
2. Use settings, procedures, and variables that are consonant with the theoretical psychophysiological processes underlying the arousal construct.
3. Specify and assess multiple physiological measures and expected patterns of psychophysiological responses.
4. Use continuous or repeated physiological measures.

Specifying an Arousal Construct

The first recommendation makes clear that investigators should abandon arousal as an implicit or symbolic construct (Averill, 1974) if it is to be assessed psychophysiologically. Ideally, the arousal construct should be specified in terms of appropriate psychophysiological theories. Since arousal is not a unitary construct in either psychophysiology or social psychology, this may seem like trying to hit a moving target with a moving weapon. However, consideration of different psychophysiological views should help investigators define the arousal construct more explicitly and allow empirical verification of its importance in specific social psychological theories.

For example, since dissonance results from cognitions, one could argue that dissonance fits Lacey's notion of sensory rejection rather than intake. Or one might view dissonance as a self-justification process in line with Graham and Clifton's defensive reaction. One might also argue that it fits best with Obrist's notion of active coping. Indeed, dissonance may reflect some combination of all three theoretical psychophysiological influences. Since there are strong similarities in the physiological response patterns associated with sensory rejection, defensive reaction, and active coping, the expected patterns associated with dissonance can be readily specified. Alternatively, the psychophysiological processes underlying dissonance may vary over time, changing perhaps from patterns of intake to patterns of rejection.

If the arousal construct cannot be specified in terms of one of these approaches, then exploratory research may be conducted to identify the physiological changes that accompany the social processes of interest. In order to avoid Type II errors, it is advisable to sample as many physiological response systems as possible. The observed patterns can then be interpreted in terms of one or more of the theoretical approaches. However, further research would be required to verify the initial patterns in an a priori manner.

Maintaining a Psychophysiologically Consonant Experimental Situation

Careful consideration of differing psychophysiological approaches to arousal suggests that researchers should avoid combining experimental stimuli that may elicit oppositional physiological responses. Otherwise, a type of multiple-treatment interference may operate in an experiment to confuse the psychophysiological picture of arousal. Presentation of relatively elaborate textual material to induce arousal (e.g. threat to self-esteem) may evoke sensory intake or orienting processes. These processes are likely to produce response patterns that conflict with the patterns expected in a threat-arousal situation (i.e., defensive reaction), thereby diminishing the utility of the psychophysiological measures. To the extent that social psychological experiments involve multifactorial treatments and elaborate procedures, maintaining a psychophysiologically consonant experimental situation can be difficult. Therefore, it is to the social psychophysiologist's advantage to keep the situation as uncomplicated and straightforward as possible, to include appropriate control groups, and to employ continuous measurement to delineate the psychophysiological processes that unfold over time.

Multiple Psychophysiological Response Measures

Since, as suggested, there is no unidimensional "magic litmus test" of arousal, a strong case can be made for using multiple rather than single electrodermal and cardiovascular measures. First, as discussed, sophisticated psychophysiological theories of arousal specify differential patterns of electrodermal and cardiovascular responses as a function of behavior and environment.

Second, as outlined above, there are multiple influences on electrodermal and cardiovascular responses. For most cardiovascular responses there are opposing SNS and PNS influences (see Table 2.1). For example, one cannot state with certainty whether a change in HR is due to SNS or PNS activity, or both. Moreover, the presence of multiple neurotransmitter systems within the SNS at the heart, the vasculature, and the sweat glands suggests that changes in the activity of one of these systems may not be indicative of changes in the activity of the other systems. Likewise, evidence of SNS efferent patterning in human skin and muscle nerves (Wallin, 1981) suggests that changes in the activity of one response system (e.g., electrodermal activity) may not be accompanied by changes in the activity of other response systems (e.g., vascular activity). In addition, for both cardiovascular and electrodermal measures there are many intrinsic influences that may confound an arousal interpretation of such measures (see Table 2.1). For example, skin conductance level and response amplitude may be influenced by hydration effects and prior EDA. Systolic and diastolic blood pressure are influenced by various cardiac and vascular effects, as well as vascular rigidity and volume loading. Using multiple measures allows the investigator to *converge* on neurally mediated changes reflecting arousal.

Third, using multiple measures ameliorates problems of individual response stereotypy. For example, although nonspecific electrodermal response frequency is under SNS control without direct PNS influences, there is a substantial subset of individuals who fail to show electrodermal responses (i.e., nonresponders or "stabiles") even under specific stimulus conditions that normally produce a response (Venables & Christie, 1980). Likewise, individuals with cardiovascular diseases may exhibit exaggerated cardiovascular responses regardless of stimulus conditions (Obrist, 1981). Since it is unlikely that irrelevant, intrinsic (i.e., nonneural) factors contributing to these individual differences will influence both EDA and cardiovascular activity, multiple autonomic measures should be assessed.

Suggested patterns and measures. Delineating patterns of psychophysiological responses to assess, and identifying specific measures to use, is a function of the psychophysiological approach (e.g., active-passive coping, intake-rejection) that provides the rationale for measurement of the arousal construct. Familiarity with these approaches is essential. An important implication is that *no change* in certain psychophysiological measures may be as important as substantial change in others, as long as the predicted theoretical pattern occurs.

One should include as many nonredundant electrodermal and cardiovascular measures of arousal as necessary in order to disentangle SNS and PNS, as well as intrinsic, influences. Conversely, one should exclude measures that are particularly susceptible to intrinsic influences. As we have argued, assessment of EDA should focus on skin conductance response frequency (number of nonspecific fluctuations) where measurement periods are sufficiently long (e.g., 15 seconds or more). The effects of hydration and prior activity on skin conductance level and response amplitude may make these measures less sensitive to SNS influences (Fowles, 1986) and hence less than ideal. Nevertheless, skin conductance response amplitude may be more appropriate than response frequency for experimental situations involving short-lived (e.g., less than 15 seconds) phasic responses to discrete stimuli.

The assessment of cardiac activity should focus on both chronotropic and inotropic performance, since they represent different degrees of SNS and PNS influence, thereby clarifying the neural interactions underlying changes in cardiac activity. Heart rate or interbeat interval is the primary chronotropic index and PEP is suggested as the primary inotropic index. Although there is no direct noninvasive measure of vascular tone, one or more measures of peripheral blood flow or pressure, such as pulse transit time, should be included to assess peripheral vascular activity and the degree of intrinsic influences on cardiac activity. For example, an increase in HR accompanied by a decrease in PEP and a decrease in PTT is a clear indication of increased SNS activation. On the other hand, an increase in HR accompanied by little or no change in PEP and PTT would suggest PNS withdrawal rather than SNS activation. It should be apparent from prior discussion that multiple neural influences make HR and diastolic blood pressure ambiguous measures of SNS activation.

Since many of the psychophysiological theories that we have discussed predict increases in EDA as a function of arousal, it may be tempting to use electrodermal measures as general indexes of arousal. There are two short-comings to this approach. First, measurement of EDA alone precludes specification of the particular response pattern evoked by a task, thus preventing identification of the theoretical psychophysiological underpinnings of the elicited response. Second, increases in EDA may not reflect generalized increases in SNS activation. The first problem could be ameliorated by including a chronotropic measure of myocardial performance, such as HR, which would, for example, permit interpretation of increases in EDA in terms of orienting versus defensive reactions or intake versus rejection. The second problem could be ameliorated by including a measure of inotropic myocardial performance, such as PEP, and/or a measure of peripheral blood flow, which would provide an indication of the generality of SNS activation.

Instrumentation. General approaches to psychophysiology laboratory setup appear elsewhere (e.g., Cacioppo, Marshall-Goodell, & Gormezano, 1983; Martin & Venables, 1980; McHugo & Lanzetta, 1983). State-of-the-art equipment would include skin conductance (Fowles et al., 1981), electrocardiographic (Jennings et al., 1981), impedance cardiographic (Sherwood et al., in press), and photoplethysmographic (Jennings et at., 1980) equipment. Many social psychologists are unlikely to have access to all of this equipment, especially impedance cardioegraphic equipment. In such cases, less sophisticated alternatives may be used. Relatively inexpensive phonocardiographic equipment (e.g., heart sounds microphone and amplifier), rather than expensive impedance cardiographic equipment, could be used conjunction with EKG and photoplethysmographic equipment to derive somewhat less precise estimates of PEP. Alternatively, EKG and photoplethysmographic equipment could be used alone to derive pulse transit time, a valid but less precise index of inotropic activity. Minimally, HR could be assessed with a simple pulse meter, and systolic and diastolic blood pressure could be assessed with readily available clinical devices. Use of such equipment results, of course, in less measurement precision and greater interpretive difficulties, making the suggested pattern approach critical.

Continuous Measurement

Psychophysiologists rely on continuous or repeated measurement for a variety of reasons. First, continuous observation increases measurement accuracy, since chance fluctuations in recordings due to electrical interference, involuntary subject movements, or spontaneous variations in physiological activity (e.g., respiratory sinus arrhythmia) can be identified and excluded. Second, repeated measurement is necessary to assess changes in psychophysiological responses within individuals over time. Between-groups comparisons of such within-subject changes are usually more powerful than between-groups comparisons of absolute levels because of large individual differences in physiological response levels. Third, repeated observation allows easier identification of novelty and habituation effects, as discussed above. Fourth, studies incorporating within-subject factors, and hence continuous psychophysiological measurement, permit computation of higher-order rate-dependent indexes of arousal such as adaptation and recovery time under various stimulus conditions. Fifth, since response times differ somewhat as a function of differences between physiological systems and individual response stereotypy, continuous measurement permits appropriate "windows" of observation. Finally, continuous assessment allows the investigator to capitalize on experimental designs in which variables are manipulated in a sequential or additive/subtractive fashion (Cacioppo & Petty, 1986). Such a strategy becomes necessary as the number of experimental treatments and the possibility of stimuli likely to engender oppositional psychophysiological processes increase.

OTHER CONSIDERATIONS

Additional issues face the potential social psychophysiologist, including the cost-effectiveness of employing psychophysiological measures and potential methodological problems specific to psychophysiological measurement. The former is, of course, not unrelated to the latter.

Cost-Effectiveness

Some benefits of using psychophysiological measures in social psychological research include: (a) relatively direct and continuous assessment of underlying processes or states; (b) increased sensitivity to subtle changes in underlying states; (c) enhancement of the validity of constructs measured imperfectly by verbal or behavioral measures; (d) less susceptibility to artifacts such as demand characteristics and experimenter bias; (e) refinement and enhancement of theories to reflect better the complex, interrelated biological and social processes underlying behavior; and (f) increased applicability of social psychology in applied areas such as health. Similar and other advantages are discussed by Cacioppo and Petty (1983a) and McHugo and Lanzetta (1983).

On the other hand, there are costs. Most of these are associated with the expense of maintaining a proper psychophysiological recording environment. Setting up a laboratory for long-term use, especially for programmatic research, reduces outlay expenses by amortizing such expenses over a relatively long period of time. And, of course, psychophysiology equipment or even whole laboratories may already be available in an institution if the investigator does some searching. In our opinion, presumed expenses too often and too easily cancel the decision to use physiological measures before the advantages and actual costs are considered.

Methodological Concerns

Using psychophysiological measures brings atypical issues to bear on social psychological research methods. These concerns affect the validity of experiments and data analysis. Special attention must be paid to design and measurement techniques in order to ward off threats to internal validity—especially maturation, testing, instrumentation, and selection—and to external validity—especially the reactive effects of experimental arrangements.

Maturation. Since psychophysiological responses are mediated by physiological systems, which themselves are moderated by biological processes related to digestion, fatigue, drugs (e.g., alcohol, caffeine, nicotine), physical environments, and so forth, the investigator must take account of diurnal variations in various behaviors such as eating, drinking, exercising, and sleeping, as well as environmental influences such as temperature and humidity. One method of controlling maturational artifacts is to run subjects in an environmentally stable, comfortable laboratory setting during time periods when such effects are minimal (e.g., 9 a.m. to 11 a.m.). Specific instructions to get enough sleep the night before and to eat breakfast (or fast) before arriving at the laboratory also may be helpful. If practical considerations demand that subjects be run throughout the day, then random scheduling and assignment of subjects is critical. In addition, maturational considerations (e.g., hunger, thirst, bladder distension) make long experimental sessions (i.e., more than two hours) problematic.

Testing. Repeated psychophysiological measurement can be problematic in two ways. First, such "testing" may change the nature of the target variable. For example, frequent, repeated blood pressure measurement using an occlusive cuff can cause temporary tissue and vascular compression in the arm. Likewise, wearing a finger photoplethysmographic transducer over time can become uncomfortable. Also, as mentioned previously, repeated elicitation of EDA may increase hydration effects on electrodermal level and response amplitude. Second, a "testing" effect may result from measuring psychophysiological responses to repeated stimuli, since habituation and adaption processes may occur.

Instrumentation. Changes can and do occur in psychophysiological measuring devices as a function of electronic noise and time. An environment that is relatively free from electronic interference is desirable. Calibration of electrophysiological recording equipment such as transducers, couplers, and amplifiers is critical, especially for amplitude-based measures such as electrodermal level and response amplitude. Maintaining proper electrode depolarization also is important. Fortunately, circuitry in modern equipment minimizes electronic noise interference and facilitates calibration.

Selection. Individual response stereotypy contributes enough to physiological response variability without adding other group differences to error variance. Gender, age, racial, and morphological (e.g., weight) differences in physiological functioning not only preclude assignment of subjects differing on these factors to different experimental conditions, but also suggest that assignment of a heterogeneous mixture of subjects to the same experimental conditions will increase error variance.

Reactive effects of experimental arrangements. If the array of equipment necessary to perform psychophysiological measurements is foreboding to the potential investigator, imagine the potential subject's perceptions. Subjects should be made comfortable both physically and psychologically. Subjects need to be assured and sometimes reassured about laboratory safety. Furthermore, investigators should refrain from making "medical diagnoses" on the basis of psychophysiological measurement.

Implications for experimental design. The aforementioned threats to internal validity can be controlled by using true experimental designs. We recommend pretest-posttest control group designs, in which subjects are assigned randomly to various treatment levels and physiological measurements are taken repeatedly at each observation point. Generally, this involves a baseline recording period (pretest), followed by experimental stimulation (treatment) and a second recording period (posttest), followed by a final baseline (recovery) period. In familiar Campbellian symbols:

| R | O_1 O_2 O_3 O_4 | XO_5 XO_6 XO_7 XO_8 | O_9 O_{10} O_{11} O_{12} |
| R | O_{13} O_{14} O_{15} O_{16} | O_{17} O_{18} O_{19} O_{20} | O_{21} O_{22} O_{23} O_{24} |

A within-subjects design of this type is also advantageous because it is sensitive to the variability of physiological responses over time and minimizes the effects of individual differences in basal physiological activity. Where subject factors such as gender or personality characteristics are of theoretical interest, analogous quasi-experimental designs are recommended. If multiple treatments are employed in a repeated-measures design, then counterbalancing is critical to minimize adaptation and novelty effects as alternative explanations for physiological changes.

CONCLUSIONS

Arousal can be used as an empirical variable in social psychological research if (a) sufficient attention is paid to possible psychophysiological bases for such arousal, (b) corresponding patterns of electrodermal and cardiovascular responses are delineated, (c) suitable measurement techniques are employed, and (d) appropriate experimental designs are used. We believe that the investment of resources required to incorporate psychophysiological methods in social psychological research will increase the value of arousal constructs in theories of social behavior beyond any value as hypothetical entities and will increase knowledge about physiological processes that accompany social behavior.

NOTE

1. It should be noted that others have proposed somewhat different classifications for electrodermal measures. For example, Cacioppo, Marshall-Goodell, and Gormezano (1983) argue that greater conceptual clarity can be achieved by categorizing physiological activity on two dimensions: phasic versus tonic, and spontaneous versus evoked. Although this taxonomy may prove more useful eventually, we have employed the traditional taxonomy suggested by Venables and Christie (1980).

REFERENCES

Austin, W., & Walster, E. (1974). Reactions to confirmations and disconfirmations of expectancies of equity and inequity. *Journal of Personality and Social Psychology, 30*, 208–216.

Averill, J. R. (1974). An analysis of psychophysiological symbolism and its influence on emotions. *Journal for the Theory of Social Behavior, 4,* 147–190.

Blascovich, J., & Katkin, E. S. (1982). Arousal-based social behaviors: Do they reflect differences in visceral perception? In L. Wheeler (Ed.), *Review of personality and social psychology* (Vol. 3, pp. 73–95). Beverly Hills, CA: Sage.

Brener, J. (1987). Behavioral energetics: Some effects of uncertainty on the mobilization and distribution of energy. *Psychophysiology, 24,* 499–512.

Bundy, R. S., & Mangan, S. M. (1979). Electrodermal indices of stress and cognition: Possible hydration artifacts. *Psychophysiology, 16,* 30–33.

Cacioppo, J. T., Marshall-Goodell, B. S., & Gormezano, I. (1983). Social psychophysiology: Bioelectrical measurement, experimental control, and analog-to-digital acquisition. In J. T. Cacioppo & R. E. Petty (Eds.), *Social psychophysiology: A sourcebook* (pp. 666–690). New York: Guilford.

Cacioppo, J. T., & Petty, R. E. (Eds.). (1983a). *Social psychophysiology: A sourcebook.* New York: Guilford.

Cacioppo, J. T., & Petty, R. E. (1983b). Foundations of social psychophysiology. In J. T. Cacioppo & R. E. Petty (Eds.), *Social psychophysiology: A sourcebook* (pp. 3–36). New York: Guilford.

Cacioppo, J. T., & Petty, R. E. (1986). Social processes. In M.G.H. Coles, E. Donchin, & S. W. Porges (Eds.), *Psychophysiology: Systems, processes, and applications* (pp. 646–679). New York: Guilford.

Cantor, J. R., Zillman, D., & Bryant, J. (1975). Enhancement of experienced sexual arousal in response to erotic stimuli through misattribution of unrelated residual excitation. *Journal of Personality and Social Psychology, 32,* 69–75.

Cline, V., Croft, R., & Courrier, S. (1973). Desensitization of children to television violence. *Journal of Personality and Social Psychology, 27,* 360–365.

Coles, M.G.H., Donchin, E., & Porges, S. W. (Eds.). (1986). *Psychophysiology: Systems, processes, and applications.* New York: Guilford.

Croyle, R. T., & Cooper, J. (1983). Dissonance arousal: Physiological evidence. *Journal of Personality and Social Psychology, 45,* 782–791.

Duffy, E. (1957). The psychological significance of the concept of "arousal" or "activation." *Psychological Review, 64,* 265–275.

Festinger, L. (1957). *A theory of cognitive dissonance.* Stanford, CA: Stanford University Press.

Fowles, D. C. (1980). The three arousal model: Implications of Gray's two-factor learning theory for heart rate, electrodermal activity, and psychopathy. *Psychophysiology, 17,* 87–104.

Fowles, D. C. (1986). The eccrine system and electrodermal activity. In M.G.H. Coles, E. Donchin, & S. W. Porges (Eds.), *Psychophysiology: Systems, processes, and applications* (pp. 51–96). New York: Guilford

Fowles, D. C., Christie, M. J., Edelberg, R., Grings, W. W., Lykken, D. T., & Venables, P. H. (1981). Publication recommendations for electrodermal measurements. *Psychophysiology, 18,* 232–239.

Gleason, J. M., & Katkin, E. S. (1978, October). *The effects of cognitive dissonance on heart rate and electrodermal response.* Paper presented at the annual meeting of the Society for Psychophysiological Research, Madison, WI.

Graham, F. K., & Clifton, R. K. (1966). Heart-rate change as a component of the orienting response. *Psychological Bulletin, 65,* 305–320.

Grossman, P., & Wientjes, K. (1986). Respiratory sinus arrhythmia and parasympathetic cardiac control: Some basic issues concerning quantification, applications and implications. In P. Grossman, K.H.L. Janssen, & D. Vaitl (Eds.), *Cardiorespiratory and cardiosomatic psychophysiology* (pp. 117–138). New York: Plenum.

Jennings, J. R., Berg, W. K., Hutcheson, J. S., Obrist, P. A., Porges, S., & Turpin, G. (1981). Publication guidelines for heart rate studies in man. *Psychophysiology, 18,* 226–231.

Jennings, J. R., Tahmoush, A. J., & Redmond, D. P. (1980). Non-invasive measurement of peripheral vascular activity. In I. Martin & P. H. Venables (Eds.), *Techniques in psychophysiology* (pp. 63–137). Chichester: John Wiley.

Kaplan, H. B., & Bloom, S. W. (1960). The use of sociological and social psychological concepts in physiological research: A review of selected experimental studies. *Journal of Nervous and Mental Disease, 131,* 128–134.

Kelsey, R. M. (1988). An investigation of the relationship between electrodermal lability and myocardial reactivity to stress. *Psychophysiology, 25,* 461–462. (Abstract)

Lacey, J. (1967). Somatic response patterning and stress: Some revisions of activation theory. In M. H. Appley & R. Trumbull (Eds.), *Psychological stress: Issues in research* (pp. 14–37). Englewood Cliffs, NJ: Prentice-Hall.

Lacey, J. I., & Lacey, B. C. (1958). Verification and extension of the principle of automatic response-stereotypy. *American Journal of Psychology, 71,* 50–73.

Larsen, P. B., Schneiderman, N., & Pasin, R. D. (1986). Physiological bases of cardiovascular psychophysiology. In M.G.H. Coles, E. Donchin, & S. W. Porges (Eds.), *Psychophysiology: Systems, processes, and applications* (pp. 122–165). New York: Guilford.

Malmo. R. B. (1959). Activation: A neuropsychological dimension. *Psychological Review, 66,* 367–386.

Martin, I., & Venables, P. H. (Eds.). (1980). *Techniques in psychophysiology.* Chichester: John Wiley.

McHugo, G. J., & Lanzetta, J. T. (1983). Methodological decisions in social psychophysiology. In J. T. Cacioppo & R. E. Petty (Eds.), *Social psychophysiology: A sourcebook* (pp. 630–665). New York: Guilford.

Mesulam, M., & Perry, J. (1972). The diagnosis of lovesickness: Experimental psychophysiology without the polygraph. *Psychophysiology, 9,* 546–551.

Newlin, D. B., & Levenson, R. W. (1979). Pre-ejection period: Measuring beta-adrenergic influences upon the heart. *Psychophysiologsy, 16,* 546–553.

Obrist, P. A. (1981). *Cardiovascular psychophysiology: A perspective.* New York: Plenum.

Pribram, K. H., & McGuinness, D. (1975). Arousal, activation, and effort in the control of attention. *Psychological Review, 82,* 116–149.

Shapiro, D., & Crider, A. (1969). Psychophysiological approaches in social psychology. In G. Lindzey & E. Aronson (Eds.), *The handbook of social psychology* (Vol 3., pp. 1–49). Reading, MA: Addison-Wesley.

Sherwood, A., Allen, M. T., Fahrenberg, J., Kelsey, R. M., Lovallo, W. R., & van Doornen, L.J.P. (in press). Methodological guidelines for impedence cardiography. *Psychophysiology.*

Steptoe, A. (1980). Blood pressure. In I. Martin & P. H. Venables (Eds.), *Techniques in psychophysiology* (pp. 247–273). Chichester: John Wiley.

Stern, R. M., Ray, W. J., & Davis, C. M. (1980). *Psychophysiological recording.* New York: Oxford University Press.

Tucker, D. M., & Williamson, P. A. (1984). Asymmetric neural control systems in human self-regulation. *Psychological Review, 91,* 185–215.

Van Toller, C. (1979). *The nervous body.* Chichester: John Wiley.

Venables, P. H., & Christie, M. J. (1980). Electrodermal activity. In I. Martin & P. H. Venables (Eds.), *Techniques in psychophysiology* (pp. 3–67). Chichester: John Wiley.

Waid, W. M. (Ed.). (1984). *Sociophysiology.* New York: Springer-Verlag.

Wallin, B. G. (1981). Sympathetic nerve activity underlying electrodermal and cardiovascular reactions in man, *Psychophysiology, 18,* 470–476.

Wegner, D. M., & Giulani, T. (1980). Arousal-induced attention to self. *Journal of Personality and Social Psychology, 38,* 719–726.

Wilder, J. (1967). *Stimulus and response: The law of initial value.* Bristol: Wright.

3

A Practical Guide to the Use of Response Latency in Social Psychological Research

RUSSELL H. FAZIO

Russell H. Fazio is Professor of Psychology at Indiana University. His research interests are in the general area of attitudes and social cognition, and include the activation of attitudes from memory, the functional value of attitudes, and the processes by which attitudes guide behavior. He has authored numerous articles reporting research in which response latency measures were employed.

Response latency is used with increasing frequency in social psychological research. Undoubtedly, a number of catalysts are responsible for this increased reliance upon latency measures. The field's recent emphasis on the cognitive processes that mediate social psychological phenomena is one such factor (Sherman, Judd, & Park, 1989). Latency measures have been employed very commonly by our colleagues in cognitive psychology as one means by which information about cognitive processes and structure can be obtained. It is only sensible that social psychological research that is concerned with underlying cognitive mechanisms would find a similar utility in latency measures. Thus the very nature of the research question has provided motivation for the use of response latency. Opportunity factors also have played a major role. Given the proliferation of microcomputers, the technology for collecting response latency data is now readily available, and many social psychology laboratories include a number of microcomputers for use as subject stations.

Given both the motivation and the opportunity, many social psychologists have employed latency measures in their recent research. For example, Smith and his colleagues have used response latency as a means of indexing the efficiency with which individuals can make a variety of judgments

AUTHOR'S NOTE: Preparation of this chapter was supported by Grant MH38832 and by Research Scientist Development Award MH00452 from the National Institute of Mental Health. I would like to thank Donal Carlston, Frank Kardes, Martha Powell, David Schneider, Eliot Smith, and Carol Williams for their helpful comments on an earlier version of this chapter.

(Smith, Branscombe, & Bormann, 1988; Smith & Lerner, 1986). Carlston and Skowronski (1986) collected latency data in the context of an experiment designed to examine associative network representations of a stimulus person. They employed latency to distinguish between alternative pathways by which the perceiver might access relevant information from memory. Judd and Kulik (1980) used response latency measures to examine the effects of attitudes on the ease with which attitudinally relevant information is processed. In my own work, the latency of responses to attitudinal inquiries has proven useful in examining issues relevant to the accessibility of attitudes from memory (see Fazio, 1989, for a review). Clearly, response latency measures constitute an addition to the variety of methodological tools that social psychologists employ.

In this chapter, I plan to discuss the use of response latency in social psychological research. However, the scope and perspective of the chapter will be delimited in that I will not consider the literature that treats reaction time as a phenomenon in and of itself. An extensive literature exists within the fields of cognitive and sensory psychology concerning reaction time and how it is affected by such variables as stimulus intensity and duration, the occurrence of warning signals, the variability and duration of foreperiods that precede stimulus presentation, the impact of trial-by-trial feedback, and the imposition of payoff structures. Excellent and technically sophisticated reviews of this literature are available (e.g., Luce, 1986; Smith, 1968).

Instead, this chapter is written from the perspective of an individual whose laboratory began to employ response latency measures nearly ten years ago—despite being initially naive about many of the potential pitfalls that surround the collection, analysis, and interpretation of latency data. Over the years, the laboratory has been forced to confront a number of such matters. As a result, one characteristic of latency measures has become very obvious to us. Despite the apparent simplicity of response latency (after all, one is simply measuring the time interval between stimulus onset and the subject's responding), latency data can be extraordinarily messy. Nevertheless, we feel that we have made progress in understanding and handling some of the problems that can arise and, consequently, have been able to address a variety of substantive issues that we could not have considered without the use of latency measures.

This chapter focuses upon some issues with which one must be concerned when using response latency, and provides some practical guidelines. I doubt that any of the solutions or practices that my laboratory has adopted as standard operating procedures are in the least bit profound. However, my hope is that pulling these issues and guidelines together will ease the difficulties that researchers who have never used latency measures might otherwise experience. The first section discusses a variety of design and procedural issues that one needs to be aware of when using response latency. A succeeding section considers issues involved in the analysis of latency data. The third section considers the general issue of interpreting latency data and provides illustrations of some conceptual matters that can be addressed with such data.

DESIGN AND PROCEDURAL ISSUES

The latency of a response is measured as the time interval between stimulus onset and the individual's response. The actual timing typically is conducted through the use of computer software that makes use of either the computer's internal clock or a real-time clock board.[1] Most often, such data are collected with the subject seated directly before a microcomputer and responding via the use of designated keys on the keyboard. Alternatively, the subject might be seated before a monitor that is controlled by a computer, which presents the stimulus and records the response that the subject makes on some response box.

However, the collection of response latency data need not be limited to stimuli consisting of computer-generated text. It is possible to collect such data with audio stimuli. For example, Fazio and Williams (1986) conducted a field study with a specially designed apparatus the components of which included a small microprocessor and a two-channel cassette recorder. One channel contained a series of tape-recorded statements to which the participant was to respond by pressing a button on a response box. An electronic marker was placed on the second channel at an appropriate location near the end of each statement. This marker served as the signal for the microprocessor to initiate timing. Thus the latency with which subjects responded to each statement could be recorded. Likewise, it is possible to employ pictorial stimuli in a response latency task. Through the use of an appropriate interface board, one can have the computer control the advancement of a slide projector. In this way, one can present photos as stimuli. The onset of the slide initiates the computer's timing sequence and the subject's pressing of a response button terminates it.

Just as the stimuli need not necessarily be computer-generated text, the response that is required of the subject need not necessarily be a key or button press. For example, the use of voice-activated switches can permit the subject's verbal enunciation of a response to serve as the terminator of the timing sequence.

Despite these potential configurations for special circumstances, the use of computer-generated text as stimuli and key or button presses as responses is certainly the most common, and the simplest, system for collecting latency data. What is far more important than the specific configuration is a variety of procedural matters that focus upon increasing the likelihood that the latency data will both reveal an effect and be interpretable.

Reducing the "Noise" in Latency Data

The major difficulty with latency data is that they tend to exhibit remarkable variability. As a result, the "signal-to-noise" ratio can be far less than is necessary to detect the presence of a true effect statistically. The "noise" emanates from a variety of sources. Individuals themselves respond at very different rates. On any given trial, an individual's attention can wander. An individual can exhibit confusion regarding the matching of his or her implicit response to the motoric response options that are available. Every effort should be undertaken to do whatever is possible to reduce this noise level. Three practices that we have adopted as a matter of course are described below.

Instructions to subjects. Some subjects will reflect and deliberate about their responses. Indeed, it sometimes appears that such subjects have arrived at a response, but then pursue some form of a checking procedure prior to actually responding. The time involved in such a checking sequence is typically not relevant to the question being addressed by the latency measure. Instead, it is a sign that such subjects have adopted a very strict decision criterion; they need to feel very confident of their judgments before responding. This behavior can produce slow latencies and a positively skewed distribution. Inattentive subjects who are not very involved in the task and who are very lackadaisical in responding can also contribute to this skewness. As Luce (1986) has stated: "Much of the art of running a good reaction-time experiment centers on gaining the cooperation of subjects . . . in maintaining a high level of attention when actually running in the experiment" (p. 51).

Variability in latencies can be diminished through the instructions provided to subjects. By inducing all subjects to respond as quickly but as accurately as possible, the experimenter can decrease the likelihood that subjects will provide very slow latencies. Obviously, what is ideal is for subjects to respond as quickly as they possibly can without committing any errors. It is this balance between speed and accuracy that one must attempt to achieve through experimental instruction. Our standard instructions emphasize both factors. After describing the nature of the stimuli that the subjects will see, detailing what is required of them to make a response, and instructing them to keep one index finger above each of the two response keys, the experimenter typically has stated: "Now there are two things that I want you to keep in mind as you do this task. First, and above all, be accurate. Don't be in such a hurry to respond that you regret your decision. Second, while being accurate, try to respond as quickly as possible. So, you should try to maximize both the speed and the accuracy of your responses." Relying upon the subject's verbal and nonverbal reactions, the experimenter reiterates these instructions if it appears that the subject has not understood clearly.

The specific wording is not critical. However, the goal that one seeks to achieve through the instructions is twofold. One aim is that the instructions lead subjects to adopt more uniform decision criteria. The second is that the instructions motivate the subjects to take the task seriously and remain attentive.

Practice trials. A series of practice trials also can be very helpful in reducing the variability in the latency data. Such trials serve to familiarize the subjects with the nature of the task. They also serve to bring the subjects' motor performance to an asymptotic level. As a result, the experimenter can increase the likelihood that the motor component of any given subject's latencies is fairly constant across the target trials.

The presence of at least one block of practice trials has become standard operating procedure in our work employing latency tasks. Indeed, typically the experimenter is given discretion to rerun the practice trials if the subject appears to have the least bit of difficulty in responding at a rapid pace. The intent is to ensure that the subjects truly understand the nature and the mechanics of the task prior to the collection of critical data.

Filler trials. Despite the benefits of appropriate experimental instructions and practice trials, individual differences in general speed of responding can still be profound and can lead to variability in the latency data. The optimal solution to this difficulty is to employ a within-subjects design. In this way, each subject can serve as his or her own control. However, the conceptual variables that are of interest in social psychology often do not lend themselves to manipulation as within-subjects factors. In such cases, it can be beneficial to include a number of filler trials in the latency task. We typically have observed correlations in the .4 to .6 range between the mean filler latencies and the target latency (e.g., Fazio, Herr, & Olney, 1984). The latencies from such trials provide a means of enhancing statistical power. The filler latencies can serve as an index of a given subject's baseline speed of responding. Such baseline assessment can reduce what would otherwise be error variance and, hence, increase the "signal-to-noise" ratio in an experimental design. Another benefit to including filler trials in a response latency task is discussed in a later section concerning the speed-accuracy trade-off.

Number of Response Options

A social psychologist planning a response latency measure needs to make a decision about the number of response alternatives to make available to the subject. Typically, latency tasks involve only two alternatives (e.g., yes/no, like/dislike). However, it is tempting to increase the number of response options so that the response itself represents the subject's position along some Likert-type scale. In this way, one could collect simultaneously both a scalar response and a latency score from each subject.

However, this strategy does pose one major difficulty. The more response alternatives that are available, the greater the likelihood that a given latency score involves a component in which the individual is concerned about the specific response that is most appropriate within some narrowed range of the available options. For example, imagine a subject being required to indicate a judgment via a 9-point scale. The subject might be instructed to use the keys labeled 1 to 9 on the keyboard to indicate the extent of liking or disliking for the stimulus object or to indicate a judgment regarding a target person along a trait dimension. Although the subject may make an implicit judgment readily ("Yes, I do like this object" or "Yes, this person is honest") and might have been able to respond relatively quickly if only a dichotomous choice had been available, the subject may spend time debating whether scale positions 6, 7, or 8 best represents his or her judgment. Such behavior will increase the variability of the observed latencies.

Obviously, the larger the scale one wishes to employ, the greater the problem. In our own work, we have employed both two-response and five-response alternatives. We have found latency data to remain sufficiently sensitive when a five-response alternative Likert scale (e.g., strongly like, like, neutral, dislike, and strongly dislike) is employed. What we typically have done in such cases is to place the labels $++$, $+$, 0, $-$, and $--$ over the relevant keys on the keyboard (usually the digit keys 4-8, only because they are in the center of the keyboard) or above the five buttons on the response box.

Using such a system, we have successfully replicated findings that stemmed from earlier research employing two-response alternatives (see

Fazio & Williams, 1986, p. 506). In addition, we have had success using both the five-options system (Fazio & Williams, 1986; Houston & Fazio, in press) and the two-options system (Fazio, Powell, & Williams, 1988a) in employing latency scores to index the accessibility of subjects' attitudes from memory. However, we have never conducted an empirical investigation that directly compared the two systems and must confess to some concern about the noise that the additional response options might introduce. The success that we have had with five options implies that the extent to which subjects deliberate about which of two adjacent response options (e.g., "strongly like" versus "like") to use is relatively minor in such a configuration.

Although it appears that a five-options system can be employed fruitfully, intuitively one must have serious doubts about any scale involving more than five intervals. Our recommendation is that one not attempt to couple any scale larger than five units with the simultaneous collection of latency data. If scalar responses of more than five intervals are desired (so as to discriminate better among subjects), then it appears more appropriate to distribute a traditional questionnaire *following* the collection of the latency data via a dichotomous response system. Indeed, this was the strategy followed by Fazio et al. (1988a) in their investigation of attitude accessibility as a moderator of the attitude-behavior relation. Indices of attitude accessibility were constructed from the latencies involved in a dichotomous, like/dislike, judgment task and attitude scores themselves were obtained from a subsequently administered set of seven-point response scales.

The Speed-Accuracy Trade-Off

One of the central issues to be kept in mind when employing response latency measures is the well-documented speed-accuracy trade-off (see Luce, 1986; Pachella, 1974). Although the relation between speed and accuracy is certainly not linear, the faster individuals respond, the more likely it is that they will make an error. The decision criterion that subjects adopt may be relatively strict or lenient. That is, subjects may feel that they need to be very sure of their judgments before responding, in which case their latencies are likely to be relatively slow, or subjects may be less cautious, and, even if they commit only negligibly more errors, their latencies are likely to be relatively fast. This trade-off constitutes one of the major reasons for emphasizing both speed and accuracy in experimental instructions, as was discussed above. Ideally, one strives for a situation in which subjects commit very few errors while responding as quickly as possible.

Although there cannot be any set criterion, generally speaking, researchers seem to regard an error rate above 10% as suspect. For example, this issue has been investigated in the context of work concerned with the relation between latency of indicating that a test stimulus was a member of a previously presented set and set size. Sternberg (1975) has argued that the slope and shape of the functions relating latency and set size change very little when subjects are instructed to increase their speed at the cost of accuracy, provided that errors do not exceed about 10%.

Unfortunately, for many of the research questions that would be of interest to social psychologists, accuracy cannot be objectively defined. For example, affective judgments of some stimulus object or target person cannot be compared to some objectively correct answer. Obtaining an estimate of the error rate in such cases is not nearly as clear as when the latency trials involve responses that truly can be considered correct or incorrect.

Although by no means perfect, one "solution" to this issue is to compare the responses that individual subjects make during the latency task to judgments that they provide on a later measure in which speed of responding is not an issue. On the assumption that this latter measure provides an indication of the individual's "true" judgments, inconsistencies between the responses provided in the latency task and these judgments can be examined. Fazio et al. (1988a) did exactly this in an experiment in which subjects made like/dislike judgments about 100 products during a latency task. At a later point in the experiment, subjects were given unlimited time to complete a questionnaire in which they rated each product along a 7-point scale. An "error" was defined as having responded "like" during the latency task but having rated the product more negatively than the neutral point on the questionnaire scale, or having responded "dislike" but assigned a rating above the neutral point. Such inconsistencies were not very frequent. On the average, subjects responded inconsistently on 7.3% of the 100 trials. The examination of inconsistent responding in this manner provides a means by which "error" rates can be approximated in research in which correct and incorrect responses cannot be defined objectively.

In research in which latencies are compared across experimental conditions, one must be concerned with the possibility that the subjects' decision criteria, and hence their positions along a speed-accuracy operating curve, may not be equivalent across conditions. This concern provides yet another reason for employing filler trials. The latencies from such trials can be relevant to the issue of whether any difference in target latency might be attributed to a difference in decision criteria across conditions. If filler latencies were not equivalent across conditions, then the manipulation may have affected the decision criteria that individuals employed. Slower filler latencies in one condition might indicate that the subjects adopted a stricter decision criteria — that is, felt a greater need to be sure of their judgment prior to responding. The absence of such a difference in filler latencies is consistent with the assumption that decision criteria, and hence positions along a speed-accuracy operating curve, were consistent across conditions. Given this reasoning, we strongly recommend employing filler trials as a test of the equivalence of decision criteria whenever there is any reason to suspect that a manipulation has the potential to affect such criteria.

The value of using filler latencies in this manner is illustrated by an experiment conducted by Fazio, Lenn, and Effrein (1984, Experiment 1). This research concerned the spontaneous formation of attitudes and, more specifically, the hypothesis that individuals would be motivated to undertake the effort of developing an attitude when a situational cue implied that it would be functional to have such a summary evaluation. The cue in this experiment involved an expectation of future questioning about the attitude objects. All subjects first worked on samples of five types of novel intellectual puzzles under the guise that the puzzles were being considered for possible use in an aptitude test of "observation skill and strategy development." Some of the subjects then completed an attitude measure in which they rated how interesting they found each puzzle type. Hence these subjects (the consolidation condition) were forced to undertake an attitude formation process. Subjects in the cue condition were not forced to complete a scale, but were led to believe that one of the psychologists who was developing the test would be visiting the lab shortly in order to discuss the puzzles and the subjects' reactions to them. It was in this way that an expectation of future questioning was fostered. The remaining subjects (no consolidation condition) neither were forced to complete the attitude measure nor received the cue.

More will be said about the logic underlying this design at a later point. What is relevant now is that the intent of the experiment was to examine the latency with which the subjects in these various conditions could respond to subsequent attitudinal inquiries about the five puzzle types. If subjects in the cue condition responded faster than subjects in the no-consolidation condition and no slower than subjects in the consolidation condition, then it would appear reasonable to conclude that the cue motivated individuals to undergo the same sort of attitude formation process that forced completion of the questionnaire involved.

However, the concern that the experimenters had about this design was the possibility that the cue would not only promote attitude formation but also alter decision criteria in the latency task. Knowing that a psychologist would be discussing the puzzle types with them might lead the subjects to adopt a more cautious decision criterion, that is, to feel greater pressure to be accurate in their responses. The stricter decision criterion fostered by the cue might mask the enhanced speed that may result from the cue's having also fostered previous attitude formation. Filler trials were employed in order to overcome this difficulty. Two common puzzle types with which subjects would have been familiar prior to the experiment—crosswords and mazes—served as the fillers. As part of the instructions that preceded the latency task, subjects had been forewarned that the trials would involve both the puzzles that they had seen earlier and some that they had not. Unless one were to argue that decision criteria change from trial to trial, the latencies from these filler trials can provide an indication of the strictness of the decision criteria that the subjects were employing.

The latency data revealed that the experimenters' concerns were justified. Filler latencies were relatively slower in the cue condition. However, an analysis of variance in which target versus filler latency served as a within-subjects factor revealed interactions between trial type and condition that confirmed the predictions. Relative to the baseline speed of responding provided by their filler latencies and the decision criteria implied therein, the subjects in the cue condition responded just as fast on the target trials as did the subjects in the consolidation condition, both of whom were faster than the subjects in the no-consolidation condition. Thus the data indicated that an expectation of future questioning was sufficient to prompt attitude formation.

This experiment illustrates the value of including filler trials when a manipulation may conceivably affect decision criteria. If only target trials had been employed, the latency data would have led to the erroneous inference that the cue had not prompted spontaneous attitude formation. By employing filler latencies and examining the target latencies in relation to these fillers, it was possible to obtain clear evidence that the cue implying functionality did exert an impact upon the subjects.

Differential Responses Across Conditions

Another issue to be concerned with when designing an experiment that employs response latency as a dependent measure is the possibility that the responses themselves will not be equivalent across the various conditions. Two conditions may differ in average latency, but if they also differ with respect to average responses, the latency difference becomes difficult to interpret. Is the latency difference a direct consequence of the experimental variable that was manipulated to create the two conditions? Or is it simply a reflection of the differential amount of time that is necessary to decide upon one response alternative over another (e.g., yes versus no)?

This issue is best considered at the time one designs the experiment. If there appears to be a strong possibility that the independent variable will produce differential responses, then the investigator should question the appropriateness of employing a latency measure. If the major concern is with the latency with which subjects can reach some decision or express some judgment, then the experiment ideally should be designed in such a way that differential responses do not occur. That is, the experimental design should be such that equivalent response patterns are to be expected across the various conditions. Further discussion of this issue will be found in the next section, which concerns the analysis of latency data.

DATA ANALYSIS ISSUES

A variety of issues regarding the analysis of latency data merit consideration. Once again, although the practices that we generally have adopted might be fairly obvious, a review of the issues that can arise when analyzing latency data may be helpful to researchers who have not conducted such work.

Skewness of Latency Data

Distributions of response times—whether within a subject and across trials or within a given trial and across subjects—are inevitably skewed. No matter how careful one is with respect to experimental instructions and no matter how many practice trials one provides, latencies on some trials will be relatively slow. Distributions typically are characterized by a fairly long tail of such slow latencies. Indeed, an occasional latency may be so slow that it clearly constitutes an outlier and leads one to wonder whether the subject "fell asleep" on that particular trial.

The question facing the researcher is whether such outliers should be disregarded and the relevant trials simply assigned a missing, or some a priori determined maximum, value. Obviously, this is a judgment call. Such "cleaning" of response latency data is not at all uncommon in cognitive psychology experiments. However, it needs to be done with extreme caution. The distribution of latencies from a given target trial should be examined routinely for the existence of subjects who responded in an extremely slow fashion. Having identified such subjects, it is then prudent to examine the individual subject's distribution of latencies across trials. In this way, one can consider whether the slow target latency merely represents a response from a subject who is generally slow in responding or whether it appears reasonable to conclude that the subject's attention wandered on that particular trial.

Whether outliers are present or not, the skewness of latency distributions has the consequence that a mean of raw latency scores is not generally an ideal measure of the central tendency. Obviously, median latencies can be examined and reported. However, if one wishes to examine means, performing some transformation of the raw latencies is desirable (see Kirk, 1986). We generally perform a reciprocal transformation of the latency scores ($1/X$, or $1/[X + 1]$ if any of the latencies are less than 1 second). Logarithmic transformations also are commonly employed (e.g., Smith & Lerner, 1986). These transformations have the consequence of bringing the tail involving slower latencies closer to the center of the distribution and making the mean a more accurate reflection of the central tendency of the distribution.

Comparing Latencies in Various Experimental Conditions

Differential responses. After conducting an experiment in which latency constitutes a dependent measure, one should examine not only the latencies themselves, but also the responses. In particular, one needs to be concerned with the issue mentioned earlier. Is the pattern of responses equivalent across conditions? One hopes that the experiment was designed in such a way that the answer is yes. However, the situation must be examined. Differential responses across conditions could stem either from subjects' actually judging the information differently or from the manipulation affecting the decision criteria that subjects in the various conditions employed and the resulting "error" rate. In either case, the latency data are then difficult to interpret.

One manner in which latencies are commonly analyzed when evidence exists of differential responses is to limit the analysis to those latencies associated with a given response. For example, only the "yes" latencies might be analyzed. Obviously, such a procedure is characterized by all the problems that social psychologists typically associate with subject attrition. Just as we would be concerned to learn that the data from 20% of the subjects from a given condition were omitted due to suspicion on the part of the subjects, one must be skeptical of omitting latency trials involving a given response. Such a procedure is most appropriate when one of the two response options overwhelmingly predominates over the alternative, as is typically the case when the trial involves an objectively correct answer. Although the error rate may be relatively low, it still may be differential across conditions.

Nevertheless, given low error rates, it may be useful to analyze only the latencies stemming from a correct response.

A second procedure has been suggested as a solution to the problem of differential responses. Pachella (1974) recommends the use of multivariate analysis of variance in such situations. The response and the latency can be treated as a bivariate dependent variable in a MANOVA. This approach may be the only reasonable recourse open to a researcher when the prevalence of one response does not predominate over the other. That is, in a latency task involving a subjective social judgment, the distribution of responses may be such that limiting the analysis to a particular response would result in the loss of too many data points. Although Pachella's recommendation is aimed at differential (and low) error rates, a multivariate analytic approach also appears reasonable for the distributed response situation. Nevertheless, this situation is best avoided by doing all that one can to design the research so that responses will be equivalent across conditions. Regardless of the type of analysis used, interpretation of latency data is problematic when differential responses occur.

Using filler latencies. The value of including filler trials in a response latency task already has been discussed. Latencies from such trials provide a means of controlling for individual differences in general speed of responding and enhancing statistical power. For example, analysis of covariance can be employed. The mean latency from filler trials can serve as a covariate, which typically will reduce the error variance markedly. Alternatively, the target latencies can be adjusted for mean filler latency by the computation of a difference score. In either case, the signal-to-noise ratio is enhanced (see Fazio, Lenn, & Effrein, 1984, as an illustration).

The relevance of filler trials to the issue of the equivalence of decision criteria across experimental conditions also has been discussed. On the assumption that decision criteria do not fluctuate from trial to trial, filler issues can be informative. The latencies from such trials should be analyzed for possible effects of the experimental manipulations. If the experimental conditions differ with respect to filler latencies, then either the manipulation has affected decision criteria or there has been a failure of randomization. In either case, it is important to examine such latencies.

Using Latencies to Identify Position Along a Continuum

Sometimes response latency is employed not as a dependent measure but as an individual difference measure. The relation between this individual difference and some other variables or phenomenon is then examined. For example, my colleagues and I have employed response latencies as a measure of the strength of the association in memory between an attitude object and the individual's evaluation of the object. The strength of these object-evaluation associations is known to be a determinant of the accessibility of the attitude from memory, that is, of the likelihood that the attitude will be activated from memory automatically upon mere observation of the attitude object (Fazio, Sanbonmatsu, Powell, & Kardes, 1986). The question of interest has been whether attitude accessibility moderates the extent of the relation between attitudes and subsequent judgments or behavior. Latencies of response to an attitudinal inquiry provided the means by which individuals could be placed along a continuum representing the accessibility of their attitudes from memory.

The major issue that arises in such research concerns the extent to which one is indexing the conceptual variable of interest versus an individual difference concerning individuals' general speed of responding. Once again, it is important to employ filler trials and to examine the extent to which the target latency covaries with the filler latencies. If substantial covariation does exist, then it is important to adjust the target latencies for individual differences in baseline speed of responding. Otherwise, one is simply identifying a continuum of generally fast versus slow responders.

In our own work, we typically have observed such covariation between target and filler latencies. In fact, this is true of every investigation that we have conducted in which individuals indicated their evaluation of an attitude object as the name of the object appeared on the screen. The one instance in which we did not observe much covariation was an investigation that employed an audio presentation of the stimuli as opposed to text presentation on a computer screen. As mentioned earlier, Fazio and Williams's (1986) investigation of the 1984 presidential election involved a specially designed apparatus that presented tape-recorded attitude statements to the respondent. An electronic marker at the end of each statement initiated the timing sequence. The average interitem correlations among the latencies to the opinion issues that were presented in this way was an insubstantial .19. This contrasts with an average interlatency correlation of .42 (Fazio et al., 1988a) and .40 (Houston & Fazio, in press) in two studies that involved the presentation of textual stimuli. Just why the Fazio and Williams investigation constitutes an exception to what appears to be a general trend is not clear. However, as is implicit in this discussion, the difference in mode of stimulus presentation may be important. The time necessary to read a visual display may enhance the amount of covariation that is observed. That is, reading time may be a fairly constant individual difference that forms a component of each response latency.

Regardless of whether presentation mode is critical or not, it is important that the relation between target and filler latencies be examined. If covariation exists, then the target latencies must be adjusted for the baseline that is provided by the filler latencies. Three possible means of adjustment that we have explored are these. First, and most obviously, one can compute the difference between the target latency and the mean filler latency. Such an index assumes that a difference score of a given value for an individual with a slow baseline is equivalent to the same difference score for an individual with a fast baseline. This assumption may not always be valid. Should an individual with a baseline of 4 seconds and a target latency of 3 be considered equivalent to a person with a baseline of 2 seconds and a target latency of 1?

The second alternative means of adjustment deals explicitly with this concern by computing a ratio index. For example, the ratio of the target latency to the sum of the target latency and the mean filler latency (target/[target + mean filler]) can be computed. Such a ratio can range from 0 to 1, with .5 indicating that the target latency was equal to the mean filler latency. The lower the ratio, the faster the subject's target latency was relative to his or her filler latencies. The two hypothetical individuals noted above would have different values on this ratio index: .43 and .33, respectively.

We can offer no specific recommendation regarding adjustment via a difference score versus a ratio score. In our view, the decision is best made on empirical grounds. The entire intent of adjustment is to remove the covariation between the target latency and the baseline speed of responding. Hence it seems appropriate to base the decision upon the size of the correlation between the adjustment index and the baseline provided by the mean of the filler latencies. Whichever index produces a correlation closer to the desired value of zero is to be preferred.

One final means of adjustment that we have employed involves the computation of z-scores. After calculating the mean and the standard deviation of the filler latencies for each subject, one can transform the target latency to a z-score relative to this mean and standard deviation. In this way, the location of the target latency within an individual subject's distribution of filler latencies can be noted. Intuitively, this appears to be the most pleasing of the possible means of adjustment. However, it does require that the latency task include a sufficient number of filler trials that one can feel confident that a reasonable estimate of the within-subject standard deviation is being obtained. Fazio et al. (1988a) successfully employed such an index in an investigation in which 90 filler trials were available for each subject.

USES OF RESPONSE LATENCY

There may be nothing scientifically less meaningful than the simple observation that subjects responded in x milliseconds. As social psychologists aware of the many influences upon scale ratings (anchoring effects, the role of context, social desirability concerns, and the like), we never conceive of drawing inferences from the simple observation that subjects' average rating on a 9-point scale was 6.5. We want to know how the scale points were labeled, the precise wording regarding the stimulus that was rated, and the context in which the rating was made. Even then, we rarely draw inferences. Instead, we compare the obtained mean to the mean in a relevant control condition. It is the design of the experiment, not the measurement tool of a rating scale, that makes the data interpretable and meaningful.

The same is true of response latency. The interpretation and meaning of latency scores depend upon the type of judgments that respondents are making, the context in which those judgments are made, and the specifics of the experimental design with respect to the conditions being compared. As Pachella (1974) has stated, "Interpretation of reaction time is dependent upon the experimental logic involved in specific situations. . . . all of the general principles of experimental design and deductive logic are applicable when reaction time is a dependent variable" (p. 45).

In what follows, three uses that have been made of response latency measures are discussed briefly. The interpretation of the latency data that seems most appropriate varies from one domain to the other as a function of the context and nature of the latency task.

Spontaneous Formation of a Construct

Response latency tasks can be useful in examining issues concerning the conditions under which individuals spontaneously form some construct. Have they spontaneously drawn some inference from the information that has been provided? Have they summarized that information into some overall judgment, as in the case of forming an attitude toward some novel object or an impression of a target person? When latency measures are to be employed for this purpose, the experimental logic and design takes advantage of an often-observed finding regarding the latency that is required to "compute" a judgment for the first time versus the latency that is required to express the judgment a second time. In a number of different experiments, it has been found that individuals who had previously been forced to develop attitudes toward novel objects, by virtue of the need to complete a questionnaire, responded more quickly to attitudinal inquiries than did individuals who were not so forced to form attitudes (Fazio, Chen, McDonel, & Sherman, 1982; Fazio, Lenn, & Effrein, 1984). Thus individuals who have previously consolidated the available information into a summary attitudinal judgment can respond more quickly to a subsequent attitudinal inquiry than can individuals who have not yet consolidated and need to do so at the time that the inquiry is posed during the response time task.

Carlston and Skowronski (1986) observed a similar effect with respect to trait inferences about a target person's honesty. Two relevant factors were manipulated orthogonally. Before viewing a videotape in which the target person performed an honest behavior, some subjects were explicitly informed that the experiment was concerned with the apparent honesty of the videotaped individuals. After viewing the tape, some subjects received an inquiry regarding the target's honesty prior to the critical trial of the response time task and others did not. These two variables had additive effects upon the latencies of response to the critical question concerning the target's honesty. Having been forewarned about the experimenter's interest in the target's honesty and having made such a judgment previously each served to enhance the speed with which subjects could respond to the later inquiry. Thus, in the two different domains of attitudes and trait inferences, it has been observed that the more relevant cognitive work that individuals perform prior to the response latency task, the greater the savings those individuals exhibit in terms of their latencies of response.

It is this general principle that serves to make response latency measures appropriate for addressing questions regarding spontaneous construct formation. It is this principle that was the basis of the experiment concerning spontaneous attitude formation that was summarized previously (Fazio, Lenn, & Effrein, 1984). As in that experiment, a condition in which subjects are not forced to consolidate but receive some relevant cue can be compared to a condition in which subjects are forced to consolidate and to a condition in which subjects neither consolidate nor receive the cue. By comparing latencies from such conditions, it is possible to discern whether a cue prompted individuals to engage in appropriate cognitive work prior to the response time task. If the consolidation and cue subjects both respond faster than the no-consolidation subjects, then one can conclude that the cue led individuals to undertake some spontaneous cognitive effort. As mentioned earlier, Fazio, Lenn, and Effrein (1984) obtained evidence that an expectation of future questioning was sufficient to prompt spontaneous attitude formation. In a second experiment employing the same design and logic, they found that an expectation of future interaction with the attitude objects also promoted spontaneous attitude formation.

This experimental logic can be applied to any situation in which one is concerned with the subjects' spontaneous formation of a construct. A recent experiment by Kardes (1988) provides yet another illustration. Kardes was interested in persuasion and, more specifically, with the conditions under which individuals would spontaneously infer the conclusion of a persuasive argument when the conclusion had not been stated explicitly. Subjects were presented with an advertisement that described various features of a fictitious compact disc player. In one version, conclusions about these various features (e.g., "Inserting a disc is easy with the CT-2000.") were not stated explicitly, but could be inferred syllogistically from the information that was presented (e.g., "The CT-2000 features . . . a motorized drawer. Other CD players lack a motorized drawer. Inserting a disc is difficult without one."). In the other version, the conclusions were stated explicitly. Kardes reasoned that individuals would spontaneously infer the conclusions only when properly motivated. In order to manipulate the presence or absence of such motivation, the ad sometimes included a boldface header intended to increase the likelihood that the subjects viewed compact disc players as both personally relevant and variable in their quality ("You will probably own a compact disc player sooner than you think. Some CD players are very bad and some are very good.").

At a later point in the experiment, subjects were presented with the conclusions concerning the compact disc player. They were asked to indicate whether the statement was or was not true as quickly as possible. When motivation had not been heightened, subjects who received explicit conclusions responded faster than did those for whom the conclusions were left implicit. However, when the motivational cue was present, this difference did not occur, implying that the cue was sufficient to induce individuals to infer the conclusions spontaneously. Having established that spontaneous inferences had been made in the high-motivation condition, Kardes was then able to address various issues regarding the consequences of such self-generation. Once again, then, response latency measures with appropriate experimental comparisons proved effective at providing an indication of whether subjects had spontaneously engaged in some relevant cognitive work while the information was being presented.[2]

Latency as a Measure of Processing Efficiency

In an impressive program of research, Smith and his colleagues have employed response latency to assess the efficiency with which individuals make social judgments (Smith et al., 1988; Smith & Lerner, 1986). The latency with which subjects can make a novel judgment provides an indication of how efficient they are at that particular judgmental procedure. The focus has been upon the effects of various forms of practice. For example, the more individuals have practiced making judgments of whether varying sets of traits match a given occupational stereotype (e.g., waitress), the faster they become at such judgments. More important, the effects of such practice have been shown to generalize to a novel stereotype. When subjects are asked to verify a different stereotype (e.g., librarian), their latencies indicate that they have benefited from their earlier practice, even though that practice involved judgments of a different occupational stereotype. Such results allowed Smith and his colleagues to draw interesting conclusions about the development of procedural efficiency. Apparently, individuals can, with sufficient practice, become very efficient at executing a particular judgmental procedure independent of the specific content of the information that is being judged.

For present purposes, the research by Smith and his colleagues provides an excellent illustration of yet another application of response latency measures. Furthermore, one can see once again that the conceptual interpretation that is appropriately given to the latency data depends upon the context of the response latency task and the nature of the comparisons that are made. Here, the speed with which subjects could make a series of judgments after undergoing varying levels of practice, and the degree to which such practice benefited performance on judgment tasks that were conceptually similar but of different content, provided an indication of subjects' general efficiency at making such judgments.

Latency as a Measure of
Associative Strength in Memory

As mentioned earlier, my own laboratory has employed latency measures primarily as a means of indexing the strength of the association in memory between an attitude object and the individual's evaluation of that object. We have found latency of response to an attitudinal inquiry to provide a reasonable approximation of the likelihood that the attitude will be activated from memory automatically upon mere observation of the attitude object (see Fazio et al., 1986). It is this variable of attitude accessibility upon which we have focused as a critical determinant of the relation between attitudes and judgments of attitudinally relevant information and the relation between attitudes and actual behavior toward the attitude object (see Fazio, 1989, for a review of this research). In this work, individuals are placed along a continuum of attitude accessibility as a function of the latency of their responses to an attitudinal inquiry. The faster individuals can respond to the target inquiry (typically adjusted for their general baseline speed of responding on filler trials), the greater the strength of the association between the attitude object and the evaluation.

More recently, we have employed a response latency task in order to examine the associative strength in memory between a category label and members of the category. For example, does mention of "credit cards" activate "Visa"? If so, then individuals should be able to indicate that "Visa" is a member of the previously specified category relatively quickly. In contrast, because the associative strength between "credit cards" and "Diners Club" is probably weaker, individuals may be slower, although just as accurate, in responding to a query about "Diners Club."

In a validation study addressing such associative strength, Fazio, Powell, and Williams (1988b) examined associations involving product categories and specific brands. The aim was to assess the degree of correspondence between a latency measure of associative strength and each of two additional measures. Subjects were randomly assigned to one of the three tasks. For those who engaged in the latency task, a trial began with the presentation of a category label, such as CREDIT CARDS; the label remained on the screen for 750 milliseconds. It was then replaced by a brand name that equally often (so as to keep the subjects honest) was or was not a member of the category. The subjects were instructed to indicate as quickly as possible whether the specific brand was a member of the preceding category by pressing either a yes or a no button. Each of 26 product categories examined in this way was followed once by a brand that, on the basis of pilot testing, was believed to be strongly associated to the category (e.g, VISA) and once by a weak associate (e.g., DINERS CLUB). For any given one of the 52 target brands, the average latency of response across subjects (following a reciprocal transformation of the scores) served as the measure of the associative strength between the product category and the brand.

These estimates of associative strength were then compared to estimates derived from the two other tasks. One task involved a free recall, naming measure. Subjects were asked to list members of a specified category. An index based upon order of output was computed, on the assumption that brands named earlier in the list were more strongly associated with the category label than were brands named later or not named at all.

The third measure that was employed involved a priming procedure in which subjects were not responding to a direct query regarding category membership. This measure was obtained by gauging the extent to which presentation of a category label as a prime facilitated recognition of a category member name as it gradually became apparent on the computer screen. This recognition threshold procedure involved brief presentation of the category label under the ruse that it was a "memory word" that the subject needed to remember until the end of the trial and then recite. A brand name that may or may not have been a member of the preceding category then appeared. However, the brand name was initially masked by a rectangular block of dots. Gradually, these masking dots disappeared until the brand name became legible. Subjects were instructed to press a key as soon as they recognized the word, and then to announce the target word and the memory word aloud. If presentation of the category label activated the brand from memory, then it should be easier to recognize the brand name when it was preceded by the category label than when it was not. The extent to which a category label facilitated recognition of a specific brand served as the measure of associative strength.

What is most relevant to the present purposes is the finding that the latency estimates of associative strength correlated substantially with both the estimates based upon the naming measure and the estimates based upon the recognition threshold measure. This finding provides convergent validity regarding the appropriateness of response latency as a measure of associative strength. We also examined the correspondence between these latency estimates and those that an earlier sample had provided regarding the same category-brand associations. The estimates from the two samples correlated .82, indicating that the measure was characterized by more than respectable reliability.

Thus latency measures appear to provide reliable and valid indications of associative strength in memory. This has been shown with respect to object-evaluation associations and category-member associations. However, the same is probably true of any memorial associations, including associations between an object and its features, a stereotype and its attributes, and a person and his or her ascribed traits or abilities.

CONCLUSION

It appears evident that response latency measures deservedly belong within social psychology's methodological toolbox. Latency measures are unquestionably noisy—both methodologically and conceptually. Nevertheless, if they are used appropriately and interpreted judiciously, latency measures can be very informative. A response latency measure can be interpreted as the time required to form some novel judgment, as an index of the degree to which individuals are efficient at performing a judgmental task, as an indication of associative strength in memory, or as a sign of the accessibility of some construct from memory. The interpretation is not inherent to the measure itself. The context and nature of the latency task and the experimental design and logic through which the latency data are viewed are what impart conceptual meaning to the measure. In part, it is this very flexibility that makes response latency such an attractive and generally useful tool. Furthermore, response latency measures permit us to address questions of mechanism, process, and memory representations that can be difficult to tackle without such a tool. The specific questions themselves remain social psychological in nature. They can, should, and do concern phenomena and constructs that have long been central to the field—attitudes, stereotypes, impression formation, attribution, and the like.

NOTES

1. Software is the one remaining obstacle with respect to the availability of resources for collecting response latency data. Most researchers, including myself, have developed their own. If my experience is at all representative, this can be an expensive and time-consuming enterprise, requiring the services of a competent programmer. However, as more and more researchers have come to rely upon the computerized control of data collection, the situation seems to be changing. A few software packages that permit the collection of latency data are now commercially available and more are likely to be marketed in the near future. The April 1988 issue of *Behavior Research Methods, Instruments, & Computers* includes a very helpful series of articles on "The Desktop Experimental Laboratory." Costin (1988) describes MacLab, a software system for the Macintosh computer. Poltrock and Foltz (1988) summarize the capabilities of what they refer to as the APT PC and APT II systems, which permit one to create and run experiments on an IBM PC and an Apple II, respectively. Finally, Schneider (1988) describes an impressively powerful and flexible software system referred to as Micro Experimental Laboratory (MEL). MEL currently runs on IBM PC-compatible computers, but a Macintosh version is to be available soon. Each of these software systems allows users to "author" computer-controlled experiments without requiring actual programming, and each is commercially

available. Butler (1988) provides a comparative evaluation of these systems and describes the strengths and weaknesses of each one.

2. Research conducted by Smith and Miller (1983) found latency data and a similar logic to be useful in addressing the general issue of whether causal attributions are made spontaneously in the course of comprehending a statement describing a target's action.

REFERENCES

Butler, D. L. (1988). A critical evaluation of software for experiment development in research and teaching. *Behavior Research Methods, Instruments, & Computers, 20,* 218–220.

Carlston, D. E., & Skowronski, J. J. (1986). Trait memory and behavior memory: The effects of alternative pathways on impression judgment response times. *Journal of Personality and Social Psychology, 50,* 5–13.

Costin, D. (1988). MacLab: A Macintosh system for psychology labs. *Behavior Research Methods, Instruments, & Computers, 20,* 197–200.

Fazio, R. H. (1989). On the power and functionality of attitudes: The role of attitude accessibility. In A. R. Pratkanis, S. J. Breckler, & A. G. Greenwald (Eds.), *Attitude structure and function* (pp. 153–179). Hillsdale, NJ: Erlbaum.

Fazio, R. H., Chen, J., McDonel, E. C., & Sherman, S. J. (1982). Attitude accessibility, attitude-behavior consistency, and the strength of the object-evaluation association. *Journal of Experimental Social Psychology, 18,* 339–357.

Fazio, R. H., Herr, P. M., & Olney, T. J. (1984). Attitude accessibility following a self-perception process. *Journal of Personality and Social Psychology, 47,* 277–286.

Fazio, R. H., Lenn, T. M., & Effrein, E. A. (1984). Spontaneous attitude formation. *Social Cognition, 2,* 217–234.

Fazio, R. H., Powell, M. C., & Williams, C. J. (1988a). *The role of attitude accessibility in the attitude-to-behavior process.* Unpublished manuscript, Indiana University.

Fazio, R. H., Powell, M. C., & Williams, C. J. (1988b). [Measuring the strength of category-member associations in memory]. Unpublished raw data, Indiana University.

Fazio, R. H., Sanbonmatsu, D. M., Powell, M. C., & Kardes, F. R. (1986). On the automatic activation of attitudes. *Journal of Personality and Social Psychology, 50,* 229–238.

Fazio, R. H., & Williams, C. J. (1986). Attitude accessibility as a moderator of the attitude-perception and attitude-behavior relations: An investigation of the 1984 presidential election. *Journal of Personality and Social Psychology, 51,* 505–514.

Houston, D. A., & Fazio, R. H. (in press). Biased processing as a function of attitude accessibility: Making objective judgments subjectively. *Social Cognition.*

Judd, C. M., & Kulik, J. A. (1980). Schematic effects of social attitudes on information processing and recall. *Journal of Personality and Social Psychology, 38,* 569–578.

Kardes, F. R. (1988). Spontaneous inference processes in advertising: The effects of conclusion omission and involvement on persuasion. *Journal of Consumer Research, 15,* 225–233.

Kirk, R. E. (1968). *Experimental design: Procedures for the behavioral sciences.* Belmont, CA: Brooks/Cole.

Luce, R. D. (1986). *Response times: Their role in inferring elementary mental organization*. New York: Oxford University Press.

Pachella, R. G. (1974). The interpretation of reaction time in information processing research. In B. H. Kantowitz (Ed.), *Human information processing: Tutorials in performance and cognition.* (pp. 41–82) Hillsdale, NJ: Erlbaum.

Poltrock, S. E., & Foltz, G. S. (1988). APT PC and APT II: Experiment development systems for the IBM PC and Apple II. *Behavior Research Methods, Instruments, & Computers, 20,* 201–205.

Schneider, W. (1988). Micro Experimental Laboratory: An integrated system for IBM PC compatibles. *Behavior Research Methods, Instruments, & Computers, 20,* 206–217.

Sherman, J., Judd, C. M., & Park, B. (1989). Social cognition. *Annual Review of Psychology, 40,* 281–326.

Smith, E. E. (1968). Choice reaction time: An analysis of the major theoretical positions. *Psychological Bulletin, 69,* 77–110.

Smith, E. R., Branscombe, N. R., & Bormann, C. (1988). Generality of the effects of practice on social judgment tasks. *Journal of Personality and Social Psychology, 54,* 385–395.

Smith, E. R. & Lerner, M. (1986). Development of automatism of social judgments. *Journal of Personality and Social Psychology, 50,* 246–259.

Smith, E. R., & Miller, F. D. (1983). Mediation among attributional inferences and comprehension processes: Initial findings and a general method. *Journal of Personality and Social Psychology, 44,* 492–505.

Sternberg, S. (1975). Memory scanning: New findings and current controversies. *Quarterly Journal of Experimental Psychology, 27,* 1–32.

4

Assessing Frequency Reports of Mundane Behaviors

CONTRIBUTIONS OF COGNITIVE PSYCHOLOGY TO QUESTIONNAIRE CONSTRUCTION

NORBERT SCHWARZ

Norbert Schwarz received degrees in sociology (Dipl.-Soz., Dr. phil.) from the University of Mannheim and in psychology (Dr. phil. habil.) from the University of Heidelberg. He has held visiting appointments at North American universities, and he currently directs a research program on cognitive aspects of survey methodology at the Zentrum für Umfragen, Methoden und Analysen (ZUMA), in Mannheim, Federal Republic of Germany, and is Privatdozent of Psychology at the University of Heidelberg. His research interests focus on human judgmental processes, in particular the interplay of affect and cognition, and the application of social cognition research to survey methodology.

Much of our knowledge about individuals' behavior is based on their direct verbal reports. From consumer behavior to health problems, and from styles of parenting to the nation's unemployment rate or the prevalence of crime, psychologists and social scientists rely on respondents' behavioral reports as their major data base for testing theories of human behavior and offering advice on public policy. Given the importance of behavioral reports, surprisingly little attention has been given to how respondents go about answering quantitative autobiographical questions, asking them, for example, how often they have done something, or how much of something they have consumed, during a specified time period. As an introduction to the issues raised in the present chapter, the reader may want to answer the following questions, which are taken from major U.S. surveys:

1. During the two-week [reference] period, on the days when you drank liquor, about how many drinks did you have? (Health Interview Survey Supplement, National Center for Health Statistics)

AUTHOR'S NOTE: Parts of the research reported here were supported by grants Schw 278/2 and Str 264/3 from the Deutsche Forschungsgemeinschaft to the author and Fritz Strack, by a Feodor Lynen Fellowship from the Alexander von Humboldt Foundation to the author, and by ZUMA's program on cognition and survey research. Thanks are extended to Barbara Bickart, Bettina Scheuring, and Fritz Strack for their helpful comments on a previous draft.

2. Now, I'd like to read you a short list of different kinds of pain. Please say for each one, on roughly how many days — if any — in the last 12 months you have had that type of pain. How many days in the last year have you had [headaches; backaches; stomach pains; joint pains; muscle pains; dental pains]? (Health Interview Survey Supplement, National Center for Health Statistics)

3. We would like to ask [your/your relative's] work history for every job and every period of unemployment that lasted 6 months or more, starting with the first full-time job [you/he] held from the age of 16, including any jobs held while in military service. [. . .] About how many hours a week did (you/he) work on that [first] job, including overtime? ("Women at Work" Study, U.S. Bureau of the Census)

4. When you were growing up, how frequently did your father attend religious services? (General Social Survey, National Opinion Research Center)

The present chapter reviews our current knowledge of the cognitive processes that underlie respondents' answers to quantitative questions such as the ones above, paying special attention to the methodological implications of the reviewed findings for questionnaire construction. Much of the research is fairly new, growing out of the recently initiated dialogue between survey researchers and cognitive psychologists (see Hippler, Schwarz, & Sudman, 1987; Jabine, Straf, Tanur, & Tourangeau, 1984, for reviews), as well as the recent interest in autobiographical memory (see Gruneberg, Morris, & Sykes, 1988; Neisser, 1982; Rubin 1986).

THE PROCESS OF QUESTION ANSWERING

Answering a quantitative autobiographical question requires that respondents undertake several tasks. First, respondents need to understand what the question refers to, and which behavior they are supposed to report. Second, they have to recall or reconstruct relevant instances of this behavior from memory. Third, if the question specifies a reference period, they must determine if these instances occurred during this reference period or not. Similarly, if the question refers to their "usual" behavior, respondents have to determine if the recalled or reconstructed instances are reasonably representative or if they reflect a deviation from their usual behavior. Fourth, as an alternative to recalling or reconstructing instances of the behavior, respondents may rely on their general knowledge, or other salient information that may bear on their task, to infer an answer. Finally, respondents have to provide their report to the researcher. They may need to map their report onto a response scale provided to them, and they may want to edit it for rea-

sons of social desirability (see Strack & Martin, 1987; Tourangeau & Rasinski, 1988, for related discussions of attitude questions).

In the first part of this chapter, each of these tasks will be discussed in
some detail. For the sake of simplicity, this discussion will assume that the
question is asked in an open response format, and that no precoded response
alternatives are provided to the respondent. As the review develops, it will
become evident that answering autobiographical questions is a process that
is highly theory-driven, and relies as much on respondents' inference strategies as on their recall of specific autobiographical details. The second part
of the chapter will then explore a specific set of inference rules, namely,
respondents' assumptions about the informational value of response alternatives provided to them by the researcher. Focusing on what respondents
learn from response alternatives, this section will address the special issues
that arise at various stages of the judgment process when respondents are
asked to report their behavior by checking the appropriate alternative from
a set of response categories in a closed answer format.

ANSWERING BEHAVIORAL QUESTIONS
IN AN OPEN RESPONSE FORMAT

Understanding the Question

The key issue at the question-comprehension stage is whether the
behavior that the respondent identifies as the referent of the question does or
does not match what the researcher had in mind. As a general rule, question
comprehension is considerably poorer than most researchers would like to
believe, even for apparently simple questions (Belson, 1981). For example,
in a British readership survey (Belson, 1968), respondents were presented
an aided recall task: "I want you to go through this booklet with me, and tell
me, for each paper, whether you happen to have looked at any copy of it in
the past three months, it doesn't matter where" (p. 2). Subsequently, respondents were asked to explain the key terms of the question. The interpretations of "looked at" ranged from "seen on a bookstall" to "read fairly fully,"
and included "like to read," "bought," and "taken regularly." The phrase "any
copy" was frequently overlooked or interpreted to mean "your own copy,"
and the reference period of three months tended to be ignored or became a
vague "recently." Belson concluded that respondents who find a question
difficult to answer are "likely to modify it in such a way that it becomes more
easy to answer" (p. 9). In particular, they are likely to interpret broad terms

less broadly than intended, and to respond to the gist of the question rather than to its exact wording. Moreover, respondents may use the response alternatives provided to them by the researcher to determine the meaning of the question, as will be elaborated below.

In addition to these general comprehension problems (see Belson, 1981; Hippler & Schwarz, 1987; Strack & Martin, 1987 for reviews of related research), respondents' definition of certain behaviors may vary depending upon *who* is supposed to engage in the behavior. For example, the concept of "paid work," which is crucial for most labor force surveys, was found to include very different activities depending on the target person's age, education, and employment history. What qualifies as "paid work" for the respondent's teenage children (e.g., baby-sitting or mowing the neighbor's lawn) does not qualify as "paid work" for the adult respondent, resulting in different definitions of the *class* of target behaviors as a function of the employment history of the target person (Schwarz, 1987). Thus the same question may result in the assessment of different behaviors, rendering the reports noncomparable.

Recalling Relevant Instances

Once respondents have formed a subjective understanding of what the question refers to, they need to retrieve relevant information about the behavior under study from memory. Ideally, most researchers would like the respondent to scan the reference period, retrieve all instances that match the target behavior, and count them in order to determine the overall frequency of the behavior during the reference period. This, however, is the route that respondents are least likely to take.

In fact, exept for rare and very important behaviors, respondents are unlikely to have detailed representations of numerous individual instances of a behavior stored in memory, and may be expected to blend details of various instances into one global representation of the behavior under study (Linton, 1982; Means, Mingay, Nigam, & Zarrow, 1988; Neisser, 1986; Wickelgren, 1976). Thus many individual episodes become indistinguishable or irretrievable, due to interference from other similar instances (Baddeley & Hitch, 1977; Wagenaar, 1986), fostering the generation of knowledgelike representations that "lack specific time or location indicators" (Strube, 1987, p. 89). The finding that a single spell of unemployment is more accurately recalled than multiple spells (Mathiowetz, 1986), for example, suggests that this phenomenon applies not only to mundane and unimportant behaviors, but also to repeated experiences that profoundly affect an individual's life.

Accordingly, a "recall and count" model does not provide an appropriate description of how people answer frequency questions about frequent behaviors or experiences. Rather, their answers are likely to be based on some fragmented recall and the application of inference rules to compute a frequency estimate, as will be described below (see Blair & Burton, 1987; Bradburn, Rips, & Shevell, 1987; Means et al.,1988).

If researchers are interested in obtaining reports that are based on recalled episodes, they may simplify respondents' task by providing appropriate recall cues. This, however, is more easily said than done. Theoretically, the most efficient recall cues are cues that match respondents' encodings of the target behavior. But, unfortunately, research on everyday memory is a relatively recent field of study and little is known about respondents' habits of encoding for specific classes of everyday events. For example, while researchers may be interested in how often respondents drink alcoholic beverages, respondents may be unlikely to encode "drinking alcoholic beverages" as a separate category. Therefore, providing them with a selection of common situations (seeing friends, watching TV, having dinner, and so on) in which they may consume alcohol may provide better recall cues (Strube, 1987). In the absence of specific knowledge about the representation of everyday behaviors, breaking down a global question into several more specific ones and using short rather than long reference periods were found to improve respondents' recall and to increase the likelihood that respondents used a recall rather than an estimation strategy.

For example, a question about how often a respondent has eaten out may be broken down into a series of separate questions about eating at different types of restaurants. A recent experiment indicated that when respondents were asked to report separately how often they had eaten dinner in Chinese, Greek, Italian, American, Mexican, and fast-food restaurants, they reported an average of 26.0 trips in a three-month period, compared to 20.5 trips reported when they were asked the more general question, "How many times have you eaten dinner in a regular or fast-food restaurant?" (Sudman & Schwarz, 1987). Moreover, when respondents were asked to report restaurant visits only for the previous month, they reported about 13.7 visits, a monthly average substantially greater than the range of 7–9 visits found by dividing the three-month totals by three.

In addition, varying the reference period and the specificity of the question affected respondents' strategies, as was previously reported by Blair and Burton (1987). When asked only about the previous month, most respondents (62%) reported that they tried to remember specific events. For the three-month period, only about one-third (32%) of those asked the general question about all restaurants tried to remember specific events, while slightly more than half (56%) reported using an estimation strategy. For respondents asked about specific types of restaurants for three months, the majority (54%) reported using a mixed strategy. Specifically, they tried to remember specific trips to some kinds of restaurants—namely, the ones rarely visited—and estimated for other types. Thus respondents were more likely to use an estimation strategy the larger the number of similar experiences, presumably because repeated similar experiences are difficult to retrieve individually.

In general, the quality of recall will improve as the retrieval cues presented in the body of the question, or on an accompanying list of examples, become more specific. There is, however, an important drawback to the use of specific questions: Respondents are likely to omit instances that do not match the specific questions or examples, resulting in underreports if the list is not exhaustive. Thus, in the above example, visits to a restaurant not included in the set of specific questions are likely to be omitted even if a final question asks if the respondent ate at any "other" restaurant (see Sudman & Bradburn, 1983).

In providing specific recall cues, it is important to note that different cues are differentially effective. Thus the date of an event is usually found to be a poor cue, whereas cues pertaining to what happened, where it happened, and who was involved have been found to be very effective (Wagenaar, 1986, 1988). In addition, recall will improve when respondents are given sufficient time to search memory, Recalling specific events, such as going out for a drink, may take up to several seconds (Reiser, Black, & Abelson, 1985), and repeated attempts to recall may result in the retrieval of additional material, even after a considerable number of previous trials (e.g., Means et al., 1988; Williams & Hollan, 1981). Unfortunately, respondents are unlikely to have sufficient time to engage in repeated retrieval attempts in most research situations (and may often not be motivated to do so even if they had the time). This is particularly crucial in the context of survey research, where the available time per question is usually less than one minute (Bradburn et al., 1987; Groves & Kahn, 1979).

Moreover, the direction in which respondents search memory has been found to influence the quality of recall. Specifically, better recall is achieved when respondents begin with the most recent occurrence of a behavior and work backward in time than when they begin at the beginning of the reference period (e.g., Loftus & Fathi, 1985; Whitten & Leonard, 1981). This presumably occurs because memory for recent occurrences is richer and the recalled instances may serve as cues for recalling previous ones. Given free choice, however, respondents tend to prefer the less efficient strategy of forward recall. Even under optimal conditions, however, respondents will frequently be unable to recall an event or some of its critical details, even if they believed they would "certainly" remember it at the time it occurred (e.g., Linton, 1975; Thompson, 1982; Wagenaar, 1986). In general, the available evidence suggests that respondents are likely to underreport behaviors and events, which has led many researchers to assume that higher reports of mundane behaviors are likely to be more valid. Accordingly, a "the more the better" rule is frequently substituted for external validity checks.

Dating Recalled Instances

After recalling or reconstructing a specific instance of the behavior under study, respondents have to determine if this instance occurred during the reference period. This requires that they understand the extension of the reference period and that they can accurately date the instance with regard to that period.

Reference periods that are defined in terms of several weeks or months are highly susceptible to misinterpretations. For example, the phrase "during the last twelve months" has been found to be construed as a reference to the last calendar year, as including or excluding the current month, and so on. Similarly, anchoring the reference period with a specific date — for example, "Since March 1, how often . . . ?" — is not very helpful because respondents will usually not be able to relate an abstract date to meaningful memories.

Not surprisingly, the most efficient way to anchor a reference period is the use of salient personal or public events, often referred to as "landmarks" (Loftus & Marburger, 1983). In addition to improving respondents' understanding of the reference period, the use of landmarks facilitates the dating of recalled instances. Given that the calendar date of an event will usually not be among its encoded features, respondents were found to relate recalled events to other, more outstanding events in order to reconstruct the exact time and day (e.g., Baddeley, Lewis, & Nimmo-Smith, 1978). Accordingly, using public events (such as the eruption of Mount Saint Helens), important personal memories that respondents were asked to think of, or outstanding dates (such as New Year's Eve) as landmarks was found to reduce dating biases (Loftus & Marburger, 1983; Means et al., 1988). A related procedure, called "bounded recall" (Neter & Waksberg, 1964), has been developed for use in repeated interviews, where data from the previous interview

serve as landmarks and recall cues. However, the high cost of repeated interviews frequently discourages its use, although Sudman, Finn, and Lannom
(1984) adapted the procedure for use in single interviews.

Without a chance to relate a recalled event to a well-dated landmark or a
personal "time line" (Means et al., 1988), time dating is likely to reflect both
"forward" and "backward telescoping." That is, distant events are assumed to
have happened more recently than they did, whereas recent events are
assumed to be more distant than they are (e.g., Brown, Rips, & Shevell,
1985, 1986). Moreover, respondents have been found to use the clarity and
vividness of their memory as a cue to the distance of the event, assuming that
events that are recalled in detail occurred more recently than events for
which memory is more impoverished (Brown, Rips, & Shevell, 1985, 1986).
This heuristic fosters forward telescoping for sensational and vivid events.

The Role of Inference Processes

Given the inappropriateness of the "recall and count" model, it is not surprising that inference strategies play a major role in answering frequency questions. As Bradburn et al. (1987) observed, "Respondents will use any
information they have in order to generate a reasonable answer" (p. 160). The
best documented strategies are the use information provided by precoded
response alternatives (discussed in detail in the second part of this chapter),
the decomposition of the recall problem into subparts, the use of the availability heuristic, and reliance on subjective theories of stability and change.

Regarding *decomposition strategies*, respondents who were asked to report
the number of restaurant visits were found to determine a rate of occurrence
for a limited time period and to multiply this rate to arrive at an estimate for
the complete reference period (Blair & Burton, 1987; Sudman & Schwarz,
1987). For example, a hypothetical respondent may first determine that she
eats out about every weekend, and that she also had dinner at a restaurant this
Wednesday, but apparently not the week before. Thus she may infer that this
makes four times a month for the weekends, and let's say twice for other occasions, thus "eighteen times during the last three months" would be an appropriate answer. Note that estimates of this type are likely to be accurate if the
respondent's inference rule is adequate, and if exceptions to the usual behavior
are rare. Thus the nature and use of inference rules involved in decomposition strategies will be a promising topic for future research.

A second inference strategy, the use of the *availability heuristic* (Tversky
& Kahneman, 1973), relies on the ease with which specific instances come
to mind. The more easily an instance of the behavior and associated details

come to mind, the more recent or frequent the behavior appears. While recent or frequent events are indeed easier to recall, ease of recall is also influenced by other factors, such as the vividness or importance of a memory. Accordingly, the recency and frequency of vivid events is likely to be overestimated, whereas the recency and frequency of pallid events are underestimated, resulting in the frequent finding that rare and vivid events are overreported whereas pallid and mundane events are underreported (Bradburn et al., 1987).

A particularly important inference strategy was identified by Michael Ross and his collaborators, who found that respondents answer retrospective questions by using their present status with regard to the attribute under study as a benchmark, and invoke an implicit theory of self to assess whether their past standing on that attribute was similar to or different from their current status (for reviews, see Ross, 1988; Ross & Conway, 1986). With regard to many variables, people hold *implicit theories of stability and change*, often related to naive conceptions of life-span development, on which considerable interpersonal agreement has been documented (Ross, 1988). These theories allow them to infer their previous attitudes and behaviors by using their current attitude or behavior as an initial estimate, which they adjust according to their implicit theory. The resulting reports of previous attitudes and behaviors are correct to the extent that the implicit theory is accurate (see also Nisbett & Wilson, 1977).

So far, this approach has been tested primarily with retrospective reports of attitudes and opinions (e.g., Markus, 1986; Ross & Conway, 1986), but it is equally applicable to retrospective reports of behaviors and experiences. Frequently, individuals assume a rather high degree of stability, resulting in underestimates of the degree of change that has occurred over time. Accordingly, retrospective estimates of income (Withey, 1954) or of tobacco, marijuana, and alcohol consumption (Collins, Graham, Hansen, & Johnson, 1985) were found to be heavily influenced by respondents' income or consumption habits at the time of interview. On the other hand, when respondents have reason to believe in change, they will detect change, even though none occurred. For example, respondents who participated in a study of skills training (that did not improve their skills on any objective measure) subsequently reported that their skills were considerably poorer *before* they participated in the program. Presumably, they used their belief in the effectiveness of the training program to infer what their skills must have been before they "improved" (Conway & Ross, 1984). Similarly, participants in a pain treatment program were found to remember more pain than they had recorded during a baseline period, again reflecting their belief in program-induced change (Linton & Gotestam, 1983; Linton & Melin, 1982). As a final example, women's retrospective reports of menstrual distress were found to be a function of their theory of the menstrual cycle: The more respondents believed that their menstrual cycles affected their well-being, the more their retrospective reports deviated from diary data obtained during the cycles (McFarland, Ross, & DeCourville, 1988).

Finally, respondents may use their general world knowledge to infer reasonable answers. Asked to report the frequency of dental visits, a respondent may refer to *normative expectations* (e.g., the expectation to have semi-annual checkups) and may adjust the resulting estimate to reflect individual deviations (e.g., "I don't go as often as I should.") (Bradburn et al., 1987, p. 160). This inference strategy is likely to result in estimates that are displaced toward the initial anchor supplied by the normative expectations, reflecting the general finding that initial anchor values dominate the resulting estimates (Tversky & Kahneman, 1974).

In general, these findings emphasize that retrospective behavioral reports are to a large degree theory driven: Respondents are likely to begin with some fragmented recall of the behavior under study and to apply various inference rules to arrive at a reasonable estimate. It will be an important task for future research to learn more about the kind of theories that respondents apply.

Editing the Answer

After having determined a private estimate of the frequency of the target behavior, the respondent has to report his or her estimate to the researcher. The communicated estimate may deviate from the respondent's private estimate due to considerations of social desirability and self-presentation. Practical steps taken to reduce response editing include various techniques to assure anonymity; wording the question in a way that implies that the undesirable behavior is "usual," thus decreasing respondents' concern (but potentially introducing other biases); using respondents' own words to label the target behavior; and embedding the question into a list of other, less sensitive ones. Sudman and Bradburn (1983, pp. 54ff.) provide a detailed discussion of various techniques employed by survey researchers.

USING RESPONSE ALTERNATIVES: WHAT RESPONDENTS LEARN FROM SCALES

The preceding discussion focused on how respondents report behavioral frequencies in response to open-ended questions, and emphasized the importance of various inference rules that respondents apply to compute retrospective estimates. In line with Bradburn et al.'s (1987) observation that respondents will "use any information they have to generate a reasonable answer" (p. 160), the following sections of this chapter will explore the inference rules that respondents apply to information that is particularly salient in the research situation: namely, the information provided by the response alternatives presented to them by the researcher.

Frequently, respondents are asked to report their behavior by checking the appropriate alternative from a list of response categories provided to them. While the selected alternative is assumed to inform the researcher about the respondent's behavior, it is frequently overlooked that a given set of response alternatives may be far more than a simple "measurement device." Rather, it may also constitute a source of information for the respondent (see Schwarz, 1988; Schwarz & Hippler, 1987). Specifically, respondents were found to assume that the range of the response alternatives provided to them reflects the researcher's knowledge of, or expectations about, the distribution of the behavior in the "real world." To the extent that respondents apply this "naive theory" of response scales, the range of the response alternatives may affect respondents' understanding of the question, their behavioral reports, and subsequent related judgments. The following sections review a series of experiments that bear on these possibilities.

Understanding the Question

Frequently, the behavior under study is ill-defined and open to interpretation. This is particularly likely when researchers are interested in subjective experiences. Assume, for example, that respondents are asked to indicate how frequently they were "really irritated" recently. Before the respondent can give an answer, he or she must decide what the researcher means by "really irritated." Does this refer to major irritations such as fights with one's spouse or does it refer to minor irritations such as having to wait for service in a restaurant? If the respondent has no opportunity to ask the interviewer for clarification, or if a well-trained interviewer responds, "Whatever you feel is really irritating," he or she might pick up some pertinent information from the questionnaire. One such piece of information may be the frequency range provided by the scale.

For example, respondents who are asked to report how often they are irritated on a scale ranging from "several times daily" to "less than once a week" may relate the frequency range of the response alternatives to their general knowledge about the frequency of minor and major annoyances. Assuming that major annoyances are unlikely to occur "several times a day," they may consider instances of less severe irritation to be the target of the question than may respondents who are presented a scale ranging form "several times a year" to "less than once every three months." Experimental data support this assumption (Schwarz, Strack, Mo, & Chassein, 1988). Respondents who reported their experiences on the former scale subsequently reported less extreme examples of annoying experiences than respondents who were given the latter scale. Thus the type of annoying experiences that respondents reported was determined by the frequency range of the response alternatives in combination with respondents' general knowledge, rather than by the wording of the question per se. Accordingly, the same question combined with different frequency scales is likely to assess different experiences.

Theoretically, the impact of the response alternatives on respondents' interpretation of the question should be more pronounced the less clearly the target behavior is defined. For this reason, questions about subjective experiences may be particularly sensitive to the impact of response alternatives because researchers usually refrain from providing a detailed definition of the target experience so as not to interfere with its subjective nature. Ironically, assessing the frequency of a behavior with precoded response alternatives may result in doing just what is avoided in the wording of the question.

Estimating Behavioral Frequencies

That a list of response alternatives may bias respondents' behavioral reports has repeatedly been observed by survey researchers (e.g., Bradburn, Sudman, & Associates, 1979) and a study on leisure time activities can serve as an illustration. In a study by Schwarz, Hippler, Deutsch, and Strack (1985, Experiment 1), a quota sample of German adults reported how many hours a day they spend watching TV. Previous research by Darschin and Frank (1982) indicated that the average daily TV consumption in West Germany was slightly more than 2 hours. To test the impact of different response alternatives, half of the sample received a scale ranging in half-hour steps from "up to ½ hour" to "more than 2½ hours," while the other half received a scale ranging from "up to 2½ hours" to "more than 4½ hours," as shown in Table 4.1.

The range of the response alternatives had a pronounced impact on respondents' reports. Specifically, only 16.2% of the respondents who were presented the low-frequency scale reported watching TV for more than 2½ hours, while 37.5% of the respondents who were presented the high-frequency scale did so.

TABLE 4.1   Reported Daily TV Consumption as a Function of
Response Alternatives (N = 132)

Low-Frequency Alternatives	%	High-Frequency Alternatives	%
Up to ½ hour	7.4	Up to 2½ hours	62.5
½ hour to 1 hour	17.7	2½ hours to 3 hours	23.4
1 hour to 1½ hours	26.5	3 hours to 3½ hours	7.8
1½ hours to 2 hours	14.7	3½ hours to 4 hours	4.7
2 hours to 2½ hours	17.7	4 hours to 4½ hours	1.6
More than 2½ hours	16.2	More than 4½ hours	0

SOURCE: Adapted from Schwarz, Hippler, Deutsch, and Strack (1985).

Mediating processes. Two processes may contribute to this finding. On the one hand, the memory research reviewed above suggests that respondents may be unlikely to have detailed episodic memories of behaviors that are as frequent and mundane as watching TV. Rather, they may base their answers on salient information that allows the computation of a reasonable estimate. One source of pertinent information that is highly salient in the research context is the range of the response alternatives provided to them. Accordingly, respondents may use the range of the response alternatives as a frame of reference to estimate their own TV consumption.

As another theoretical possibility, respondents may be sensitive to self-presentational concerns when responding. They may be reluctant to check a response alternative that seems extreme in the context of the scale and thus reflects a presumably unusual behavior. This has been suggested by Bradburn and Danis (1984) in a discussion of higher reports of alcohol consumption in an open than in a closed response format (Bradburn et al., 1979).

Both hypotheses implicitly assume that respondents use the range of the response alternatives to infer which behavior is "usual." In general, respondents were found to assume that the behavior of the "average" person is represented by the values stated in the middle range of the response scale, and that the extremes of the scale also represent the extremes of the distribution—at least as long as these values do not appear obscure in the context of the respondents' lay theories (Schwarz et al., 1985; Schwarz & Hippler, 1987).

A number of experimental studies have investigated how these assumptions mediate the impact of response alternatives: Is the impact of response alternatives on behavioral reports mediated by self-presentation considerations or by respondents' use of the range of the response alternatives as a frame of reference in estimating frequencies that are difficult to reconstruct from memory?

Self-reports versus proxy reports. One way to differentiate between the two proposed mechanisms is to compare the impact of response alternatives on reports of one's own behavior (self-reports) and on reports about the behavior of other persons (proxy reports). In general, the two process assumptions lead to opposite predictions for both types of reports. If the impact of response alternatives is mediated by self-presentation concerns, scale effects should be *stronger* when respondents report their own behavior than when they report the behavior of friends or distant acquaintances. This follows from the assumption that they are presumably more concerned about self-presentation than about the image they present of others.

If respondents use the values presented in the scale to compute an estimate, on the other hand, the impact of scale range should be more pronounced the less other information is available that could be used to compute an answer. Therefore, the effect of scale range should be *smaller* when respondents report their own behavior than when the report the behavior of friends or distant acquaintances, because they can draw upon a broader base of information that allows the reconstruction of relevant episodes for self-reports.

In one study, American undergraduates were asked to report their own weekly TV consumption, the weekly TV consumption of a close friend, or the weekly TV consumption of a "typical undergraduate" of their university on a scale ranging from "up to 2½ hours per week" to "more than 10 hours" or on a scale ranging from "up to 10 hours" to "more than 25 hours" (Schwarz & Bienias, in press, Experiment 1). As predicted by the frame of reference hypothesis, the impact of scale range was most pronounced when respondents estimated the TV consumption of a "typical undergraduate." Specifically, 71% provided estimates of more than 10 hours per week on the high-frequency response scale, but only 13% did so on the low-frequency scale, resulting in a difference of 58 percentage points. The impact of scale range was least pronounced, on the other hand, when respondents reported their own TV consumption, with a difference of 32 percentage points. This pattern of results is opposite to the one predicted by the self-presentation hypothesis, which holds that self-reports should be most strongly affected. Reports about the behavior of close friends fell between these extremes, as both hypotheses would predict, with a difference of 37 percentage points.

These findings suggest that respondents use the range of the response alternatives as a frame of reference in estimating behavioral frequencies, and that the less other information they have, the more likely they are to rely on this frame. In this regard, it is informative to note that most of the respondents in the "friends" condition chose their roommates as target persons. It therefore comes as little surprise that their estimates of their friends' behaviors were only slightly more susceptible to scaling effects than their self-reports.

In summary, the impact of the range of the response alternatives increased as the availability of relevant information about the target behavior decreased. This conclusion is further supported by a study that used an individual difference approach to explore the impact of information accessibility and self-presentation concerns.

Private and public self-consciousness. Previous research in personality psychology has indicated that individuals who focus attention on the self provide more accurate self-reports, presumably because relevant self-knowledge is cognitively more accessible to them (see Wicklund, 1982, for a review). This suggests that these individuals should be less influenced by the ranges of the response scales provided to them because they may have better access to relevant self-related information. Such a finding would parallel the results of the previous study, further supporting the hypothesis that the impact of scale range decreases as respondents' available knowledge about the behavior under investigation increases.

However, individuals differ not only in the extent to which they pay attention to their own behaviors and feelings, but also in the extent to which they pay attention to the impression they give to others. According to the self-presentation hypothesis, individuals who care a lot about their public image should be more affected by scale range than individuals who pay less attention to what others think of them.

Accordingly, individuals' disposition to pay attention to what others think of them and their disposition to focus on their own behaviors and feelings were assessed with the "public" and "private self-consciousness" scales developed by Fenigstein, Scheier, and Buss (1975). Specifically, American college students reported their weekly TV consumption on one of the previously described high- or low-frequency response scales and their reports were analyzed as a function of their private and public self-consciousness scores (Schwarz & Bienias, in press, Experiment 3).

As predicted by the frame of reference hypothesis, the impact of scale range was more pronounced for respondents who scored low on private self-consciousness than for respondents who scored high on private self-consciousness. Specifically, 51% of the respondents who scored *low* on private self-consciousness reported watching TV for more than 10 hours per week when given the high-frequency response scale, while only 13% of them did so when given the low-frequency scale, resulting in a difference of 38 percentage points. In contrast, respondents who scored *high* on the private self-consciousness scale were not significantly affected by the range of the response scales provided to them. This finding presumably reflects the higher accessibility of self-related information under high self-consciousness, and suggests that these respondents used information recalled from memory, rather than information provided by the scales, to estimate their TV consumption. To this extent, the present results parallel the findings of the self-reports versus proxy reports study by indicating that the impact of response alternatives decreases as the accessibility of other information increases. Finally, respondents' public self-consciousness – that is, their disposition to focus attention on what others think of them – did not affect the impact of the frequency range of the response scales.

Conclusion. In combination, these findings suggest that respondents use the range of the response alternatives provided to them as a frame of reference in estimating their own behavioral frequencies. Accordingly, the less other information is easily accessible in memory, the more pronounced is the impact of response alternatives on respondents' reports. Self-presentation concerns, on the other hand, do not seem to play a major role, at least not with nonthreatening questions such as the ones used here. It is conceivable, however, that self-presentation concerns that may be elicited by highly threatening questions will be compounded if the respondent discovers that his or her report requires the endorsement of a response alternative that seems extreme in the context of the list. Thus response alternatives may also affect behavioral reports at the editing stage of the judgmental process, although strong empirical evidence for this possibility has not yet been provided.

How strongly response alternatives bias respondents' reports will depend upon how much the scale deviates form respondents' actual behavioral frequencies. Theoretically, a precoded scale that matches respondents' actual behavioral frequencies may be expected to increase the validity of the obtained estimates. Note, however, that the effects of a given response scale may be different for different subpopulations. To the extent that the actual frequency of a behavior varies across subpopulations, a set of response alternatives constructed on the basis of pretest data is unlikely to match the actual behavior of extreme groups, which are likely to be underrepresented in pretests with limited sample sizes. Because the range of the scale may be used by all respondents as a frame of reference in estimating behavioral frequencies, it may therefore tend to obscure differences between subpopulations.

Comparative Judgments

If respondents use the range of response alternatives to make inferences about the distribution of the behavior in the population, we may also expect response alternatives to affect a wide range of related judgments to which these inferences may be relevant. Most important, checking one from an ordered set of response alternatives may be equivalent to determining one's own location in a distribution. For example, many of the respondents who reported their daily TV consumption on the low-frequency scale shown in Table 4.1, were likely to check a response category in the upper range of that scale. This may have suggested to them that they watch more TV than many other people. In contrast, respondents who received the high-frequency scale were likely to check a category in the lower range of that scale, which may have suggested to them that they watch less TV than is "usual." If so, the range of the response scale, and respondents' own placement on the scale, may provide comparison information, and respondents may use this information for subsequent judgments to which such information may be relevant. The range of the response alternatives therefore may not only determine the responses given to the particular question to which they pertain, but influence answers to subsequent questions as well.

To test these considerations, respondents of the leisure-time study described above (Schwarz et al., 1985, Experiment 1) were asked to evaluate how important a role TV plays in their own lives. As expected, respondents reported a higher importance of TV in their own lives when the low-frequency range suggested a low TV consumption to be typical than when the high-frequency range suggested that many people watch a lot of TV. Note that this was true even though the former respondents reported watching less TV than the latter, as discussed above.

In a related study, the range of the response scale used to report one's own TV consumption affected respondents' subsequent evaluation of their leisure time even under conditions where the crucial response scale and the leisure time question were separated by several buffer items (Schwarz et al., 1985, Experiment 2). In this study, respondents reported higher satisfaction with the variety of things they do in their leisure time when they had previously reported their own TV consumption on the high-frequency scale, which suggested to them that they watch less TV than average, than when they had given their report on the low-frequency scale. Thus it seems that the impact of the range of the response alternatives on subsequent comparative judgments is rather robust (see also Schwarz & Scheuring, in press).

Theoretically, the impact of the response alternatives on comparative judgments should be more pronounced the less comparison information is easily available from other sources. In addition, researchers should be aware that precoded response alternatives may bias respondents' comparative judgments even under conditions where the set of response alternatives perfectly matches the actual distribution of behavior, thus introducing little bias in behavioral reports. While individuals who were not exposed to the response scale may use varying standards of comparison (e.g., based on their reference group), exposure to a given response scale may result in the use of the salient comparison information provided by the scale. To this extent, judgments obtained from a sample that was exposed to the response scale may differ from judgments prevailing in the population to which one may want to generalize the obtained results.

And What About the Users of a Respondent's Report?

However, respondents are not the only ones who use the range of response alternatives as a frame of reference in making comparative judgments. Rather, potential users of a respondent's report are also likely to be affected by the response scale in their interpretation of the reported behavior. In one study, experienced physicians and advanced students of medicine were more likely to assume that having a given physical symptom twice a week requires medical attention when this frequency was reported on a low- rather than a high-frequency range scale (Schwarz, Bless, Bohner, Harlacher, & Kellenbenz, 1988, Experiment 1). For example, practicing physicians were more likely to recommend that a fictitious patient should see a doctor if the patient reported vomiting twice a week on a low- rather than high-frequency range scale. Thus experienced professional users of symptom checklists evaluated the same frequency report differently, depending on the context provided by the frequency range of the response scale.

CONCLUSIONS

What are the implications of the reviewed findings for questionnaire construction? Most important, the reviewed findings demonstrate that respondents are unlikely to answer quantitative autobiographical questions on the basis of a "recall and count" procedure. While researchers may increase the likelihood that respondents will attempt to use a recall and count strategy by asking specific questions pertaining to a well-anchored short reference period, respondents will usually base their answers on some fragmented recall from which they attempt to infer a plausible estimate using various inference strategies. In doing so, respondents "use any information they have to generate a reasonable answer" (Bradburn et al., 1987, p. 160). Accordingly, the traditional distinction between "opinion questions," which are presumably answered on the basis of somewhat unreliable judgmental processes, and "factual questions," which are presumably answered on the basis of more reliable recall from memory, is misleading. As much as answering opinion questions requires a considerable degree of recall (see, e.g., the discussions by Bodenhausen & Wyer, 1987; Schwarz & Strack, in press; Strack & Martin, 1987; Tourangeau & Rasinski, 1988), answering quantitative "factual" questions requires a considerable degree of inference and judgment. A judgmental approach to retrospective reports, emphasizing the inference and estimation strategies that underlie respondents' reports, may therefore prove to be an important supplement to current research on autobiographical memory, and is likely to improve our understanding of basic judgmental processes as well as the collection of retrospective data in theory testing and applied social and psychological research.

REFERENCES

Baddeley, A. D., & Hitch, G. J. (1977). Recency reexamined. In S. Dornic (Ed.), *Attention and performance* (Vol. 6, pp. 647–667). Hillsdale, NJ: Erlbaum.

Baddeley, A. D., Lewis, V., & Nimmo-Smith, J. (1978). When did you last . . . ? In M. M. Gruneberg, P. E. Morris, & R. N. Sykes (Eds.), *Practical aspects of memory* (pp. 77–83). London: Academic Press.

Belson, W. A. (1968). Respondent understanding of survery questions. *Polls, 3,* 1–13.

Belson, W. A. (1981). *The design and understanding of survey questions.* Aldershot: Gower.

Blair, E., & Burton, S. (1987). Cognitive processes used by survey respondents to answer behavioral frequency questions. *Journal of Consumer Research, 14,* 280–288.

Bodenhausen, G. V., & Wyer, R. S. (1987). Social cognition and social reality: Information acquisition and use in the laboratory and the real world. In H. J. Hippler, N. Schwarz, & S. Sudman (Eds.), *Social information processing and survey methodology* (pp. 6–41). New York: Springer-Verlag.

Bradburn, N., & Danis, C. (1984). Potential contributions of cognitive research to survey questionnaire design. In T. B. Jabine, M. L. Straf, J. M. Tanur, & R. Tourangeau (Eds.), *Cognitive aspects of survey methodology: Building a bridge between disciplines* (pp. 101–129). Washington, DC: National Academy Press.

Bradburn, N. M., Rips, L. J., & Shevell, S. K. (1987). Answering autobiographical questions: The impact of memory and inference on surveys. *Science, 236,* 157–161.

Bradburn, N., Sudman, S., & Associates (1979). *Improving interviewing methods and questionnaire design*. San Francisco: Jossey-Bass.

Brown, N. R., Rips, L. J. & Shevell, S. K. (1985). The subjective dates of natural events in very-long-term memory. *Cognitive Psychology, 17*, 139–177.

Brown, N. R., Rips, L. J., & Shevell, S. K. (1986). Public memories and their personal context. In D. C. Rubin (Ed.), *Autobiographical memory* (pp.137–158). Cambridge: Cambridge University Press.

Collins, L. M., Graham, J. W., Hansen, W. B., & Johnson, C. A. (1985). Agreement between retrospective accounts of substance use and earlier reported substance use. *Applied Psychological Measurement, 9*, 301–309.

Conway, M., & Ross, M. (1984). Getting what you want by revising what you had. *Journal of Personality and Social Psychology, 47*, 738–748.

Darschin, W., & Frank, B. (1982). Tendenzen im Zuschauerverhalten. Teleskopie-Ergebnisse zur Fernsehnutzung im Jahre 1981. *Media Perspektiven, 4*, 276–284.

Fenigstein, A., Scheier, M. F., & Buss, A. H. (1975). Public and private self-consciousness: Assessment and theory. *Journal of Consulting and Clinical Psychology, 43*, 522–527.

Groves, R. M., & Kahn, R. L. (1979). *Surveys by telephone: A national comparison with personal interviews*. New York: Academic Press.

Gruneberg, M. M., Morris, P. E., & Sykes, R. N. (Eds.). (1988). *Practical aspects of memory: Current research and issues* (Vol. 1). Chichester: John Wiley.

Hippler, H. J., & Schwarz, N. (1987). Response effects in surveys. In H. J. Hippler, N. Schwarz, & S. Sudman (Eds.), *Social information processing and survey methodology* (pp. 102–122). New York: Springer-Verlag.

Hippler, H. J., Schwarz, N., & Sudman, S. (Eds.). (1987). *Social information processing and survey methodology*. New York: Springer-Verlag.

Jabine, T. B., Straf, M. L., Tanur, J. M., & Tourangeau, R. (Eds.). (1984). *Cognitive aspects of survey methodology: Building a bridge between disciplines*. Washington, DC: National Academy Press.

Linton, M. (1975). Memory for real-world events. In D. A. Norman & D. E. Remelhart (Eds.), *Explorations in cognition* (pp. 376–404). San Francisco: Freeman.

Linton, M. (1982). Transformations of memory in everyday life. In U. Neisser (Ed.), *Memory observed: Remembering in natural contexts* (pp. 77–91). San Francisco: Freeman.

Linton, S. J., & Gotestam, K. G. (1983). A clinical comparison of two pain scales: Correlation, remembering chronic pain and a measure of compliance. *Pain, 17*, 57–65.

Linton, S. J., & Melin, L. (1982). The accuracy of remembering chronic pain. *Pain, 13*, 281–285.

Loftus, E., & Fathi, D. C. (1985). Retrieving multiple autobiographical memories. *Social Cognition, 3*, 280–295.

Loftus, E. F., & Marburger, W. (1983). Since the eruption of Mt. St. Helens, has anyone beaten you up? *Memory and Cognition, 11*, 114–120.

Loftus, E. F., Smith, D. K., Johnson, D. A. & Fiedler, J. (1988). Remembering "when": Errors in the dating of autobiographical memories. In M. M. Gruneberg, P. E. Morris, & R. N. Sykes (Eds.), *Practical aspects of memory: Current research and issues* (Vol. 1, pp. 234–240). Chichester: John Wiley.

Markus, G. B. (1986). Stability and change in political attitudes: Observed, recalled, and explained. *Political Behavior, 8*, 21–44.

Mathiowetz, N. A. (1986, June). *Episodic recall and estimation: Applicability of cognitive theories to survey data.* Paper presented at the Social Science Research Council Seminar on Retrospective Data, New York.

McFarland, C., Ross, M., & DeCourville, N. (1988). *Retrospective vs. current reports of menstrual distress.* Unpublished manuscript, University of Waterloo.

Means, B., Mingay, D. J., Nigam, A., & Zarrow, M. (1988). A cognitive approach to enhancing health survey reports of medical visits. In M. M. Gruneberg, P. E. Morris, & R. N. Sykes (Eds.), *Practical aspects of memory: Current research and issues* (Vol. 1, pp. 537–542). Chichester: John Wiley.

Neisser, U. (Ed.). (1982). *Memory observed.* San Francisco: Freeman.

Neisser, U. (1986). Nested structure in autobiographical memory. In D. C. Rubin (Ed.), *Autobiographical memory* (pp. 71–88). Cambridge: Cambridge University Press.

Neter, J., & Waksberg, J. (1964). A study of response errors in expenditure data from household interviews. *Journal of the American Statistical Association, 59,* 18–55.

Nisbett, R. E., & Wilson, T. D. (1977). Telling more than we can know: Verbal reports on mental processes. *Psychological Review, 84,* 231–259.

Reiser, B. J., Black, J. B., & Abelson, R. P. (1985). Knowledge structure in the organization and retrieval of autobiographical memories. *Cognitive Psychology, 17,* 89–137.

Ross, M. (1988). *The relation of implicit theories to the construction of personal histories.* Unpublished manuscript, University of Waterloo.

Ross, M., & Conway, M. (1986). Remembering one's own past: The construction of personal histories. In R. M. Sorrentino & E. T. Higgins (Eds.), *Handbook of motivation and cognition* (pp. 122–144). New York: Guilford.

Rubin, D. C. (Ed.). (1986). *Autobiographical memory.* Cambridge: Cambridge University Press.

Schwarz, N. (1987, April). *Cognitive aspects of labor surveys in a multi-national context* (OECD Document MAS/WP 7[87]4).Report commissioned for the ninth meeting of the Working Party on Labor Statistics, Organization for Economic Cooperation and Development, Paris.

Schwarz, N. (1988). Was Befragte aus Antwortalternativen lernen. *Planung und Analysen, 15,* 103–107.

Schwarz, N., & Bienias, J. (in press). What mediates the impact of response alternatives on frequency reports of mundane behaviors? *Applied Cognitive Psychology.*

Schwarz, N., Bless, H., Bohner, G., Harlacher, U., & Kellenbenz, M. (1988). Response scales as frames of reference: The impact of frequency range on diagnostic judgments. *ZUMA-Arbeitsbericht, 6.*

Schwarz, N., & Hippler, H. J. (1987). What response scales may tell your respondents. In H. J. Hippler, N. Schwarz, & S. Sudman (Eds.), *Social information processing and survey methodology* (pp. 163–178). New York: Springer-Verlag.

Schwarz, N., Hippler, H. J., Deutsch, B., & Strack, F. (1985). Response categories: Effects on behavioral reports and comparative judgments. *Public Opinion Quarterly, 49,* 388–395.

Schwarz, N., & Scheuring, B. (in press). Judgments of relationship satisfaction: Inter- and intraindividual comparisons as a function of questionnaire structure. *European Journal of Social Psychology.*

Schwarz, N., & Strack, F. (in press). Evaluating one's life: A judgment model of subjective well-being. In F. Strack, M. Argyle, & N. Schwarz (Eds.), *The social psychology of well-being*. London: Pergamon.

Schwarz, N., Strack, F., Mo, G., & Chassein, B. (1988). The range of the response alternatives may determine the meaning of the question. *Social Cognition, 6,* 107–117.

Strack, F., & Martin, L. (1987). Thinking, judging, and communicating: A process account of context effects in attitude surveys. In H. J. Hippler, N. Schwarz, & S. Sudman (Eds.), *Social information processing and survey methodology* (pp. 123–148). New York: Springer-Verlag.

Strube, G. (1987). Answering survey questions: The role of memory. In H. J. Hippler, N. Schwarz, & S. Sudman (Eds.), *Social information processing and survey methodology* (pp. 86–101). New York: Springer-Verlag.

Sudman, S., & Bradburn, N.M. (1983). *Asking questions*. San Francisco: Jossey-Bass.

Sudman, S., Finn, A., & Lannom, L. (1984). The use of bounded recall procedures in single interviews. *Public Opinion Quarterly, 48,* 520–524.

Sudman, S., & Schwarz, N. (1987). Contributions of cognitive psychology to marketing research. *ZUMA-Arbeitsbericht 9.*

Thompson, C.P. (1982). Memory for unique personal events: The roommate study. *Memory and Cognition, 10,* 324–332.

Tourangeau, R., & Rasinski, K. A. (1988). Cognitive processes underlying context effects in attitude measurement. *Psychological Bulletin, 103,* 299–314.

Tversky, A., & Kahneman, D. (1973). Availability: A heuristic for judging frequency and probability. *Cognitive Psychology, 5,* 207–232.

Tversky, A., & Kahneman, D. (1974). Judgment under uncertainty: Heuristics and biases. *Science, 85,* 1124–1131.

Wagenaar, W. A. (1986). My memory: A study of autobiographical memory over six years. *Cognitive Psychology, 18,* 225–252.

Wagenaar, W. A. (1988). People and places in my memory: A study on cue specificity and retrieval from autobiographical memory. In M. M. Gruneberg, P. E. Morris, & R. N. Sykes (Eds.), *Practical aspects of memory: Current research and issues* (Vol. 1, pp. 228–232). Chichester: John Wiley.

Whitten, W. B., & Leonard, J. M. (1981). Directed search through autobiographical memory. *Memory and Cognition, 9,* 566–579.

Wickelgren, W. A. (1976). Memory storage dynamics. In W. K. Estes (Ed.), *Handbook of learning and cognition processes* (Vol. 4, pp. 321–362). Hillsdale, NJ: Erlbaum.

Wicklund, R. A. (1982). Self-focused attention and the validity of self-reports. In M. P. Zanna, E. T. Higgins, & C. P. Herman (Eds.), *Consistency in social behavior* (pp. 149–172). Hillsdale, NJ: Erlbaum.

Williams, M. D., & Hollan, J. D. (1981). The process of retrieval from very long term memory. *Cognitive Science, 5,* 87–119.

Withey, S. B. (1954). Reliability of recall of income. *Public Opinion Quarterly, 18,* 31–34.

5

Computer Simulation
of Social Interaction

GAROLD STASSER

Garold Stasser is an Associate Professor of Psychology at Miami University. His interest in group decision making dates back to his graduate training at the University of Illinois, where he received his Ph.D. in 1977. His other research interests include information flow in discussion groups and models of group productivity.

Computer simulation has a fairly long history in the social and cognitive sciences. Guetzkow, Kotler, and Schultz (1972) and Dutton and Starbuck (1971) provided case studies of early examples and discussions of methodological issues pertaining to computer simulation. Abelson (1968) spoke directly to the use and usefulness of computer models in social psychology. Oddly, the application of computer models in social psychology seemed to decline in the years following the publication of these works. This decline is puzzling for two reasons. First, Abelson (1968) made a convincing case for the value of computer simulation in a handbook readily available to social psychologists. He noted, for example, that computer models can synthesize various theoretical propositions about different aspects of social behavior into a single model, and they can accommodate both qualitative and quantitative variables and relationships. Moreover, the process of developing a computer model can identify gaps and inconsistencies in the theoretical ideas that are embodied in the model. Once a computer model is operative, it provides a powerful tool for "thought experimentation" (Davis & Kerr, 1986).

A second reason that the decline of interest in computer simulation seems odd is that other developments during the 1970s should have facilitated the move to computer simulation techniques. Computer literacy was on the rise both in the general population and among social scientists. Also, computing equipment and computing time were becoming more readily available. While computer simulation waned in social psychology during this era, it flourished in the cognitive sciences (see Barr & Feigenbaum, 1981).

AUTHOR'S NOTE: Work on this chapter was supported by a National Science Research grant (BNS-8721844). Send correspondence to Garold Stasser, Department of Psychology, Miami University, Oxford, OH 45056. I would like to thank James Davis, Reid Hastie, and Clyde Hendrick for their comments on an earlier draft of this chapter.

More recently, there are indications that social psychologists have renewed their interest in the computer simulation. During the past few years, several computer models have been published in social psychological journals and books. Although it is impossible to describe these models adequately in this chapter, I refer to sources where more complete descriptions are available. My intent in this chapter is not to provide an exhaustive review of computer models. My main objectives are (a) to characterize the process of developing and testing computer models, (b) to outline the theoretical and methodological roles of computer simulation, and (c) to identify the benefits of using computer simulation in social psychology. The intended audience is not those who have worked with or read extensively about computer models, but rather those who are not so familiar with the application of computer simulation in social science. As such, my hope is to stimulate interest so that readers will explore further by sampling from the works referenced herein.

THE PROCESS OF COMPUTER SIMULATION: AN ILLUSTRATIVE EXAMPLE

The process of developing a computer model is most easily portrayed by offering an example. For this purpose, let me present a simple model that illustrates how a computer model integrates various conceptual ideas about behavior into a coherent representation of a social system. It is convenient to think of model construction as starting with a definition or description of the domain of social behavior to be modeled—the referent social system. A social system can be defined at the several levels of analysis encompassed by social psychology: individuals in social environments (Hastie, 1988; Heise, 1987; Smith, 1988), dyads (Huesmann & Levinger, 1976), small groups (Penrod & Hastie, 1980; Stasser & Davis, 1981), and organizations or communities (Abelson & Bernstein, 1963; Carley, 1986).

Referent social system. For my example, the referent social system is a small group such as a jury, committee, panel, or board that is faced with the task of deciding among various options or courses of action. Characteristically, such groups discuss the merits of the decision options before reaching a decision. One presumed function of discussion is to provide adequate information upon which to base a decision. Each member brings his or her own ideas, facts, experiences, and arguments, and it is hoped that the group can benefit from these multiple sources of information by constructing a comprehensive and unbiased picture of the relative merits of the options. In view of this presumed function, we might ask: Does group discussion contain a representative sample of members' knowledge and experience?

Conceptual model. A social system ordinarily includes many component processes that occur over time. For the group decision-making example, these components include prediscussion information distribution (who knows what prior to discussion), discussion (what is said during discussion), individual choice (what members prefer, given what they know, at any point in time), and collective choice (how members' preferences are combined to yield a group decision). Each of these components could be further divided into subcomponents. For example, discussion entails memory processes (recall) and social processes (editing recall in response to real or imagined social pressures), and individual choice entails information integration and judgment. Indeed, each of the components identified for the social system that I have in mind has been treated by others as the system of interest. Sociologists have formulated even more general theories of information diffusion within communities and organizations (see Carley, 1988); these more general theories provide ways of representing distribution of information among group members before discussion. And psychologists have models of memory and judgment that are relevant to the individual choice component (Hastie, 1988). Thus what is a system and what is a component of that system is a relative distinction that depends on the domain of interest and the level of analysis.

Keeping matters simple, let us assume that members are haphazardly exposed to a pool of information that is equally available to all members of a broader social unit (e.g., an organization or community). Each member's prior experience gives him or her a sample of this information. Within the framework of the model, discussion might proceed in one of two ways. One could be termed a *fact-finding orientation* and operationalized as a random search and retrieval process: When a member speaks, any piece of information in memory is as likely as any other to be selected. Another way can be labeled a *debate orientation* and is predicated on the notion that members bring to the group not only information but also tentative preferences. This submodel supposes that members will contribute information that is consistent with their current preferences.

A simple conception of *individual* choice is that members prefer the alternative for which they currently have the most supporting information. *Collective* choice can be represented as a voting process in which members vote for their current preferences and the group decides when they all agree (or, alternatively, when some quorum agrees as specified by an operative decision rule such as "majority rule"). Of course, this model of collective choice ignores such things as strategic voting and compliance with social pressures. In developing a computer model, such additional complexities can often be incorporated after the basic model is operative.

Computer model. The conceptual model, with its description of various component processes, provides the ingredients of a computer model. The computer program should emulate the processes suggested by each component and do so in a way that allows the component processes to function as an integrated system. For illustrative purposes, I wrote a program that gave expression to the ideas contained in the foregoing conceptual model.

Figure 5.1 presents an abbreviated flowchart of the Information Sampling (IS) simulation program. For simplicity's sake, the program accommodates only two decision alternatives (A and B) and portrays information as supporting either A or B. Input includes the proportion of A-supporting items in the original information pool (APOOL), group size (GRPSIZE), the number of items in members' memories (MEMSIZE), maximum discussion length (MAXDISC), and members' rule for selecting contributions to discussion (RULE). Two rules for selecting discussion contributions are incorporated in the model; these rules correspond to the aforementioned fact-finding and debate orientations. One is a RANDOM selection process in which members randomly select from the items they have remaining in their memories at each discussion round. The other is a PREFERENCE selection rule in which members contribute information that supports their current preferences. Output includes the discussion length, group decision (A, B, or NONE, indicating a stalemate), and the proportion of A items contained in discussion.[1]

Translating ideas to program routines often exposes "loose ends." For example, if the PREFERENCE selection rule were based solely on the notion that members contribute information that supports their current preferences, it would not be adequate to cover all contingencies. For one, it is possible for members to deplete all of their preference-supporting information after several rounds of discussion. In that event, do they add nothing to discussion (by passing or simply repeating previously mentioned items) or do they contribute preference-opposing information by default? I chose the latter option for the present simulation. Similarly, given the way that individual choice is modeled, it is possible for members to be indifferent if they have equal amounts of supporting information for both alternatives. I resolved this impasse by having the computer program select randomly from an indifferent member's memory.

The IS program composes a group by sampling MEMSIZE items from the information pool for each of the GRPSIZE members. This step uses a

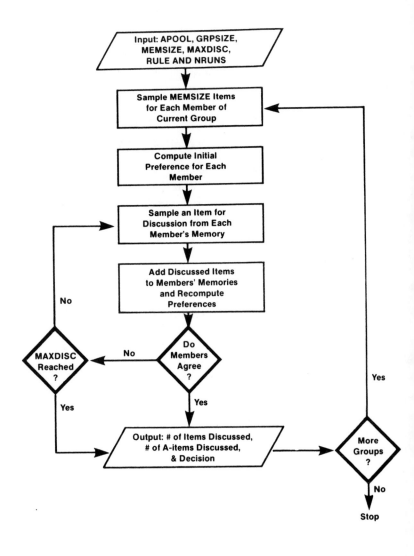

Figure 5.1   An abbreviated flowchart for the Information Sampling Model.

common simulation technique called a Monte Carlo procedure (for a more thorough discussion of Monte Carlo techniques, see Dutton & Briggs, 1971). The program generates a pseudorandom number (RANNUM) between 0 and 1 for each item sampled. Since APOOL percentage of the items in the pool are A-supporting items, the program compares RANNUM to APOOL. If RANNUM is less than APOOL, an A item is sampled; otherwise, a B item is sampled.

After the group is composed in this manner the IS program simulates discussion by having each member in turn select an item from memory to discuss. If the RANDOM rule is operative, the program employs the Monte Carlo procedure again, comparing the random number generated to the proportion of A items in a member's memory. If the PREFERENCE rule is operative, a simulated member simply contributes an item that supports his or her current preference. During a simulated discussion, the program maintains a record of the total number, as well as the number of A items, that are discussed. At the end of each round of discussion a "vote" is taken by recomputing members' preferences given the new information that was discussed and determining if they agree. If they agree, discussion is stopped, the results of the discussion are output, and the simulation moves to the next group. If they do not agree, the program moves to the next round of discussion.

Table 5.1 summarizes illustrative results from two simulation runs; each run simulated the discussions of 100 3-person groups. For both runs, each member had 16 items sampled from a pool in which 60% of the information favored A, and maximum discussion length was set at 8 rounds. One simulation used the RANDOM selection rule, while the other used the PREFERENCE rule. Notice that under both rules, most simulated groups agreed on A, which is in a sense the correct decision because A had more support in the original pool. However the RANDOM rule generated 14% stalemates, while 10% of the PREFERECENCE-rule groups agreed on the incorrect B option.

The simulated data for discussion content are interesting when compared to the composition of the original information pool (60% A-supporting items). Both rules tended to generate discussions that consisted of more than 60% of A items. This overrepresentation was particularly evident for the PREFERENCE selection rule, but the fact that it occurred at all for the RANDOM rule is surprising. It seems that a RANDOM selection rule should generate discussions that, on the average or in the long run, yield the same proportion of A items as there is in the original pool. However, about two-thirds of the RANDOM-rule discussions consisted of more than 65% A items; in fact, on the average, 0.67 of these RANDOM-rule discussions

TABLE 5.1 Distributions of Discussion Content and Group Decisions for Simulated Three-Person Groups Under RANDOM and PREFERENCE Discussion Rules

	RANDOM Rule	*PREFERENCE Rule*
Proportion of discussion that was A information[a]		
0.0	0	1
0.1	0	0
0.2	0	4
0.3	10	4
0.4	2	1
0.5	12	0
0.6[b]	13	2
0.7	39	13
0.8	4	19
0.9	2	0
1.0	18	56
Group decisions		
A	83	90
B	3	10
None	14	0

a. Proportions are rounded to the nearest tenth.
b. Of the available information, 60% supported A (i.e., APOOL = .6).

were A items, which is significantly greater than the 0.6 proportion in the original pool, $t(99) = 3.35$, $p < .01$. Note also that under both rules there was a tendency for simulated discussions to be polarized—to either over- or underrepresent A items by a sizable amount.

The IS Model, although simple, illustrates three important features of computer simulation. First, the computer program is precise. This precision pertains not only to the output (as illustrated in Table 5.1), but also to the fact that the program will not tolerate the gaps and generalities that can remain obscured in a verbal description of the conceptual model (Hastie 1988; Stasser, 1988). Precision in a computer model has the advantage of making clear how the social process is being represented. This clarity in turn makes the shortcomings of the model obvious. Thus it is clear that the IS model of group discussion needs work. Recognizing such deficiencies in a model is a benefit in scientific endeavors where the goal is to develop increasingly successful theories.

Second, computer models readily accommodate complexity. The IS model is simplistic, but using a computer program to represent the process did not force me to be so simpleminded. Indeed, the medium invites complexity, and the challenge in developing a computer model is knowing when, where, and how to add complexity. As models evolve, a danger is that they will become too complex and unwieldy, often obscuring the essential parts of the model and defying any claims to parsimony.

Finally, even this simple example shows how intuitions and verbally argued deductions can be challenged by computer simulations. It is possible to argue convincingly that the two-stage random sampling process in the RANDOM-rule IS model (first randomly sampling from the original pool to form the content of members' memories, and then randomly sampling from memories to form the content of discussion) should result in unbiased discussions. Why then did the RANDOM-rule simulations result in so many discussions that overrepresented A items? Additional runs determined that this overrepresentation occurred because the simulated discussions were stopped when the group reached a consensus. When the simulation program was changed to obtain discussions of a fixed length (e.g., 3 rounds), this bias did not occur under the RANDOM selection rule. Therefore, the seemingly reasonable assumption that discussions will be unbiased if members are unbiased in their selection of information to discuss is challenged when we recognize that groups tend to discuss to agreement rather than to discuss for a fixed amount of time.

THE ANATOMY OF A COMPUTER MODEL

Abelson (1968) presented a rather detailed description of the process of model development. His description of the common features of dynamic models provides a guide for dissecting and comprehending computer models. The *units* are the elements that "embody or carry" the social or psychological process of primary interest. *Properties* are a set of variables that represent attributes or characteristics of the units. In the IS model, the primary units are the group members. The properties of these members include their preferences and the numbers of A and B items in their memories. *Processes* are the relationships among and transformations of the units' properties over time. For example, discussion is a process in the IS model during which an item from each member's memory is selected and placed in a "common" memory that members share. Individual choice is a process in which preferences are computed and recomputed based on the contents of individual and shared memory locations. Typically, processes are interwoven such that what happens during one iteration of a process can affect later iterations of that process and other processes. For example, in the PREFERENCE version of the IS model, what a member says during one iteration of discussion potentially affects others' preferences and thus what they are likely to say during their turns. It is this interaction of model components over time that imparts a dynamic character to computer models.

Simulating multiple processes occurring over time often results in distinct *phases* that are distinguished by qualitatively different processes and usually correspond to different segments or routines in a simulation program. In its first phase, the IS model forms a group; in its second phase, it simulates discussion. Indeed, the discussion phase consists of several subphases as the program cycles repeatedly from discussion round to preference revision to voting.

Finally, a computer model uses *inputs* and yields *outputs*. While the idea of an input to a program is familiar to most, the identification of inputs to a computer model is not a trivial matter. Inputs not only define the starting conditions of the simulation but also frequently control processes during the simulation. For example, the APOOL variable in the IS model specifies a starting condition, whereas the RULE variable determines how the discussion process will be simulated. Many input variables have a status like that of an independent variable in an empirical study. They are variables that for conceptual reasons are believed to affect the social and psychological processes under study. In the IS model, group size was included as an input variable not only to increase the generalizability of the model but also in recognition of the fact that group size is an important theoretical variable in the study of group process (Steiner, 1972). Therefore it is possible to see if the simulation results (Table 5.1) for three-person groups generalize to other group sizes by changing the GRPSIZE variable and running new simulations.

Sometimes input variables are included simply as a matter of convenience or necessity. In the IS model, the "maximum discussion length" variable was included because, in the natural course of events, group discussions terminate at some point even when agreement fails to emerge. However, an appropriate "universal" limit on discussion length did not seem to be a sensible resolution and therefore this limit was left to the discretion of the program user (which has the added benefit of allowing the user to impose different values over multiple simulations to see if, or how much, limiting the discussion really matters).

As computer models evolve from simple shells (such as the IS model) to more elaborate and complex representations, the number of input variables typically increases, permitting a wider range of conditions to be simulated and more independent (causal, antecedent) factors to be studied. Carley's (1988) CONSTRUCT1 and Stasser's (1988) DISCUSS models are examples of what a mature IS model might look like; both of these models permit the user to specify many input values and to design rather complicated patterns of information distribution prior to the simulation of interaction.

However, this increase in the number of input variables is not inevitable. Frequently, convenience variables (such as maximum discussion length in the IS model) become obsolete as the model incorporates more social and psychological processes. For example, one might identify processes that plausibly account for how a group terminates discussion in the absence of agreement, and then replace the arbitrary limit used in the IS model with a more meaningful and interesting solution. (See Hastie, Penrod, & Pennington, 1983; Stasser, 1988, for approaches to simulating the termination of dicussion in an apparent stalemate.)

Output variables are of two types. The more obvious kind are those that reflect the consequences or outcomes that are of interest (group decisions and the content of discussion in the IS example). A mature model will often record and report the values of many dependent, as well as meditating, variables of the process. For example, the Hastie et al. (1983) JUS model of jury decision making outputs verdicts, voting switches, deliberation times, patterns of preference change across deliberation, and growth rates of factions.

Another kind of output variable is used for debugging and monitoring the action of the program to ensure it is functioning as intended. The necessity of debugging variables is apparent during the initial development of a computer program. However, as I will contend below, a useful computer model is never a finished product; it should always be amenable to revision and further development. Thus debugging output should always be readily available so that functioning of the program can be checked constantly as changes are made.

THE ROLE OF COMPUTER SIMULATION

Ostrom (1988) identified two possible views of the role that computer simulation can have in the conduct of a social science. In one view, computer simulation is a *method* for examining our theories. This view places simulation alongside other methods — such as laboratory experimentation and measurement techniques — to be employed as needed or desired to monitor the progress of our theoretical ideas. An extreme version of this view is the contention that computer simulations are nothing more than surrogates for experimentation when studying real people is too costly or impossible. Another view is exemplified by Ostrom's (1988) argument that a computer model is a *theory*. From this view, a computer model is an abstract, conceptual representation that, like any theory, is subject to varying degrees of confirmation and disconfirmation when tested against empirical observations. And, also like any theory, a computer model should be open to revision, refinement, and extension in the light of new evidence. Whether we view a computer model as a methodological tool or a theoretical expression depends on our purposes.

Computer Model as Method

A series of articles by Kalick and Hamilton (1986, 1988) and Aron (1988) illustrate the use of computer simulation as a method. Substantively, the articles focus on the apparently conflicting empirical evidence for the matching hypothesis of mate selection (which suggests that individuals seek mates who are no more or less attractive than themselves). Kalick and Hamilton (1986) reviewed a number of experimental studies that, in the balance, gave little support to the notion of matching. These studies suggested that, regardless of people's own attractiveness, they tend to prefer more attractive partners. To the contrary, correlational studies have found a substantial degree of positive correlation between the attractiveness of existent couples, suggesting that matching does occur.

Kalick and Hamilton (1986) noted, however, that the observation of similarity between partners does not necessarily mean that they were motivated to select similar partners. They suggest that in a community of eligible partners each could prefer attractive mates and act according to that preference, but the negotiation of mutually acceptable partnerships would give rise to a process wherein partners would tend to be similar in attractiveness. To explore this possibility, Kalick and Hamilton developed the RAN-MATCH simulation of mate selection. They described the program in some detail; I will summarize its features here only briefly. The program forms a pool of eligible mates; each potential mate is assigned an attractiveness value. The simulation then randomly pairs the potential mates and a date (successful pairing) occurs if, and only if, both partners agree to the relationship. In one version of the model, the probability of each partner's agreement increases as a positive function of the other's level of attractiveness (simulating a preference for attractive partners). In another version, the probability of agreement increases as the difference between the partners' attractiveness decreases (simulating a preference for matching). The simulation progresses through rounds of "date" proposals until all (or some percentage) of the eligible partners are successfully paired for dates.

Kalick and Hamilton (1986) demonstrated that, even when eligible dates were "motivated" to choose more attractive partners, the correlation between partners' levels of attractiveness was substantial by the time 80% of the couples were successfully formed. Subsequently, Aron (1988) challenged some of the assumptions that Kalick and Hamilton made in the development and application of their RAN-MATCH simulation. Kalick and Hamilton (1988) responded by revising their model to address some of these criticisms, running additional simulations, and concluding, as they did in their original article, that correlations between the attractiveness of partners need not imply that partners favored similar others in selecting mates.

These articles form an instructive case study of computer simulation as method. The intent was not to elaborate or extend existing theories of mate selection and interpersonal attraction. The intent was to understand better the implications of these theories, particularly in regard to the apparently contradictory experimental and correlational evidence. The advantage of simulation in this sort of endeavor stems mainly from the computer's computational flexibility and power and its bookkeeping efficiency.

Moreover, the RAN-MATCH program, by taking advantage of the flexibility inherent in simulation, can easily incorporate modifications and refinements. For example, RAN-MATCH has a "prettier at closing time" option that adjusts the probabilities of acceptance as a function of the number of unsuccessful matchings a couple has experienced. Moreover, RAN-MATCH can easily accommodate different assumptions about key elements such as the distribution of attractiveness levels in the population and the functional relationship between the probability of acceptance and the attractiveness of the potential partner. Indeed, Kalick and Hamilton (1986) listed eight specific ways that their model could be extended to make the simulations more elaborate and "lifelike." All of these proposed extensions are feasible given the flexibility of computer simulation, and none is merely cosmetic.

As Kalick and Hamilton (1986) noted, the purpose of the simulation technique in their application was "to help delineate the relations between 'molecular' events and outcomes in a macroscopic system" (p. 679). In other words, simulations can provide a bridge between a theory about individual behavior and group-level (community, societal) manifestations of that behavior. These authors also mentioned the value of "placing conceptual models in motion" in order to understand better some of their concrete implications (Kalick & Hamilton, 1988). "Placing in motion" is an apt phrase, because the simulation process literally unfolds across time. In the final analysis, however, computer simulation as a method places a distinct emphasis on translating a verbal theory into a series of computational steps and the strength of inference from simulation results depends on the reasonableness or adequacy of this translation. Theory is master and computer model is servant.

Computer Model as Theory

Ostrom (1988; see also Hastie, 1988) advocated a more active role for computer simulation. In his view, computer languages form a third symbol system for representing theoretical ideas, and he compared the utility of this system with the symbol systems of natural language and mathematics. It is not the case that computer models necessarily divorce themselves from verbally and mathematically expressed ideas; one can transport ideas from one symbol system to another. But it is also not the case that computer models are necessarily subservient to verbal and mathematical expressions of theoretical ideas. Computer models can often incorporate quantitatively complex relationships that are difficult to express in natural language and qualitative relationships that are difficult to accommodate in mathematical systems. In a real sense, computer models combine the flexibility that characterizes natural language with the precision and deductive power that characterizes mathematical systems (Hastie, et al., 1983). Therefore, Ostrom (1988) contended that viewing computer simulation as simply a research method is a mistake. In fact, one need not go far afield from social psychology to find computer models being treated, without apology, as theoretical statements (see, for example, the portrayal of Newell, Laird, & Rosenbloom's, 1987, SOAR model as a unified theory of cognition; Waldrop, 1988a, 1988b).

A recent issue of the *Journal of Experimental Social Psychology* presented three computer models that are theoretical statements (Hastie, 1988; Smith, 1988; Stasser, 1988; see also Smith-Lovin & Heise, 1988). These models integrate various theoretical ideas that have been previously presented in verbal and mathematical formulations. For example, Stasser's (1988) DISCUSS model of group decision making incorporates theoretical notions drawn from social influence, verbal learning, information processing, small group communication, and group decision making. In developing the model, the primary emphasis was on integration of ideas into a functioning whole, not on a slavish reproduction of these ideas as they had been expressed elsewhere. Ideally, a computer model provides a coherent, internally consistent, and comprehensive representation of the social psychological processes under study. This ideal is no more or less relevant when theories are expressed in the natural language or mathematical notation.

Computer models play several roles that we traditionally ascribe to theories. First, they provide a mode or medium for communicating conceptual ideas (Hastie et al., 1983; Ostrom, 1988). Second, they can account for past empirical results, often summarizing and explaining what seem to be puzzling and contradictory outcomes. Similarly, they can recast past results, giving them new meaning or interpretations (Smith, 1988; Stasser, 1988). Third, computer models are subject to disconfirmation and revision in the light of empirical evidence; see, for example, Judd and Park's (1988) empirical examination of predictions obtained from Linville, Fischer, and Salovey's (1987) PDIST model of in-group/out-group perceptions.

Fourth, computer models, once they are placed in motion, can interpolate among, and extrapolate beyond, existing data sets (Davis & Kerr, 1986). This ability is particularly useful when data are sparse and costly to obtain. Fifth, they provide a framework for addressing applied questions. This function is nicely illustrated by Hastie, et al. (1983), who employed the JUS model of jury decision making to examine the possible effects of jury size on verdicts (see also Carley, 1986, for an organizational example).

Finally, computer models can motivate and guide future empirical investigations. This function can be served in several ways. As mentioned above, the process of constructing a model often highlights gaps in our knowledge. Similarly, a process or variable that we had never thought of as being important may emerge as a central or critical element in the computer model. In either case, the natural response is to redirect empirical efforts in order to understand better previously ignored facets of the process. Moreover, the model gives us a way of forecasting the effects of independent variables on outcomes of interest. Rather than relying solely on our intuitions and "armchair speculations" in addressing such issues as likely effect sizes and necessary sample sizes to yield reasonable power, we can run a computer simulation of the process, varying the levels of independent variable(s) of interest. Because computer simulations are precise and can monitor multiple outcomes, simulating tentatively planned research gives a sense of how much effect an independent variable is likely to have on which dependent variables (see Stasser, 1988, for an example).

EVALUATING MODELS

Whether a computer model is employed as a method or as a theoretical expression, one cannot avoid the issue of deciding whether or not the model is a good one. There are several criteria for making such a judgment. One could be termed the *criterion of plausibility*, which asserts that the model's representation of a process, and the assumptions made about the process, should be reasonably consistent with prevailing ideas and available evidence (Hastie, 1988). This criterion is clearly subjective and in most cases is dealt with through formal and informal dialogue in the scientific community. Another criterion is a model's heuristic value, its ability to promote thinking and research. A computer model, like any theoretical expression, can be implausible in some ways and still contribute to the progress of understanding by reframing issues, revealing unconsidered possibilities, and sharpening our insights about the relationships among theoretical constructs. Plausibility and heuristic value are important, but in an empirical social science the model should be confronted with data at some point.

Goodness of Fit

A typical strategy for examining the empirical validity of a model is to compare the predictions of the model with the observed outcomes of a study (or several studies). The predictions of the model are treated as a statistical hypothesis, and the credibility of this hypothesis is evaluated using a statistical test. To illustrate more concretely, consider the predictions in Table 5.1 obtained from the IS model. The model predicts that, under the conditions simulated using the PREFERENCE rule, 90% of the groups will decide A and 10% will decide B. Suppose that I were to devise an experiment in which 20 three-person groups were given a decision task similar to the one envisioned in the model and found that 16 groups decided A and the remaining 4 decided B. I could then compute the value of a standard goodness-of-fit statistic (e.g., a chi-square statistic; Hays, 1988) comparing the predicted frequencies obtained from the model with the actual observed frequencies of decision outcomes. The basic decision rule is to reject the model as an adequate account of data if the value of the statistic is unlikely (e.g., if p level is less than .20 or .10); otherwise, retain the model as a sufficient explanation of the observed data.

While this approach has the advantage of being familiar to those with traditional statistical training in psychology, there are some problems in applying it to model testing. First, the relationship between alpha level (or significance level) and scientific caution is reversed. We are most familiar with null hypothesis testing where the usual motivation is to reject the null hypothesis because it implies that our independent variables are not having their anticipated effects on a dependent variable. When our motivation is to reject the null hypothesis, using low alpha levels (commonly set at .05 or .01 by convention) to judge the statistical significance of our results is viewed as being cautious, rigorous, or stringent. Indeed, we are suspicious of anyone who uses an alpha level greater than .05 and applaud those who use very low (stringent) levels such as .001 or .0001.

In evaluating a model, however, we are often more interested in accepting than in rejecting the hypothesis that was derived from the model. That is, our motivation is often to accumulate evidence for, not against, the model. And a rigorous or stringent test is one that requires a close correspondence between the model's hypothesis and the obtained results. Thus a rigorous statistical test is one that demands a relatively likely value of the test statistic before we accept the model as adequate. As a result, a rigorous model test might employ an alpha level as high as .25.

The fact that we are often interested in providing evidence *for* a model presents a second problem that arises when applying hypothesis-testing logic. One lesson that our traditional statistics courses teach is that accepting the null hypothesis has ambiguous implications, particularly when statistical power is low or unknown. A similar lesson applies when testing a hypothesis based on computer simulations, and model tests that use statistical hypothesis-testing procedures present a dilemma. If we design our empirical test with too few observations and thus limited power, we will almost certainly end up supporting the model by a statistical test even when the model is a poor one. But if the test is very powerful, we will almost certainly reject the model because even relatively small (and perhaps trivial by theoretical or practical standards) discrepancies between predicted and observed outcomes will yield a "significant result." (Note that the problem of a very powerful statistical test rejecting a good model is aggravated by using higher alpha levels such as .25.) The point is that heavy reliance on significance tests can be grossly misleading.

One way around this dilemma is to consider patterns of predicted and observed outcomes under several conditions or across several studies and to evaluate models using multiple outcomes (for examples, see Hastie et al. 1983; Stasser & Davis, 1981). Another way is to test different versions of a model or different models competitively with the data. Some of these models or submodels should be tested precisely because they are thought to be deficient in substantive ways. Such theoretically deficient or *baseline* models provide a context for evaluating the theoretically favorite versions. If a favorite model is accepted while baseline models are rejected, there is evidence that the success of the favorite model is not due solely to an insensitive test. Similarly, if all models are rejected by conventional statistical criteria but the favorite theoretical model does markedly better than the baseline models, there is at least the suggestion that the theoretical model is on the right track but needs fine-tuning. (See Stasser, 1988, and Stasser & Davis, 1981, for examples of competitive model testing; see Bentler & Bonett, 1980, and Bonett & Bentler, 1983, for a more complete discussion of these issues in the context of structural equation modeling.)

Turing Tests

Although most of the examples considered here lend themselves in one way or another to statistical analyses, it is conceivable that simulations of social behavior could yield patterns of discrete and qualitative outcomes that are not easily represented in a statistical test. For example, an interaction between two individuals might be characterized as an episode of behaviors (action and reaction over time) sampled from a repertoire of possible actions presumed available at each of several choice points. However, the same underlying process may produce distinctly different patterns from one real-life, or simulated, episode to another. Abelson (1968) suggests using some variant of a Turing test to accommodate such possibilities. Basically, the test involves judges viewing two outputs—one from a simulation and one constructed from actual behavior. The task is to identify which of the outputs is simulated, and to the degree that the judges fail to distinguish reliably between the two, the simulation model is supported. Abelson (1968) discusses some more elaborate versions of this approach and some of the problems in its application.

Setting Input Parameters

The success of a model in predicting observed data depends in part on selecting appropriate values for input variables. Sometimes the appropriate values are obvious, given the conditions under which the observations are made. At other times, one may be able to specify only a range of plausible or meaningful values. Consider again the IS model. Suppose that we had data from six-person groups who discussed and decided which of two products was better. Suppose further that we had the following data for each group: each member's preference before discussion, the content of discussion, and the group's decision. To simulate these discussions using IS, the group size parameter obviously should be set to six. But how much of the collective pool of information supports product A (APOOL), and how many items of salient information did the members typically bring to discussion (MEMSIZE)?

There are two basic approaches to specifying the values of input parameters, paralleling the distinction that Kerr, Stasser, and Davis (1979) make between *model fitting* and *model testing*. In model fitting, parameters are assigned values that maximize the fit of the model's prediction to the observed data. Applying this approach to the above example, we might systematically vary APOOL and MEMSIZE over a range of plausible values and locate, if we can, a combination of values that yields an accurate set of simulation predictions for the discussion content, prediscussion preferences, and group decisions. In model testing, parameter values are determined by prior analyses or independently collected data. For example, we may have designed the two products under consideration in the above example so that each had a specified set of desirable and undesirable features. This knowledge could guide our choice for APOOL. Or we might have had an independent sample of individuals simply recall, in an unstructured, free-recall format, as much as they could about each product. These data could be used to obtain estimates of both APOOL and MEMSIZE.

In practice, most attempts to specify indeterminate (or free) parameter values are a hybrid of model fitting and testing, The values of input parameters are determined by fitting the model to one kind of data (e.g., setting APOOL using prediscussion preferences) and then testing the fit of the model's predictions to other kinds of data (e.g., discussion content and group decisions). Or, alternatively, the parameters might be set using the data obtained in one condition or from a subset of the total sample, and tested against the data from other conditions or the remainder of the sample. Hastie et al.'s (1983) evaluation of the JUS model with jury data is a good example of such a hybrid approach; they used the data from juries deliberating under a unanimity rule to estimate parameters and tested the fit of the model with data for juries using two-thirds- and five-sixth-majority rules.

Sensitivity Analysis

In spite of valiant attempts to obtain input parameter estimates, there may remain a degree of uncertainty about the appropriateness of the specific values used in a simulation. This uncertainty is quite likely when the focus turns from empirical validation to generalizing beyond the available data—

that is, when the model is used to design future research, to explore conditions for which empirical data are lacking, to study applied problems, and the like. In these cases, there may be few, if any, concrete anchors for some parameter values; yet one would like some assurance that the conclusions reached are not the result of an unfortunate combination of input values. Or one may want to know how, and to what degree, the conclusions are affected by different patterns of input. Sensitivity analyses entail (a) identifying a range of plausible values for each parameter under question, (b) selecting several values within the plausible range (at least the extreme values), and (c) running a simulation for each possible combination of input values (as in a factorial designed experiment). The results from these multiple simulations can be used to assess the generalizability of conclusions and to bracket the effects of the variables represented by the parameters under study (see Stasser, 1988, for an example).

COMPUTER SIMULATION: A PANACEA?

I have briefly characterized the nature of computer models and simulation and distinguished between the methodological and theoretical roles of computer models. I have argued that simulation techniques offer several advantages, such as precision and clarity of theoretical expression, computational and deductive power, and accommodation of complexity. I agree, however, with Hastie (1988), who stated: "Simulation modeling is not a miracle cure for theoretical ills. Good theorizing will always require intelligence, creativity, and style from human theorists" (p. 445).

There are pitfalls to be avoided. First, using computer models to articulate theories not only permits complexity, but invites it. Thus parsimony is in danger of being ignored. As a model evolves, one should add complexity judiciously, taking care to incorporate fundamental processes and to avoid cluttering the model with unnecessary or peripheral routines. Similarly, one should avoid creating such a tortuous tangle of program steps and routines that the important elements and relationships in the model are obscured. A danger signal is the feeling that one needs to study the model rather than the phenomena that the model is intended to represent.

Computer models should do more than simply represent theory; a useful model should also promote theoretical thinking. This heuristic function seems to be short-lived in the development of many models. Once a model is published, attention often turns to making the model generally available for use (see Frijda, 1967): how the computer code should be distributed, how the program can be made more "user friendly," and so forth. These practical questions regarding the marketing of the program are important, but they tend to promote the sense that the computer model is finished. Viewing the model as a finished product defeats one of the major benefits of simulation. Like any theoretical statement, computer models should be subject to revision in response to new questions and new data.

Finally, as Ostrom (1988) and Hastie (1988) noted, computer simulation may not be appropriate for all domains of social psychology. There should be strong theory supported by empirical evidence to guide the development of the major components in a model. If theories are primitive, as they must be in emerging areas of interest, or if an area is in theoretical disarray, computer simulation offers little help. Moreover, simulation offers less advantage when interest is restricted to only a few variables (e.g., attraction and similarity) than when a system of interdependent variables is under study.

It is clear that computer simulation is not a panacea—it does not offer a remedy for all of our theoretical shortcomings. Nonetheless, it does offer several benefits. As a mode of theoretical expression, computer language combines the flexibility of natural language and the precision and deductive power of mathematics. As a result, various theoretical propositions, some expressing qualitative and others quantitative relationships, can be integrated into one model. The process of translating theoretical ideas into a computer program not only identifies missing links and inconsistencies, it might also refine our ideas and suggest new perspectives. Just as important, a simulation program typically yields predictions about a number of aspects of the modeled behavior, and these predictions are precise. Multiple outcomes and precise predictions set the stage for strong empirical tests of the model and the ideas that it represents. Finally, computer models provide a way of going beyond that existing empirical record. We can explore new combinations of independent variables and obtain estimates of effect sizes. Such exploratory simulation is useful for planning empirical research and for obtaining tentative answers to applied questions. While there are dangers and pitfalls to be avoided when using simulation techniques, the real danger is that social psychologists will continue to overlook the value of computer simulation and to forego its benefits.

NOTE

1. A listing of the IS program is available in both SAS and Fortran languages. A copy may be obtained by writing to the author.

REFERENCES

Abelson, R. P. (1968). Simulation and social behavior. In G. Lindzey & E. Aronson (Eds.), *Handbook of social psychology* (Vol. 2, pp. 274–356). Reading, MA: Addison-Wesley.

Abelson, R. P., & Bernstein, A. (1963). A computer model of community referendum controversies. *Public Opinion Quarterly, 27*, 93–122.

Aron, A. (1988). The matching hypothesis reconsidered again: Comment on Kalick and Hamilton. *Journal of Personality and Social Psychology, 54*, 441–446.

Barr, A., & Feigenbaum, E. A. (Eds.). (1981). *The handbook of artificial intelligence* (Vol. 1). Los Altos, CA: Kaufmann.

Bentler, P. M., & Bonett, D. G. (1980). Significance testing and goodness of fit in the analysis of covariance structures. *Psychological Bulletin, 88*, 588–606.

Bonett, D. G., & Bentler, P. M. (1983). Goodness-of-fit procedures for the evaluation and selection of log-linear models. *Psychological Bulletin, 93*, 149–166.

Carley, K. M. (1986). Measuring efficiency in a garbage can hierarchy. In J. March & R. Weissinger-Baylon (Eds.), *Ambiguity and command: Organizational perspective on military decision making* (pp. 165–194). Boston: Pitman.

Carley, K. M. (1988). *Social and cognitive stability* (Social and Decision Sciences Working Paper Series). Department of Social and Decision Sciences, Carnegie-Mellon University.

Davis, J. H., & Kerr, N. L. (1986). Thought experiments and the problem of sparse data in small group performance research. In P. S. Goodman (Ed.), *Designing effective work groups* (pp. 305–349). San Francisco: Jossey-Bass.

Dutton, J. M., & Briggs W. G. (1971). Simulation model construction. In J. M. Dutton & W. H. Starbuck (Eds.), *Computer simulation of human behavior.* New York: John Wiley.

Dutton, J. M., & Starbuck, W. H. (Eds.). (1971). *Computer simulation of human behavior.* New York: John Wiley.

Frijda, N. H. (1967). Problems in computer simulation. *Behavioral Science, 12*, 59–67.

Guetzkow, H., Kotler, P., & Schultz, R. L. (Eds.). (1972). *Simulation in social and administrative science: Overviews and case-examples.* Englewood Cliffs, NJ: Prentice-Hall.

Hastie, R. (1988). A computer simulation of person memory. *Journal of Experimental Social Psychology, 24*, 423–447.

Hastie, R., Penrod, S. D., & Pennington, N. (1983). *Inside the jury.* Cambridge, MA: Harvard University Press.

Hays, W. L. (1988). *Statistics* (4th ed.). New York: Holt, Rinehart & Winston.

Heise, D. R. (1987). Affect control theory: Concepts and model. *Journal of Mathematical Sociology, 13*, 1–33.

Huesmann, L. R., & Levinger, G, (1976). Incremental exchange theory: A formal model for progression in dyadic social interaction. In L. Berkowitz & E. Walster (Eds.), *Equity theory: Toward a general theory of social interaction* (Vol. 19, pp. 191–229). New York: Academic Press.

Judd, C. M., & Park, B. (1988). Out-group homogeneity: Judgments of variability at the individual and group levels. *Journal of Personality and Social Psychology, 54*, 778–788.

Kalick, S. M., & Hamilton, T. E. (1986). The matching hypothesis reexamined. *Journal of Personality and Social Psychology, 51*, 673–682.

Kalick, S. M., & Hamilton, T. E. (1988). Closer look at a matching simulation: Reply to Aron. *Journal of Personality and Social Psychology, 54*, 447–451.

Kerr, N. L., Stasser, G., & Davis, J. H. (1979). Model Testing, model fitting, and social decision schemes. *Organizational Behavior and Human Performance, 23*, 399–410.

Linville, P. W., Fischer, G. W., & Salovey, P. (1987). *The PDIST model of ingroup/outgroup perception.* Paper presented at the annual meeting of the Society of Experimental Social Psychology, Charlottesville, VA.

Newell, A., Laird, J., & Rosenbloom, P. (1987). SOAR: An architecture for general intelligence. *Artificial Intelligence, 33*, 1–64.

Ostrom, T. M. (1988). Computer simulation: The third symbol system. *Journal of Experimental Social Psycholog, 24*, 381–392.

Penrod, S. D., & Hastie, R. (1980). A computer model of jury decision making. *Psychological Review, 87*, 133–159.

Smith, E. R. (1988). Category accessibility effects in a simulated exemplar-based memory. *Journal of Experimental Social Psychology, 24*, 448–463.

Smith-Lovin, L., & Heise, D. R. (Eds.). (1988) *Analyzing social interaction: Advances in affect control theory.* New York: Gordon & Breach.

Stasser, G. (1988). Computer simulation as a research tool: The DISCUSS model of group decision making. *Journal of Experimental Social Psychology, 24*, 393–422.

Stasser, G., & Davis, J. H. (1981). Group decision making and social influence: A social interaction sequence model. *Psychological Review, 88*, 523–551.

Steiner, I. D. (1972). *Group process and productivity.* New York: Academic Press.

Waldrop, M. M. (1988a). Toward a unified theory of cognition. *Science, 241*, 27–29.

Waldrop, M. M. (1988b). SOAR: A unified theory of cognition. *Science 241*, 296–298.

6

Meta-Analysis and the Integrative Research Review

HARRIS COOPER

Harris Cooper is Professor of Psychology and Research Associate at the University of Missouri. In addition to studying knowledge synthesis and dissemination, he has authored substantive research reviews in social, clinical, personality, and educational psychology, and in several other behavioral science disciplines. He also studies applications of social psychology to classroom instruction. He was the first recipient of the American Educational Research Association's Early Career Award. He is a consulting editor for several psychology and education journals, and is a member of the Advisory Committee for the Russell Sage Foundation's Program in Research Integration.

Research in the social sciences has undergone a period of rapid expansion. One result is a narrowing of the range of expertise of many scholars. Consequently, social scientists now rely more on integrative research reviews to acquire knowledge in topic areas other than their areas of specialization. Meta-analysis, a set of procedures for integrating the quantitative results from multiple studies, has improved the quality of such research reviews. However, meta-analysis introduces new issues in research interpretation and cannot in itself ensure that a review is superior in quality.

This chapter begins by placing meta-analysis in a broad historical context. The current state of meta-analytic techniques is then described, followed by sections on issues that are unresolved or are emerging in the practice of meta-analysis. The chapter concludes with a return to broader issues concerning criteria for evaluating the quality of knowledge syntheses in general and meta-analyses in particular.

A general theme of the chapter is that in writing research reviews, social scientists need to think about what distinguishes good from bad reviews. Few formal efforts of this sort have been carried out in the past, but they are crucial for assessing the value of existing meta-analyses and for promoting the generation of higher-quality research reviews in the future.

META-ANALYSIS IN CONTEXT

The growing role of literature reviews in defining knowledge. The *Psych-INFO* reference data base uses the term "literature review," or a variation thereof, to identify one category of document. A recent study of descriptors used in *PsychINFO* found that the percentage of documents described as literature reviews remained steady between the years 1967 and 1978, ranging from 0.5% to 1.7% (Cooper, 1986a). However, from 1978 to 1983 *PsychINFO* showed a dramatic increase in the use of the term, from 2.3% to 4.3%. Since 1980, the document type "literature review" has been assigned to 1 in 25 documents cataloged by the system (also see Mazella & Malin, 1977).

The expanding role of literature reviews in our definition of knowledge is a response to the increase in human resources and research activity in the social sciences (Garvey & Griffith, 1971). The growth in the social science knowledge base appears to have had two effects on individual scholars. First, social scientists attempt to keep up with developments in narrowing areas of specialization. Second, and consequently, researchers rely to a greater extent on literature reviews to remain abreast of developments in related fields. Also, regardless of the capacities of individuals, expanding literatures necessitate the collecting, evaluating, and synthesizing of scholarship in order to bring coherence and perspective to problem areas. Indeed, Price (1965) suggested that a literature review needs to be constructed for every 30 to 40 papers "to replace those research papers that have been lost from sight behind the research front" (p. 61).

The different types of literature reviews and their relative frequency. The term *literature review* encompasses a broad array of scholarly products. Table 6.1 presents a taxonomy meant to capture important distinctions in literature reviews. The taxonomy was developed through interviews with experts in the knowledge synthesis process and with reviewers performing knowledge integrations in diverse social science disciplines (Cooper, 1988). The taxonomy categorizes reviews according to six characteristics: (a) focus, (b) goal, (c) perspective, (d) coverage, (e) organization, and (f) audience.

Based on responses from authors of reviews abstracted in *PsychINFO* and ERIC, it was found that over half of all reviews primarily focused on research outcomes (Cooper, 1988). Further, one-fourth of the reviews had as a goal the creation of generalizations based on the synthesis of others' scholarship. This focus and goal formed the largest intersection of any two categories of review—one reviewer in six stated that the integration of research outcomes for the purpose of drawing general conclusions was the reason for undertaking the review. This focus and goal are also the ones commensurate with the use of meta-analysis.

The emergence of meta-analysis as an accepted procedure for accomplishing research integrations. In 1976, Glass introduced the term *meta*-analysis to stand for "the statistical analysis of a large collection of analysis

TABLE 6.1 A Taxonomy of Literature Reviews

Characteristic	Categories
Focus	research outcomes
	research methods
	theories
	practices or applications
Goal	integration
	generalization
	conflict resolution
	linguistic bridge building
	criticism
	identification of central issues
Perspective	neutral representation
	espousal of position
Coverage	exhaustive
	exhaustive with selective citation
	representative
	central or pivotal
Organization	historical
	conceptual
	methodological
Audience	specialized scholars
	general scholars
	practitioners or policymakers
	general public

SOURCE: Cooper, H. M. (1988). "Organizing Knowledge Syntheses: A Taxonomy of Literature Reviews." Published by permission of Transaction Publishers, from *Knowledge in Society*, Vol. 1, No. 1. Copyright © 1988 by Transaction Publishers.

results from individual studies for purposes of integrating the findings" (p. 3). However, procedures for performing meta-analysis existed long before 1976 (see Olkin, in press). Indeed, methods for estimating and combining experimental effects and correlations have existed since the turn of the century (e.g., Pearson, 1896). Methods for combining results of inference tests (e.g., p-levels) date back to the 1930s (Fisher, 1932), and social psychologists were among their early proponents. *The American Soldier* (Stouffer, Suchman, DeVinney, Star, & Williams, 1949) contained a formula for combining probability levels across studies, as did the first *Handbook of Social Psychology* (Mosteller & Bush, 1954).

Until recently, applications of quantitative synthesis procedures were rare (see Bangert-Drowns, 1986; Rosenthal, 1984). It took the expansion of the empirical data base and the growing need for research reviews to provide impetus for the general use of meta-analysis. Initial interest in meta-analysis in psychology was stimulated by the appearance of two applications: a review of the effectiveness of psychotherapy by Smith and Glass (1977) and a review of interpersonal expectancy effects by Rosenthal and Rubin (1978). Also, proponents of meta-analysis demonstrated that traditional review procedures led to inaccurate or imprecise characterizations of the literature, even when the size of the literature was relatively small (Cooper, 1979; Cooper & Rosenthal, 1980).

Meta-analysis did not go uncriticized. Some critics opposed quantitative synthesis using arguments similar to those used to oppose primary data analysis (Barber, 1978; Eysenck, 1978; Mansfield & Bussey, 1977). Others linked meta-analysis with more general reviewing procedures that are inappropriate, but not necessarily related to the use of statistics in reviews (see Cook & Levitan, 1981; Cooper & Arkin, 1981). These arguments included the contention that it is inappropriate to compute average effects or correlations across studies varying in methodology and that meta-analysis remains a subjective procedure although it cloaks conclusions in the manteau of science. Several of these issues are addressed later in this chapter.

In the 1980s, several refinements in meta-analytic techniques have enhanced their acceptability. These include (a) the development of unique statistical theory and analytic procedures for performing meta-analyses (Hedges & Olkin, 1985; Rosenthal, 1984), (b) the integration of quantitative techniques with narrative and descriptive ones (Light & Pillemer, 1984), and (c) the placement of quantitative procedures into a broader framework that views research reviewing as a scientific endeavor (Cooper, 1982, 1989).

Evidence indicates that the application of meta-analysis to topics in psychology is growing and has not reached asymptote. According to Guzzo, Jackson, and Katzell (1987), the number of articles and dissertations that were indexed using the term "meta-analysis" has increased steadily in the past decade and reached nearly 100 for the year 1985. Within personality and social psychology, an informal survey of *PsychINFO* revealed approximately 100 independent meta-analyses conducted through the first half of 1987. About half of these were on topics in social psychology and half in personality psychology. Greenberg and Folger (1988) state that "if the current interest in meta-analysis is any indication, then meta-analysis is here to stay" (p. 191).

THE CURRENT STATE
OF META-ANALYTIC PROCEDURES

The elements of meta-analysis. At the center of Glass's analysis of analyses was the effect size. Cohen (1977) defined an effect size as "the degree to which the phenomenon is present in the population, or the degree to which the null hypothesis is false" (pp. 9–10). In meta-analysis, effect sizes are (a) calculated for the outcomes of studies (or sometimes comparisons within studies), (b) averaged across studies to estimate general magnitudes of effect, and (c) compared between studies to discover if variations in study outcomes exist and, if so, what features of studies might account for them. Some meta-analyses also integrate the results of statistical inference tests. This is done by combining across studies the probability values associated with tests of related hypotheses. Procedures for combining p-levels will be examined first.

Combining probabilities across studies. Suppose a research reviewer is interested in whether men and women differ in their response to conformity-inducing experimental manipulations. The reviewer is able to locate 16 studies, each of which tested for a sex difference. Of these, 10 studies reported nonsignificant differences between the sexes and 6 reported significant differences, indicating females were more conforming. Of the 6 significant differences, 4 were significant at $p < .05$, one at $p < .01$, and one at $p < .005$ (all two-tailed). Can the reviewer reject the null hypothesis that no sex difference exists?

Rosenthal (1978) cataloged seven methods for combining the results of inference tests so that an overall test of the null hypothesis can be obtained. All seven methods require that the inferences tests (a) relate to the same hypothesis, (b) are independent, and (c) meet the initial statistical assumptions made by the primary researchers.

Of the seven methods, the most serviceable and frequently applied is called the method of Adding Zs. In its simplest form, the Adding Zs method involves (a) converting the (one-tailed) p-level for each inference test to its associated Z-score (with direction retained), (b) summing the Z-scores, (c) dividing the sum by the square root of the number of inference tests, and (d) looking up the p-level associated with this cumulative Z-score. This p-level is the probability that a series of studies with these results could have been generated if all of the studies actually tested a null relation. In the example given above (taken from Cooper, 1979), the cumulative Z-score is 2.35, $p < .02$ (two-tailed).

Rosenthal (1978) also gave a formula for the Adding Zs method that allows a reviewer to weight inference tests differentially so that they make unequal contributions to the cumulative result. The weights can be based on any criterion the reviewer chooses, including, for example, the methodological rigor of the individual studies. There is also a statistic, called the Fail-safe N, that allows the reviewer to calculate the number of studies that collectively sum to an exact null finding (i.e., $p = .50$) that would change a significant cumulative result to a nonsignificant one (see Cooper, 1979; Rosenthal 1979).

Vote-counting procedures are related to combined probability procedures. Hedges and Olkin (1980) described four ways to perform vote counts in research synthesis. Three of these use as their data only studies that report significant findings. As such, they lack statistical power and are susceptible to producing results affected by publication biases. The fourth procedure involves (a) counting the number of positive and negative results, regardless of significance, and (b) applying the sign test to determine if one direction appears in the literature more often than would be expected by chance. This method has the advantage of using all studies in the vote count but suffers because it does not weight a study's contribution by its sample size. Still, it can be an informative complement to a combined probability analysis, and can even be used to generate an effect size estimate (see Hedges & Olkin, 1985).

Estimating effect sizes. Proponents of meta-analysis claim that one of the procedure's principal benefits lies in the estimation of effect sizes. Rather than asking simply whether or not a treatment difference is reliably greater than zero (indicated by statistical significance), the effect size tells the magnitude of the treatment difference. Indeed, because the parameter estimates contained in meta-analyses are often based on extremely large numbers of research participants, the likelihood of not rejecting the exact null hypothesis becomes exceedingly small, while estimates of effect size become highly reliable.

Although numerous estimates of effect size are available, two dominate the literature. The first, called the d-index by Cohen (1977; also see Glass, McGaw, & Smith, 1981; Hedges & Olkin, 1985), is a scale-free measure of the separation between two group means. Calculating the d-index for any study involves dividing the difference between the two group means by either their average standard deviation or the standard deviation of the control group. For example, Cooper, Burger, and Good (1981) examined the difference between boys' and girls' locus-of-control beliefs concerning academic achievement. Across 10 studies they found the average d-index was .08 favoring girls. Thus the average academic locus-of-control score of girls in these studies was .08 standard deviations above the average score for boys.

The second effect size metric is the r-index or correlation coefficient. It measures the degree of linear relation between two variables. For example, Cooper and Hazelrigg (1988) found eight studies that sought to determine if an experimenter's need for social influence was correlated with the amount of biased responding the experimenter obtained from subjects performing a photo-rating task. On average, the r-index was .15 for the eight studies. The average correlation was computed by (a) transforming r-indexes to Z-scores (to normalize their distribution) (b) weighting Z-scores by their sample size, (c) dividing the sum of the weighted Z-scores by the sum of the weights, and (d) converting the resulting Z-score back to a correlation coefficient.

State-of-the-art meta-analytic procedures call for the weighting of effect sizes when they are averaged across studies. The reason is that studies yielding more precise estimates—that is, those with larger sample sizes—should contribute more to the combined result. Both Hedges and Olkin (1985) and Rosenthal (1984) provide procedures for calculating the appropriate weights. Also, Hedges and Olkin (1985) describe how confidence intervals for effect sizes can be estimated. These can be used in place of combined *p*-levels to reject the null hypothesis that the difference between two means, or the size of a correlation, is zero.

Examining variance in effect sizes. Another advantage of performing a statistical integration of research is that it allows the reviewer to test hypotheses about why the outcomes of studies differ. Inevitably, effect sizes from different studies will vary. Without the aid of statistics, the reviewer simply examines the difference in outcomes across studies, groups them informally by study features, and decides (based on an "interocular inference test") whether the feature is a significant predictor of variation in outcomes. At best, this method is imprecise. At worst, it leads to incorrect inferences. In contrast, meta-analysis provides a formal means for testing whether different features of the studies explain variation in their outcomes.

Three statistical procedures for examining variation in effect sizes appear in the literature. The first approach applies standard inference tests, like ANOVA or multiple regression. The effect size is used as the dependent variable and study features are used as independent or predictor variables. This approach has been criticized based on the untenability of the underlying assumptions (See Hedges & Olkin, 1985).

The second approach compares the variation in obtained effect size with the variation expected due to sampling error (Hunter, Schmidt, & Jackson, 1982). This approach involves calculating not only an estimate of the observed variance in effects but also the expected variance, given that all observed effects are estimating the same population value (this expected value is a simple function of the average effect size estimate, the number of estimates, and the total sample size). Proponents of this procedure generally eschew any tests to judge whether significant differences exist between the two estimates. This approach also includes adjustments to effect sizes to account for methodological artifacts.

The third approach, called homogeneity analysis, is probably most useful to social psychologists. It provides the most complete guide to making inferences about a research literature. Because effect sizes are imprecise, they will vary somewhat even if they all estimate the same population parameter. Therefore, a homogeneity analysis first applies significance tests to determine whether sets of effect sizes exhibit more variance than expected by sampling error (the same expected value explicitly calculated in the approach described above). Next, homogeneity analysis allows the reviewer to test whether study features explain variation in effect sizes. Analogous to ANOVA, studies can be grouped by features and the average effect sizes for groups can be tested for homogeneity. For example, Cooper and Hazelrigg (1988) used this approach to see if different study features were associated with the magnitude of correlations between experimenters' personalities and the appearance of experimenter bias. They found that the size of the correlation was higher in studies that provided incentives to experimenters for obtaining the "correct" result.

It is relatively simple to carry out a homogeneity analysis because computer packages (e.g., SAS, SPSSX) can be used to generate the statistics. The formulas for homogeneity analysis are described in Hedges and Olkin (1985), Cooper (1989), Rosenthal (1984), and Wolf (1986).

In sum, a generic meta-analysis might contain four separate sets of statistics: (a) combinations of the p-levels of independent inference tests and Failsafe Ns, (b) a frequency analysis of positive and negative results and a sign test, (c) estimates of average effect sizes with confidence intervals, and (d) homogeneity analyses examining study features that might moderate study outcomes. A good meta-analysis generally contains all four components, but the need for combined probabilities and sign tests diminishes as the body of literature grows or if the author provides confidence intervals around effect size estimates.

Other elements of integrative research reviewing. The interest in quantitative procedures for combining results of studies serves to highlight a host of related issues concerning the systematicity and objectivity of research reviews. To clarify these issues, Cooper (1982, 1989) conceptualized the research review as a data gathering exercise and, as such, applied to it evaluative criteria similar to those employed to judge primary research. Table 6.2 presents this conceptualization.

Similar to primary research, a research review involves problem formulation, data collection, data evaluation, data analysis and interpretation, and public presentation. During the problem formulation stage of a review, the most important decisions concern how to define the constructs of interest and, relatedly, what research operations will be viewed as relevant. Another important decision concerns how much detail to retain on the methodological and conceptual distinctions that appear in the literature. The data collection stage involves the procedures used to gather the relevant literature. Reviewers can vary in both the searching strategies they use and how they interpret search outcomes (Cooper & Ribble, 1989). Data evaluation involves making decisions about the value to the synthesis of individual studies. Typically, studies are evaluated according to their age, the quality of their research designs and measurements, and how rigorously their treatments were implemented, as well as other criteria. Data analysis is where meta-analysis enters the process. Here, the reviewer decides what criteria will be used for making inferences about the literature as a whole. Public presentation concerns report writing and editing—what to leave in and out of the description of the review.

Cooper (1982, 1989) further argued that each stage of reviewing raises an independent set of issues. Like primary research, the decisions made at each stage can engender or guard against threats to the validity of the review's conclusions.

UNRESOLVED ISSUES IN META-ANALYSIS

When conducting primary research, investigators encounter decision points that present multiple choices about how to proceed. The same is true for conducting integrative research reviews. Some of these decisions will be easy to make, the choice being dictated by topic area considerations and the nature of the research base. Other decisions will be less clear. Three choice points have been most perplexing for meta-analysts. One occurs during data collection, one during data evaluation, and one during data analysis. They involve (a) the exhaustiveness of the literature search, (b) the use of methodological quality as a rule for including or excluding studies from reviews, and (c) how to determine whether separate tests of hypotheses are actually independent of one another. All sides of each issue will be presented here; my own suggested resolutions can be found in Cooper (1989).

Stage Characteristics	\<Stage of Research\>				
	Problem Formulation	*Data Collection*	*Data Evaluation*	*Analysis/Interpretation*	*Public Presentation*
Research question asked	What evidence should be included in the review?	What procedures should be used to find relevant evidence?	What retrieved evidence should be included in the review?	What procedures should be used to make inferences about the literature as a whole?	What information should be included in the review report?
Primary function in review	Constructing definitions that distinguish relevant from irrelevant studies	Determining which sources of potentially relevant studies to examine	Applying criteria to separate "valid" from "invalid" studies	Synthesizing valid retrieved studies	Applying editorial criteria to separate important from unimportant information
Procedural differences that create variation in review conclusions	(1) Differences in included operational definitions. (2) Differences in operational detail	Differences in the research contained in sources of information	(1) Differences in quality criteria. (2) Differences in the influence of non-quality criteria	Differences in rules of inference	Differences in guidelines for editorial judgment
Sources of potential invalidity in review conclusions	(1) Narrow concepts might make review conclusions less definitive and robust (2) Superficial operational detail might obscure interacting variables	(1) Accessed studies might be qualitatively different from the target population of studies (2) People sampled in accessible studies might be different from target population of people	(1) Nonquality factors might cause improper weighting of study information (2) Omissions in study reports might make conclusions unreliable	(1) Rules for distinguishing patterns from noise might be inappropriate (2) Review-based evidence might be used to infer causality	(1) Omission of review procedures might make conclusions irreproducible (2) Omission of review findings and study procedures might make conclusions obsolete

SOURCE: Cooper, H., "Scientific Guidelines for Conducting Integrative Research Reviews." *Review of Educational Research*, 1982, 52, pp. 291–302. Copyright 1982. American Educational Research Association, Washington, D.C. Reprinted by permission.

Publish or perish. Research reviewers disagree about how exhaustive a literature search needs to be. Some reviewers go to great lengths to locate as much relevant material as possible. Others are less thorough. Typically, the disagreement centers on the importance of including unpublished research in syntheses.

Those in favor of limiting syntheses to published material only argue that publication is an important screening device for maintaining quality control. Because published research has been reviewed for quality, it gives us the best evidence available. Also, including unpublished research typically does not change the nature of the general conclusions drawn by reviewers. Therefore, the studies found in unpublished sources do not warrant the additional time and effort needed to obtain them.

Those arguing that research should not be judged based on publication status also give two rationales for their decision. First, even if publication status does relate to the quality of research, there will still be much overlap between the distributions of published and unpublished reviews along the quality dimension. Superior studies sometimes are not submitted or are turned down for publication for other reasons. Inferior studies sometimes find their way into print. Application of the publish or perish rule may lead to the omission of numerous high-quality studies and will not ensure that only high-quality studies are included in the review. Second, when performing a meta-analysis, both the reliability of effect size estimates, expressed through the size of confidence intervals, and tests for effect size moderators will depend on the amount of available data. Therefore, reviewers may impede unnecessarily their ability to make confident statistical inferences by excluding unpublished studies.

Table 6.3 presents the results of a survey that asked research reviewers what searching techniques they used in preparing their reports (Cooper, 1986a). Authors of 57 reviews published in journals and books covering psychology and education were asked whether they used each of fifteen different searching strategies, and, if so, how useful they found the strategy, and how central or significant were the references it yielded.

On average, reviewers reported using between six and seven search techniques. The most frequently used technique, and the one yielding the most central references, was examination of past reviews. Computer searches of reference data bases were viewed as most useful, and were used by a surprisingly large number of reviewers (61%). Other analyses indicated three independent styles of literature searching: (a) the bibliographic search, placing heavy emphasis on reference lists compiled by others; (b) the personal contact search, relying on information provided directly to the reviewer by other

TABLE 6.3 Use, Utility, and Centrality of Different Sources of References

Use[a]	Utility[b]	Source of References	Centrality[c]
35	2.6	computer search of abstract data bases (e.g., ERIC, Psychological Abstracts)	3.1
32	4.0	manual search of abstract data bases	4.5
5	4.5	computer search of citation index (e.g., SSCI)	3.7
8	4.0	manual search of citation index	3.1
53	2.7	references in review papers written by others	2.6
47	3.9	references in books written by others	3.4
40	3.3	references in nonreview papers from journals you subscribe to	3.4
31	4.0	references in nonreview papers you browsed through at the library	4.3
44	4.8	communication with people who typically share information with you	4.3
20	5.4	formal requests of scholars you knew were active in the field (e.g., solicitation letters)	4.5
22	6.1	information from conversations at conferences or with students	5.6
18	5.6	topical bibliographies compiled by others	5.6
15	6.3	browsing through library shelves	5.8
5	7.2	general requests to government agencies	5.2
9	7.3	comments from readers/reviewers of past work	5.5

SOURCE: Cooper (1986a).
a. The number of reviewers (out of 57) who said they used the source to locate references.
b. The average ranking of the source with regard to the number of references it yielded (only by authors who used the source).
c. The average ranking of the source with regard to the "significance" or "centrality" of the references it yielded (only by authors who used the source).

scholars; and (c) the manual search, tapping primarily printed sources. Further, the search strategies reviewers used were related to both their expertise and the nature of the citations in the review. Of course, these results reveal the normative practices of reviewers and not necessarily a guide to what ought to be done.

Judging the quality of primary studies. Another area of controversy in meta-analysis is related to the publication issue. All research reviewers agree that the quality of a study should dictate how heavily it is weighted when inferences about a literature are drawn. However, there is disagreement about whether studies should be excluded from reviews entirely if they are flawed.

Proponents of excluding flawed studies often employ the "garbage in-garbage out" axiom (Eysenck, 1978). They argue that amassing numerous flawed studies cannot replace the need for better-designed ones. Others argue that reviewers should employ the principle of best evidence used in law. This principle argues that "the same evidence that would be essential in one case might be disregarded in another because in the second case there is better evidence available" (Slavin, 1986, p. 6). Thus a reviewer evaluates the entire literature and then bases decisions on only those studies that are highest in quality, even if these are not ideal.

Opponents of excluding studies contend that flawed studies can, in fact, accumulate to valid inferences. This might happen if the studies do not share the same design flaws but do come to the same result. Further, global decisions about what makes a study good or bad are fraught with difficulty. There is ample evidence that even the most sophisticated researchers can disagree about the dimensions that define quality and how these dimensions apply to particular studies (see Gottfredson, 1978). And finally, opponents of exclusion contend that the effect of research design on study outcomes is an empirical question. Rather than leaving studies out based on disputable, global judgments of rigor, the operational details of studies can be examined empirically for their relation to outcomes through homogeneity analyses. Then, if studies with more desirable features produce results different from other studies, inferences about the literature can be adjusted accordingly.

Identifying independent hypothesis tests. Meta-analysts must make decisions concerning how to handle multiple effect sizes coming from the same study. These effect sizes may share method variance that makes them nonindependent data points. The problem is that the assumption that effects are independent underlies the meta-analysis procedures described earlier.

Sometimes a single study can contain multiple estimates of the same relation because (a) more than one measure of the same construct is used and the measures are analyzed separately or (b) results are reported separately for different samples of people. Taken a step further, a reviewer might consider as not independent separate but related studies in the same report, or multiple reports from the same laboratory.

There is a disagreement among meta-analysts about how to handle nonindependent tests. Some reviewers treat each effect size as independent, regardless of the number that come from the same study (Glass et al., 1981). They assume the effect of violating the independence assumption is not great. Others use the study as the unit of analysis (Rosenthal, 1984). In this strategy, a mean or median result is calculated to represent the study. Still other meta-analysts advocate a shifting unit (Cooper, 1989). Here, each study is allowed to contribute as many effects as there are categories in the given analysis, but effects within any category are averaged.

Recently, application of generalized least squares regression has been suggested as a solution to the problem of nonindependence (Raudenbush, Becker, & Kalaian, 1988). The key to using this procedure lies in the reviewer's ability to estimate credibly the actual degree of relation among nonindependent results (see Hedges & Olkin, 1985, chap. 10, for a related procedure).

EMERGING ISSUES IN META-ANALYSIS

Like theories, social research methods are dynamic entities. They undergo revision, become more precise, and find extension to new domains of application. Four developments in the application and interpretation of meta-analysis are discussed below: (a) the development of procedures for substantively interpreting the meaning of effect sizes, (b) using role-playing methodologies to extend the hypothesis-testing capabilities of meta-analysis, (c) statistical synthesis of complex forms of data, and (d) the synthesis of syntheses.

Guidelines for interpreting the magnitude of effects. Numerical estimates of effect are of little value unless they can be infused with substantive meaning. While meta-analytic techniques have greatly improved the reliability of effect size estimates, much less progress has been made in their interpretation.

The first set of guidelines available to help interpret effect size were provided by Cohen (1988), who proposed effect size values "to serve as operational definitions of the qualitative adjectives 'small', 'medium', and 'large'" (p. 12). He recognized that judgments of "largeness" and "smallness" require a comparison between the item under consideration and some other item, or contrasting element. Therefore, in operationally defining these adjectives he compared different magnitudes of effect "with a subjective average of effect sizes as are encountered in the behavioral sciences" (p. 13).

Cohen defined a small effect as $d = .2$ or $r = .1$, which he said is representative of personality, social, and clinical psychology research. A large effect of $d = .8$ or $r = .5$ is more likely to be found in sociology, economics, and experimental or physiological psychology. According to Cohen, then, a social psychologist might interpret an effect size of $r = .1$ to be small when compared to all behavioral sciences but also about average when compared to other social psychological effects.

Cohen's benchmarks probably do not agree with the conventional wisdom of most personality psychologists. Most researchers would predict the "typical" or average correlation involving a personality construct to be $r = .3$, not $r = .1$. In a study of citations made in social psychology textbooks, Cooper and Findley (1982) found the average correlation to be $r = .48$, closer to Cohen's definition of a large social science effect. Of course, the source of these effect sizes means they are probably overestimates of all effects within the discipline.

While Cohen was careful to stress that his conventions are to be used as a last resort, many meta-analysts have adopted his benchmarks without assessing their applicability to the particular circumstance. At the time Cohen offered his guidelines, holding an effect size up against a criterion as broad as "all behavioral sciences" might have been the best contrasting element available. Today, with so many meta-analytic estimates of effect at hand, such a comparison holds little information.

Cooper (1981) suggested an alternative to Cohen's benchmarks. Instead of a single set of criteria, multiple contrasting elements should be used as yardsticks to interpret effect sizes. These should include some that (a) are broader than the treatment or predictor variable under consideration (e.g., How does the effect of alcohol on aggression compare to other influences on aggression, in general?), (b) are different from the treatment but within the same subclass (e.g., How does the effect of mood on helping compare to the effect of empathy on helping?), and (c) share the same treatment or predictor but vary in outcome measure (e.g., Do men and women differ more on social attitudes or social behaviors?). Cooper also suggested that effect sizes need to be interpreted in relation to the methodology used to generate them (e.g., the sensitivity of the research design, the trustworthiness of measures).

Of course, judgments of "size" are not synonymous with judgments of "merit." The relative merit of different treatments or explanations involves components in addition to effect sizes. In applied settings involving treatment effects, most notable among these are (a) the cost of particular treatments and (b) the value placed on changes the treatment is meant to influence.

Levin and colleagues have begun the task of establishing the relative cost-effectiveness of educational interventions (Levin, 1987; Levin, Glass, & Meister, 1987). They compared the cost-effectiveness of computer-assisted instruction, cross-age tutoring, reductions in class size, and increases in daily instructional time. First, they established an estimate of the magnitude of effect of each intervention over a constant treatment duration. Then, they calculated the cost per student of replicating each intervention. Finally, a cost-effectiveness ratio was established by calculating the effect size gain obtained for each $100 cost per student.

The situation is a bit less complex when theory-related predictors of behavior are at issue (e.g., the predictors of aggression or helping behavior). Here, measures of effect translate more directly into the "power of prediction" criterion often used to distinguish among theories. However, estimates of effect size for theory-related predictors still must be evaluated in light of methodological differences in the studies used to generate them.

In sum, evaluations of the merit, explanatory power, and cost-effectiveness of treatments and predictors are multifaceted and depend on which of numerous criteria are perceived as relevant. As treacherous as these judgments are, they are made every day. Discussion and debate about how best to carry them out is likely to occupy scholars' attention for some time to come.

Role playing in meta-analysis. Another issue in meta-analysis has emerged directly from its application in social psychology. It involves the use of role players to assess the psychological meaning of differences among experimental contexts. Study coders are asked to infer, using passages extracted from methods sections, how an experimental manipulation might have been interpreted by the actual subjects in a study. For example, Carlson and Miller (1987) asked coders to estimate how sad, guilty, angry, or frustrated different experimental manipulations might have made subjects in studies of the effects of mood on helping. Differences in the coders' assessments were then related to differences in study outcomes. The results were offered to shed light on the different theories' relevance or accuracy.

These "high-inference" judgments about studies create issues for research reviewers not engendered by the "low-inference" data retrieval typically associated with meta-analysis (e.g., experimental design, sample size, test statistic values). First, special attention must be paid to the reliability of high-inference judgments. Second, judges are being asked to play the roles of research subjects, and the validity of role-playing methodologies per se is still a controversial issue (Greenberg & Folger, 1988). Thus the value of role-player coding in meta-analysis is likely to cause considerable debate in the future. However, high-inference codings potentially add a new dimension to the reviewer's ability to interpret research literatures. Therefore, the pros and cons of the procedures deserve explication.

Statistical synthesis of complex forms of data. The statistical procedures for meta-analysis described above focus on integrating bivariate results from experimental and descriptive research. There exists a parallel set of synthesis procedures within applied psychology meant to help assess the generalizability of test instrument validity (Schmidt & Hunter, 1977). Yet to be developed, however, are techniques for the summarization of a host of more complex statistical procedures.

Meta-analysis methodologists are just now beginning to turn their attention to the integration of output from statistical techniques such as multiple regression, multivariate analyses of variance, structural equations, and factor analysis (see Driskell & Mullen, 1988). Each of these techniques will present a unique set of problems, in regard to both the statistical theory needed to perform the integration and its practical application. For instance, present-day meta-analysts find incomplete and nonuniform standards of data reporting to be one of their most vexing problems. It is likely to be even more troublesome as the data to be synthesized become more complex.

The synthesis of syntheses. With the number of meta-analyses growing, the opportunity has arisen for the comparison of findings across related quantitative syntheses. However, the only efforts at the synthesis of syntheses have appeared in the field of education, not psychology. Walberg (1986) proposed a theory of educational productivity that contains nine components required to optimize affective, behavioral, and cognitive learning. He used the components in his model to organize the results of dozens of meta-analyses, to examine the consistency of meta-analyses that replicated one another, and to compare the magnitudes of effect found associated with different components of the model.

The problems arising from the synthesis of syntheses represent a new challenge for meta-analysts. Yet, some of its potential benefits — for aiding in effect size interpretation, for comparing the explanatory value of theories, and for generating in applied settings reliable estimates of treatment effects over multiple outcomes — indicate it is a likely area of future methodological development.

JUDGING THE QUALITY
OF INTEGRATIVE RESEARCH REVIEWS

Perhaps the most important, and perplexing, question stemming from the increased dependence on literature reviews concerns how to distinguish good reviews from bad ones.

Quality standards for meta-analysis. Within the confines of integrative research reviewing some progress toward applicable standards for quality judgments has been made. For instance, the model of integrative reviewing as scientific research presented in Table 6.2 leads directly to several explicit questions about reviewing methods that relate to quality: (a) Do the operations appearing in the literature fit the reviewer's abstract definition? (b) Is enough attention paid to the methodological details of the primary studies? (c) Was the literature search thorough? (d) Were primary studies evaluated using explicit and consistent rules? (e) Were valid procedures used to combine the results of independent studies?

Sacks, Berrier, Reitman, Ancona-Berk, and Chalmers (1987) used a related scheme to evaluate the quality of 86 meta-analyses in medicine. A checklist containing 23 items, the origin of which was not detailed, was divided into six general areas of meta-analysis methodology—meta-analysis design (e.g., protocol, literature search), combinability of the separate studies, control of bias, statistical analysis, sensitivity analysis (i.e., multiple tests of data using various assumptions), and application of results. Results indicated that only 28% of the meta-analyses addressed all six areas, while 59% addressed five of the six areas. The authors concluded that "an urgent need exists for improved methods in literature searching, quality evaluation of trials, and synthesizing of results" (p.450).

Quality standards for literature reviews. While detail and rigor of the synthesis plan may be necessary conditions for judging a research review as superior in quality, these criteria are certainly not sufficient (see Cooper, in press). Several attempts have been made to pin down more general notions about how to determine the quality of reviews. These efforts have been both conceptual and empirical in nature and have tried to expand (a) the definition of knowledge synthesis encompassed by the quality criterion and (b) what is meant by the term *quality*.

One attempt used the taxonomy of literature reviews described above (see Table 6.1; Cooper, 1988). The first seven winners of the American Educational Research Association's Research Review Award were categorized to see if there were any consistencies among award-winning reviews. Little consistency was found. The seven reviews ran the gamut of focuses, goals, perspectives, coverages, organizations, and audiences.

Strike and Posner (1983) proposed that a good synthesis, whether of empirical research or abstract ideas, requires both intellectual quality and utility. First, a synthesis should clarify and resolve rather than obscure inconsistencies within the material being synthesized. Second, a synthesis should result in a progressive problem shift, involving greater explanatory power, expanded scope of application, and increased capacity to pursue unsolved problems. Finally, a synthesis should demonstrate consistency, parsimony, and elegance. It should answer the questions asked; readers should sense that they got what they came for.

While Strike and Posner's standards are highly abstract, there is some empirical support for them. As part of a larger study of the knowledge synthesis process, Cooper (1986b) asked post-master's degree graduate students in education and psychology to read six reviews of the desegregation research that covered the same set of 19 studies. One set of reactions to the reviews concerned evaluations of their quality.

On uniform rating scales, readers judged the quality of five separate aspects of the papers, but results revealed that the judgments were highly related – reviews perceived as superior on one dimension were also perceived as superior on the other dimensions. Further, quality judgments were not strongly related to the reviewers' or readers' position on desegregation or their general political beliefs. Instead, a review's quality was associated with readers' confidence in their interpretation of the review. Reviews seen as more interpretable were given higher quality ratings.

Readers were also asked to provide open-ended comments on the papers. These were subjected to an informal content analysis to discover what quality dimensions the readers generated on their own. The dimensions that emerged included (a) organization, (b) writing style, (c) clarity of focus, (d) use of citations, (e) attention to variable definitions, (f) attention to study methodology, and (g) manuscript preparation.

Cozzens (1981) polled readers about what made a review useful. She found no relation between the rated usefulness of a review and the kind of publication in which it appeared. She did find interactions between the characteristics of reviews and the intended use of them. For instance, if a review was used to follow developments in one's own specialty, comprehensiveness was valued but the reputation of the author was irrelevant. However, if the review was used to follow less familiar work, brevity was important, as was the standing of the author in the field.

In sum, the general criteria that have been offered for good research reviewing range from the lofty pursuits of resolving conflict and stimulating progressive problem shifts to the mundane concerns of presenting material effectively. However, efforts to integrate and apply these criteria are few and far between. Social research methodologists need to continue to identify and systematize criteria for evaluating research reviews, and need to use these standards to assess the quality of meta-analyses. Both products should provide impetus for and facilitate the generation of higher-quality meta-analyses in the future. As the role of reviews in our definition of knowledge expands, our ability to distinguish good from bad reviews will increase in importance.

REFERENCES

Bangert-Drowns, R. L. (1986). Review of developments in meta-analytic methods. *Psychological Bulletin, 99,* 388-399.

Barber, T. (1978). Expecting expectancy effects: Biased data analyses and failure to exclude alternative interpretations in experimenter expectancy research. *Behavioral and Brain Sciences, 3,* 388-390.

Carlson, M., & Miller, N. (1987). Explanations of the relation between negative mood and helping. *Psychological Bulletin, 102,* 91-108.

Cohen, J. (1988). *Statistical power analysis in the behavioral sciences.* Hillsdale, NJ: Erlbaum.

Cook, T., & Levitan, L. (1981). Reviewing the literature: A comparison of traditional methods with meta-analysis. *Journal of Personality, 48,* 449-471.

Cooper, H. M. (1979). Statistically combining independent studies: A meta-analysis of sex differences in conformity research. *Journal of Personality and Social Psychology, 37,* 131-146.

Cooper, H. M. (1981). On the effects of significance and the significance of effects. *Journal of Personality and Social Psychology, 41,* 1013-1018.

Cooper, H. M. (1982). Scientific guidelines for conducting integrative research reviews. *Review of Educational Research, 52,* 291-302.

Cooper, H. M. (1986a). Literature searching strategies of integrative research reviewers: A first survey. *Knowledge: Creation, Diffusion, Utilization, 8,* 372-383.

Cooper, H. M. (1986b). On the social psychology of using research reviews: The case of desegregation and black achievement. In R. S. Feldman (Ed.), *The social psychology of education* (pp. 341-363). Cambridge: Cambridge University Press.

Cooper, H. M. (1988). Organizing knowledge syntheses: A taxonomy of literature reviews. *Knowledge in Society, 1,* 104-126.

Cooper, H. M. (1989). *Integrating research: A guide for literature reviews* (2nd ed.). Newbury Park, CA: Sage.

Cooper, H. M. (in press). Moving beyond meta-analysis. In K. W. Wachter & M. L. Straf (Eds.), *The future of meta-analysis.* New York: Russell Sage.

Cooper, H. M., & Arkin, R. A. (1981). On quantitative reviewing. *Journal of Personality, 49,* 225-230.

Cooper, H. M., Burger, J. M., & Good, T. L. (1981). Gender differences in the academic locus of control beliefs of young children. *Journal of Personality and Social Psychology, 40,* 562-572.

Cooper, H. M., & Findley, M. (1982). Expected effect sizes: Estimates for statistical power analysis in social psychology. *Personality and Social Psychology Bulletin, 8,* 168-173.

Cooper, H. M., & Hazelrigg, P. (1988). Personality moderators of interpersonal expectancy effects: An integrative research review. *Journal of Personality and Social Psychology, 55,* 937-949.

Cooper, H. M., & Ribble, R. G. (1989). Influences on the accuracy of literature searches for research syntheses. *Knowledge: Creation, Diffusion, Utilization, 10*, 179–21.

Cooper, H. M., & Rosenthal, R. (1980). Statistical versus traditional procedures for summarizing research findings. *Psychological Bulletin, 87*, 442–449.

Cozzens, S. E. (1981). *User requirements for scientific reviews* (Grant Report No. IST-7821947). Washington, DC: National Science Foundation.

Driskell, T. E., & Mullen, B. (1988). *Status, expectation and behavior: Meta-analytic review and test of the theory.* Manuscript submitted for publication.

Eysenck, H. (1978). An exercise in mega-silliness. *American Psychologist, 33*, 517.

Fisher, R. A. (1932). *Statistical methods for research workers.* London: Oliver & Boyd.

Garvey, W., & Griffith, B. (1971). Scientific communication: Its role in the conduct of research and the creation of knowledge. *American Psychologist, 26*, 349–361.

Glass, G. V (1976). Primary, secondary, and meta-analysis of research. *Educational Researcher, 5*, 3–8.

Glass, G. V, McGaw, B., & Smith, M. L. (1981). *Meta-analysis in social research.* Beverly Hills, CA: Sage.

Gottfredson, G. (1978). Evaluating psychological research reports. *American Psychologist, 33*, 920–934.

Greenberg, J., & Folger, R. (1988). *Controversial issues in social research.* New York: Springer-Verlag.

Guzzo, R. A., Jackson, S. E., & Katzell, R. A. (1987). Meta-analysis analysis. In B. M. Staw & L. L. Cummings (Eds.), *Research in organizational behavior* (Vol. 9, pp. 407–442). Greenwich, CT: JAI.

Hedges, L. V., & Olkin, I. (1980). Vote-counting methods in research synthesis. *Psychological Bulletin, 88*, 359–369.

Hedges, L. V., & Olkin, I. (1985). *Statistical methods for meta-analysis.* Orlando, FL: Academic Press.

Hunter, J. E., Schmidt, F. L., & Jackson, G. B. (1982). *Meta-analysis: Cumulating research findings across studies.* Beverly Hills, CA: Sage.

Levin, H. M. (1987). Cost-benefit and cost-effectiveness analysis. *New Directions for Program Evaluation, 34*, 83–99.

Levin, H. M., Glass, G. V, & Meister, G. R. (1987). Cost-effectiveness of computer-assisted instruction. *Evaluation Review, 11*, 50–72.

Light, R. J., & Pillemer, D. B. (1984). *Summing up: The science of research reviewing.* Cambridge, MA: Harvard University Press.

Mansfield, R., & Bussey, T. (1977). Meta-analysis of research: A rejoinder to Glass. *Educational Researcher, 6*, 3.

Mazella, A., & Malin, M. (1977). *A bibliometric study of the review literature* (Grant Report No. DS176-05834). Washington, DC: National Science Foundation.

Mosteller, F., & Bush, R. R. (1954). Selected quantitative techniques. In G. Lindzey (Ed.), *Handbook of social psychology* (Vol. 1, pp. 280–334). Reading, MA: Addison-Wesley.

Olkin, I. (in press). History and goals. In K. W. Wachter & M. L. Straf (Eds.), *The future of meta-analysis.* New York: Russell Sage.

Pearson, K. (1896). Mathematical contributions to the theory of evolution, III. Regression, heredity and panmixia. *Philosophical Transactions of the Royal Society of*

London Series A, 187, 253–318. (Reprinted in *Karl Pearson's early statistical papers* [1948]. Cambridge: Cambridge University Press.)

Price, D. J. (1965). Networks of scientific papers. *Science, 149,* 510–515.

Raudenbush, S. W., Becker, B. J., & Kalaian, H. (1988). Modeling multivariate effect sizes. *Psychological Bulletin, 103,* 111–120.

Rosenthal, R. (1978). Combining results of independent studies. *Psychological Bulletin, 85,* 185–193.

Rosenthal, R. (1979). The "file-drawer problem" and tolerance for null results. *Psychological Bulletin, 86,* 638–641.

Rosenthal, R. (1984). *Meta-analytic procedures for social research.* Beverly Hills, CA: Sage.

Rosenthal, R., & Rubin D. (1978). Interpersonal expectancy effects: The first 345 studies. *Behavioral and Brain Sciences, 3,* 377–415.

Sacks, H. S., Berrier, J., Reitman, D., Ancona-Berk, V. A., & Chalmers, T. C. (1987). Meta-analyses of randomized controlled trials. *New England Journal of Medicine, 316,* 450–455.

Schmidt, F. L., & Hunter, J. E. (1977). Development of a general solution to the problem of validity generalization. *Journal of Applied Psychology, 62,* 529–540.

Slavin, R. E. (1986). Best evidence synthesis: An alternative to meta-analytic and traditional reviews. *Educational Researcher, 15,* 5–11.

Smith, M. L., & Glass, G. V (1977). Meta-analysis of psychotherapy outcome studies. *American Psychologist, 32,* 752–760.

Stouffer, S. A., Suchman, E. A., DeVinney, L. C., Star, S. A., & Williams, R. M., Jr. (1949). *The American soldier: Vol. 1. Adjustment during army life.* Princeton, NJ: Princeton University Press.

Strike, K., & Posner, G. (1983). Types of syntheses and their criteria. In S. Ward & L. Reed (Eds.), *Knowledge structure and use: Implications for synthesis and interpretation* (pp. 343–361). Philadelphia: Temple University Press.

Walberg, H. J. (1986). Synthesis of research on teaching. In M. C. Wittrock (Ed.), *Handbook of research on teaching* (pp. 214–229). Washington, DC: American Educational Research Association.

Wolf, F. W. (1986). *Meta-analysis: Quantitative methods for research synthesis.* Beverly Hills, CA: Sage.

Design Issues in Dyadic Research

DAVID A. KENNY

David A. Kenny studied with Donald T. Campbell at Northwestern University, where he received his Ph.D. in social psychology in 1972. He has taught at Arizona State University and Harvard University and was a Fellow at the Center for Advanced Study in the Behavioral Sciences. He is the author of three books, the most recent being *Statistics for the Social and Behavioral Sciences* (Scott Foresman, 1987). He is currently Professor of Psychology at the University of Connecticut.

Two-person social interaction represents the core of social psychology. When we observe people in natural settings, they spontaneously form two-person units (Bakeman & Beck, 1974; James, 1953). Also, the standard topics in social psychology—person perception, influence, attraction, aggression, helping, and bargaining—most often involve two people. Even the study of personality can be viewed as the study of two-person social interaction (Malloy & Kenny, 1986).

In this chapter, the designs that can be used to study two-person interaction are detailed. Considered first are designs in which people interact with only one partner. For these designs people could interact once with the same partner (confederate design), a few partners (nested design), or each with a different partner (standard design). Considered second are designs in which people interact with multiple partners. In ordinary multiple-partner designs, each person interacts with every other person (round-robin design) or people are divided into groups and each person interacts with the members of the other group (block design). In some cases, a subset of the dyads can be considered as special, for example, best friends or marital partners. Three designs for special dyads are considered: dyad round-robin, dyad within-block, and dyad between-block. Finally, people can interact with others in a group in which each person has an assigned role (family design).

To make the discussion of research designs concrete, a general example will be considered: the research topic of interruptions. In this chapter four important questions will be considered: First, are men more likely to interrupt

---

AUTHOR'S NOTE: The research reported here was supported in part by National Science Foundation grant BNS-8807462 and National Institute of Mental Health grant MH R01-4029501. I wish to thank Norman Anderson, Bryan Hallmark, William Ickes, and Deborah A. Kashy for helpful comments on a previous version of this chapter.

than women? This question will be referred to as the *sex difference* question. (Some readers may prefer to study an experimental variable such as status. They can, throughout this chapter, substitute status for sex.) Second, if one member of the dyad repeatedly interrupts his or her partner, is that person interrupted by the partner? This question will be referred to as the *reciprocity* question. Third, is it the case that some people are more likely to interrupt or that in some relationships there are more interruptions? This question will be referred to as the *variance* question. At issue is whether interruptions occur at the level of the individual or at the level of the relationship. Fourth, are we more likely to interrupt someone we dislike than someone we like? This question will be referred to as the *correlation* question. The sex difference question is a type of correlation question, but gender is dichotomous and fixed, whereas dislike for one's partner is random and continuous. (See the Appendix to this chapter for a discussion of random effects.)

It is impossible to cover in a single chapter all issues relevant to the design of dyadic research. One issue not covered is the design and analysis of sequential studies. For instance, is a person more likely to interrupt his or her partner if the person was recently interrupted? While not covered in this chapter, sequential statistics can be measured for each dyad and then analyzed using dyad as the unit of analysis (Kenny, 1988). Also not covered is the analysis of ordinal and nominal dependent variables. In this chapter, the concentration is on issues of design, and the reader is referred to other sources for details concerning the statistical analysis.

One major design issue concerns whether each person interacts with only one person or with more than one person. A second design issue concerns whether the dyad is symmetric or asymmetric. A dyad is said to be symmetric if the researcher chooses not to distinguish the two people; a dyad is said to be asymmetric if the two people are identified by a distinguishing characteristic. For example, a married couple is asymmetric because the individuals can be distinguished by their gender, while same-sex roommates are symmetric. A third important design issue is one- versus two-sided data structures. Dyadic data are said to be two-sided if the responses of both interactants are measured and one-sided if the response from only one interactant is measured.

SINGLE-PARTNER DESIGNS

There are three major types of dyadic designs in which people interact with a single partner. All the people can interact with the same partner (confederate design), with some of the same partners (nested design), and with all different partners (standard design). These three design types are diagrammed in Table 7.1.

Confederate Design

For the confederate design all subjects interact with the same partner. The one common partner is often a confederate whose behavior is highly standardized by the experimenter. For instance, the confederate might be instructed not to interrupt the subject. Problems in standardizing the confederate's behavior are discussed by Duncan and Fiske (1985). Ordinarily in the confederate design, the data are one-sided. That is, data are only gathered from the subject and not from the confederate.

Sex differences in interruptions could be measured using the confederate design, but they would be of limited generalizability. The results would be limited to the one confederate and to that confederate's sex. Moreover, because the confederate's behavior was standardized, the interaction may not be very natural, a constraint that further limits generalizibility. Reciprocity cannot be measured because the measurement is one-sided. Variance cannot be apportioned to person or relationship because each person interacts with only one partner. The correlation between the liking of the confederate and the number of interruptions could be measured, but there would be limited generalizability. Moreover, because the confederate's behavior was standardized, there would be a restriction in the range of the disliking variable.

Nested Design

In the nested design all subjects do not interact with the same person; instead, there are multiple confederates. For instance, there may be six partners, three male and three female. (It is also possible to employ the nested design and not use confederates; for example, people can be nested within teachers, targets, judges, therapists, and so on.) If the number of confederates is small, say fewer than eight, for reasons of power one probably should treat confederate as a fixed factor. In a fixed analysis, confederate is treated as a factor in the analysis, but, strictly speaking, the results apply only to the specific confederates studied. If the number of confederates is greater than eight, one can employ the Kenny and La Voie (1985) analysis in which confederate is treated as random. (See the Appendix for a discussion of random variables.) If confederate is treated as a random factor, correlations and variances can be computed for both confederates and subjects within confederates.

TABLE 7.1 Three Single-Partner Designs

Confederate Design

Person	Partner 7
1	X
2	X
3	X
4	X
5	X
6	X

Nested Design

Person	Partner 10	11	12
1	X		
2	X		
3	X		
4		X	
5		X	
6		X	
7			X
8			X
9			X

Standard Design

Person	Partner 7	8	9	10	11	12
1	X					
2		X				
3			X			
4				X		
5					X	
6						X

NOTE: X indicates collected data.

The nested design provides greater generalizability than the confederate design. This is especially true if the number of confederates is large enough to be treated as a random factor. Too often in confederate studies, we do not select and train enough confederates to treat confederate as a random factor. For example, assume that there are male and female confederates, and assume that female confederates are interrupted more often than male confederates. If confederate is treated as a random factor, then a significant sex of confederate effect can be generalized across subjects and confederates. If confederate is treated as a fixed factor in the analysis, then a significant effect of confederate sex refers only to the particular confederates studied. That is, it is known only that those particular female confederates are interrupted and not females in general.

Because data from the nested design are generally one-sided (only the subject's responses are measured), the reciprocity question cannot be answered. If the data are two-sided, the reader should consult Kenny and Albright (1987).

Variance can be assigned to confederate and subject within confederate: Confederate variance means that some confederates are interrupted more than others, and subject within confederate variance indicates that some subjects interrupt a particular confederate more than other subjects interrupt that confederate.

The correlation question can be addressed at two levels, assuming that confederate is treated as random: First, are the confederates who are liked more interrupted less? Second, for a particular confederate, do the people who like him or her more interrupt him or her less?

Standard Design

In the standard design, both members of the dyad are subjects and the data are typically two-sided. (Unfortunately, all too often data from this design are treated as if they were one-sided to simplify the analysis.) The analysis of the standard design is discussed extensively by Kenny (1988). There are three types of standard designs that can be used to study sex differences in interruptions. First, each dyad can contain one male and one female. To measure the sex difference, a repeated measure analysis of variance would be used. Dyad would be the unit of analysis and sex would be the repeated measure. Second, each dyad can be same-sexed; that is, both members are male or both members are female. Interruptions would be averaged across dyad members, and sex would be a between-dyad variable. Third, some of the dyads could be same-sexed and others could be opposite-sexed. There are then three different dyad types—male-male, female-female, and male-female—and so sex is both a within- and between-dyad variable. This type of design is called a Kraemer and Jacklin (1979) design, and its analysis is also discussed by Kenny (1988). A Kraemer and Jacklin design, while more complicated to analyze than the other two types of designs, is preferable because it subsumes the other two types of designs. Most important, the

Kraemer and Jacklin design unconfounds the effects of whether males tend to interrupt more than females (regardless of sex of partner) and whether females tend to be interrupted more than males.

When all dyads contain one male and one female, reciprocity can be assessed by a simple correlation. However, when some of the dyads contain same-sex members, that is, the dyad is symmetric, problems arise in measuring reciprocity. In particular, it is not clear whose score to use as the X variable and whose score to use as the Y variable. To solve this problem reciprocity can be measured by the intraclass correlation (Kenny, 1988).

In the standard design, variance cannot be apportioned to person and relationship because people interact with only one partner. Correlation can be measured for individuals and dyads by a procedure detailed by Kenny and La Voie (1985). One can measure whether people who dislike their partners interrupt them more and whether, in dyads, when there is more dislike, there are more interruptions.

MULTIPLE-PARTNER DESIGNS

The basic model for multiple-partner designs is the social relations model (Kenny & La Voie, 1984). In this model each person interacts with more than one subject. For instance, one can measure the number of times John interrupts Mary. According to the model, the number of times that John interrupts Mary depends on how frequently people interrupt each other (a constant), how frequently John tends to interrupt others (an actor effect), how frequently Mary is interrupted by others (a partner effect), and how frequently John interrupts Mary after the constant, the actor, and the partner effects are removed (the relationship effect). All of these components are random effects (see the appendix).

A major advantage of multiple-partner designs is that variance can be apportioned between individuals (actor and partner) and dyads (relationship). Thus it can be determined whether behavior is based on individual differences or on relational features.

Reciprocity can be measured in two ways. It can be measured at the individual level: Are people who interrupt others also interrupted by others? Reciprocity at the dyad level measures the correlation between person A's relationship effect toward B with B's relationship effect toward A. If person A interrupt person B more than A interrupts others and more than others interrupt B, does B interrupt A more than B interrupts others and more than A is interrupted?

In considering multiple-partner designs, distinctions can be made among ordinary designs, special-dyad designs, and family designs. In ordinary designs people are all interchangeable. In special-dyad designs, each person has a special relationship with one other person. In a family design, each person in the group has a fixed role.

Ordinary Designs

There are two basic types of designs[1] that permit the estimation of social relations parameters: the round-robin and block designs.

In a *round-robin* design, each person is paired with every other person in the group, as in the top diagram of Table 7.2. The round-robin design is the prototypical multiple-partner design. In order to be able to estimate actor, partner, and relationship variance as well as the actor-partner correlation and dyadic reciprocity, the minimum group size is four, but if dyadic reciprocity can be assumed to be zero, the group size can be as small as three. It may be reasonable to assume no dyadic reciprocity if the people observe but do not interact with each other.

In a *block* design, individuals in each group are divided into two subgroups. Every person in one subgroup interacts with all of the people in the other subgroup but with none of the others in the person's own subgroup. So in Table 7.2, people 1 and 2 are in one subgroup and 3 and 4 in the second. The minimum subgroup size is two. There are three major types of block designs: half block, symmetric, and asymmetric.

In the *half block* design, data from only one of two blocks are gathered. In Table 7.2, if only the data from the block with people 1 and 2 as actors and with 3 and 4 as partners are gathered, the design would be a half block. So only the observations of the upper block of X's are gathered. In a half block design, the data from only one of the two interactants are gathered and, therefore, the data are one-sided. For some research questions a half block design is necessary. For example, in studies of parent-child or therapist-patient interactions, sometimes the behavior of only the child or patient is observed. Because the data in the half block design are one-sided, reciprocity cannot be measured.

For the symmetric and asymmetric block designs both blocks of data are gathered. For the *symmetric block* designs, assignment into the two subgroups is either random or arbitrary, and one cannot distinguish the people in the two subgroups. For instance, DePaulo, Kenny, Hoover, Webb, and Oliver (1987) used a symmetric block design. They began with a group of six

TABLE 7.2 Ordinary Multiple-Partner Designs

Round-Robin Design

	Partner			
Actor	1	2	3	4
1	–	X	X	X
2	X	–	X	X
3	X	X	–	X
4	X	X	X	–

Block Design

	Partner			
Actor	1	2	3	4
1	–	–	X	X
2	–	–	X	X
3	X	X	–	–
4	X	X	–	–

NOTE: Dashes indicate uncollected data. All other data are gathered.

women, they created two subgroups of three women, and each woman interacted with the women in the other subgroup.

In the *asymmetric block* design the two subgroups can be distinguished by some natural variable (male versus female) or by some experimental variable (leader versus follower). For instance, Oliver (1988) studied cross-sex interactions. He had groups of two men and two women for whom he created all possible male-female dyads. There were then two blocks of data. One block consisted of the males' ratings of their female partners and the other consisted of the females' ratings of their male partners.

The round-robin and block designs can be combined into a block-round-robin design. For instance, Whitley, Schofield, and Snyderman (1984) measured liking in a racially integrated classroom setting. The within-race data are round-robin in structure and the between-race data are asymmetric block in structure. The block-round-robin design is particularly useful in studying intergroup relations. For the block-round-robin design there must be at least four people in each subgroup and eight people in total.

We now consider how the round-robin and block designs can be used to answer the four basic questions posed at the beginning of the chapter. To measure sex differences in interruptions when only same-sex dyads are to be studied, either a round-robin or a block design can be used. If only opposite-sex dyads are to be studied, then an asymmetric block design can be used. Design and analysis issues become more complicated when both same- and opposite-sex dyads are run in the same group. In terms of analysis, one can estimate the Kraemer-Jacklin parameters and use group as the unit statistical analysis. (For an illustration, see DiPilato, West, and Chartier, 1988.) In terms of design, a round-robin design with two men and two women has the disadvantage of having half as many same-sex dyads as opposite-sex dyads. A block or a block-round-robin design is to be preferred over a round-robin design because the number of same- and opposite-sex dyads can be kept comparable.

If the block-round robin design is used, one can measure dyadic reciprocity for all three dyad types: male-male, female-female, and male-female. This design requires a minimum of eight people, four males and four females. Moreover, with a block-round-robin design, we can determine whether a person who interrupts males also interrupts females.

The correlation question can be addressed in three ways: actor, partner, and relationship. For actor, we ask whether people who interrupt others are disliked by others. For partner, we ask whether people who are interrupted are also disliked. At the relationship level there are two correlations. First, if a person interrupts the partner, is he or she disliked by his or her partner? Second, if a person is interrupted by the partner, does he or she dislike the partner?

There are a number of important design issues in the collection of multiple-partner data: Self data, order effects, group size, and number of groups. In rating studies the subject may rate him- or herself, and so there are self data. If there are self data, the investigator should consider having people rate or judge self last, because the judgment of self could be disrupting.

The effect of order of interactions or ratings has not been given much consideration in previous studies using the social relations model. However, in the few times that order effects have been studied (La Voie, 1981; Oliver, 1988), minimal order effects have been found. Handling order in the round-robin design is problematic. If self data are not gathered or are always gathered last, as was just suggested, it is impossible to counterbalance partner and position. In most rating research the target is confounded with a position. For instance, partner A is always rated first by all actors, partner B second, and so on. While it is possible to examine the effect of position on ratings, it appears that this has never been done.

Another important design issue is the number of subjects per group. For the round-robin design, there must be at least four people per group (three if dyadic reciprocity can be assumed to equal zero). However, using the minimum of four is risky because if there are missing data and a person must be omitted from the analysis, the entire group's data would be lost. Practical considerations often dictate the sample size. A reasonable recommendation is from five to nine. If the group size is large, then there are many more dyads than there are individuals, and so dyadic effects are estimated with far greater precision than individual-level effects. If the focus is on relationship effects, then large group sizes are desirable; if, however, the focus is on individual effects, moderate group sizes are preferable.

A second factor to consider is the number of groups. One important rule of thumb is that the fewer the number of partners each actor has, the greater the number of groups that are needed. Round-robin designs, then, require fewer groups than the block design because more observations per person are gathered. The symmetric block design requires fewer groups than the asymmetric block design because data are pooled in the symmetric designs, whereas for the asymmetric design the results are estimated for each block. For most applications, a total of 6 groups is the minimum, while 15–20 is a reasonable goal. (If the purpose of the study is to compare parameter estimates for different groups, then 15–20 groups are needed for each condition.) The more people in a group, the fewer groups need be run. For instance, Miller and Kenny (1986) studied only one group composed of 45 people.

Special-Dyad Designs

Not all dyads are the same. Some might be called special and others might be called ordinary. Examples of special dyads are married couples, roommates, best friends, parent-child, and patient-therapist. In this section I consider data from a group of people each of whom is paired with one other special partner and each of whom is also paired with other people who can be considered "ordinary."

Special-dyad studies have examined whether children obey strangers as much as their parents (Landauer, Carlsmith, & Lepper, 1970), whether people reciprocate disclosure as much to strangers as to a spouse (Dindia, Fitzpatrick, & Kenny, 1989), and how friendship is qualitatively different from acquaintance (Kenny & Kashy, 1989). Table 7.3 presents the three possible designs for special-dyad studies. For each of the three designs, people (1,2), (3,4), (5,6) and (7,8) are members of special dyads; for instance, they are married to each other. The interaction between members of special dyads is denoted by x and the interaction between members of ordinary dyads is denoted by o. The design at the top of Table 7.3 is the dyad round-robin design. All possible interactions are gathered.

TABLE 7.3 Designs for the Study of Special Dyads

Dyad Round-Robin Design

	Partner							
Actor	1	2	3	4	5	6	7	8
1	—	x	o	o	o	o	o	o
2	x	—	o	o	o	o	o	o
3	o	o	—	x	o	o	o	o
4	o	o	x	—	o	o	o	o
5	o	o	o	o	—	x	o	o
6	o	o	o	o	x	—	o	o
7	o	o	o	o	o	o	—	x
8	o	o	o	o	o	o	x	—

Dyad Within-Block Design

	Partner							
Actor	1	2	3	4	5	6	7	8
1	—	—	—	—	x	o	o	o
2	—	—	—	—	o	x	o	o
3	—	—	—	—	o	o	x	o
4	—	—	—	—	o	o	o	x
5	x	o	o	o	—	—	—	—
6	o	x	o	o	—	—	—	—
7	o	o	x	o	—	—	—	—
8	o	o	o	x	—	—	—	—

Dyad Between-Block Design

	Partner							
Actor	1	2	3	4	5	6	7	8
1	—	x	—	—	o	o	o	o
2	x	—	—	—	o	o	o	o
3	—	—	—	x	o	o	o	o
4	—	—	x	—	o	o	o	o
5	o	o	o	o	—	x	—	—
6	o	o	o	o	x	—	—	—
7	o	o	o	o	—	—	—	x
8	o	o	o	o	—	—	x	—

NOTE: o indicates a datum from an ordinary dyad observation, x indicates a datum from a special dyad observation, and dashes indicate uncollected data. Special dyads are (1,2), (3,4), (5,6), and (7,8).

In a block design, people are assigned to two different subgroups and they interact with the people in the other subgroup. The two members of the special dyad can be in the same subgroup (dyad between-block design) or they can be members of different subgroups (dyad within-block design). In the dyad within-block design members of a special dyad interact with different people, while in the dyad between-block design they interact with the same people.[2] So if married couples are the special dyads, in a dyad within-block design, each husband would interact with his own wife as well as all the other wives and each wife would interact with all of the husbands; in the dyad between-block design, each couple would interact with both members of two other couples.

There are a number of factors that should be considered in choosing which special-dyad design to use. The dyad within-block design requires the fewest dyads and is also the easiest to analyze. But this design does not permit the estimation of certain effects that the other two designs can estimate. For instance, in the husband-wife study described in the previous paragraph, there are no same-sex interactions, and so information about that type of dyad is lost. The dyad within-block design may be required if some interactions would not be informative. This is more likely when the dyads are asymmetric. For instance, if one is studying adult-child interactions, it may not be sensible to have children interact with children and adults interact with adults. In such a case, one should use the dyad within-block design.

In some cases with the dyad block design, data from only one of the two blocks are collected. For instance, Landauer et al. (1970) measured only the compliance of the child in mother-child interactions. This design might be called dyad half block. When the special dyad is asymmetric, the dyad block design becomes dyad asymmetric block and the dyad round-robin design becomes the dyad block-round-robin design.

The dyad round-robin and the dyad between-block designs provide full information and can estimate the myriad parameters described in Kenny (1990). The advantage of the dyad between-block design is that it requires fewer interactions, and the advantage of the dyad round-robin design is that effects are estimated with greater precision. One should then prefer the dyad round-robin design when data collection costs are low and the dyad between-block design when they are high.

There can be more than 4 special dyads, but if there are fewer many of the parameters described by Kenny (1990) cannot be estimated. The sample sizes required for special-dyad designs are rather excessive. In an analysis by Kenny (1990), there were very few significant effects with 6 groups and 24 special dyads. Kenny and Kashy (1989) did obtain significant results with

16 groups and 119 special dyads. In special-dyad designs, the effective sample size is not the person but the special dyad.

Now considered are the four questions about interruptions. The special dyad to be used in this example is husband and wife. Assume that it is found that husbands repeatedly interrupt their wives. There are a number of possible explanations for this result that can be teased out by a special-dyad study. We can learn whether the sex difference is unique to marital dyads, to opposite sex dyads, due to the fact that males interrupt partners of both sexes, or due to the fact that females are interrupted by both sexes. Clearly the finding that husbands interrupt their wives is subject to a host of alternative explanations.

Reciprocity of interruptions can be measured separately for married couples and strangers. If the dyad round-robin or dyad between-block design is employed, one can measure reciprocity for male-male, female-female, and male-female dyads.

It is also possible to separate actor, partner, and relationship variance for couples and strangers, so it can be determined if a man who interrupts his wife also interrupts others.

The correlation between liking and interrupting can also be measured for both couples and strangers. For instance, at the relationship level, it can be determined whether liking leads to fewer interruptions for both couples and strangers.

We can also determine whether when a male tends to interrupt someone, his spouse also tends to interrupt that person. That is, we can determine if the marriage partners have similar relational styles. Moreover, it can be determined whether husbands and wives have similar interruption rates and similar rates of being interrupted.

Family Designs

In a family design all the people in each group can be distinguished by role or status. For instance, the group can be mother, father, son, and daughter, hence the name family design. Members can be distinguished by factors other than their family roles. For instance, the group members might be distinguished by organizational rank or by personality type. The design is still dyadic because each family member interacts with or rates every other family member.

Examples of the family design can be found in work by Stevenson, Leavitt, Thompson, and Roach (1988), who studied play activities in families; Cook and Dreyer (1984), who studied approval statements in three-person families; Cook, Kenny, and Goldstein (1989), who studied negative affect in families with troubled adolescents; and Sabatelli, Buck, and Kenny (1986), who studied nonverbal communication in married couples.

Imagine a four-person family: mother, father, son, and daughter, as in Table 7.4. There are a total of 12 scores. The score FD would indicate how frequently the father (F) interrupts the daughter (D), and SM would measure how frequently the son (S) interrupts the mother (M).

Table 7.4 illustrates the various sources of variance. An x in the table means that the source of variance is present in the measure. The first source of variance is a constant or mean, and it measures the tendency for there to be more interruptions in some families than there are in other families. The second factor measures the extent to which some mothers interrupt family members more than other mothers. Note that the three measures for which the mother is the actor (MF, MS, and MD) have mother actor variance. In a similar fashion, the actor factors can be defined for father, son, and daughter. So, for instance, the daughter actor effect reflects the fact that some daughters interrupt other family members more than other daughters.

The partner effect for a given mother measures the extent to which her interaction partners interrupt her more than other mothers are interrupted. Partner variance can also be measured for father, mother, and daughter.

Table 7.4 can be viewed as a factor loading matrix. There are a total of nine common factors (the mean, four actor factors, and four partner factors). Each measure then loads on three of the nine factors. For instance, SF loads on the constant, son actor, and father partner factors. For each measure there is a unique factor that measures the relationship effect.

A person's actor factor may be correlated with his or her partner factor. For mother, this would measure the extent to which a mother who interrupts family members is also interrupted by them. Moreover, relationship effects from the same dyad can be correlated. It can then be asked, for example, If a husband tends to interrupt his wife frequently, does she interrupt him frequently?

These designs can be analyzed by confirmatory factor analysis (Kenny, 1979). Unlike traditional exploratory factor analysis, confirmatory factor analysis requires the researchers to state explicitly what measures load on what factor and what factors are correlated with each other. The researcher-specified factor loadings for this four-person family model are given in Table 7.4. The common factors are uncorrelated with each other except that each role's actor and partner effects may be correlated. Reciprocal relationship effects can be estimated by correlating the unique factors. If there are four or more people in each family, a mean or constant factor can be estimated.

Sex differences is the family design can be measured in a variety of ways.

TABLE 7.4   Loading Matrix for Four-Person Family Study

			Factor						
			Actor				*Partner*		
Variable	C	M	F	S	D	M	F	S	D
MF[a]	X	X					X		
MS	X	X						X	
MD	X	X							X
FM	X		X			X			
FS	X		X					X	
FD	X		X						X
SM	X			X		X			
SF	X			X			X		
SD	X			X					X
DM	X				X	X			
DF	X				X		X		
DS	X				X			X	

NOTE: F = father, M = mother, S = son, D = daughter, and C = constant.

a. The rate at which the mother interrupts the father. Each of the remaining eleven variables is interpreted similarly.

We can ask whether male family members interrupt more and are interrupted less than female family members. We can also ask if there are more interruptions in opposite-sex dyads than in same-sex dyads. Family should be the unit in these analyses.

We can measure reciprocity for each of the six dyad types. It may be the case that same-sex dyads show reciprocity of interruptions whereas opposite-sex dyads show compensation; that is, one member of the dyad repeatedly interrupts the partner while the partner infrequently interrupts the other.

Variance is measured for each family role. So actor and partner variance can be measured for mother, father, son, and daughter. At the relationship level, variance can be measured for both people in the six dyads.

We can also obtain 32 different answers to the correlation question: 4 each for both actor and partner and 24 at the relationship level. The actor correlation for sons would ask whether sons who tended to interrupt their partners frequently were disliked by their partners. The partner correlation for sons would measure whether sons who were frequently interrupted were disliked. For each of the six dyad types, there are four relationship correlations. An example of these four correlations for mother-daughter dyads are as follows:

1. If a mother interrupts her daughter more than other mothers interrupt their daughters, does the mother like her daughter less than other mothers like their daughters?

2. If a mother interrupts her daughter more than other mothers interrupt their daughters, does the daughter like her mother less than other daughters like their mothers?

3. If a daughter interrupts her mother more than other daughters interrupt their mothers, does the daughter like her mother less than other daughters like their mother?

4. If a daughter interrupts her mother more than other daughters interrupt their mothers, does the mother like her daughter less than other mothers like their daughters?

Although there are 24 possible relationship-level correlations between disliking and interruption, in most applications they would be pooled into a smaller number.

A type of "confederate" can be used in a family design. For instance, one could have a husband and wife interact with two people, one male and one female, both of whom are strangers to each other and to the marital dyad. Members of this quartet could interact with each other and the number of interruptions could be measured. A variant of this design was employed by Sabatelli et al. (1986). With this design one can assess the extent to which there is more reciprocity of interruptions in the stranger dyads than in the married couples.

In family studies the sample size is the number of families. Minimally one would expect as many families as variables. For four-person families the number of variables is 12, and if the correlation question is addressed the number of variables is 24. Although it is difficult to gather this type of data, clearly one should attempt to obtain sample sizes of at least 30.

CONCLUSION

This chapter has elaborated many different ways to answer the four questions posed in the introduction. For instance, the question of whether men interrupt others more than women do can be tested by a wide variety of different designs. In some of those designs the sex difference is measured more than once. For instance, in the Kraemer and Jacklin design, the sex difference is measured for same- and opposite-sex partners. Quite clearly, researchers can learn much more from their data if they take the time to analyze those data properly. They could also learn much more if they take the time to collect the proper data.

APPENDIX:
STATISTICAL PROPERTIES OF RANDOM EFFECTS

Social and personality psychologists are not used to thinking about random effects. What follows is a fairly nontechnical description of a random effect. The problem considered here is the measurement of variance due to groups.

Imagine a study with four groups, labeled I, II, III, and IV, with four subjects in each group, 16 subjects total. The raw data are as follows:

    I: 6, 5, 3, 2
   II: 8, 7, 9, 6
  III: 1, 3, 5, 4
   IV: 5, 7, 8, 6

The group means for the four groups are 4.0, 7.5, 3.25, and 6.5, respectively. The variance of the group means is 4.057.

What would happen if we recomputed the variance of the group means but instead sampled three of the four scores form each group? If we computed the variance from all 256 possible sets of three-person groups, the variance would increase to 4.257. Let us now consider what the group variance would be if there were two people in each group. If we computed the variance from all 1,296 possible two-person groups, the average variance is 4.656. For the one-person groups the variance increases to 5.854. So we see that the smaller the group, the larger the variance:

group size:	1	2	3	4
variance:	5.854	4.656	4.257	4.057

We want an estimate of group variance that is independent of group size. As the group size increases, the variance approaches the value of what the group variance would be if there were an infinite number of people per group. We can extrapolate that value for our hypothetical study using a formula given in Kenny and La Voie (1985):

$$4.057 - \frac{2.396}{4} = 3.458$$

where 4.057 is the variance in the group means for the whole sample, 2.396 is the pooled variance within groups, and 4 is the group size. This, then, is the estimate of the variance due to group if group is treated as a random factor. The estimate of group variance is a *forecast* of what the variance would be if there were an infinite number of people in each group.

All the formulas used to estimate variances of random effects involve real variances that are used to approximate a hypothetical variance. Such a forecast generally always involves a subtraction. It is then possible for the estimate of group variance (as well as other estimates of the variance of a random factor) to result in a negative value. Generally, a negative variance is interpreted as a zero or a very small variance. Negative variances should never happen when one is computing the variance of a set of numbers, but they do occur when one uses real variances to forecast a hypothetical variance. This does not necessarily invalidate the method.

A related set of problems can occur when one correlates two random effects. Let us call the above variable X and now consider for the same 16 people a second variable Y:

> I: 4, 3, 5, 6
> II: 7, 9, 8, 7
> III: 2, 4, 6, 3
> IV: 7, 6, 5, 6

The means for the four groups are 4.5, 7.75, 3.75, and 6.0. Let us compute the covariance between X and Y (which is the numerator of the correlation coefficient) for group sizes 1 through 4:

group size:	1	2	3	4
covariance:	3.401	3.453	3.470	3.479

We see that unlike the variance of X, the covariance between X and Y increases, if only slightly, as the sample size increases. (If the data were configured differently, the covariance could be made to decrease with increasing sample size.) Again we seek an estimate of what the covariance would be if the group sizes were infinitely large. Again using Kenny and La Voie (1985), the forecast is as follows:

$$3.479 - \frac{-.1042}{4} = 3.505$$

where 3.479 is the covariance between the group means, $-.1042$ is the pooled covariance within groups or the covariance between individual scores with the means subtracted, and 4 is the group size. This is again a hypothetical covariance or a forecast of what the covariance would be if group sizes were large.

A correlation is defined as the covariance divided by the product of the variables' standard deviations. We have learned that the forecast covariance is 3.505 and that the forecast variance of X is 3.458. It can be shown that the forecasted variance of Y is 2.740. Taking the square roots of the variances, the correlation between the group effects is 3.505/(1.860*1.655), which equals 1.14. Just as with the variances of random variables there can be surprises, so can there be with correlations between random variables.

Real correlations can never be larger than one, but the forecasts derived from random variable components can be. Such bigger-than-life correlations can come about in two ways. First, if the true correlation is large and near one, the estimated correlation can be larger than one. Second, if group variance is very small or even near zero, then the forecast of the correlation is not very reliable. Not only are correlations of 1.14 possible, but values as large as 25.38 can occur. These out-of-range correlations do not reflect a strong relationship; rather, they indicate only little or no random variation. To distinguish between these two explanations, a test of statistical and practical significance is needed to establish whether there is variation in the component. If there is significant random variation in both variables, then the likely explanation for the out-of-range correlation is that the true correlation is near one. If there is no significant variance in one of the variables, then the correlation should not be interpreted.

Given that the computed correlation is 1.14, it is clear that this is not an ordinary Pearson product-moment correlation. One must not apply the standard test of significance on such a correlation.

One can avoid the problems of negative variance and correlations larger than one by assuming a fixed-effects model, but such a model has two problems: the magnitude of the effect depends on sample size, and the results of various levels are confounded. Avoiding bias and confounding seems to be a small price to pay for an occasional out-of-range estimate.

It is reasonable to assume that some variables are fixed. Most experimental and demographic variables can be assumed to be fixed. The values are fixed in the sense that either the experimenter or the subject makes the assignment to groups on the basis of the score. The interplay of fixed and random variables is discussed by Kenny (1985, 1987).

NOTES

1. A third design presented by Kenny and La Voie (1984) is the circle design. In that design person i interacts with person i − 1 and i + 1. Also, person 1 interacts with person n. While the social relations parameters can be estimated using this design, estimates appear to be fairly unstable, and so this design is not recommended.

2. The terms *dyad within-block* and *dyad between-block* can be confusing. The term *dyad within-block* is used because dyads are crossed with blocks as in a within-subjects design, and the term *dyad between-block* is used because dyads are nested within blocks as in a between-subjects design.

REFERENCES

Bakeman, R., & Beck, S, (1974). The size of informal groups in public. *Environment & Behavior, 6,* 378–390.

Cook, W., & Dreyer, A. (1984). The social relations model: A new approach to the analysis of family-dyadic interaction. *Journal of Marriage and the Family, 46,* 679–687.

Cook, W., Kenny, D. A., & Goldstein, M. J. (1989). *Parental affective style risk and the family system: A social relations model analysis.* Unpublished manuscript, University of California, Los Angeles.

DePaulo, B., Kenny, D. A., Hoover, C., Webb, W., & Oliver, P. V. (1987). Accuracy of person perception: Do people know what kind of impressions they convey? *Journal of Personality and Social Psychology, 52,* 303–315.

Dindia, K., Fitzpatrick, M., & Kenny, D. A. (1989). *Self disclosure in couples and strangers: A social relations analysis.* Unpublished manuscript, University of Wisconsin – Milwaukee.

DiPilato, M., West, S. G, & Chartier, G. M. (1988). Person perception of type As and Bs: A round robin analysis. *Journal of Social and Personal Relationships, 5,* 263–266.

Duncan, S., Jr., & Fiske, D. W. (1985). *Interaction structure and strategy.* Cambridge: Cambridge University Press.

James, J. (1953). The distribution of free-forming small group size. *American Sociological Review, 18,* 569–570.

Kenny, D. A. (1979). *Correlation and causality.* New York: Wiley-Interscience.

Kenny, D. A. (1985). The generalized group effect model. In J. Nesselroade & A. von Eye (Eds.), *Individual development and social change: Explanatory analyses* (pp. 343–357). Orlando, FL: Academic Press.

Kenny, D. A. (1987). *Fixed effects in the social relations model.* Unpublished manuscript, University of Connecticut.

Kenny, D. A. (1988). The analysis of data from two person relationships. In S. Duck (Ed.), *Handbook of personal relationships* (pp. 57–77). London: John Wiley.

Kenny, D. A. (1990). What makes a relationship special? In T. Draper & A. C. Marcos (Eds.), *Family variables: Conceptualization, measurement, and use.* Newbury Park, CA: Sage.

Kenny, D. A., & Albright L. A. (1987). Accuracy in interpersonal perception: A social relations analysis. *Psychological Bulletin, 102,* 390–402.

Kenny, D. A., & Kashy, D. A. (1989). *Interpersonal perception between friends and acquaintances: A matter of quality or quantity?* Unpublished manuscript, the University of Connecticut.

Kenny, D. A., & La Voie, L. (1984). The social relations model. In L. Berkowitz (Ed.), *Advances in experimental social psychology* (Vol. 18, pp. 142–182). Orlando, FL: Academic Press.

Kenny, D. A., & La Voie, L. (1985). Separating group and individual level effects. *Journal of Personality and Social Psychology, 48,* 339–348.

Kraemer, H. C., & Jacklin, C. N. (1979). Statistical analysis of dyadic social behavior. *Psychological Bulletin, 86,* 217–224.

Landauer, T. K., Carlsmith, J. M., & Lepper, M. (1970). Experimental analysis of the factors determining obedience of four-year-old children to adult females. *Child Development, 41,* 601–611.

La Voie, L. (1981). *The analysis of social interaction: Individual and interactive effects in same-and mixed-aged dyads.* Unpublished doctoral dissertation, University of Connecticut.

Malloy, T. E., & Kenny, D. A. (1986). The social relations model: An integrative method for personality research. *Journal of Personality, 54,* 199–225.

Miller, L. C., & Kenny, D. A. (1986). Reciprocity of self-disclosure at the individual and dyadic levels: A social relations analysis. *Journal of Personality and Social Psychology, 50,* 713–719.

Oliver, P. V. (1988). *Effects of need for social approval on first interaction among members of the opposite sex.* Unpublished doctoral dissertation, University of Connecticut.

Sabatelli, R. M., Buck, R., & Kenny, D. A. (1986). A social relations analysis of nonverbal communication accuracy in married couples. *Journal of Personality, 53,* 513–527.

Stevenson, M. B., Leavitt, L. A., Thompson, R. H., & Roach, M. A. (1988). A social relations model analysis of parent and child play. *Developmental Psychology, 24,* 101–108.

Whitley, B. E., Schofield, J. W., & Snyderman, H. N. (1984). Peer preferences in a desegregated school: A round robin analysis. *Journal of Personality and Social Psychology, 46,* 799–810.

8

Covariance Structure Modeling in Personality and Social Psychological Research

AN INTRODUCTION

MICHAEL D. COOVERT
LOUIS A. PENNER
ROBERT MacCALLUM

Michael D. Coovert is an Assistant Professor of Psychology at the University of South Florida. He received an undergraduate degree in computer science and psychology from Chaminade University of Honolulu, an M.S. in psychology from Illinois State University, and a Ph.D. in psychology (computer science minor) from the Ohio State University. His research interests include quantitative methods, attribution theory, cognition, human-computer interaction, and artificial intelligence.

Louis A. Penner is currently Professor and Chair of the Department of Psychology at the University of South Florida. He received his master's from Miami University (Ohio) in 1966 and his Ph.D. in social psychology from Michigan State University in 1969. His research interests include prosocial behavior, individual differences in social behavior, and the consistency of social behavior across time/situations. He is the author of two social psychology textbooks and a monograph on treatment programs for the elderly.

Robert MacCallum received his Ph.D. in quantitative psychology from the University of Illinois in 1974. He is in his fifteenth year as a member of the faculty in psychology at The Ohio State University, and holds the rank of Professor. His research interests are in the theory, development, and evaluation of quantitative methods, particularly covariance structure modeling, factor analysis, and multidimensional scaling. He has published more than 20 research papers on these topics and is currently coauthoring a book (with Ledyard Tucker) on factor analysis.

The goal of this chapter is to provide a conceptual introduction to covariance structure modeling (CSM), an analytic technique of considerable value

AUTHORS' NOTE: We are grateful to Michael Brannick, Kathleen McNelis, Glenn Reeder, Paul Spector, J. S. Tanaka and two anonymous reviewers for their comments on earlier drafts of this chapter, Mary LaLomia for her assistance with the figures, and Madeline Altabe and David Ho for their help with the literature survey. We also thank Kenneth Bollen for providing us with a draft of his forthcoming text and Steven Breckler for the unpublished data used in the analyses in this chapter.

for theory and research in personality and social psychology. Initially, we define and describe CSM, and present arguments for the contributions it can make to personality/social research. There follow sections on the mathematical framework for CSM, and some of the concepts and issues that are important to its understanding and use. The introductory material is not overly technical, and readers with some familiarity with psychometric theory, multiple regression, path analysis, and factor analysis will have little trouble with it. We present the mathematical and statistical material at a conceptual level throughout the chapter, but a deeper understanding of later sections would be greatly aided by some experience with the technique. We especially encourage the reader to run the programs listed in the Appendix so their output can be referred to during the course of the chapter. Readers whose appetites are whetted can find more extensive and detailed introductions to CSM in books by Bollen (in press), Everitt (1984), Hayduk (1987), and Loehlin (1987), as well as the manuals that accompany the CSM software (e.g., LISREL 7; see Jöreskog & Sörbom, 1988). Also in this volume, Tanaka, Panter, Winborne, and Huba provide an excellent discussion of some of the conceptual questions personality/social psychologists might have about this technique and its applicability to their research areas and methods.

BASIC CONCEPTS

Defining CSM

The analytic technique we call covariance structure modeling is also known by a number of other names. Perhaps the most common name is structural equation modeling (Bielby & Hauser, 1977; Duncan, 1975; Goldberger & Duncan, 1973; Tanaka et al., this volume). Essentially the same technique has been called causal modeling (Bentler, 1980; Reichardt & Gollob, 1986), latent variable models (Everitt, 1984), and LISREL, an acronym that stands for *li*near *s*tructural *rel*ations (Hayduk, 1987; Jöreskog & Sörbom, 1988).

CSM, like many other statistical techniques, permits the researcher to test the viability of a conceptualization of how a set of variables covary or how the variables are related in various ways. However, it differs from other techniques in important ways. The major difference concerns the type of information yielded by the technique. The goal of CSM extends beyond simply determining the degree of covariation between a small number of directly measured variables, as is the case in more common correlational techniques. Its primary objective is to *determine the plausibility of a model* proposed about the nature of relationships within a set of variables. This set of variables typically contains both observed (or measured) variables and unobserved (or latent) variables. Conceptually, latent variables are equivalent to hypothetical constructs. Whereas techniques such as analysis of variance or multiple regression consider only measured variables, CSM considers both latent variables and measured variables.

An important aspect of CSM is that a researcher can evaluate models in which one (or more) latent variable(s) mediates the relation between other latent variables. A *mediator* variable is one that accounts for, or explains the relation between other variables (Baron & Kenny, 1986). Figure 8.1 presents a schematic representation of a model that contains a mediated relationship. The figure is based on a generalized version of Fishbein and Ajzen's (1975) model of how attitudes are related to behavior. In this model the variable *intention* mediates the relationship between the variables *affect* and *cognition* and the variable *behavior*.

As Kenny (1986) points out, much of what interests personality/social psychologists are the mediational mechanisms responsible for the phenomena under investigation. But as Fiske, Kenny, and Taylor (1980) noted, the analytic technique usually employed by personality/social psychologists, analysis of variance, cannot establish a link between a mediator and a dependent measure.

The ability of CSM to include latent variables in an analysis illustrates yet another advantage of CSM over more commonly used analytic techniques. Personality/social researchers have long struggled with issues of construct validity for operations used to represent the constructs of interest. In a typical study of social phenomena, variables are operationalized in only one way, and so the construct is inextricably confounded with the method chosen to measure it. Researchers employing CSM typically obtain multiple indicators for each latent variable in a model. For a model to be viable in CSM, separate operationalizations of a given latent variable must converge with one another to form a meaningful entity. Thus, while CSM creates additional burdens on the researcher, in terms of identifying/developing multiple measures of the constructs, the findings are more likely to be based on valid measures of the constructs than findings generated by single measures of the constructs.

In preparation for this chapter, a questionnaire concerned with the use of CSM was sent to a random sample of contemporary personality/social researchers. The survey results indicated that despite the considerable

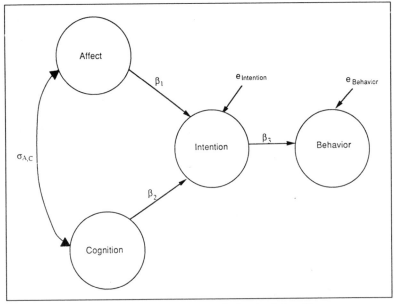

Figure 8.1   Structural model containing a mediational relationship.

potential value of CSM for personality/social research, it remains largely unknown and is viewed with suspicion by many people with limited familiarity with it.

We suspect that the relative newness of this technique, the mathematics underlying it, and the fact that it was developed primarily in nonexperimental areas all contribute to this suspicion and general lack of knowledge. In addition, however, there may be two or more basic philosophical reasons for the relative dearth of personality/social research employing CSM.

First, considerable skepticism is evoked by any technique that claims that causality can be assessed by correlational data. This concern about CSM is, however, based on a misunderstanding of what is meant by *causality* in this context. The implication seems to be that CSM can magically tell us which of two simultaneously measured variables is the cause and which is the effect. Neither CSM nor any other technique can prove causality. As Bielby and Hauser (1977) and Kenny (1979, 1986) noted, causal inference is the result of human thought or experimental control, not statistical techniques. Although statistics cannot prove causality, they can provide results that may lead to an inference of causality. The most that CSM can do is to tell the researcher that a causal model is extremely unlikely or, alternatively, is plausible, but it cannot prove causality. Proof of causation is not the intent of CSM or causal modeling in general (Asher, 1983).

The second reason for lack of use of CSM appears to be more the result of semantic confusion than any substantive problem with CSM as an analytic technique. Sometimes CSM is characterized as a *confirmatory technique,* but "confirmation" of a model means only that it is a viable one. A model cannot be *confirmed* by CSM; it can at best be *not disconfirmed.*

Uses of CSM

There are several ways CSM may be employed by personality/social researchers. Most generally, CSM may be used to examine theories about the structural relationships among latent variables. A typical question of interest is whether the relationship between two latent variables is direct versus mediated through some other variable(s). For example, Moreland and Zajonc (1979) examined different models of the direct and indirect effects of the frequency of stimulus exposure on affective reactions to that stimulus. A special situation arises in the use of CSM for confirmatory factor analysis (CFA). A full discussion of how CFA differs from exploratory factor analysis is beyond the scope of this chapter (see Long, 1983a), but the basic difference is that in exploratory factor analysis one tries to determine the factor structure underlying a set of variables, while in CFA a specific model of the factor structure is proposed and statistically tested. For example, Lennox and Hoyle (1989) used CFA to investigate whether Snyder's self-monitoring scale (Snyder & Gangestad, 1986) measured one factor or three correlated factors. Another use of CSM is in conjunction with the multitrait-multimethod technique to evaluate the construct validity of a set of measures (Widaman, 1985). Rather than conducting a subjective visual inspection of correlations, CSM can be used to draw more objective conclusions about convergent and discriminant validity.

CONCEPTS AND ISSUES IN COVARIANCE STRUCTURE MODELING

Models

As noted previously, in CSM a model is proposed about a specific pattern of relationships among a set of measured and latent variables in some population. There are two different components to the proposed model. The first component is the *measurement model*; it concerns how the measured or indicator variables are related to the unmeasured or latent variables. Typically, a measured variable serves as an indicator of only one latent variable. For example, in Figure 8.1, a person's response to the semantic differential could serve as an indicator for the latent variable *cognition*, but it would not serve as an indicator of the latent variable *intention*. The second component is the *structural model*; it concerns how the latent variables are related to one another. Whereas indicator variables are always directly related to latent variables, latent variables may be related directly or indirectly (i.e., through a mediator variable); and they may be correlated with one another, or not related at all. For example, in Figure 8.1, *affect* and *cognition* are directly related to *intention*, but only indirectly related to *behavior*. Also, *affect* and *cognition* are correlated.

Both component models also specify the direction of the relations between the relevant variables. If a relationship is directional, this means that one variable influences another. This relationship is often viewed as a causal influence, but not necessarily one of rigorous cause-effect. One of the basic assumptions of CSM is that the latent variables influence the measured variables. Therefore, all relationships specified in the measurement model are directional from the latent to the measured variables. In the structural model, nondirectional relationships are also possible. In a nondirectional relationship, such as a correlation, two variables are related, but no directional influence is specified as is the case between *affect* and *cognition* in the figure. Latent variables that are influenced by the other variables in the model are called *endogenous* or *dependent*. In Figure 8.1, *intention* and *behavior* are endogenous variables. The other latent variables in Figure 8.1, *affect* and *cognition*, are *exogenous* or *independent* latent variables.

Errors

Another important consideration of CSM is the notion of errors. Generally, two types of errors play a role in a model. The first type is *errors in variables*. As previously stated, measured variables serve as indicators of latent variables, but measured variables are imperfect indicators and will contain some error. Part of this error will be error of measurement, or the part of the measured variable that is unreliably measured. There may also be a component of the measured variable that is influenced by a specific factor(s), not specified in the model. As an example, imagine two separate indicators of the latent variable *behavior* in Figure 8.1. One is a score on a (perfectly reliable) self-report measure of behavior in response to some attitude object (e.g., a snake); the other is a (perfectly reliable) observation of actual behavior (e.g., how close the person would come to a snake). It is possible that an individual's score on the self-report measure could be influenced by reading ability, but this would be unlikely for the behavioral observation. Reading ability can be considered a specific influence on the obtained score on the questionnaire, and one that is reliably measured. Thus error in variables reflects an inability to predict due to both reliably measured specific factors and error of measurement. Some authors refer to these influences as *disturbance terms* (Bollen, in press; James, Mulaik, & Brett, 1982).

A second type of error is *errors in equations*. CSM is a linear technique and, as such, it specifies that the relations between the variables are linear. These linear relations are rarely perfect and any latent variable or measured variable in the model that is expressed as a linear function of other variables will not be perfectly predicted, resulting in a residual term. This is an error in estimation/prediction, or an error in the equation. Errors in variables and errors in equations are conceptually very different, and each type is represented separately in CSM.

Path Diagrams

One very useful tool for specifying the relationships among variables in a model is a path diagram. As noted earlier, Figure 8.1 is a path diagram of a structural model, based on Fishbein and Ajzen's (1975) conceptualization of how attitudes are related to behavior. In this model, *affect* and *cognition* are separate and correlated latent variables, with the relationship between them being nondirectional. Each has a direct, directional influence on the latent variable *intention* and, through it, they indirectly influence the latent variable *behavior*. (In path diagrams, nondirectional relations are represented by two-headed arrows [e.g., $\longleftrightarrow$]; directional relations are represented as single-headed arrows [e.g., $\longrightarrow$].) Also shown in Figure 8.1 are the notations for parameters (i.e., path coefficients between the latent variables, and correlations/covariances between the latent variables). For example, β_1, represents the regression weight between *affect* and *intention*, and $\sigma_{A,C}$ represents the correlation/covariance between *affect* and *cognition*. Errors in equations (single-headed arrows leading to the circles that represent the dependent latent variables) are also presented in Figure 8.1.

In Figure 8.2, the measurement model has been added to the structural model. (Also, the various parameters of the model are now being repre-

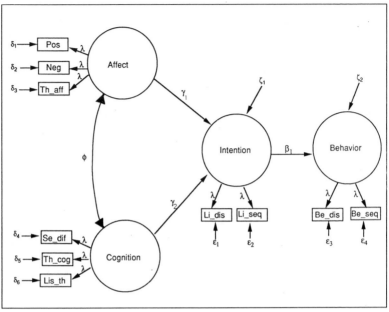

Figure 8.2   Measurement model added to the structural model.

sented with the notation system of LISREL. The LISREL program for conducting CSM will be employed in the next section of this chapter.) Each
latent variable is now represented by at least two measured or indicator variables. (In path diagrams, latent variables are represented by circles and measured variables are represented by squares or rectangles.) The specific
indicators for each of the latent variables are described in detail by Breckler
(1984) and are summarized in Table 8.1.[1]

The indicator variables in Figure 8.2 are labeled with their abbreviations
from Table 8.1, and the parameters that indicate the influence of the latent
variables on the measured variables are labeled λ. These parameters represent the influence of the latent variables on the measured variables. They are
the same as factor loadings in factor analysis: weights that represent the
influence of the common factor on variables. Finally, δ_1--δ_6 and ϵ_1--ϵ_4 are
errors in the independent and dependent indicator variables, respectively.

TABLE 8.1 Latent and Indicator Variables Used in the Model of the Relationship Between Attitude and Behavior

Latent Variables	Indicator Variables
Affect	(1) Pos: rating of positive emotions in response to snakes
	(2) Neg: rating of negative emotions in response to snakes
	(3) Th_aff: response to Thurstone items about affective reaction to snakes
Cognition	(1) Se_dif: semantic differential rating of snakes
	(2) Th_cog: response to Thurstone items about characteristics of snakes
	(3) Lis_th: number of favorable and unfavorable thoughts about snakes
Intention	(1) Li_dis: rating of likelihood one would approach snake
	(2) Li_seq: rating of likelihood one would touch snake
Behavior	(1) Be_dis: distance from pictures of a snake
	(2) Be_seq: degree of physical contact with a live snake

MATHEMATICAL REPRESENTATION OF THE MODEL

Clearly, a wide variety of models could be identified that fit into the framework described in the previous sections. In general, a covariance structure model can be defined as a hypothesis about a specific pattern of relationships among a set of measured and latent variables. Given such a model, there are two central objectives of CSM. The first is to estimate the parameters of the model (e.g., coefficients representing influences of variables on other variables). The second is to evaluate the fit of the model to the data; that is, to assess the degree to which the data are consistent with the model. In order to achieve these objectives, it is necessary to construct a mathematical framework capable of representing the general class of models just described. While several such frameworks have been proposed (e.g., Bentler & Weeks, 1980; Jöreskog, 1974, 1977; McArdle & McDonald, 1984), this chapter uses the framework developed by Jöreskog (1974, 1977) and implemented by the LISREL computer program (Jöreskog & Sörbom, 1988). Essentially, LISREL determines the viability of a proposed model by translating a path diagram of the relations between measured and latent variables into equations that describe the same model. The adequacy of these equations is then mathematically evaluated by determining how well the matrix generated by the equations matches a matrix that is empirically generated. Thus LISREL provides information on whether the equations, and thus the proposed model, are viable. However, as noted earlier, it does *not* prove or disprove the model.

At the core of LISREL is a set of three general matrix equations. The first two equations concern the "measurement model" component of the proposed model. The third equation concerns the "structural model" component of the proposed model. These equations, like simple linear regressions, attempt to predict the value of some entity based on the linear combination of variables weighted by parameters. It is important to realize, however, that certain components of the equations (the latent variables) are not directly measured.

We begin our discussion of LISREL by considering the the two equations that represent the measurement component of a proposed model. Recall that this component of the model concerns how the measured or indicator variables are related to the latent variables. Consider equation 1, which describes the manner in which the latent independent variables influence the indicators of these variables:

$$x = \Lambda_x \xi + \delta \qquad [1]$$

This equation proposes that the indicator variables (x) are equal to the influence of the latent variables (ξ) on their indicator variables, plus error in the indicator variables (δ). Therefore **x** is a column vector (a matrix composed of a single column of numbers representing scores for a random individual on a set of variables) containing the entries $x_1, x_2, \ldots, x_q$, which are the q indicators for the independent variables. Λ_x is a $q \times n$ matrix (a matrix with q rows and n columns) containing the coefficients that represent the effects of the independent latent variables on their indicators. ξ is a column vector containing n independent latent variables: $\xi_1, \xi_2, \ldots, \xi_n$, those latent variables that, according to the investigator's hypothesis, are not affected by any other variables in the model. Finally, δ is a $q \times 1$ vector of errors in the indicators.

Equation 2 describes the portion of the measurement model concerned with the influence of the dependent latent variables on their indicator variables:

$$y = \Lambda_y \eta + \epsilon \qquad [2]$$

y is a column vector containing $y_1, y_2, \ldots, y_p$, which are the p indicators (the dependent measured variables) of the dependent latent variables. Λ_y is a $p \times m$ matrix of coefficients representing the effects of the dependent latent variables on their indicators. η is a column vector containing m dependent latent variables: $\eta_1, \eta_2, \ldots, \eta_m$. The dependent latent variables are those that, according to the investigator's hypothesis, are affected by at least one other latent variable in the model. ϵ is a $p \times 1$ vector of errors in these indicators. Thus the measurement model component of the proposed model defines each measured variable as a linear combination of the latent variables plus an error term. Equations 1 and 2 can each be thought of as equivalent to the common factor model, where each measured variable is represented as a linear combination of common factors (latent variables), plus an error term.

The final equation in CSM, concerned with the "structural model" component of the proposed model, describes the relations among the latent variables:

$$\eta = B\eta + \Gamma\xi + \zeta \qquad [3]$$

This equation says that the latent dependent variables are equal to the linear combination of the influence of the other dependent latent variables, the independent latent variables, and some residual. More specifically, in this equation, B is a matrix of coefficients representing the effect of each dependent latent variable (η) on each of the other dependent latent variables. (In the case of Figure 8.2, for example, this would be the effect of the mediational latent variable *intention* on the latent variable *behavior*.) The matrix Γ is an $m \times n$ matrix of coefficients representing the effect of each independent latent variable (ξ) on each dependent latent variable (η). For Figure 8.2, the influence of *affect* and *cognition* on *intention* would be contained in Γ. Finally, ζ is a vector containing residuals, or "errors in equations," for each of the dependent latent variables.

Σ is the name of the population covariance matrix; it contains the actual variances and covariances between the measured variables contained in the model. As noted earlier, in CSM, an estimate of this matrix is produced and then the degree to which it matches the sample covariance matrix is evaluated. According to CSM, the population variances and covariances of the measured variables are dependent upon the matrices just presented and four matrices concerned with the covariances between the latent variables and the measured variables. These matrices and the symbols used to represent each of them in LISREL are as follows: (a) $\Phi = E(\xi\xi')$, a covariance matrix for the independent latent variables; (b) $\theta_\delta = E\ (\delta\delta')$, a covariance matrix for the errors of measurement in the independent measured variables; (c) $\theta_\epsilon = E\ (\epsilon\epsilon')$, a covariance matrix for the errors of measurement in the dependent measured variables; and (d) $\Psi = E\ (\zeta\zeta')$ a covariance matrix for the errors in equations for the dependent latent variables.

Jöreskog and Sörbom (1988) have shown that, given some related mathematical assumptions, the population covariance matrix, Σ, for the measured variables is a function of the eight matrices — Λ_x, Λ_y, B, Γ, θ_δ, θ_ϵ, Φ, and Ψ — we have just presented.

Since the mathematical function that actually produces the Σ matrix is quite complex, it will not be presented here; it can be found in many sources, including Long (1983b) and Jöreskog and Sörbom (1988). The critical point is that this equation states that the variances and covariances of the measured variables in the population (i.e., the entries in the Σ matrix) are direct mathematical functions of the entries in the eight parameter matrices. Because of the central role of these eight matrices in CSM, the nature of these matrices in terms of the meanings of their rows, columns, and entries is summarized in Figure 8.3. If the model specified by the equations held perfectly in the population, there would be numerical values of the parameters that, when substituted into this function, would exactly reproduce the population variances and covariances of the measured variables (Σ). Put somewhat differently, the relationships proposed by the model would exactly match the actual relationships among the measured variables in the population. But since we do not expect the model to hold perfectly in the population or the sample, the problem becomes how to obtain values of the parameters that, when substituted into the model, most closely reproduce the observed variances and covariances.

Before we discuss the ways in which this is done, we need to note that one does not need to estimate *all* the parameters in each of the eight matrices. Rather, for any given model, only a relatively small number of the parameters contained in the matrices may need to be estimated; that is, the particular hypothesized model will involve only a subset of the possible relations that could be defined. The matrices in the equations contain three kinds of parameters: *free, fixed, and constrained*. A *free parameter* is one for which the value is unknown and needs to be estimated, in the same way a factor loading or regression weight is estimated. An example of this would be the coefficient representing the "strength" of the path between the latent variable *cognition* and the latent variable *intention* (see Figure 8.2). A *fixed parameter* is one for which the value is set by the researcher to some specified numerical value (based on the proposed model); a typical example would be

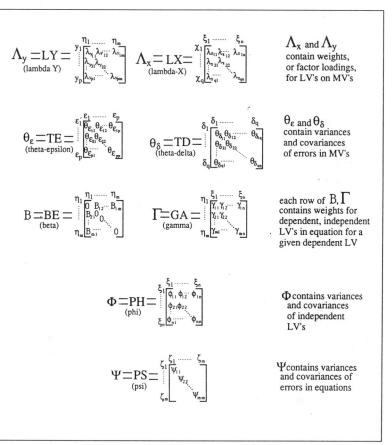

Figure 8.3   Eight parameter matrices employed by LISREL.

a coefficient fixed at zero because a particular influence is hypothesized to be *not* present. For example, there is no path specified between the independent latent variable *affect* and the dependent latent variable *behavior*. Finally, *constrained parameters* are those that are to be estimated but with the constraint that they are equal; for example, one might constrain the influences of *affect* and *cognition* on *intention* to be equal. Thus, based on the researcher's hypothesized model, each parameter in the eight matrices of Figure 8.3 can be specified as being fixed, free, or constrained.

In order to make all of this a bit clearer, we will show how the matrices presented in Figure 8.3 can be used to represent the model represented in Figure 8.2. For the purposes of this example, assume the measured variables serving as indicators are those described earlier (see Table 8.1). Equations 1, 2, and 3 for Figure 8.2 are presented in Figure 8.4. The eight LISREL parameter matrices for the proposed model are shown in Figure 8.5. Matrices Λ_x and Λ_y represent the effects of the latent variables on their respective indicators. (The reason for one nonzero loading being fixed at 1.0 in each column of these matrices will be explained below.) Coefficients in matrices B and Γ represent directional influences of latent variable on other latent variables. Entries in Φ represent variances and covariances of the independent and dependent latent variables. Diagonal entries in θ_δ and θ_ϵ represent the error variances in the independent and dependent measured variables, respectively. Finally, diagonal entries in Ψ represent the variances of the errors in equations for the two dependent latent variables. Matrices θ_δ, θ_ϵ, and Ψ are diagonal in this example because the model hypothesized no nonzero covariances within the various kinds of errors. Note also that this example as presented contains no constrained parameters.

It is important to recognize that the framework is a very general one, and that a wide range of models can be represented by specifying fixed, free, and constrained parameters in these eight matrices.

At this time, we encourage the reader to run the programs listed in the Appendix.[2] Values from the output will be used in examples throughout the remainder of the chapter.

CRITICAL ISSUES IN CSM

In carrying out covariance structure modeling, there are several critical issues of which the researcher must be aware. These include identification, parameter estimation, and assessment of fit. Each issue is considered below.

Identification

Generally, whenever there is a system of equations that contain unknowns, one must determine if there exists a unique solution for the unknowns. If a model is *identified*, there is a unique solution for all the parameters that are estimated. If a model is not identified, there are alternative solutions whose parameter estimates vary, but fit the model equally well. For example, consider a model expressed by the mathematical equa-

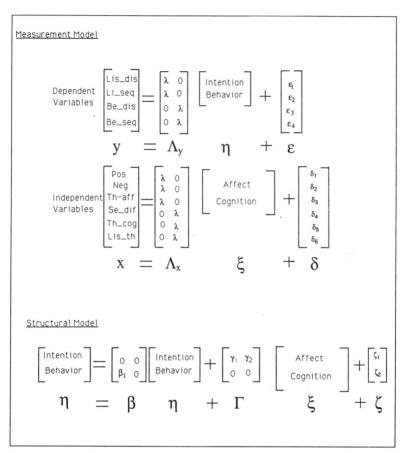

Figure 8.4   Specification of equations 1, 2, and 3 for the example model.

tion $3a + b = 5$. This model is *underidentified* because there are an infinite number of solutions for the unknowns in the equation. In this example, a characteristic of underidentification is that the number of equations is less than the number of unknowns. In the case where there exist as many equations as unknowns, a model may be *just identified*. Consider the following model: $3a + b = 5$; $a + b = 3$. In this instance, there is a single unique solution for unknowns ($a = 1$; $b = 3$); just identified models fit exactly. Finally, a model may be *overidentified* when there are more equations than unknowns.

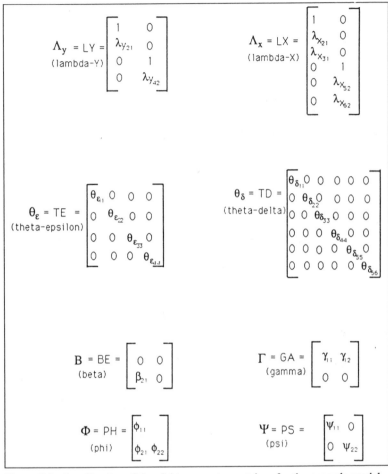

Figure 8.5 Specification of the eight parameter matrices for the example model.

Consider the following model: $3a + b = 5$; $a + b = 3$; $a + 2b = 10$. There is no longer one unique solution for this system of equations. One might, however, propose one of these solutions and see how well it fits the overidentified model. Note that in overidentified models one cannot usually obtain a perfectly fitting solution for the unknowns. Instead, one can define a "best" solution and evaluate how well that solution fits.

Let us consider the relevance of this issue in CSM. A covariance structure model can be considered to be a system of equations, each equation containing some unknowns (parameters). Given the expression of the model defining Σ as a function of the eight parameter matrices, there will be one equation for each distinct entry in Σ, and as many unknowns as there are distinct parameters to be estimated. The number of distinct entries in Σ will be $[(p + q)(p + q + 1)] / 2$. If t represents the number of parameters to be estimated, then a necessary condition for identification is that:

$$t \leq [(p + q)(p + q + 1)] / 2 \qquad [4]$$

If this condition does not hold, the model is underidentified, meaning at least one parameter value will not have a unique solution. If the condition is satisfied, the model may be identified or overidentified. An additional necessary condition for identification involves the scales of measurement for the latent variables. Since a latent variable is a hypothetical construct that is not measured, its scale is arbitrary. But since some of the parameters of the model involve latent variables, it is necessary for the scale of each latent variable to be established. This can be easily accomplished by the researcher when the model is specified. A simple and common way to achieve this is to define one of the nonzero entries in each column of Λ_x and Λ_y as fixed at 1.0. This serves to equate the unit of measurement of the given latent variable (column) with the chosen measured variable (row). This procedure was followed in Figure 8.5 and 8.6.

The conditions just defined are necessary but not sufficient conditions for identification. Proving identification can be done only on a case-by-case basis. More detailed discussions of this important issue can be found in Bollen (in press, chap. 4), Everitt (1984, pp. 36–37), Hayduk (1987, pp. 139–150), and Kenny (1979, pp. 34–41). Also, while the LISREL program does provide the user with information about identification in a given model, the LISREL checks for identification are not fail-safe. Ideally, the researcher should verify that necessary and sufficient conditions for identification are satisfied.

Parameter Estimation

As stated earlier, a major task in CSM is to estimate the parameters of the model. Recall that the model defines the population covariance matrix as a function of the entries in the eight parameter matrices defined above. In practice, of course, we will not observe Σ, but rather a sample covariance matrix, S, containing sample variances and covariances of the measured variables. We wish to find estimates of the parameters so that the model fits the sample data as well as possible. More specifically, we wish to find parameter estimates that, when substituted into the equation of the model, yield a "model estimate," $\hat{\Sigma}$, of the population covariance matrix that will be as close to the sample covariance matrix, S, as possible. This estimation problem can be approached in different ways, to be described shortly. Thus there is a two-step process in evaluating a model. First, the best estimates of the parameters are obtained, and second, how well the resulting solution fits the actual data is evaluated. We will first present three methods for obtaining parameter estimates and then discuss ways to assess how well a resulting solution fits the sample covariance matrix.

Maximum likelihood. This estimation procedure assumes that our sample of observations is obtained from some population and the distribution of variables in that population is multivariate normal. A likelihood function can be defined that represents the multivariate normal distribution as a function of data and parameters (free parameters of the specified model). Given data (sample covariances), parameters can be estimated to maximize the value of the likelihood function. Another way of stating this is that parameter estimates may be obtained that maximize the likelihood the differences between the estimates and observed values are attributed to sampling fluctuation. A maximum likelihood solution, then, is a solution that maximizes the probability that the discrepancy between one's estimate of some population characteristic and "observed sample information could have arisen as a mere sampling fluctuation" (Hayduk, 1987, p. 130). The example model with maximum likehood estimates for the parameters is presented in Figure 8.6. (The reader should note the number in the figure for errors are variances of those error estimates.)

Generalized least squares. If one has a sample covariance matrix S and estimates for all parameters of the specified model, $\hat{\Sigma}$ can be computed. Optimally, we want the model estimates in $\hat{\Sigma}$ to be identical to the sample covariances for each pair of variables. A residual covariance can be determined for each pair of variables by subtracting the estimated covariance between each pair of variables form the observed covariance for those same variables ($s_{jk} - \hat{\sigma}_{jk}$). The better the fit, the smaller those differences will be. An overall fit can be determined by squaring those differences and summing over all the pairs of variables. If the model fits perfectly, the sum of those squared residuals will be zero. The worse the fit, the larger the number will be.

Generalized least squares estimates are obtained by finding those param-

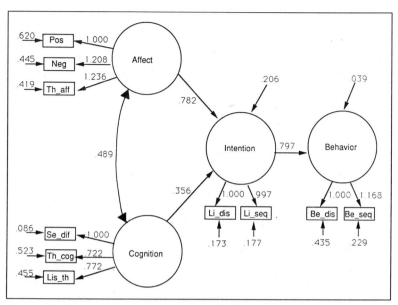

Figure 8.6 Example model with maximum likelihood parameter estimates.

eter estimates that yield a minimum sum of squares residual, where the residuals are weighted to correct for unequal variances and nonzero covariances in the disturbance terms. An advantage of both maximum likelihood and generalized least squares procedures is that their estimates are scale invariant and scale free (Bollen, in press, chap. 4).

Asymptotically distribution free. The maximum likelihood and generalized least squares estimation methods are based on classical normal theory, meaning that the measured variables are assumed to have a normal distribution in the population, and that the resulting estimates have desirable statistical properties when that assumption is satisfied. Recent work by Browne (1982, 1984), Bentler (1983a), and others has yielded techniques for parameter estimation that produce estimates with desirable properties when the population distribution is from a general family of nonnormal distributions. This approach, called asymptotically distribution free (ADF) estimation, is a variation on generalized least squares and is available in LISREL 7. A primary disadvantage is that it can be very expensive to run in terms of computing costs.

Goodness-of-Fit Measures

For a researcher, the primary goal of CSM is often to determine if the model offers a plausible explanation of the relationships that exist in the observed data. If the model fits the sample data well, inferences can be drawn regarding the viability of the model. If the model does not fit well, problems may exist with the data or with the model itself.

Generally, a researcher will be interested in two different aspects of fit. The first are overall measures to assess how well, in general, the model is fitting the data. The second are detailed measures of fit focusing on specific parameters. It should be pointed out that prior to the assessment of either general or specific indices of fit, the solution should be inspected for other problems, such as underidentification and improper estimates (e.g., negative variances). Once these have been ruled out, the researcher can be more confident in conclusions drawn from fit measures.

Chi-square. If one uses the estimation procedures described above, the asymptotic distribution of the employed fitting function (F), multiplied by $(N - 1)$ is approximately distributed as chi-square with degrees of freedom equal to $\{[(p + q) (p + q + 1)]/2\} - t$; where t is equal to the number of free parameters, and p and q equal the number of independent and dependent measured variables, respectively. In our example, the degrees of freedom would equal: $\{[(6 + 4) (6 + 4 + 1)]/2\} - 24 = 31$. It is therefore possible to perform a statistical test (chi-square) of the hypothesis that the stated model holds exactly in the population. (It is important to realize this is a different null hypothesis from one typically employed by psychologists.) *If the chi-square is significant, this means the estimated covariance matrix is significantly different from the sample matrix.* The model thus is not a viable one and the hypothesis is rejected because, statistically, the proposed model is not a plausible one. The chi-square for the model in the example is $\chi^2_{31} = 48.59, p < .023$, indicating that statistically the model is not a plausible one. A nonsignificant chi-square, on the other hand, would indicate that, statistically, the model is a plausible one for explaining the relationships that exist in the data. A nonsignificant chi-square does not mean the model should be immediately accepted. As noted several times in this chapter, other statistically plausible models may exist (MacCallum, 1986). There is, however, a problem with this index of fit. Since the null hypothesis is virtually always false to some degree, almost any model will be rejected when the sample size is large. Because of this, the descriptive measures of fit discussed in the next section have been proposed.

A second use of the chi-square statistic is to compare different models where one model is *nested* in another model. One model is nested in a second if the free parameters of the first are a subset of those of the second. For example, let us name the model in Figure 8.2, M_k. Now imagine the same model with an additional path between *affect* and *behavior*. We will call this model M_j. In this example, M_k is nested within M_j. The usefulness of nested models for comparison purposes is that the difference in chi-square between the two models is itself distributed as a chi-square with degrees of freedom equal to the difference in degrees of freedom between the two models. Thus $\chi^2_{k,j} = \chi^2_k - \chi^2_j$; with $df_{k,j} = df_k - df_j$. The null hypothesis being tested is that M_j and M_k are equivalent models. If the chi-square is significant, the additional parameter in M_j is significant and this model explains the relationships that exist in the data better than the nested model. Model M_j can be tested by freeing the path between *affect* and *behavior* (by modifying the program as indicated in the Appendix). The chi-square for the modified model is $\chi^2_{30} = 47.56$, $p < 022$. $\chi^2_{k,l}$ (48.59 − 47.56) = 1.03, with degrees of freedom (31 − 30) = 1. This is well below the critical value, so the addition of the path is not significant and the modified models does not explain the relationships found in the data better than the more parsimonious original model.

Descriptive Measures of Fit

Because the chi-square test is very sensitive to sample size and will almost always reject a model on statistical bases (Bentler & Bonett, 1980; Jöreskog, 1981), other methods have been developed to indicate how well, in a practical sense, a model fits the data. That is, while not inferential indicators of fit, they do provide useful estimates of how well the model fits the data. Although there are a number of such overall fit measures (e.g., Bentler & Bonett, 1980; Bollen, in press; but see also Balderjahn, 1988; Hayduk, 1987; Tanaka & Huba, 1985), we will focus on three widely employed measures, ρ, Δ, and root mean square residual (RMR).

Prior to discussing these measures, it is necessary to introduce a special model called the *null model*. A null model is most often defined as the most restricted model possible. The null model simply represents the hypothesis that the measured variables are not correlated in the population. Obviously, it is a nonsubstantive model that almost always fits the data very poorly; its chi-square and degrees of freedom (χ^2_0, df_0) are used only as a point of reference for the evaluation of the substantive model of interest. The program for computing a null model for the example is given in the Appendix. Using the data provided by Breckler (1984), this model produces a chi-square with 45 degrees of freedom: $\chi^2_{45} = 729.45$, $p < .000$.

ρ (*rho*). Bentler and Bonett (1980) provided two measures for reflecting practical fit of a model to the data. The first measure, ρ, is an extension of a fit index originally proposed by Tucker and Lewis (1973). The value of ρ for model k is obtained as follows:

$$\rho = Q_0 - Q_k / Q_0 - 1 \qquad [5]$$

where $Q_0 = \chi^2_0 / df_0$ and $Q_k = \chi^2_k / df_k$. This fit measure can be thought of as comparing the difference in fit between the null model and model k to the difference in fit between the null model and a theoretically correct model. In practice, rho should be equal to or greater than .90, preferably much higher, to indicate a practical fit of the model to the data. For our example, ρ indicates the model fits nicely in terms of practical fit, $\rho = .963$; $[(729.45/45) - (48.59/31)] / [(729.45/45) - 1]$.

Δ (*delta*). Bentler and Bonett (1980) also proposed Δ as a second measure of practical fit. Delta is different from rho in that it is a normed fit index (bound to range between 0 and 1) that does not require a statistical basis for assessing the fit of the model. The value of Δ can be obtained as follows:

$$\Delta = F_0 - F_k / F_0 \qquad [6]$$

where F is the obtained minimum value of the fitting function (e.g., maximum likelihood, generalized least squares) for the given model. Recall that $\chi^2 = (N - 1) * F$, so the values of F in equation 6 are obtained by dividing χ^2 by $(N - 1)$. As with rho, delta should equal or exceed .90 for a model to explain the relationships in the data practically. Delta also indicates a good practical fit of the model: $\Delta = .933$; $[(729.45/104) - (48.59/104)] / (729.45/104)$.

Root mean square residual. The third estimate of overall fit compares the elements ($\hat{\sigma}_{ij}$) of the population matrix ($\hat{\Sigma}$) generated by the model with the elements (s_{ij}) of the sample matrix (**S**). An evaluation of our model can be made by examining how similar s_{ij} is to $\hat{\sigma}_{ij}$. An overall determination for how well the model fits the data may be made through examination of how closely these values correspond. For each pair of variables there will be a residual covariance ($s_{ij} - \hat{\sigma}_{ij}$). This will produce $S - \hat{\Sigma}$, a matrix of these residuals which is used to determine goodness of fit. To obtain RMR, square those differences, sum them, and divide by the number of variances and covariances, and then take the square root. If there is very good fit, the number will be very small (s_{ij} and $\hat{\sigma}_{ij}$ will be very close to each other). The smaller the RMR, the better. If perfect fit existed, RMR would be zero. One thing to keep in mind when using RMR is that there is some dependence on the magnitude of the elements in the covariance matrix. If they are all on widely different scales, RMR can fluctuate because of these scale differences. Interpretation of RMR, therefore, is to a certain extent a function of the magnitude of values in the matrix. For example, in a *correlational* data matrix, RMR = .05 would be fairly good. Each correlation is being fit at an average error of .05. Here one knows the bounds of the scales because the data are correlations. For our example model, RMR = .054, indicating acceptable fit of the model according to this criterion. In the null model, RMR = .507, indicating, as expected, very poor fit.

Detailed Information About Fit

A particular model may fit well overall, but there might be specific parameters, such as a proposed direct influence of one latent variable on another where the model does not fit well. If the model fits poorly overall, detailed information about specific parameters would be especially important to know because such information may suggest ways in which the model may be modified for subsequent examination. There are several different types of information available in the LISREL program about individual parameters.

t-values. For each free parameter of the model, the approximate standard error of that parameter estimate can be obtained. This measure shows how much the estimate varies from sample to sample. Optimally, we would like the standard error to be a small value, indicating stability across samples. A test can be performed of the hypothesis that the parameter is zero in the population. The test is simply the parameter estimate divided by its standard error. LISREL calls these t-values and computes them for each free parameter. If the absolute value of t is greater than or equal to 2, the hypothesis that the free parameter is zero in the population is rejected. Examination of the t-values for the example model indicate they are all greater than $|2|$. Thus all estimated parameters are significant. If $|t| < 2$, this hypothesis cannot be rejected; the parameter could have been fixed at zero and it would not have made much difference in the overall fit of the model. The parameter could subsequently be fixed at zero instead of letting it be free, allowing for a more parsimonious model. For example, in the modified model discussed above the t-value for the path between *affect* and *behavior* equaled − .94. Thus it is not significantly different from zero in the population and could be fixed to zero (as in the original model).

Modification index. For each fixed zero parameter (i.e., a parameter with a value set to zero by the researcher), a modification index (MI) can be obtained; this is the minimum change in the overall χ^2 if the corresponding fixed parameter were freed. Wherever there are large MI values, the corresponding fixed parameter could be freed to improve the model. When using MIs, three rules should be followed. First, only one parameter should be changed at a time; one change can affect all other estimates and MIs. Second, only changes that are substantively meaningful should be made. A parameter should never be freed only on the basis of statistical information. A theoretical justification must exist for each parameter that is estimated. Third, MIs are distributed approximately as a χ^2 with 1 degree of freedom. The critical value for the χ^2 with one degree of freedom is about 6 or 7. Since these are estimates, an MI should be at least 8 or 9 before one considers freeing that parameter. Examination of the modification indices for the example model indicated that the *Th__cog* and *Lis__th* measured variables could be allowed to load on the *affect* latent variable. There was, however, in this example no theoretical justification for estimating either parameter and thus the model should not be changed.

Residuals. Residuals $(\mathbf{S} - \hat{\mathbf{\Sigma}})$ are important in that examination of them will allow the researcher to determine which relationships fit well and which do not. Small residuals indicate good fit while large residuals indicate poor fit. Normalized residuals are provided by LISREL. A normalized residual can be considered a significance test defined as the residual divided by the approximate standard error for that residual. If the normalized residual is larger than two, it indicates the relationship does not fit very well. The model should be reconsidered, as it may not be properly specified.

Standard errors. When parameter estimates are obtained, it is important to examine their standard errors. Large standard errors may signify underidentification in coefficients (Hayduk, 1987, pp. 141) or multicolinearity among the measured variables (Jöreskog and Sörbom, 1988).

Squared multiple correlation (SMC). As was shown above, a model can be represented as a system of equations. For every equation a SMC can be determined. The SMCs represent strengths in relationships. In the measurement model, there is a linear relationship between measured variables and latent variables. An SMC will be obtained for each measured variable and can be interpreted as the proportion of variance in the measured variable accounted for by the latent variable. If the SMCs are large, there is a good deal of variance in the measured variable explained by the latent variable, signaling that the indicators provide a valid measure of the latent variable. These are equivalent to communalities in the common factor model.

In a measurement model, the optimal situation is when the SMCs are relatively large and proportionally equal for each latent variable and across the latent variables. If one latent variable has indicators with SMCs for measured variables lower than the values other latent variables have, this can cause a problem in that the given latent variable may not be represented accurately by its indicators. In the structural model, there will be one SMC for each structural equation. The SMC is equal to the proportion of variance in a dependent latent variable accounted for by other latent variables in the equation.

Two things should be remembered about SMCs. First, they are computed by taking functions of variances, and these are not restricted to be positive. If they are negative, this is a symptom of a serious problem in the model or the data. Second, an SMC is not really a goodness-of-fit index. The LISREL model only estimates SMCs; it does not attempt to maximize them. Thus SMCs could be low and one could still have a model that fits the data well. As a result, a researcher may or may not be interested in them.

Improper Solutions and Nonconvergence

When fitting a covariance structure model to sample data,, several things can occur that are symptomatic of problems with the model and/or data. One such event is nonconvergence of the fitting algorithm. Nonconvergence means that the computer program has not been able to find a solution for the parameter estimates that will minimize the value of the fitting function, within a preset limit on the number of iterations. Another such event is the occurrence of an "improper solution," which is a solution in which at least one parameter estimate has a value outside of its logical bounds—for instance, a variance estimate that is negative. The general view of such events is that they reflect serious problems with the model and/or data. With regard to the model, it may be poorly specified and not correspond closely to the real world. With regard to the data, the sample size may be too small, or there may be a great deal of "noise" in the data, such as a high level of error of measurement or sampling error. Thus when an attempt to fit a model does not converge, or yields an improper solution, the researcher is advised to reevaluate the model and the nature of the data.

Specification Searches

When a model is found to fit the sample data poorly, a commonly employed strategy is to carry out modification of the model so as to attempt to obtain a revised model that fits the data adequately. This process, often called a *specification search*, most often involves adding new parameters to the original model, but may also involve other steps, such as deleting variables. Decisions about adding parameters to a model are usually made by identifying fixed parameters with large modification indices (discussed above).

Specification searches are very beguiling because they can yield a model that fits the data well. One must recognize that such searches are *data driven* and *exploratory*. This situation implies that resulting models cannot be tested statistically with any validity, that their goodness of fit and substantive meaning must be evaluated with caution, and that their validity and replicability are open to question. Final models resulting from specification searches must be cross-validated before any real validity can be claimed (Bentler, 1980; Cliff, 1983; Cudeck & Browne, 1983).

Research by MacCallum (1986) has indicated that when a true model does exist in the population and the initial model fit to a sample is misspecified, there is a relatively low probability of finding the true model via a specification search unless (a) sample size is large, (b) there are very few specification errors in the initial model, and (c) each modification is well justified on substantive and logical grounds. Thus one must not approach the use of CSM with the notion that one can arbitrarily specify an initial model, then modify it as needed so as to obtain a valid model that fits the data well. Rather, it is necessary to specify the initial model very carefully, obtain data from a large sample, and make any specification search very short and highly defensible on substantive grounds.

Power

The statistical concept of power (i.e., the probability of detecting whether a null hypothesis is false) is quite relevant in CSM since one is often testing hypotheses about a given model or about differences between alternative models. When a null hypothesis about a particular model, or about a difference between models, is not rejected, that does not necessarily mean that the hypothesis is true. It is possible, for instance, that the power of the test is too low and that a Type II decision error has been made. Recent work has led to the development of methods for determining power of tests of given null hypotheses versus some specified alternative hypothesis in CSM (e.g., Matsueda & Bielby, 1986; Satorra & Saris, 1985). The evaluation of power by such methods can provide the researcher with information that can lead him or her to have more (or less) confidence in the outcome of a particular test. In addition, these methods provide a capability for evaluating the sensitivity of the hypothesis tests to certain types of model misspecifications. The power of the tests depends to some extent on the particular manner in which the model is misspecified.

Alternatives to LISREL

Although LISREL is arguably the best known approach, other representations and computer programs exist. Bentler and Weeks (1980; see also Bentler 1983b) proposed a representation that is more general than that of LISREL. Every variable in the system (even errors) is considered as either dependent or independent. This allows for the definition of only three parameter matrices (instead of eight) and only one matrix equation (instead of three). The Bentler-Weeks approach is implemented by the EQS program (version 3.0), which has several advantages over the LISREL program. No knowledge of matrix algebra is required to use EQS, and it allows for generation of path diagrams, has the ability to use distribution-free theory techniques for the estimation of parameters, and allows for inequality constraints on parameters and tests of multivariate normality. A drawback of the program is that it does not allow for the analysis of multiple samples. The program is available for mainframe, mini-, and microcomputers and through the BMDP statistical software.

The COSAN program (Fraser & McDonald, 1988) is based on the covariance structure model of McDonald (1978, 1980, 1985) and McArdle and McDonald (1984). A current advantage of the program over LISREL is its ability to allow nonlinear constraints between parameters.

A simpler version of LISREL, termed SIMPLIS, has been introduced as an attempt to remove the Greek notation and matrix algebra (Jöreskog & Sörbom, 1986). It is faster and easier to use than LISREL. However, due to its limited output, it may be of little use to most investigators and could lead to improper application of the technique (Hayduk, 1987).

The Latent Variable Path Model (Lohmoller, 1988) and the program, PLS, is meant to be complementary to LISREL, EQS, and COSAN. PLS is capable of handling large models in fairly quick computational time and appears immune to the generation of negative error variances (or Heywood cases).

A final program called LINCS (linear covariance structure analysis) is available from Schoenberg and Arminger (1988). The program includes the LISREL model as a special case, and a menu-driven student version is under development.

CONCLUSIONS

Although the roots of CSM can easily be traced back at least to the beginning of the twentieth century (e.g., Spearman's work on factor analysis and Wright's work on path analysis), the mathematical formulae that underlie it and the computer programs used to carry it out have been developed only relatively recently. Like any new discovery or innovation, CSM holds both peril and promise. In the hands of someone who is relatively unfamiliar with the technique and its assumptions or unaware of the critical importance of theory when using CSM, it can be very dangerous weapon. Unfortunately, reviews of studies that have used CSM have concluded that this is often the rule rather than the exception (Bielby & Hauser, 1977). Further, there may be limitations to the usefulness of CSM in dealing with certain kinds of data that are of interest to the personality/social researcher. For example, there is still debate over the ability of CSM to represent appropriately the interactions that are often of primary interest in laboratory studies of social processes (see Kenny & Judd, 1984; Tanaka et al., this volume). In sum, CSM is not a panacea for the problems that confront research in personality and social psychology. As suggested numerous times in this chapter, the model one tests and the modifications one makes in that model must be driven by theory. If this is not done, then this confirmatory technique becomes, de facto, an exploratory technique; and in the absence of cross-validation this exploration is often of little value. As Hayduk (1987) stated, "LISREL and [CSM] complement, but do not replace knowledge of one's data set and theoretical subject areas" (p. xiv).

At the same time, it is our strong belief that, when properly used, CSM offers great promise for empirical research and theory building. By formally evaluating the structure of the relations among the measured variables and the latent variables, CSM enables one to address explicitly such issues as biases attributed to measurement and/or specification error within a hypothesized model. Thus theory building can proceed in a more direct fashion than is possible with techniques that permit only indirect inferences about hypothetical constructs that underlie a theory.

As highlighted by the example employed in this chapter, one particular strength of CSM is that it permits a researcher to study how the relations among one set of latent variables might be mediated by other latent variables. Mediational processes play a crucial role in almost all major theories in personality/social psychology, but analysis of variance and similar techniques can test such processes only crudely (Fiske et al., 1980; Kenny, 1986). Given this, it is difficult to overstate the value of a technique that can test a proposed mediational mechanism.

In conclusion, we believe CSM to be one of the most significant methodological tools made available to psychologists in recent years. Indeed, we agree with Bentler (1980), who stated that CSM deserves as much recognition in graduate training and psychological research as commonly employed techniques such as analysis of variance.

APPENDIX:
LISREL PROGRAM CODE FOR EXAMPLE MODELS

```
1.   CSM EXAMPLE MODEL - UNPUBLISHED BRECKLER DATA
2.   DA NG=1 NI=10 NO=105 MA=CM
3.   LABELS
4.   *
5.   Be_dis Be_seq Pos Neg Th_aff Li_dis Li_seq Se_dif
     Th_cog Lis_th
6.   CM SY
7.   *
8.   1.00
9.   .66 1.00
10.  .45 .35 1.00
11.  .47 .55 .42 1.00
12.  .48 .47 .57 .53 1.00
13.  .68 .77 .43 .58 .57 1.00
14.  .63 .78 .44 .67 .57 .82 1.00
15.  .56 .65 .46 .60 .60 .71 .70 1.00
16.  .33 .47 .22 .40 .33 .45 .42 .69 1.00
17.  .50 .56 .48 .51 .62 .65 .61 .69 .44 1.00
18.  SE
19.  6 7 1 2 3 4 5 8 9 10 /
20.  MO NX=6 NY=4 NE=2 NK=2 LX=FU,FI LY=FU,FI BE=FU,FI
     GA=FU,FI C
21.  TD=DI,FR TE=DI,FR PS=DI,FR PH=SY,FR
22.  LK
23.  Affect Cogniton
24.  LE
25.  Intenton Behavior
26.  FR LY 2 1 LY 4 2
27.  FR LX 2 1 LX 3 1 LX 5 2 LX 6 2
28.  FR BE 2 1
29.  FR GA 1 1 GA 1 2
30.  VA 1. LY 1 1 LY 3 2 LX 1 1 LX 4 2
31.  OU TV MI SS RS EF
```

```
CSM EXAMPLE MODIFIED MODEL - CHANGE LINE 29 ABOVE TO
FR GA 1 1 GA 1 2 GA 2 1
```

```
CSM EXAMPLE NULL MODEL - DELETE LINES 19-30 AND INSERT LINE
   BELOW AS LINE
```

```
MO NX=10 NK=10 LX=ID TD=ZE PH=DI,FR
```

NOTES

1. Breckler's interest was in a different structural model. We are utilizing his unpublished data for illustrative purposes.

2. Individuals unable to run the programs listed in the Appendix may receive a copy of the printouts by requesting them from Michael D. Coovert, Department of Psychology, University of South Florida, Tampa, FL 33620-8200.

REFERENCES

Asher, H. B. (1983). *Causal modeling* (2nd ed.). Beverly Hills, CA: Sage.

Balderjahn, I. (1988). A note to Bollen's alternative fit measure. *Psychometrika, 53,* 283–285.

Baron, R. M., & Kenny, D. A. (1986). The moderator-mediator distinction in social psychological research: Conceptual, strategic, and statistical considerations. *Journal of Personality and Social Psychology, 51,* 1173–1182.

Bentler, P. M. (1980). Multivariate analysis with latent variables: Causal modeling. *Annual Review of Psychology, 31,* 419–456.

Bentler, P. M. (1983a). Some contributions of efficient statistics in structural models: Specification and estimation of moment structures. *Psychometrika, 48,* 493–517.

Bentler, P. M. (1983b). Simultaneous equation systems as moment structure models. *Journal of Econometrics, 22,* 13–42.

Bentler, P. M., & Bonett, D. G. (1980). Significance tests and goodness fit in the analysis of covariance structures. *Psychological Bulletin, 88,* 588–606.

Bentler, P. M., & Weeks, D. G. (1980). Linear structural equations with latent variables. *Psychometrika, 45,* 289–307.

Bielby, W. T., & Hauser, R. M. (1977). Structural equation models. *Annual Review of Sociology, 3,* 137–163.

Bollen, K. A. (in press). *Structural equation modeling with latent variables.* New York: John Wiley.

Breckler, S. J. (1984). Empirical validation of affect, behavior, and cognition as distinct components of attitudes. *Journal of Personality and Social Psychology, 47,* 1191–1206.

Browne, M. W. (1982). Covariance structures. In D. M. Hawkins (Ed.), *Topics in applied multivariate analysis* (pp. 72–141). Cambridge: Cambridge University Press.

Browne, M. W. (1984). Asymptotically distribution free methods for analysis of covariance structures. *British Journal of Mathematical and Statistical Psychology, 37,* 62–83.

Cliff, N. (1983). Some cautions concerning the application of causal modeling methods. *Multivariate Behavioral Research, 18,* 115–126.

Cudeck, R., & Browne, M. W. (1983). Cross-validation of covariance structures. *Multivariate Behavioral Research, 18,* 147–187.

Duncan, O. D. (1975). *Introduction to structural equation models.* New York: Academic Press.

Everitt, B. S. (1984). *An introduction to latent variable models.* London: Chapman-Hall.

Fishbein, M., & Ajzen, I. (1975). *Belief, attitude, intention, and behavior: An introduction to theory and research*. Reading, MA: Addison-Wesley.

Fiske, S., Kenny, D., & Taylor, S. E. (1980). Structural models for the mediation of salience effects on attribution. *Journal of Experimental Social Psychology, 18,* 105–127.

Fraser, C., & McDonald, R. P. (1988). COSAN: Covariance structure analysis. *Multivariate Behavioral Research, 23,* 263–265.

Goldberger, A. S., & Duncan, O. D. (1973). *Structural equation models in the social sciences*. New York: Seminar.

Hayduk, L. A. (1987). *Structural equation modeling with LISREL: Essentials and advances*. Baltimore: Johns Hopkins University Press.

James, L. R., Mulaik, S. A., & Brett, J. M. (1982). *Causal analysis: Assumptions, models and data*. Beverly Hills, CA: Sage.

Jöreskog, K. G. (1974). Analyzing psychological data by structural analysis of covariance matrices. In R. C. Atkinson, D. H. Krantz, R. D. Luce, & P. Suppes (Eds.), *Contemporary developments in mathematical psychology* (Vol. 2, pp. 1–56). San Francisco: Freeman.

Jöreskog, K. G. (1977). Structural equation models in the social sciences: Specification, estimation, and testing. In P. R. Krishnaiah (Ed.), *Applications of statistics* (pp. 265–287). Amsterdam: North-Holland.

Jöreskog, K. G. (1981). Analysis of covariance structures. *Scandinavian Journal of Statistics, 8,* 65–92.

Jöreskog, K. G., & Sörbom, D. (1986). *SIMPLIS: A fast and simple version of LISREL, preliminary version*. Uppsala, Sweden: University of Uppsala, Department of Statistics.

Jöreskog, K. G., & Sörbom, D. (1988). *LISREL 7: A guide to the program and applications*. Chicago: SPSS Inc.

Kenny, D. A. (1979). *Correlation and causality*. New York: Wiley-Interscience.

Kenny, D. A. (1986). Quantitative methods for social psychology. In G. Lindzey & E. Aronson (Eds.), *The handbook of social psychology* (3rd ed., pp. 487–508). New York: Random House.

Kenny, D. A., & Judd, C. M. (1984). Estimating the nonlinear and interactive effects of latent variables. *Psychological Bulletin, 96,* 201–210.

Lennox, R. D., & Hoyle, R. H. (1989). *Latent structure of the Self-Monitoring scale*. Unpublished manuscript, University of North Carolina, Chapel Hill.

Loehlin, J. C. (1987). *Latent variable models: An introduction to factor, path, and structural analysis*. Hillsdale, NJ: Erlbaum.

Lohmoller, J. B. (1988). The PLS program system: Latent variables path analysis with partial least squares estimation. *Multivariate Behavioral Research, 23,* 125–127.

Long, J. S. (1983a). *Confirmatory factor analysis*. Beverly Hills, CA: Sage.

Long, J. S. (1983b). *Covariance structure models: An introduction to LISREL*. Beverly Hills, CA: Sage.

MacCallum, R. (1986). Specification searches in covariance structure modeling. *Psychological Bulletin, 100,* 107–120.

Matsueda, R. L., & Bielby, W. T. (1986). Statistical power in covariance structure models. In N. B. Tuma (Ed.), *Sociological methodology* (pp. 120–158). San Francisco: Jossey-Bass.

McArdle, J., & McDonald, R. P. (1984). Some algebraic properties of the reticular action model for moment structures. *British Journal of Mathematical and Statistical Psychology, 37,* 234–254.

McDonald, R. P. (1978). A simple comprehensive model for the analysis of covariance structures: *British Journal of Mathematical and Statistical Psychology, 31,* 59–72.

McDonald, R. P. (1980). A simple comprehensive model for the analysis of covariance structures: Some remarks on applications. *British Journal of Mathematical and Statistical Psychology, 33,* 161–183.

McDonald, R. P. (1985). *Factor analysis and related methods.* Hillsdale, NJ: Erlbaum.

Moreland, R. L., & Zajonc, R. B. (1979). Exposure effects may not depend on stimulus recognition. *Journal of Personality and Social Psychology, 37,* 1085–1089.

Reichardt, C. S., & Gollob, H. F. (1986). Satisfying the constraints of causal modeling. In W. M. Trochim (Ed.), *Advances in quasi-experimental design and analysis* (pp. 91–107). San Francisco: Jossey-Bass.

Satorra, A., & Saris, W. E. (1985). Power of the likelihood ratio test in covariance structure analysis. *Psychometrika, 50,* 83–90.

Schoenberg, R., & Arminger, G. (1988). LINCS: Linear covariance structure analysis. *Multivariate Behavioral Research, 23,* 271–273.

Snyder, M., & Gangestad, S. (1986). The nature of self-monitoring: Matters of assessment, matters of validity. *Journal of Personality and Social Psychology, 51,* 125–139.

Tanaka, J. S., & Huba, G. J. (1985). A fit index for covariance structure models under arbitrary GLS estimation. *British Journal of Mathematical and Statistical Psychology, 38,* 197–201.

Tucker, L. R., & Lewis, C. (1973). A reliability coefficient for maximum likelihood factor analysis. *Psychometrika, 38,* 1–10.

Widaman, K. F. (1985). Hierarchically nested covariance structure models for multitrait-multimethod data. *Applied Psychological Measurement, 9,* 1–26.

9

Theory Testing in Personality and Social Psychology with Structural Equation Models

A PRIMER IN 20 QUESTIONS

J. S. TANAKA
A. T. PANTER
WAYNE C. WINBORNE
G. J. HUBA

J. S. Tanaka is Associate Professor of Psychology at New York University. His interests are multivariate statistics, latent variable models, and the interface of personality and cognition.

A. T. Panter is Assistant Professor at the L. L. Thurstone Psychometric Laboratory in the Department of Psychology at the University of North Carolina, Chapel Hill. Her primary research interest focuses on models of the person responding process in personality assessment.

Wayne C. Winborne is a doctoral candidate in social/personality psychology at New York University and Research Coordinator at the Center for Law and Social Justice at Medgar Evers College, City University of New York. His research focuses on racially motivated violence, ethnic differences in cognitive style, and survey methodology in underrepresented populations.

G. J. Huba is President and Founder of the Measurement Group, in Culver City, California, a private consulting firm specializing in test development and research methodology.

Structural equation modeling (SEM) methods are reasonably well known to personality and social psychologists. Bentler (1980) and Maruyama and McGarvey (1980) provided early nontechnical introductions to this field. More recent guides include Hayduk (1987), Judd, Jessor, and Donovan

AUTHORS' NOTE: We wish to thank Richard Bagozzi, Peter Bentler, Kenneth Bollen, Harry Gollob, David Kenny, Richard Lennox, John Nesselroade, and Charles Reichardt for providing us with helpful materials in the preparation of this chapter, and Clyde Hendrick, Will Shadish, Lou Penner, Mike Coovert, John Bargh, Diane Ruble, Jim Uleman, the students in the fall 1989 latent variable course at New York University, and several anonymous reviewers for helpful comments on earlier drafts. Address all correspondence to J. S. Tanaka, Department of Psychology, New York University, 6 Washington Place, 7th Floor, New York, NY 10003; (212) 998-7824; BITNET: PSJST@NYUCCVM.

(1986), the excellent text of Loehlin (1987), a special section of *Child Development* (Connell & Tanaka, 1987), and the review chapter by Coovert, Penner, and MacCallum in this volume. These topics are sometimes discussed under other aliases, including latent variable models, covariance (or moment) structure models, factor-analytic simultaneous equation models (FASEM), and linear structural relations (LISREL; Jöreskog & Sörbom, 1988) models.

Previous reviews of this area have typically discussed the logic and general mechanics of SEM, covering topics such as estimation methods, model specification and fit, and computer program use. These reviews are necessary to educate a broader readership about the mechanics of these methods. However, personality and social psychologists remain wary of employing these methods in their own research programs. The methodology has been dismissed as unnecessarily complex, and applications have been described as both atheoretical and overly empirical. More fundamentally, experimental psychologists have dismissed these models as irrelevant to their work, seeing no connection between them and their standard analysis of variance (ANOVA) designs.

Our perspective is that many of the existing reviews of SEM have addressed the "what" and the "how" of the method. What seems lacking in this literature is an integrative link between these methods and theory in personality and social psychology. The purpose of this chapter is to discuss why personality and social psychologists should consider structural equation principles in their research programs. We address this "why" by outlining conditions under which SEM might help clarify theory testing.

We begin with the broadest possible perspective on the issues of SEM. Discussions of experimental design, model specification, measurement, model evaluation, and model testing are then developed. When appropriate, we illustrate how these points have been pursued. Possible misuses and popular criticisms of these methods are considered. The chapter also reviews the most recent developments in SEM, including the problems of (a) nonnormal data, (b) small samples, (c) ordered-categorical and dichotomous variables, and (d) assessment of change. We conclude by explicating our belief about the utility of these methods for testing relations underlying personality and social psychological phenomena.

The chapter is organized around 20 questions regarding SEM that are likely to be raised in the context of a research program. Each question is asked and then briefly answered. A more complete elaboration follows each brief answer. We have multiple goals in this chapter, but our primary one is to demonstrate how SEM is entirely compatible with personality and social psychological theory—even if an investigator never gets to the point of running the computer programs needed to implement these methods.

OVERVIEW:
STRUCTURAL EQUATIONS AND LATENT VARIABLES

(1) What is structural equation modeling?

Answer: All of the familiar statistical models for data are SEMs and therefore can be conceptualized in terms appropriate for these techniques.

In this chapter, we employ the term *structural equation modeling (models)* or *SEM* as a summary term for the family of linear statistical models that includes ANOVA, multiple regression, and other common multivariate statistics. This is an extension of a general linear model framework that views ANOVA models as a special case of multiple regression (e.g., Cohen & Cohen, 1983). This description of SEM differs somewhat from classic uses of this term, which generally refer only to path-analytic or latent variable models. More specifically, our use of SEM is not intended necessarily to imply issues about causality (see Question 8). We view the class of structural equation models more broadly as linear regression models, which may involve both observed and unobserved (latent) variables. To illustrate this point, consider the simple *t*-test, which is written in equation form as follows:

$$Y = \alpha + \beta X + e \qquad [1]$$

where Y denotes the dependent or outcome variable, α is the overall (grand) mean, X is a dummy independent variable coding group membership (e.g., an individual gets a "score" of 0 for control group membership or 1 for experimental group membership), β assesses the magnitude of the difference between the two groups, and e denotes other influences not accounted for by the model (i.e., "error"). This is an SEM where we hypothesize that the between-group difference can be expressed in this simple linear form.

The use of statistics should reflect an explicit choice of a particular SEM. The simple *t*-test is a *structural model* where observations on an outcome variable are hypothesized to be described fully by group membership. While it is possible that other variables may ultimately explain this difference, they have been excluded in this particular test. Analogous SEMs can be written to describe the ANOVA model and the multiple regression model, as well as multivariate extensions of these models such as the multivariate analysis of variance model and the factor analysis model.

(2) Why is it important to think in terms of models?

Answer: Models explicate investigators' biases and assumptions about hypothesized psychological processes.

The primary reason for thinking in terms of SEM is that it requires researchers to be straightforward about the mechanisms they postulate. Since any hypothesized model represents a closed system, all "important" sources of variability are assumed to be included. To the extent that the postulated model omits potentially important variables (e.g., in the *t*-test model, effects resulting from individual differences), the model is misspecified and will lead to errors in effect estimation and interpretation.

In the *t*-test model, observed differences on the outcome variable are assumed to be solely a function of group membership. Within a particular group (i.e., within the control or experimental group), all individuals are assumed to be interchangeable, since individual-level variation is hypothesized *not* to have an impact on outcome processes. Random assignment is assumed to control for individual-level variability and is viewed as relatively less important compared to processes that are assessed at the group level.

With these assumptions revealed, inconsistencies can be identified between the theory being tested and the model chosen to test this theory. For example, researchers must be aware of whether they are working from a perspective that postulates that responses to situations are in part idiographically determined or from a perspective that suggests that such variation has little importance to the model. This is just a restatement of the classic tension between the focus on social processes in social psychology and the focus on individual differences in personality psychology. The strength of an SEM approach is that important constructs reflecting both social processes and individual differences can be explicitly integrated into a single model.

(3) How does SEM fit into this modeling perspective?

Answer: The goal of SEM is to increase the validity of research findings by more closely estimating the relations that exist among psychological constructs.

Recent developments in social science methodology have been directed toward more rigorously establishing relations between constructs of interest. For example, the expanding literature on meta-analysis focuses on aggregated effects obtained for the same phenomenon over multiple studies (e.g., Cooper, this volume; Hedges & Olkin, 1985; Light & Pillemer, 1984). Like meta-analysis, SEM is aimed toward improving our knowledge about relations among psychological constructs. Unlike meta-analysis, SEM's goals are directed toward the correct specification and translation of psychological theory into empirical testing and evaluation. It attempts to attain this goal by forcing investigators to be explicit about constructs of interest, their assessment, and their interrelations. One goal of SEM is to gear investigative efforts toward obtaining the best possible estimates of these relations.

(4) How do latent variables fit in the conceptual picture?

Answer: Latent variables are central to thinking in personality and social psychology. Phenomena such as personality, attitudes, affect, motivation, and cognitive structures are all latent variables whose existence is inferred from observed behaviors.

Almost all of the psychological processes of both contemporary and historical interest in personality, social psychology, and social cognition are unobserved. Often, these unobserved processes are hypothesized to mediate observed responses (stimulus-organism-response or S-O-R theory). Historically, concepts such as needs, drives, and ego have been employed to describe the origins of observed behavior. Recent contributions in social cognition and personality have developed this theme further (e.g., Cantor & Kihlstrom, 1987; Fiske & Taylor, 1984). For example, cognitive structures have been postulated as explanatory constructs guiding social judgments (see Higgins & Bargh, 1987; Uleman & Bargh, 1989). Similarly, latent variables such as attitudes (e.g., Chaiken & Stangor, 1987; Petty & Cacioppo, 1986), motivation (e.g., Sorrentino & Higgins, 1986), affect (e.g., Isen, 1984; Izard, Kagan, & Zajonc, 1984), and personality traits and dispositions (e.g., Pervin, 1985; Snyder & Ickes, 1985) have been invoked in personality and social psychological theory throughout its history. These variables are indirectly observed and must be inferred from observed behavior.

(5) How do latent variables relate to the data I collect?

Answer: Researchers in personality and social psychology have become used to searching for the "common" aspects of a phenomenon as they exist across different operationalizations of a construct. The SEM approach formalizes this notion in a single, simultaneously estimated model that is less subject to both statistical and investigator bias.

Often, we proceed by inference from observed behaviors to unobserved constructs. Consider an investigator who chooses a single measured behavior to assess a latent construct of interest. In this situation, the behavior is assumed to have a one-to-one correspondence with the postulated underlying construct; that is, the measure is assumed to capture all of the variability in the hypothesized latent variable (e.g., a depression inventory is identical to the latent variable, depression). However, the conceptualization of a construct can be very different from its measurement in a single indicator. Single-criterion approaches confound the construct with its assessment (e.g., Campbell & Fiske, 1959; Huba & Hamilton, 1976).

This notion can be demonstrated when a hypothetical construct of interest (e.g., attitude, personality disposition, motivational or affective state) is thought to underlie a single observed behavior (e.g., completing a measure, engaging in a behavior, being exposed to certain situational constraints or experimental manipulations). We can contrast this situation with that generally associated with SEM. These models consider simultaneous multiple indicators of a latent variable, permitting triangulation on the construct of interest. Ideally, these multiple assessments will come from multiple sources and/or methods in an attempt to separate the "true" variance from other, extraneous sources (e.g., method variance).

The importance of such a multiple operationalist perspective is recognized by researchers who, in the course of a research program, seek multiple dependent or independent variables to evaluate their theoretical constructs (see Houts, Cook, & Shadish, 1986). This can be considered a search for "common" variance, the extent to which a broad set of observed behaviors reflect the same construct. However, this strategy of inferring "common" variance is subject to two kinds of bias in both across- and within-study investigations. For example, statistical bias can arise when each independent operationalization is an imperfect indicator of the unobserved construct (across studies) or an incorrect statistical model is chosen to look at data (within study).

Examples of investigator bias have also been well documented. In the meta-analysis literature (see Cooper, this volume), this bias has been discussed in the selective aggregation of only published research findings (across studies). A parallel issue has been discussed by, for example, Campbell and Fiske (1959) regarding the dangers of monomethod assessments (within study).[1]

(6) Do latent variables best approximate our psychological constructs?

Answer: Yes, but only latent variables with multiple indicators provide a better empirical representation of an underlying construct relative to a latent variable with a single indicator.

There is a general misconception that latent variable analyses somehow provide "better" or "truer" answers to hypothesized questions. This statement's truth lies in the empiricist belief that what can be observed in data is "better" than what is assumed to exist. Standard research paradigms assume the existence of an underlying latent variable, operationalized in a particular way (e.g., an attitude), as well as relations among latent variables (e.g., an attitude-behavior link). If we have simultaneous multiple methods for assessing the latent variable, it is preferable to either a situation where we must simply assume that such a relation exists on the basis of a single piece of information or a situation where we obtain multiple measures via the same method (monomethod bias). Further, possible statistical biases due to measurement error are addressed by explicitly modeling observed variable unreliabilities (e.g., Huba & Bentler, 1983).

However, as several critics of SEM have pointed out, this does not mean that latent variables with multiple indicators are the "truth" or that one has magically moved from the observed data level to the theoretical construct level (e.g., see Baumrind, 1983; Cliff, 1983; Freedman, 1987). Structural equation models with latent variables allow us to *approximate* theoretical constructs. This empirical perspective can be differentiated from the non-empirical assumption of equating a construct with a measure. However, conclusions are still dependent upon the particular measured indicators that are chosen. These models certainly are not a panacea for bad data or poor operationalization of theory. The effect of incorrectly specifying a latent variable leads to the same kind of interpretational errors associated with an incorrect experimental manipulation.

(7) As a psychologist who does laboratory research, why do I need to know about structural equation models?

Answer: Structural equation models are everywhere in some shape or form. The extent to which simultaneous multiple operationalizations are employed in experimental methodology will determine the general utility of these methods in the laboratory. Routine use of these multiple operationalizations will increase SEM's utility in laboratory settings.

Many psychologists have chosen to think about two nonoverlapping research strategies, the experimental and the nonexperimental (Cattell, 1967; Cronbach, 1957). The experimental method has been typified by its interest in group-level phenomena and controlled experimental manipulations. The nonexperimental component has been associated with the study of individual differences or with research designs that are "undercontrolled." Latent variable SEMs traditionally have been employed in the context of nonexperimental data (e.g., Kenny, 1979), and, as a result, many psychologists have come to believe that these methods are appropriate only when data are obtained in these settings. This is clearly not the case, however, as Fiske, Kenny, and Taylor (1982) and Geiselman, Woodward, and Beatty (1982) have demonstrated, along with more recent examples by Bagozzi and Yi (1988b) and Neuberg (1989).

As demonstrated above in the discussion of Question 1, all familiar statistical models that psychologists generally employ are special cases of SEMs. Latent variables are either explicitly represented in the modeling process or implicitly operationalized in the discussion of research results. Thus the idea that these models are for nonexperimental data only is simply incorrect. One concern that has been raised is whether samples are large enough in the typical lab study to employ SEM. As an example, Geiselman et al. (1982, Experiment 1) employed 20 subjects to test one of the models in their paper. Question 13, below, provides a more extended discussion of the sample size issue.

It is true that use of the particular computer programs that implement these methods (e.g., LISREL, COSAN, EQS) may not be appropriate in every application. Many of the familiar statistical methods such as ANOVA or multiple regression have both simpler computer programs and a statistical theory developed especially for these particular methods. The personality and social psychology literature is abundant with SEM examples, usually in one of these simpler forms (e.g., ANOVA, *t*-test, regression).

Latent variable SEM's contribution to experimental methodology depends on the extent to which the multiple indicators of constructs are employed. The studies of Fiske et al. (1982) looking at attributional models, Neuberg (1989) looking at impression accuracy, Bagozzi and Yi (1988a) studying attitude availability, and Geiselman et al. (1982) looking at the structure of memory are excellent examples of SEM applications in laboratory settings. The last study, in particular, shows how both behavioral (e.g., recall) and physiological (e.g., galvanic skin response and pupil dilation) indicators can be employed to test relations hypothesized to exist among constructs (e.g., memory and attention).

(8) How "causal" are these models anyway?

Answer: Causal inference is a property of experimental design characteristics, not statistical models. Even in the most straightforward, well-controlled experimental designs, issues of causality are not simple, as demonstrated in the recent work of Holland (1986, 1988; Holland & Rubin, 1983).

Researchers tend to be well versed in the positive aspects of control in their designs (e.g., alleviation of selection bias, control of unintended sources of variables, or the "third" variable problem). This control, as traditionally conceptualized in ANOVA-like terms, rules out alternative explanations for a set of findings and permits statements about a variable or a set of variables "causing" a specified outcome. Conversely, studies that do not have this same level of control do not permit causal statements about relations among the constructs examined.

Correlation does not imply causality; however, early advocates in the latent variable literature (e.g., Heise, 1975; Kenny, 1979) seemed to imply that these models held great promise for analyzing correlational designs, allowing more rigorous interpretation of data. While not uniformly agreed upon by all authors (e.g., Bentler, 1980), describing SEM as "causal models" has caught on in the literature (e.g., Glymour, Scheines, Spirtes, & Kelly, 1987; James, Mulaik, & Brett, 1982).

SEM alone cannot compensate for or eliminate aspects of designs that would facilitate or preclude the causal interpretation of an effect. Holland (1986, 1988; Holland & Rubin, 1983) has formalized conditions necessary for drawing conclusions about causal processes. As these papers show, a number of relatively stringent (and potentially unattainable) conditions must exist to demonstrate a "causal" effect for any experimental design.

(9) Do latent variables always "cause" observed measures?

Answer: Different research problems might lead to hypotheses about cause or effect indicators. While specific statistical models exist that are closer in spirit to effect indicator models, they could also be incorporated in traditional SEM frameworks.

Some authors have questioned the usual SEM assumption that measured variables are imperfect manifestations of latent variables (e.g., Bollen & Lennox, 1988; Cohen, Velez, Marchi, Cohen, & Teresi, 1986). Some of this concern stems from problems arising in applications of SEM. For example, in the life-events domain, one might expect different life-event occurrences to be conceptually related to each other. However, it is not necessarily the case that different life events should be hypothesized as emanating from a common underlying and unobserved latent process. Thus Bollen and Lennox (1988) and Cohen et al. (1986) make a distinction between cause indicator models, where measured variables are hypothesized as functions of latent variables plus error, and effect indicator models, where measured variables linearly combine to form a latent variable.

While the former model has predominated in the SEM literature, there is research relevant to the specification of the latter type of model (e.g., Lohmöller, 1989; Schönemann & Steiger, 1976; Wold, 1981). The principal-component-based strategy implied by Bollen and Lennox (1988) and Cohen et al. (1986) could also be implemented in traditional SEM schemes by including component scores for measured variables hypothesized to operate as effect indicators.

(10) What is meant by the "confirmatory/exploratory" distinction?

Answer: The confirmatory/exploratory distinction is a useful concept only at a high level of abstraction and has little to do with the actual research process. Following Cattell (1988), we prefer to think of these models as tools for both testing and exploring construct interrelations, although obviously not with the same data.

The confirmatory/exploratory distinction that is often made with respect to SEM is a broad description of a research approach. The confirmatory approach involves testing a specific hypothesis. The exploratory approach seeks to elucidate what, if any, patterns exist in data. As discussed by Cattell (1988), this categorization operates only at the highest level of abstraction and probably has very little to do with the research process as it develops in practice.

Undeniably, there has been a great deal of "data snooping" and post hoc model building in the SEM literature to date. The relative ease with which computer programs can identify and alter models to optimize fit may encourage this practice (e.g., the automatic model modification in the LIS-REL program). The potential dangers of such a strategy have been discussed by La Du and Tanaka (1989), Luijben, Boomsma, and Molenaar (1987), and MacCallum (1986).

Consider the SEM of a 2×2 experimental design using the ANOVA, where an investigator's hypothesis concerns the interaction term. Standard computer programs test not only the interaction term, but both main effects, which, by hypothesis, were not of interest. A truly "confirmatory" approach to this problem, following Rosenthal and Rosnow (1985), might look only at the specific comparisons of interest implicated by the hypothesized interaction. Statistical evaluation and interpretation of the main effects upon discovering statistical significance represents comparable degrees of data snooping.

(11) Aren't the usual statistical models "good enough"?

Answer: Stimulus-response (S-R) theories and their representation within statistical models such as the ANOVA represent the vestiges of a disciplinary focus that no longer predominates. Our standard statistical models are "good enough" only if we are theoretically willing to retreat to S-R representations. Recent developments in elaborating process models of phenomena in personality and social psychology force us to be explicit when modeling these hypothesized mediating constructs.

Regression and ANOVA models are a fundamental part of the statistical armamentarium of all psychologists. However, is it necessarily the case that these basic models adequately fulfill the needs of current psychological theories? In other words, is there a congruence between psychological theories and statistical models used to test those theories?

We believe there is a large conceptual chasm between contemporary theory in personality and social psychology and statistics, and that this can be bridged through an appreciation of latent variable SEM.

As previously noted, there is no question that models involving cognitive mediation of social stimuli currently predominate in the literature (e.g., Fiske & Taylor, 1984; Higgins & Bargh, 1987; Markus & Zajonc, 1985). These process-oriented, sociocognitive models emphasize the role of the individual perceiver in generating responses. Further, these models, which implicate the role of cognitive factors, extend from fairly complex judgments and attributions (e.g., Trope, 1986; Wyer & Srull, 1986, 1989) to "simpler" processes of responding to a set of questionnaire items (e.g., Hippler, Schwarz, & Sudman, 1987).

Although these theories are S-O-R in nature, the statistical models used to evaluate them have remained, for the most part, at the S-R level. ANOVA-based models, for example, are interested only in the relation between independent variables and a single dependent variable. They do not model the possibility of mediating (as opposed to moderating; e.g., Baron & Kenny, 1986) effects of the cognitive process variables, central to contemporary personality and social psychology theory. Taylor and Fiske (1981) noted this concern when they stated that mediational cognitive phenomena would necessarily require psychologists to move beyond the ANOVA in order to achieve a greater congruence between psychological theory and statistical models.

STRUCTURAL EQUATION MODEL PRAGMATICS

(12) Why is hypothesis testing different in these models?

Answer: The goodness-of-fit chi-square statistic employed in model evaluation involves a null hypothesis that the "model fits" the data; thus a goal of hypothesis testing could be viewed as "accepting" the null hypothesis.

However, two points must be taken into account. First, null hypotheses can never be "accepted"; one is merely presenting evidence about the consistency of a particular model with a given set of data. Second, rather than focusing on absolute model fit, emphasis should be placed on the comparative evaluation of multiple models.

Model evaluation in SEM is different from standard null hypothesis testing in at least two ways. First, the fundamental unit of analysis in these models is not an individual's data, but the information contained in the variances and covariances of measured variables (and, occasionally, the means; see Question 16). Thus, unlike ANOVA/regression models, degrees of freedom for SEM are not a function of total sample size, but rather of the total number of variances and covariances among observed variables. Sample size never explicitly appears in degrees of freedom calculations for these models.

Second, the overall determination of model fit in SEM is a goodness-of-fit chi-square statistic. One looks for values of the chi-square statistic that are small relative to the model's degrees of freedom, leading to an obtained probability level that is *greater* than the conventional .05 alpha level. The null hypothesis in these models is that "the model fits."[2] Thus one wishes to "accept" the null hypothesis that a particular model is congruent with a set of observed data.

This approach differs from our usual introduction to statistical hypothesis testing, where the null hypothesis is one we wish to reject. For example, in the two-group *t*-test, one sets up the null hypothesis of "no treatment effect." Introductory statistics texts caution heavily against a temptation to "accept" the null hypothesis, since a failure to reject the null hypothesis does not necessarily imply that the null hypothesis is true.

Concluding that a particular latent variable model is consistent with some data does not imply that it is the correct model for the data. Returning to a point made in Question 6, the "truth" has not been discovered. A researcher can conclude only that the model represents one plausible representation for the observed data. There may be other untested models that provide an equivalent, or perhaps better, fit to the data.

The focus of model testing and evaluation is not the absolute fit of any particular model, but the *comparative* fit of a priori specified competing models (e.g., Jöreskog, 1974). Thus it is not sufficient to note that a particular model achieves a level of statistical consistency with the data; one must also note that it represents the data *better* than some competing model. Neuberg (1989) presents a good example of the systematic comparison of alternative models. The definition of *better* can vary from investigator to investigator, but we take it to mean a reasonable and more parsimonious model that is consistent with a given set of data (e.g., James et al., 1982).

(13) Don't these models require large sample sizes?

Answer: Because of the mixed recommendations regarding appropriate sample sizes for these models, as well as some problems in adopting a strict inferential framework due to issues of statistical power, we propose that investigators adopt a less inferentially driven approach to model testing, particularly when samples are small.

A number of conflicting recommendations exist in the literature regarding the minimum sample size required for appropriate statistical inference. For example, Boomsma (1983) concluded that sample sizes of 100 are minimally acceptable and that samples of size 200 or greater were preferred. In contrast, Geweke and Singleton (1980) showed that much smaller samples could be used. Tanaka (1987) has suggested that a focus on absolute sample size was inappropriate without a specification of other factors such as the model size, including the number of measured and latent variables included in a model.

Another way of thinking about the sample size issue draws from the statistical power literature (e.g., Cohen, 1988). It is well known from ANOVA/regression models that increased sample sizes are associated with increased statistical power and the greater likelihood of rejecting the null hypothesis. Substantively important but moderate size effects are often not statistically detectable (i.e., significant) in small samples.

Identical logic applies for SEM. However, the hypothesis testing strategy for these models requires that we "accept" the null hypothesis (in the sense that we have previously defined). It will be "easy" to draw conclusions about model fit when samples are small (i.e., when statistical power is low), and tested models are likely to fit. While more elaborate statistically-based discussions of power in SEM can be found (e.g., Matsueda & Bielby, 1986; Saris, Satorra, & Sörbom, 1987), this summary briefly describes some of the problems involved in sample size and hypothesis testing in these models.

(14) What is meant by a "less" inferential approach?

Answer: Small samples require more careful considerations of the conditions for valid statistical inference. When sample size is small relative to the number of variables, we recommend a deemphasis on statistical inference as the sole focus of model evaluation.

We believe that SEM can be used successfully in small samples, as long as an appropriate degree of conservatism accompanies interpretation of findings. Often, the nature of a research problem constrains the sample size available for a particular investigation. For example, one might be interested in a particular low-incidence population (e.g., rape victims, clinically depressed students) where samples will be small. Conventional wisdom regarding sample size in SEM has suggested that these methods are unavailable in these situations. We view this position as extreme, akin to suggesting that any statistical analysis is not justified in a small sample.

A positive relation exists between the quality of inference made from a sample of data and its size. Thus when limited information is available, weaker inferential statements about data should be made. Such an approach emphasizes the descriptive aspects of data such as effect magnitudes rather than formal hypothesis-testing criteria. A strategy consistent with this "less" inferential approach is suggested by Tanaka (1987).

There are, however, limits to how small a sample can be to successfully employ any statistical model. For example, we would not recommend modeling in samples where the number of variables is greater than the number of subjects. This situation would clearly represent a case where insufficient information is available to evaluate a model.

LATENT VARIABLES AND THE NATURE OF DATA

(15) Must the data I have be normally distributed?

Answer: Alternative strategies of dealing with nonnormal data exist, although the choice of whether these methods are employed in practice should be arbitrated by the relative emphasis on statistical versus substantive conclusions. Whether considering questions of data nonnormality or "less than" interval-level measurement, statistical conclusions in SEM appear to be nonrobust. Despite possible differences in statistical findings, the magnitude of obtained effects is likely to be unaffected.

Two types of data requirements can be specified in SEM: (1) conceptual requirements of multiple indicators in these models and (2) distributional assumptions required for appropriate statistical inference.

Measured variable indicators required in latent variable SEM are chosen to maximize the representativeness of the latent variable. As discussed by Patterson and Bank (1986), these indicators are best obtained via multiple methods and not through use of single items or small clusters of homogeneous items. If diverse sources of information are used, the latent variable casts a broader nomological net (see Cronbach & Meehl, 1955).

A second data requirement addresses distributional assumptions. As with almost all familiar inferential tests (e.g., *t*-tests, *F*-tests), appropriate statistical inference requires normally distributed outcome variables. On occasion, data nonnormality has been addressed by appealing to the robustness of statistical tests for distributions that deviate from normality or that are not continuously distributed. Some recent theoretical (e.g., Bentler, 1983; Browne, 1982; Muthén, 1984) and empirical (e.g., Huba & Harlow, 1986, 1987; Tanaka & Huba, 1987) work in SEM allows for critical examination of these robustness arguments.

Beyond normality: ADF estimation. Browne (1982) outlined a general inferential theory for SEM applicable for nonnormal data. Bentler (1983) and Browne (1984) subsequently extended this logic. Applications based on the assumption of observed data normality such as maximum likelihood have predominated in the field, primarily due to historical precedence. These assumptions parallel the assumption of normally distributed variables in models such as ANOVA. The asymptotically distribution-free (ADF) estimator of Browne and Bentler relaxed these distributional assumptions, although at the cost of requiring additional information from the data.

A number of empirical studies have examined the ADF estimator's behavior (e.g., Huba & Harlow, 1986, 1987; Tanaka & Huba, 1987) and have yielded two general robustness findings with nonnormal data: (a) When nonnormal data are used with methods assuming data normality, statistical inference in SEM will be negatively affected, but (b) the *substantive* interpretation of findings is likely to be unaffected.

Measurement in latent variable models. The previous discussion has assumed continuously measured indicators. Much of the item-level data collected in areas such as attribution theory, personality and attitude assessment, and person perception come in dichotomous or ordered categorical form. For example, several popular personality measures possess a dichotomous response format. Moreover, 5-point and 7-point scales are ubiquitous in personality and social psychology research. The general assumption has been that 7- (or 5- or 11-) point scales provide a good approximation to continuously distributed data.

This problem is endemic not only to assessment literatures. In many studies, the outcome measure of interest is the occurrence/nonoccurrence of some behavior, a dichotomous variable that does not easily fit into our standard statistical procedures. Muthén (1984, 1987), in the LISCOMP model, provides an SEM framework for the analysis of dichotomous, ordered categorical, and continuous measured variable indicators and their mixtures.

Some of the studies that have considered robustness of standard SEM procedures to data nonnormality also have considered the robustness question with respect to noncontinuously measured data (e.g., Huba & Harlow, 1986, 1987). These studies found that statistical inference can be incorrect when standard SEM methods employ dichotomous or ordered categorical data, although substantive conclusions remained unaffected.

Applications of these models to personality and social psychological phenomena are under way. For example, Panter and her associates (Panter, 1988; Panter & Tanaka, 1987; Panter, Tanaka, & Waller, 1989; Tanaka, Panter, & Winborne, 1988) have applied the LISCOMP model to assessment instruments such as the Beck Depression Inventory (Beck, Ward, Mendelson, Mock, & Erbaugh, 1961), the Self-Monitoring Scale (Snyder, 1987), and the Need for Cognition (Cacioppo & Petty, 1982).

(16) What about information regarding means?

Answer: Mean information is readily available in SEM, although it has been underutilized to date.

With a few exceptions (e.g., McArdle & Epstein, 1987; Sörbom, 1974; Tanaka & Bentler, 1983; Tanaka et al., 1988), the analysis of mean information in SEM has been underutilized. Such underuse stems from the underlying SEM's origins in factor analysis and multiple regression, both of which tend to employ correlational data and ignore mean information. Such a focus is at odds with ANOVA, where evaluation of mean information is standard. Not only can mean information be represented in SEM, but rather complex interactive mean hypotheses have been entertained in these model (see Tanaka & Bentler, 1983).

What additional substantive knowledge is gained through examining means? The work of McArdle and his associates demonstrates some benefits of including mean information. They have modeled longitudinal growth in intellectual ability using SEM with mean information (e.g., McArdle, 1988; McArdle & Epstein, 1987). By including mean information, they were able to examine the developmental pattern of intellectual growth across time points, allowing for the assessment of each individual's similarity to the average intellectual growth. If only covariances or correlations had been examined, only data regarding an individual's rank order within the group would have been available. This would have yielded only the well-documented (and noninformative) high-stability coefficient for ability measures.

Finally, the SEM approach lets us lay to rest the truism that "ANOVAs look at means, and regressions look at correlations." This thinking is, in part, due to the lack of emphasis placed on interpreting intercept terms in regression models. As an example, consider the *t*-test of equation 1. There, the control group mean is given by α and the experimental group mean is given by $\alpha + \beta$, since β is the increment in y's mean given experimental group membership (i.e., the "treatment effect").

Now assume the regression situation where x is a continuously measured variable. Typically, the interpretive focus on such a model would be on the statistical significance of β, ignoring the intercept term α. However, an alternative interpretation is that predicted means on y could be obtained for *every* observed value of x by calculating $\alpha + \beta x$. In fact, the regression line is nothing more than the line connecting each of these predicted means for every observed x. Since all values of x are taken into account, it is richer, more valuable, and statistically more powerful (Cohen, 1983) than the common practice in personality and social psychology of median (or tertiary) splits to get a particular two- (three-) point mean comparison.

(17) Should I analyze correlations or covariances?

Answer: The appropriate statistical methods for the analysis of correlation structures are not widely available. Further, the analysis of correlations unnecessarily discards metric information that could be useful in across-group or across-sample comparisons. While examining models based on correlations may ease model interpretability, investigators should be appropriately wary of statistical conclusions based on correlations rather than covariances.

A standard approach in psychological measurement and statistics (e.g., Cohen & Cohen, 1983) assumes that a variable's metric is arbitrary and that standardizing variables does not harm conclusions drawn about models. Despite the flexibility in computer programs about whether correlation or covariance matrices are analyzed, standard inferential statistical theory applies only for the analysis of covariance information (see Browne, 1982). A separate literature exists on the analysis of correlational structures (Cudeck, 1989; De Leeuw, 1983).

Covariances contain not only associational information between two variables, but also metric information. Operating in a correlational metric is likely to ease initial interpretation, since all variables are in the same standard metric and thus can be readily compared. However, across-sample results, which are particularly critical in the single-operationalization, multiple-study approach to construct validity, are invalidated by this loss of variance information (e.g., Tanaka & Bentler, 1983).

STRUCTURAL EQUATION MODELS
AND THE ANALYSIS OF CHANGE

An area where SEM undeniably has contributed is in the analysis of longitudinal development (e.g., Gollob & Reichardt, 1987; Hertzog & Nesselroade, 1987; Nesselroade, 1988; Nesselroade & Baltes, 1979), although even these developments are not without their critics (e.g., Rogosa & Willett, 1985; Willett 1988).

(18) Do longitudinal methods matter in cross-sectional data?

Answer: Longitudinal data problems do not occur only in longitudinal data. Failing to take into account the lagged effects of a variable in a cross-sectional data set can be demonstrated to have deleterious effects.

In research methods courses, problems that arise in the analysis of longitudinal data are often seen as the unique domain of developmental psychologists. Recent work by Gollob and Reichardt (1987; Reichardt & Gollob, 1986) in the context of their "latent longitudinal" model showed that, even in cross-sectional data, "longitudinal" data problems can arise.

In a series of papers, Reichardt and Gollob (1986, 1987; Gollob & Reichardt, 1987) demonstrated that failing to take into account time-lagged effects in cross-sectional data can result in a serious model specification error, leading to erroneous conclusions about obtained effects. Because such effects are, by definition, not measured in cross-sectional designs, Reichardt and Gollob recommend multiple analyses on a set of data where time-lagged effects are estimated across a range of possible values as a way of calibrating the impact of the possible magnitude of the missing effect.

There is another perspective on the question of change that has generally been ignored in personality and social psychology. Specifically, this kind of change occurs within the context of what would typically be considered cross-sectional research and deals with the effect of sequential presentation of stimuli. Concerns regarding this point have been raised in the context of on-line presentation of stimuli (Holender, 1986), the application of social cognition principles to questionnaire design (Hippler et al., 1987), responses in personality assessment (Knowles, 1988), and psychophysiological responding (Vasey & Thayer, 1987).

Types of change. Harris's (1963) influential monograph has led methodologists to be careful about the locus of change. A unit of analysis focus helps to delineate the kinds of change hypothesized to occur and the statistical models being considered to analyze that change. We have found that a fruitful way to think about different types of change is at the interindividual or the intraindividual level (e.g., see Tanaka, in press).

(19) What is meant by "interindividual versus intraindividual" change?

Answer: Structural equation models can be constructed to look either at interindividual or intraindividual change depending on the particular hypotheses raised in the context of a research program. However, it must be noted that these different research perspectives on change have implications for what one means by *change.* This distinction has been articulated recently in the SEM literature (e.g., McArdle, 1988; Nesselroade, 1988; Rogosa & Willett, 1985, 1988).

Consider the within-subjects *t*-test where subjects are measured before and after some experimental treatment. It is often said in these studies that "subjects serve as their own controls." However, the analytic focus in these studies is the *average* difference observed across the sample of subjects. An assumption is that this average change fully describes the change process; all subjects are assumed to change in the same way at the same rate. There is no question, however, that assessing change is a critical issue in the context of personality and social psychology (e.g., personality development, person perception, stereotype perseverance).

The autoregressive SEM approach that has been suggested as a method of analyzing longitudinal designs – such as the cross-lagged panel designs of Campbell and Stanley (1966) and the alternative models suggested by Jöreskog (1974) and Kenny and Campbell (1989) – shares this focus on the study of interindividual processes. Thus a variable's stability across time or its cross-lagged relation with another variable is assumed to describe relations hypothesized to be true for all subjects.

This interindividual perspective can be compared to the approach adopted in some recent studies of affect (e.g., Zevon & Tellegen, 1982) or mother-child dyadic interaction (Hooker, Nesselroade, Nesselroade, & Lerner, 1987) that look at the relations that exist within a particular unit of analysis (an individual in the first example, mother-child dyads in the second) over multiple observations. This intraindividual perspective is interested in dynamic change occurring within a unit of analysis over time. It should not be concluded that interest in interindividual or intraindividual change represents mutually exclusive categories, since most psychological theories implicate both. While the simultaneous analysis of interindividual and intraindividual growth does not have an extensive literature, some work is being done in this area (e.g., Wood & Nesselroade, 1988). It is also likely that solutions to the problem of the simultaneous analysis of inter- and intraindividual change will be informed by the developing methodological literature on so-called hierarchical linear models (e.g., Bock, 1989; Bryk & Raudenbush, 1987; Goldstein, 1987).

FINAL NOTES

(20) Will my research suffer if I still don't use latent variable models?

Answer: Our feeling is that much of the contemporary empirical literature in personality and social psychology does not take into account the important and interesting effects that are postulated by its theories. For example, while mediational, process-oriented models dominate contemporary thought in our area (e.g., Fiske & Taylor, 1984; Higgins & Bargh, 1987; Pervin, 1985; Wyer & Srull, 1986, 1989), our research and statistical methods often do not explicitly consider mediational effects (see Taylor & Fiske, 1981). By thinking in terms of models and, in particular, SEM, we can develop better congruences between theory and practice in personality and social psychology.

We have attempted to make a number of points in this chapter that we hope will compel researchers in personality and social psychology to think in terms of SEM and latent variables. These include the facts that (a) many central constructs in our field are latent variables, even when they are not directly analyzed in this way; (b) these models do not necessarily operate in a confirmatory mode; (c) the quality of statistical inference in these models can vary as a function of sample size; (d) a variety of data distributions can be analyzed in these methods; and (e) these methods can be useful in analyzing change. We recognize that not all psychologists and research programs will necessarily employ latent variable SEMs. However, we do find that the ability to think in SEM terms is compatible with many conceptualizations of research and theory.

Our thinking is captured by one basic point. Psychologists are always thinking in terms of models. Structural equation latent variable models represent a way of moving from psychological thought to empirical action.

NOTES

1. We wish to thank Will Shadish for drawing our attention to this important distinction.

2. Alternatively, a reviewer has suggested that the null hypothesis tests residuals (i.e., the null hypothesis is that residuals are zero). Thus rejecting the null hypothesis implies that significant associations among variables are not accounted for by the model.

REFERENCES

Bagozzi, R. P., & Yi, Y. (1988a). *Availability of the attitude object as a moderator of the role of intentions in the attitude-behavior relation.* Unpublished manuscript, University of Michigan, Department of Marketing and Behavioral Science.

Bagozzi, R. P., & Yi, Y. (1988b). *On the use of structural equation models in experimental designs.* Unpublished manuscript, University of Michigan, Department of Marketing and Behavioral Science.

Baron, R. M., & Kenny, D. A. (1986). The moderator-mediator variable distinction in social psychological research: Conceptual, strategic, and statistical considerations. *Journal of Personality and Social Psychology, 51*, 1173-1182.

Baumrind, D. (1983). Specious causal attributions in the social sciences: The reformulated stepping-stone theory of heroin use as exemplar. *Journal of Personality and Social Psychology, 45*, 1289-1298.

Beck, A. T., Ward, C. H., Mendelson, M., Mock, J., & Erbaugh, J. (1961). An inventory for measuring depression. *Archives of General Psychiatry, 4*, 561-571.

Bentler, P. M. (1980). Multivariate analysis with latent variables: Causal modeling. *Annual Review of Psychology, 31*, 419-456.

Bentler, P. M. (1983). Some contributions to efficient statistics in structural models: Specification and estimation of moment structures. *Psychometrika, 48*, 493-517.

Bock, R. D. (Ed.). (1989). *Multilevel analysis of educational data.* San Diego: Academic.

Bollen, K., & Lennox, R. (1988). *Conventional wisdom on measurement: A structural equation perspective.* Manuscript submitted for publication.

Boomsma, A. (1983). *On the robustness of LISREL (maximum likelihood estimation) against small size and nonnormality.* Amsterdam: Sociometric Research Foundation.

Browne, M. W. (1982). Covariance structures. In D. M. Hawkins (Ed.), *Topics in applied multivariate analysis* (pp. 72-141). Cambridge: Cambridge University Press.

Browne, M. W. (1984). Asymptotically distribution-free methods for the analysis of covariance structures. *British Journal of Mathematical and Statistical Psychology, 37*, 62-83.

Bryk, A. S., & Raudenbush, S. W. (1987). Application of hierarchical linear models to assessing change. *Psychological Bulletin, 101*, 147-158.

Cacioppo, J. T., & Petty, R. E. (1982). The Need for Cognition. *Journal of Personality and Social Psychology, 42*, 116-131.

Campbell, D. T., & Fiske D. W. (1959). Convergent and discriminant validation by the multitrait-multimethod matrix. *Psychological Bulletin, 56*, 81-105.

Campbell, D. T., & Stanley, J. C. (1966). *Experimental and quasi-experimental designs for research.* Chicago: Rand McNally.

Cantor, N., & Kihlstrom, J. F. (1987). *Personality and social intelligence.* Englewood Cliffs, NJ: Prentice-Hall.

Cattell, R. B. (1967). *The scientific analysis of personality.* Baltimore: Penguin.

Cattell, R. B. (1988). Psychological theory and scientific method. In J. R. Nesselroade & R. B. Cattell (Eds.), *Handbook of multivariate experimental psychology* (2nd ed., pp. 3-20). New York: Plenum.

Chaiken, S., & Stangor, C. (1987). Attitudes and attitude change. *Annual Review of Psychology, 38*, 575-630.

Cliff, N. (1983). Some cautions concerning the application of causal modeling methods. *Multivariate Behavioral Research, 18*, 115–126.

Cohen, J. (1983). The cost of dichotomization. *Applied Psychological Measurement, 7*, 249–253.

Cohen, J. (1988). *Statistical power analysis for the behavioral sciences* (2nd ed.). Hillsdale, NJ: Erlbaum.

Cohen, J., & Cohen, P. (1983). *Applied multiple regression/correlation analysis for the behavioral sciences* (2nd ed.). Hillsdale, NJ: Erlbaum.

Cohen, P., Velez, C. N., Marchi, M., Cohen, J., & Teresi, J. (1986). *Opening the black box: Some methodological pitfalls in the application of latent variable analysis.* Unpublished manuscript, New York State Psychiatric Institute.

Connell, J. P., & Tanaka, J. S. (Eds.). (1987). Structural equation models in developmental psychology [Special section]. *Child Development, 58*. 1–175.

Cronbach, L. J. (1957). The two disciplines of scientific psychology. *American Psychologist, 12*, 671–684.

Cronbach, L. J., & Meehl, P. W. (1955). Construct validity in psychological tests. *Psychological Bulletin, 52*, 281–302.

Cudeck, R. (1989). The analysis of correlation matrices using covariance structure models. *Psychological Bulletin, 105*, 317–327.

De Leeuw, J. (1983). Models and methods for the analysis of correlation coefficients. *Journal of Econometrics, 22*, 113–137.

Fiske, S. T., Kenny, D. A., & Taylor, S. E. (1982). Structural models for the mediation of salience effects on attribution. *Journal of Experimental Social Psychology, 18*, 105–127.

Fiske, S. T., & Taylor, S. E. (1984). *Social cognition.* Reading, MA: Addison-Wesley.

Freedman, D. A. (1987). As others see us: A case study in path analysis. *Journal of Educational Statistics, 12*, 101–128.

Geiselman, R. E., Woodward, J. A., & Beatty, J. (1982). Individual differences in verbal memory performance: A test of alternative information-processing models. *Journal of Experimental Psychology: General, 111*, 109–134.

Geweke, J. F., & Singleton, K. J. (1980). Interpreting the likelihood ratio statistic in factor models when sample size is small. *Journal of the American Statistical Association, 75*, 133–137.

Glymour, C., Scheines, R., Spirtes, P., & Kelly, K. (1987). *Discovering causal structure.* Orlando, FL: Academic Press.

Goldstein, H. (1987). *Multilevel models in education and social research.* London: Griffin.

Gollob, H. F., & Reichardt, C. S. (1987). Taking account of time lags in causal models. *Child Development, 58*, 80–92.

Harris, C. W. (Ed.). (1963). *Problems in measuring change.* Madison: University of Wisconsin Press.

Hayduk, L. A. (1987). *Structural equation modeling with LISREL: Essentials and advances.* Baltimore: Johns Hopkins University Press.

Hedges, L., & Olkin, I. (1985). *Statistical methods for meta-analysis.* Orlando, FL: Academic Press.

Heise, D. R. (1975). *Causal analysis.* New York: John Wiley.

Hertzog, C., & Nesselroade, J. R. (1987). Beyond autoregressive models: Some implications of the trait-state distinction for the structural model of developmental change. *Child Development, 58,* 93–109.

Higgins, E. T., & Bargh, J. A. (1987). Social cognition and social perception. *Annual Review of Psychology, 38,* 369–425.

Hippler, H. J., Schwarz, N., & Sudman, S. (Eds.). (1987). *Social information processing and survey methodology.* New York: Springer-Verlag.

Holender, D. (1986). Semantic activation without conscious identification in dichotic listening, parafoveal vision, and visual masking: A survey and appraisal. *Behavioral and Brain Sciences, 9,* 1–23.

Holland, P. W. (1986). Statistics and causal inference. *Journal of the American Statistical Association, 81,* 945–970.

Holland, P. W. (1988). Causal inference, path analysis, and recursive structural equation models. In C. C. Clogg (Ed.), *Sociological methodology 1988* (pp. 449–484). Washington, DC: American Sociological Association.

Holland, P. W., & Rubin, D. B. (1983). On Lord's paradox. In H. Wainer & S. Messick (Eds.), *Principles of modern psychological measurement* (pp. 3–25). Hillsdale, NJ: Erlbaum.

Hooker, K., Nesselroade, D. W., Nesselroade, J. R., & Lerner, R. M. (1987). The structure of intraindividual temperament in the context of mother-child dyads: P-technique factor analyses of short-term change. *Developmental Psychology, 23,* 332–346.

Houts, A. C., Cook, T. D., & Shadish, W. R. (1986). The person-situation debate: A critical multiplist perspective. *Journal of Personality, 54,* 52–105.

Huba, G. J., & Bentler, P. M. (1983). On the usefulness of latent variable causal modeling in testing theories of naturally occurring events (including adolescent drug use): A rejoinder to Martin. *Journal of Personality and Social Psychology, 43,* 604–611.

Huba, G. J., & Hamilton, D. L. (1976). On the generality of trait relationships: Some analyses based on Fiske's paper. *Psychological Bulletin, 83,* 868–876.

Huba, G. J., & Harlow, L. L. (1986). Robust estimation for causal models: A comparison of methods in some developmental datasets. In P. B. Baltes, D. L. Featherman, & R. M. Lerner (Eds.), *Life span development and behavior* (Vol. 6, pp. 69–111). Hillsdale, NJ: Erlbaum.

Huba, G. J., & Harlow, L. L. (1987). Robust structural equation models: Implications for developmental psychology. *Child Development, 58,* 147–166.

Isen, A. M. (1984). Toward understanding the role of affect in cognition. In R. S. Wyer & T. K. Srull (Eds.), *Handbook of social cognition* (pp. 179–236). Hillsdale, NJ: Erlbaum.

Izard, C. E., Kagan, J., & Zajonc, R. E. (Eds.). (1984). *Emotions, cognition, and behavior.* New York: Cambridge University Press.

James, L. R., Mulaik, S. A., & Brett, J. M. (1982). *Causal analysis: Assumptions, models, and data.* Beverly Hills, CA: Sage.

Jöreskog, K. G. (1974). Analyzing psychological data by structural analysis of covariance matrices. In D. H. Krantz, R. C. Atkinson, R. D. Luce, & P. Suppes (Eds.), *Contemporary developments in mathematical psychology: Measurement, psychophysics, and neural information processing* (Vol. 2, pp. 1–56). San Francisco: Freeman.

Jöreskog, K. G., & Sörbom, D. (1988). *LISREL 7: A guide to the program and applications.* Chicago: SPSS.

Judd, C. M., Jessor, R., & Donovan, J. E. (1986). Structural equation models and personality research. *Journal of Personality, 54,* 149–198.

Kenny, D. A. (1979). *Correlation and Causality.* New York: John Wiley.

Kenny, D. A., & Campbell, D. T. (1989). On the measurement of stability in over-time data. *Journal of Personality, 57,* 445–481.

Knowles, E. S. (1988). Item context effects in personality scales: Measuring changes the measure. *Journal of Personality and Social Personality, 55,* 312–320.

La Du, T. J., & Tanaka, J. S. (1989). Influence of sample size, estimation method, and model specification on goodness-of-fit assessment in structural equation models. *Journal of Applied Psychology, 74,* 625–635.

Light, R. J., & Pillemer, D. B. (1984). *Summing up: The science of reviewing research.* Cambridge, MA: Harvard University Press.

Loehlin, J. C. (1987). *Latent variable models.* Hillsdale, NJ: Earlbaum.

Lohmöller, J.-B. (1980). *Latent variable path modeling with partial least squares.* Heidelberg: Physica-Verlag.

Luijben, T., Boomsma, A., & Molenaar, I. (1987). Modification of factor analysis models in covariance structure analysis. *Heymans Bulletins Psychologische Instituten R. U. Groningen* (HB-87-851-EX).

MacCallum, R. (1986). Specification searches in covariance structure modeling. *Psychological Bulletin, 100,* 107–120.

Markus, H., & Zajonc, R. (1985). The cognitive perspective in social psychology. In G. Lindzey & E. Aronson (Eds.), *The handbook of social psychology* (3rd ed., Vol. 1, pp. 137–230). New York: Random House.

Maruyama, G., & McGarvey, B. (1980). Evaluating causal models: An application of maximum-likelihood analysis of structural equations. *Psychological Bulletin, 87,* 502–512.

Matsueda, R. L., & Bielby, W. (1986). Statistical power in covariance structure models. In N. B. Tuma (Ed.), *Sociological methodology 1986* (pp. 120–158). Washington, DC: American Sociological Association.

McArdle, J. J (1988). Dynamic but structural equation modeling of repeated measures data. In J. R. Nesselroade & R. B. Cattell (Eds.), *Handbook of multivariate experimental psychology* (2nd ed., pp. 561–614). New York: Plenum.

McArdle, J. J., & Epstein, D. (1987). Latent growth curves within developmental structural equation models. *Child Development, 58,* 110–133.

Muthén, B. (1984). A general structural equation model with dichotomous, ordered categorical, and continuous latent variable indicators. *Psychometrika, 49,* 115–132.

Muthén, B. O. (1987). *LISCOMP: Analysis of linear structural equations using a comprehensive measurement model – User's guide.* Mooresville, IN: Scientific Software.

Nesselroade, J. R. (1988). Some implications of the trait-state distinction for the study of development over the life span: The case of personality. In P. B. Baltes, D. L. Featherman, & R. M. Lerner (Eds.), *Life-span development and behavior* (Vol. 8, pp. 163–189). Hillsdale, NJ: Erlbaum.

Nesselroade, J. R., & Baltes, P. B. (Eds.). (1979). *Longitudinal research in the study of behavior and development.* New York: Academic Press.

Neuberg, S. L. (1989). The goal of forming accurate impressions during social interactions: Attenuating the impact of negative expectancies. *Journal of Personality and Social Psychology, 56,* 374–386.

Panter, A. T. (1988, June). *Item-level analyses of ordered categorical data: Assessing the structure of dysphoric affect.* Paper presented at the Symposium on Applications of Clustering/Scaling Methods, Classification Society of North America, New York.

Panter, A. T., & Tanaka, J. S. (1987, April). *Statistically appropriate methods for analyzing dichotomous data: Assessing self-monitoring.* Paper presented at the annual meeting of the Eastern Psychological Association, Arlington, VA.

Panter, A. T., Tanaka, J. S., & Waller, N. G. (1989). *Applications of dichotomous variable factor analysis to psychological domains.* Manuscript in preparation.

Patterson, G. R., & Bank, L. (1986). Bootstrapping your way in the nomological thicket. *Behavioral Assessment, 8,* 49–73.

Pervin, L. A. (1985). Personality: Current controversies, issues, and directions. *Annual Review of Psychology, 36,* 83–114.

Petty, R. E., & Cacioppo, J. T. (1986). The elaboration likelihood model of persuasion. In L. Berkowitz (Ed.), *Advances in experimental social psychology* (Vol. 19, pp. 123–205). Orlando, FL: Academic Press.

Reichardt, C. S., & Gollob, H. F. (1986). Satisfying the constraints of causal modeling. In W.M.K. Trochim (Ed.), *Advances in quasi-experimental design and analysis* (pp. 91–106). San Francisco: Jossey-Bass.

Reichardt, C. S., & Gollob, H. F. (1987). Taking uncertainty into account when estimating effects. In M. M. Mark & R. L. Shotland (Eds.), *Multiple methods in program evaluation* (pp. 7–22). San Francisco: Jossey-Bass.

Rogosa D. R., & Willett, J. B. (1985). Satisfying a simplex structure is simpler than it should be. *Journal of Educational Statistics, 10,* 99–107.

Rosenthal, R., & Rosnow, R. L. (1985). *Contrast analysis.* New York: Cambridge University Press.

Saris, W. E., Satorra, A., & Sörbom, D. (1987). The detection and correction of specification errors in structural models. In C. C. Clogg (Ed.), *Sociological methodology 1987* (Vol. 17, pp. 105–129). Washington, DC: American Sociological Association.

Schönemann, P. H., & Steiger, J. H. (1976). Regression component analysis. *British Journal of Mathematical and Statistical Psychology, 29,* 175–189.

Snyder, M. (1987). *Public appearances, private realities: The psychology of self-monitoring.* New York: Freeman.

Snyder, M., & Ickes, W. (1985). Personality and social behavior. In G. Lindzey & E. Aronson (Eds.), *The handbook of social psychology* (3rd ed., Vol. 2, pp. 883–947). New York: Random House.

Sörbom, D. (1974). A general method for studying differences in factor means and factor structure between groups. *British Journal of Mathematical and Statistical Psychology, 27,* 229–239.

Sorrentino, R. M., & Higgins, E. T. (Eds.). (1986). *Handbook of motivation and cognition.* New York: Guilford.

Tanaka, J. S. (1987). "How big is big enough?": Sample size and goodness of fit in structural equation models with latent variables. *Child Development, 58,* 134–146.

Tanaka, J. S. (in press). Measurement of change. In J. Rappaport & E. Seidman (Eds.), *The handbook of community psychology.* New York: Plenum.

Tanaka, J. S., & Bentler, P. M. (1983). Factor invariance of premorbid social competence across multiple populations of schizophrenics. *Multivariate Behavioral Research, 18,* 135–146.

Tanaka, J. S., & Huba, G. J. (1987). Assessing the stability of depression in college students. *Multivariate Behavioral Research, 22,* 5–19.

Tanaka, J. S., Panter, A. T., & Winborne, W. C. (1988). Dimensions of the Need for Cognition: Subscales and gender differences. *Multivariate Behavioral Research, 23,* 35–50.

Taylor, S. E., & Fiske, S. T. (1981). Getting inside the head: Methodologies for process analysis in attribution and social cognition. In J. H. Harvey, W. Ickes, & R. F. Kidd (Eds.), *New directions in attribution research* (Vol. 3, pp. 459–524). Hillsdale, NJ: Erlbaum.

Trope, Y. (1986). Identification and inferential process in dispositional attributions. *Psychological Review, 93,* 239–257.

Uleman, J. S., & Bargh, J. A. (Eds.). (1989). *Unintended thought.* New York: Guilford.

Vasey, M. W., & Thayer, J. F. (1987). The continuing problem of false positives in repeated measures ANOVA in psychophysiology: A multivariate solution. *Psychophysiology, 24,* 479–486.

Willett, J. B. (1988). Questions and answers in the measurement of change. *Review of Research in Education, 15,* 345–422.

Wold, H. (1981). Soft modeling: The basic design and some extensions. In K. G. Jöreskog & H. Wold (Eds.), *Systems under indirect observation II* (pp. 1–54). Amsterdam: North-Holland.

Wood, P. K., & Nesselroade, J. R. (1988, April). *Simultaneous modeling of intra-and inter-individual variation in covariance structures.* Paper presented at the annual meetings of the American Educational Research Association, New Orleans.

Wyer, R. S., Jr., & Srull, T. K. (1986). Human cognition in its social context. *Psychological Review, 93,* 322–359.

Wyer, R. S., Jr., & Srull, T. K. (1989). *Memory and cognition in its social context.* Hillsdale, NJ: Erlbaum.

Zevon, M. A., & Tellegen, A. (1982). The structure of mood change: An idiographic/nomothetic analysis. *Journal of Personality and Social Psychology, 43,* 111–122.

Personal Design in Social Cognition

10

NORMAN H. ANDERSON

Norman H. Anderson is Professor of Psychology, University of California, San Diego. He obtained his Ph.D. at Wisconsin and has taught at Yale, Indiana, and UCLA. His research interests include social cognition, developmental psychology, judgment-decision theory, and psychophysics. He is an inveterate hiker and student of Shakespeare.

This chapter is concerned with *experimental analysis* of *individual persons*. Individuals differ, often sharply, in their attitudes, motivations, and values. However much attitudes, motivations, and values may ultimately derive from society, they exist and function within individual persons; they cannot be well understood except within the experiential framework of the individual.

This basic fact of individual differences lies as a quagmire in the path of psychological science. Three main strategies for navigating this quagmire have been tried. The experimental strategy sought to capitalize on the power of experimental method for causal analysis. The dominant experimental approach, however, was predicated on an assumption about general laws of behavior that would hold across individuals and even across species. Too often, this experimental strategy relied on standard group design that consigned individual differences to the statistical error term, thus burying much that needed study.

The strategy of differential psychology did focus squarely on individual differences, but with methods of correlation and personality tests that have little power for cognitive analysis. Strategies of phenomenology, ranging from the historical school of introspection to case histories in the psychoanalytic tradition and to contemporary action theories, have given primary attention to the person. These strategies are severely limited, however, because much of everyday cognition is not accessible to phenomenological scrutiny. Whereas the dominant experimental approach failed to take adequate account of the individual, phenomenological approaches generally lack the analytical power needed for theory of social cognition.

AUTHOR'S NOTE: Preparation of this chapter was supported in part by Grant PHS HD22932-02. I wish to thank Clyde Hendrick and Richard P. McGlynn for invaluable comments on preliminary drafts.

243

What is needed is a strategy that can combine experimental method with phenomenology. This is the aim of *personal design*, which uses experimental method to study the individual at the individual level. Personal design is defined in ideal form by four properties: experimental design, individual analysis, personal values, and personalized task and/or stimuli. An experiment is thus to be performed on a single person, using a task and/or stimuli chosen to be meaningful within the experiential framework of that person, and the person's data are analyzed in terms of personal values.

The theoretical foundations of personal design are presented in the first section of this chapter. (Alternative approaches to individual design are considered in chapters by Jaccard and Dittus and by Michela in this volume.) A short section on experimental illustrations is then presented, followed by discussion of practical research problems.

THEORETICAL FOUNDATIONS OF PERSONAL DESIGN

Personal design is based on a conceptual approach to cognition that may be characterized as *information integration*. People are assumed to translate stimulus events in the world around them into *information* relative to goal-directed judgment and action. Because several items of information are typically relevant, these must be *integrated* to produce a single judgment. It has been found that people often use algebraic rules for integration, for example, adding or averaging the information. In fact, much of human judgment, even by young children, appears to follow a general *cognitive algebra*. This cognitive algebra has provided a foundation for a unified, general theory of social cognition.

This conceptual approach faces the two fundamental problems noted in the next section. Following this, the topic of blame will be used as a concrete illustration (anticipating two experimental illustrations). A more formal presentation will then be given of *functional measurement,* which provides an effective methodology for cognitive algebra and for personal design.

Two Fundamental Problems

Personal design faces two fundamental problems: *personal values* and *multiple determination*. Individual differences are manifest in people's values. A wife's feelings of affection for her husband differ in many ways from his feelings for her. Moreover, the wife's feelings also differ from those her husband attributes to her. To understand the phenomenal world of the individual, it is necessary to take cognizance of the personal values of that individual.

The second problem, multiple determination, arises because our actions usually depend on several variables. In a mate, we look for appearance, affection, and understanding; these and other variables operate together to determine our marriage satisfaction. Appearance itself is also subject to multiple determination, for "good looks" depends on facial structure, gesture, makeup, grooming, and so forth. Understanding judgment and action cannot get far without capability for handling multiple determination.

Blame Schema

The problem of blame provides a good domain for personal design. Its importance in social/personality theory is clear, for blame is pervasive in everyday life, both in blaming others and avoiding blame ourselves. From a psychological perspective, blame is an intimate component of social/personality structure. From a sociological perspective, blame is part of the continuous policing by which society maintains itself. People are typically open and vocal about blaming and excusing, moreover, which makes them more amenable to personal design.

Blame also brings out the two basic problems: *multiple determination* and *personal values*. Two well-known determinants of blame for some harmful action are the amount of damage and the intent or motivation of the harmdoer. More blame is usually attributed when greater damage is done; more blame may also be attributed when the action stemmed from malice than when it stemmed from carelessness. Other variables may also influence blame, such as social obligation, sex and age of the harmdoer, exhibitions of remorse, and so on. All these variables provide information that is integrated into the overall reaction of blame. To illustrate the essential issues, however, only the two determinants *damage* and *intent* need to be considered.

An example of personal design appears in Leon's (1984) study of blame summarized later in Figure 10.3. Damage and Intent were manipulated in a 3×3 factorial design. Each of the nine cells of the design thus represented the misdeed of a story child with different levels of intent and damage caused. Each person in the experiment made blame judgments for each of the nine story children.

These blame judgments depend on the values of the two determinants, damage and intent. But these values are personal. The mothers considered a broken window more serious than a broken pot, whereas their sons considered the two about equally serious. Any two mothers, moreover, will generally differ in their attribution of intent. Personal design aims to analyze the blame judgments within the personal value system of each mother and each son.

In a symbolic way, the problem of blame may be written:

$$\text{Blame} = I(\text{Damage, Intent})$$

where I stands for the integration function, and Damage and Intent are two variables to be integrated to yield a judgment of blame. This symbolism makes clear a basic problem for theory of blame attribution, namely, to determine the nature of the integration function. Because the integration function defines how the person organizes the task and the stimulus field, it is called a *schema* (Anderson, 1978, in press-f).

Consider the hypothesis of a simple addition schema:

$$\text{Blame} = \text{Damage} + \text{Intent}$$

This equation will be called the basic blame schema. The first problem, of course, is how to test whether blame attribution really does follow this addition schema.

The obvious approach to testing the blame schema is to measure the three terms and check whether Damage plus Intent add up to equal Blame. But this direct approach faces formidable difficulties, and it has rarely succeeded. Among other difficulties, it requires linear (equal interval) scales of the personal values of the three terms for each individual subject in the experiment.

Fortunately, a solution is available under certain conditions with *functional measurement theory*. Functional measurement can provide a rigorous test of the blame schema with exact allowance for the personal values of the blamer. This test is simple. It may be applied to many other questions. Most important, this functional measurement approach has had substantial empirical success.

Functional Measurement Theory

Two measurement problems. Measuring personal values is actually a twofold problem, an important distinction that may be explained with the integration diagram of Figure 10.1. Between the field of stimulus information, at the left of the diagram, and the overt response, at the right, lie three stages of processing: *valuation*, *integration*, and *action*. In the valuation stage, the actual stimulus variables, denoted by capital S, are processed for meaning and value relative to the operative goal. This valuation processing yields their subjective representations, denoted by lowercase s. In the integration stage, these several subjective stimuli are integrated to yield an implicit response, denoted by lowercase r. Finally, in the action stage, the implicit response is transformed into an overt response, denoted by capital R.

In terms of the blame schema, s_1 would be stimulus information about the harmful consequences of the action and s_2 would be information about the intentions of the harmdoer. These are the objective stimuli, which are evaluated to yield the corresponding personal values, s_1 and s_2, or s_{Damage} and s_{Intent}. The integration of these personal values yields the implicit feeling of blame, r, with R being the observable blaming response.

In this notation, the blame schema may be written:

$$r = s_{Damage} + s_{Intent}$$

This equation makes clear that there are two measurement problems, one for stimuli, the other for the response. On the stimulus side, personal values must be allowed for the stimulus information about damage and intent. On the response side, the overt blaming response, R, should be a veridical measure of r, which denotes the implicit feeling of blame.

The importance of response measurement may be illustrated with the common rating method. Ratings are subject to well-known biases that may distort underlying feelings. On a 20-point scale, for example, the psychological difference between 10 and 11, in the middle of the scale, may be rather less than the psychological difference between 18 and 19, near the end of the scale. If each unit interval on the rating scale corresponds to an equal difference on the underlying psychological dimension, then the observable R is a veridical, linear measure of r. If this linear (equal-interval) property can be established, the observable response will provide a veridical picture of the unobservable cognition. The linearity property thus provides a key to cognitive analysis and a base for personal design. How this linearity property can be established is illustrated with the following parallelism theorem.

Parallelism theorem. The parallelism theorem provides a simple way to solve the two measurement problems just discussed. To illustrate, consider a 3 × 3, Intent × Damage design. The three Intent stimuli are denoted by I1,

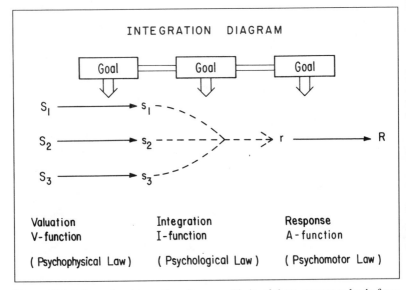

Figure 10.1 Information integration diagram. Chain of three operators leads from observable stimulus field, $\{S_i\}$, to observable response, R. Valuation operator, V, transforms observable stimuli, S_i, into subjective representations, s_i. Integration operator, I, transforms subjective stimulus field $\{s_i\}$, into implicit response, r. Action operator, A, transforms implicit response, r, into observable response, R. Adapted from N. H. Anderson, *Foundations of information integration theory.* Copyright 1981 Academic Press. Used by permission.

I2, and I3; the three Damage stimuli are denoted by D1, D2, and D3. One person is asked to judge blame for the nine Intent-Damage combinations in the nine cells of this 3×3 design.

The theoretical hypothesis is that the person follows the addition schema for blame. If this hypothesis is true, this person's judgments will exhibit a *pattern of parallelism* when plotted as a factorial graph. This parallelism property may be seen in Table 10.1, which list the theoretical responses predicted by the addition schema. The nine entries correspond to the nine cells of the 3×3 design; each entry is the sum of a row value, for Intent, and a column value, for Damage. These theoretical values exhibit a critical pattern: *The row differences are constant across columns.* In the first column, subtracting the bottom from the top row yields $(s_{I1} + s_{D1}) - (s_{I3} + s_{D1}) = s_{I1} - s_{I3}$. In the second column, also, $(s_{I1} + s_{D2}) - (s_{I3} + s_{D2}) = s_{I1} - s_{I3}$, and similarly for the third column. In short, the addition schema implies constant row differences, *regardless of what the personal values may be* (Anderson, 1981, Section 1.2). In graphical form, constant row differences is equivalent to parallelism; hence the term *parallelism property.*

In practice, of course, we observe only nine numbers, that is, the nine blame judgments. But if the nine numbers are generated by an additive process, then they must exhibit parallelism. If the hypothesized blame schema holds, therefore, then the nine blame judgments must exhibit parallelism. Thus the property of parallelism provides a diagnostic test of the additive rule. This test is made directly on the raw response; prior knowledge of the personal values of the stimuli is not needed because they are automatically taken into account in the parallelism.

There is, however, one important problem that has been slurred over. If the blame schema is correct, then the parallelism property will hold for the implicit feeling of blame, r. But what we observe is the overt response, R. It is straightforward to show that the parallelism property will also hold for R if it is measured on a linear (equal-interval) scale, that is, if R is a linear function of r.

In practice, therefore, the situation is this. We hypothesize that some judgment, such as blame, obeys an addition schema. We test a person with what we hope is a linear (equal-interval) response scale. If these observed responses exhibit parallelism, we take this as joint support for the joint hypothesis of an additive integration schema and a linear response.

Observed parallelism is not mathematical proof of the addition schema, but it is very strong evidence. If the underlying schema is nonadditive, then the data will generally be nonparallel—certainly so if the response scale is linear. If the response scale is not linear, then the data will generally be nonparallel—certainly so if the underlying schema is additive. It is logically possible, of course, that nonadditivity in the integration schema just cancels nonlinearity in the response to yield net parallelism. Subject to this reservation, however, observed parallelism is strong support for additivity and linearity taken together.

One additional implication of the parallelism theorem is notable: It provides linear (equal interval) scales of the personal stimulus values. These are just the *marginal means* of the factorial data table (Anderson, 1981, Section 1.2.3; see the discussion of Figure 10.2 below). In this way, it is possible to solve both problems of measurement, stimulus as well as response. This provides the personal values of the individual.

TABLE 10.1 Parallelism Theorem Illustrated

	D1	D2	D3
I1	$s_{I1} + s_{D1}$	$s_{I1} + s_{D2}$	$s_{I1} + s_{D3}$
I2	$s_{I2} + s_{D1}$	$s_{I2} + s_{D2}$	$s_{I2} + s_{D3}$
I3	$s_{I3} + s_{D1}$	$s_{I3} + s_{D2}$	$s_{I3} + s_{D3}$

Numerical example. A numerical example of parallelism analysis using hypothetical data is shown in Figure 10.2. The task was to judge how much a story child should be blamed for throwing a rock that injured another boy. Intention of the story child was varied across three levels: *carelessness*, intent to *scare*, and intent to *harm*. The damage was also varied across three levels: *bruised shin*, *bloody nose*, and *black eye*.

The factorial graph for Person C. H. is shown at the left of Figure 10.2. The three points on the top curve, labeled *harm*, show the blame assigned to the three story children who threw the rock with deliberate intention of harming the other child. These three points show how assignment of blame depended on the level of damage, which is listed on the horizontal axis. Thus C. H. considers bloody nose substantially worse than bruised shin, but considers black eye the same as bloody nose.

The middle curve, labeled *scare*, shows the blame assigned the three story children who only intended to scare the other child, not actually hit him with the rock. The *scare* curve lies considerably below the *harm* curve, considerably above the *careless* curve; thus C. H. considers intent to scare considerably more blamable than carelessness yet considerably less blamable than intent to harm. Still, the three points on each curve exhibit the same effects of the levels of harm already noted for the top curve.

The critical feature of the factorial graph for C. H. is that the three curves are parallel. This implies, by virtue of the parallelism theorem, that C. H. assigns blame using the addition schema. Exactly the same applies to the factorial graph for R. P. McG. at the right of Figure 10.2. These three curves are also parallel, which implies that R. P. McG. also assigns blame by using the addition schema.

However, the factorial graphs for the two persons do look rather different. This difference in appearance reflects their different personal values. To see the differences in personal values for harm, compare the shape of the *careless* curve between the two persons. For C. H., bloody nose and black

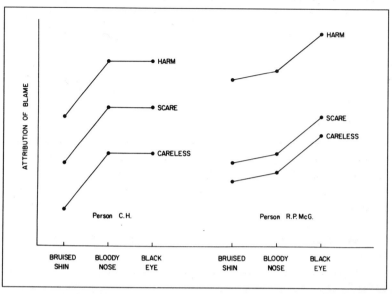

Figure l0.2. Hypothetical data to illustrate parallelism analysis. The three curves in each factorial graph represent one person's assigments of blame for nine story children, specified by a 3 × 3, Intent × Damage design. The parallelism in each factorial graph shows that both persons followed the same addition schema, Blame = Intent + Damage. The different shapes of the two graphs reflect differences in personal values of Intent and Damage.

eye are equally bad, as reflected in the flat right-hand segment of the curve, and both are much worse than bruised shin. If these were real data, one would suspect that C. H. considers head injury much more serious than injury elsewhere on the body. For R. P. McG., on the other hand, the difference between bruised shin and bloody nose is small, whereas black eye is much worse. If these were real data, one might speculate that R. P. McG. thought about the possibility of long-term damage to the eye.

Personal values for intent are also different. These are shown by the relative elevations of the three curves. For R. P. McG., the *scare* curve is rather close to the *careless* curve and far below the *harm* curve. These relative elevations means that R. P. McG. considers deliberate intent to harm

very blamable, but considers intent to scare only a little worse than carelessness. For C. H., in contrast, the *scare* curve lies midway between the other
two; this implies that the difference in blame value between *harm* and *scare*
equals the difference in blame value between *scare* and *careless*.

The personal values just discussed are measurable on true linear (equal-
interval) scales for each person separately. This follows from the parallelism
theorem. Hence the elevations of the three points on each curve are a linear
scale of the blame values for the Damage variable; these elevations mirror
the *marginal means* of the factorial design. Similarly, the relative elevations
among the three curves are a linear scale of the blame values for the Intent
variable. This illustrates how personal design can establish nomothetic laws
of behavior that allow for—and measure—idiographic values.

Functional measurement. The functional measurement procedure just
illustrated with Figure 10.2 solves the two measurement problems already
discussed in relation to Figure 10.1: measurement of the stimuli and measurement of the response. This can be done for the individual person. The
parallelism analysis may be applied to a single person's data. The stimulus
values are that person's own values of Intent and Damage; the response is
that person's own attribution of Blame. Where personal design is practicable, therefore, functional measurement offers a unique analytical method.

The logic of functional measurement rests on the integration function.
This logic makes psychological measurement an organic component of substantive inquiry. In the blame experiment, measurement of the personal values of Intent, Damage and Blame ultimately rests on nothing more than the
algebraic structure of the blame schema. Measurement is thus accomplished
as an integral part of investigating the attribution of blame.

Functional measurement inverts the customary view, epitomized in
Thurstonian paired comparisons, which sees measurement as a methodological preliminary to substantive inquiry. The customary view seems natural, for it takes the first step to be stimulus measurement, much as in physical
science. The functional measurement view, in contrast, may seem strange,
for it makes measurement derivative from the integration function. Because
of this difference in direction of approach, Thurstonian scaling theory,
among others, has neglected the fundamental problem of multiple determination, and has not really solved the measurement problem (see Anderson,
1981, Section 5.3).

Functional measurement is well grounded empirically. Some illustrations appear in the later empirical studies. More general discussion of the
measurement logic, together with empirical applications in many areas of

psychology, are given in Anderson (1981, chaps. 1, 5). Experimental procedure, design, statistical analysis, and estimation are treated in Anderson (1982).

Cognitive algebra. The logic used in the parallelism theorem may be extended to other algebraic rules. Subtraction rules, of course, also imply parallelism, since subtraction is just adding a negative value. The other basic algebraic operation, namely, multiplication, implies a factorial graph with a linear fan pattern, as does a division rule. In general, inspection of the factorial graph can often reveal the underlying integration process in a transparent way, as illustrated below with Figure 10.3.

Cognitive algebra has provided a unifying framework for a cognitive theory of everyday life. Algebraic rules are common throughout the social/personality domain: person cognition, moral judgment, attribution of cause and of blame, attitudes and stereotypes, and group dynamics. Cognitive algebra has also been prominent in other domains: judgment-decision theory, psychophysics, intuitive statistics, and developmental psychology. The same theoretical perspective has been useful across all these areas.

There is much more in the mind than cognitive algebra, of course, especially the knowledge systems considered below. Objections to cognitive algebra are discussed in Anderson (1982, Section 7.1). The main value of cognitive algebra, however, is perhaps less in the intrinsic interest of algebraic cognition than in qualitative, conceptual implications of these algebraic rules. One implication of an algebraic rule is that the conceptual terms of the rule are true cognitive entities. The argument is that an exact addition rule, for example, would be unlikely unless the terms being added were not merely correlated with cognition but had an exact correspondence. Thus the empirical success of the blame schema confers a measure of construct validity on the concepts of Blame, Intent, and Damage. Cognitive algebra thus begins the process of transforming vague verbalisms of everyday life into exact scientific concepts. In this and other ways, cognitive algebra is a tool for cognitive analysis.

Averaging theory. One algebraic rule requires special comment, namely, the ubiquitous averaging rule. The blame schema, strictly speaking, involves an averaging process. Damage and Intent are averaged to yield Blame, not added or summed. In fact, most addition rules in social judgment have actually turned out to be averaging rules. This averaging-adding issue is tangential to this chapter, however, and will be passed by with two somewhat technical comments.

First, averaging differs from adding in that averaging produces parallelism only under the *equal weighting* condition, which requires that all the levels of any one factor be equally important, that is, have equal weight. In some situations, however, different levels of a stimulus factor will have unequal importance, and such *differential weighting* is not uncommon (Anderson, 1981, Section 4.4). For example, more negative stimulus levels sometimes have greater weight, the well-known negativity effect. Differential weighting produces systematic deviations from parallelism. This nonparallelism is related to the importance weights, however, and so is predictable from averaging theory. Indeed, it was the inability of adding and summation rules to account for predictable nonparallelism that led to their demise (Anderson, 1981, Section 1.6). Averaging theory, in contrast, provided a unified account of both parallelism and nonparallelism.

The basic blame schema follows an averaging rule with equal weighting for intent and for damage. Hence it yields parallelism, as illustrated below in Figure 10.4. The variable of recompense, however, involves differential weighting and so yields nonparallelism (Hommers & Anderson, 1988, in press). For simplicity, however, the basic blame schema will be referred to as an addition schema in this chapter.

A remarkable property of the averaging rule is that it can yield valid comparisons of qualitatively different variables. In the blame schema, Intent and Damage are qualitatively different, yet the averaging rule can measure both on a common scale. The personal value of a given level of Intent may thus be measured and compared with the personal value of a given level of Damage. Similarly, the relative importance of Intent and Damage can be measured. Measurement of relative importance is a subtle, elusive problem. Most current methods have severe conceptual flaws. The *b*-weights from regression analysis, for example, are confounded with the units of their corresponding values scales, and so are not generally valid measures of psychological importance (see Anderson, 1982, chap. 6; Anderson & Zalinski, 1988). Averaging theory can provide valid measures of relative importance.

Knowledge Systems and Values

The conceptual base for personal design includes the concept of *knowledge systems*. These are organized informational structures, such as attitudes, stereotypes, and roles. Such knowledge systems have a primary function in the valuation operation of Figure 10.1. Thus each member of a dating couple continually evaluates the speech and actions of the other member, as well as of the self. These evaluations are mediated by their attitudes toward gracious living, for example, by their stereotypes about the place of women in the family, and by their role systems for interaction.

It is important, therefore, to distinguish between a knowledge system and its functional manifestations in judgment and action. Most theories of attitudes define attitude as a one-dimensional evaluative response (see Anderson, 1988). This definition closes the door to cognitive theory. Considered as a knowledge system, an attitude is more complex and qualitatively different from the various attitudinal judgments it subserves. Cognitive algebra focuses on one-dimensional responses, but it does not stop there. It aims to use such one-dimensional responses as a tool for analysis of knowledge systems (Anderson, in press-b).

This same view applies to personality traits, which are also considered knowledge systems. The trait of honesty, for example, is considered a functional system that helps guide one's behavior in diverse social situations. Although reducing this system to a crude, one-dimensional trait score may have practical utility, such reduction should not be confused with the concept of honesty as a knowledge system, which recognizes that "honest" behavior depends on the situation.

Nomothetic-Idiographic Unity

Personal design combines the nomothetic approach, which seeks general laws of behavior, with the idiographic approach, which emphasizes uniqueness of the individual.

The nomothetic approach seeks for regularities across individuals, whereas the idiographic approach seeks for meaningfulness within individuals. Nomothetic studies are typically oriented toward analysis of stimulus effects and often take average responses across individuals as primary data. Idiographic studies are typically oriented toward individual dynamics. Those who employ the nomothetic approach tend to view it as the proper scientific way; those who advocate the idiographic approach tend to view it as the only meaningful psychological way.

Integration theory combines both nomothetic and idiographic approaches. The valuation operation allows for individual differences, including the multitude of hereditary, environmental, and chance factors that make one individual different from another. Furthermore, it emphasizes person-environment interaction, especially as a determinant of the response dimension and the valuation operation. Nevertheless, regularities across individuals may still be expected, particularly in the form of the integration operation. Individual differences then appear in the parameters of the integration rule. (Anderson, 1981, p. 92)

The logic of this joint nomothetic-idiographic approach was given in the discussion of Figure 10.2. An empirical example appears below in the discussion of a study of wife-husband similarity presented in Figure 10.4: Nearly all 40 persons exhibited the parallelism pattern, which indicates generality of the blame integration schema across persons; these same persons, however, showed extreme individual differences in their moral values. The integration analysis demonstrated the nomothetic generality of the integration rule at the same time that it measured the idiographic differences of value.

A similar rule-value distinction applies to within-person generality. Each individual will exhibit an idiographic complexity of values, because values depend on situations and goals. Yet some nomothetic generality of integration rules across situations may be expected. Here again, idiographic values and nomothetic rules go hand in hand in the theoretical analysis.

Cognitive Theory of Everyday Life

The theory of information integration seeks to explain everyday feeling and thinking in something like their own terms. Integration theory differs from most phenomenological approaches, however, in requiring more than phenomenological validity. Phenomenology is not enough, as shown by its obstinate failures in the meaning constancy investigations in person cognition (Anderson, 1981, chap. 3; Hendrick & Costantini, 1970). In person cognition, cognitive algebra was a key to understanding phenomenology.

Cognitive algebra can help in constructing a cognitive theory of everyday life. The terms of an algebraic rule are typically everyday concepts, as in the foregoing blame schema. But the valuation and integration processes are often not conscious. Analysis of these valuation and integration processes is essential for theory of everyday life. In this, cognitive algebra has had some success.

The focus on everyday life leads to a *functional perspective* on cognition that complements mainstream cognitive theory in four major ways. First, the goal-oriented character of everyday life requires a conception of functional memory, which is quite different from the traditional concept of reproductive memory (Anderson, 1981, Section 4.2, 1989, in press-b). Second, mainstream cognitive theory emphasizes molecular structure, as epitomized in the many studies of letter-word recognition, but says little about molar concepts of everyday life, as epitomized in the blame schema (Anderson, in press-d; Hommers & Anderson, 1988, in press). Moreover, cognitive algebra has provided the only definite and exact analysis of the recently popular but elusive concept of schemas, especially in attribution theory (Anderson, in press-f). Finally, affect and emotion, which have received inhospitable indifference in mainstream cognitive theory, are treated as signal information about goals in the theory of information integration, subject to the same processes of valuation and integration as nonaffective information.

EXPERIMENTAL ILLUSTRATIONS OF PERSONAL DESIGN

Personal design is still in process of development. The three studies reviewed here were only partly personalized, but each one illustrates some problems of method and analysis that need consideration.

Mother-Son Similarity with Factorial Design

Seven-year-old boys follow the same blame schema as their mothers (Leon, 1984). Individual analyses of the mothers' factorial graphs revealed three subgroups, characterized by different forms of the blame schema. The three corresponding subgroups of sons showed similar blame schemas. This novel approach to social learning may be extended to study many aspects of family life.

Schema analysis. The design of Leon's experiment may be seen in the top left panel of Figure 10.3. Mothers judged blame for story children in a 3 × 3, Intent × Damage design, with the intent and damage information given in simple, declarative form. Each curve represents one level of intent, ranging from malice (M) to accident (A), as labeled by each curve. The three points on each curve represent the three levels of damage listed on the horizontal axis, namely, no damage, broken pot, or broken window.

Each mother's data were analyzed individually to determine her personal integration rule. For 18 mothers, the factorial graphs showed a pattern of parallelism. This pattern points to an Intent + Damage schema, by virtue of the parallelism theorem. The pooled data for these 18 mothers are shown in the top left panel of Figure 10.3. Their 18 sons also followed the addition schema: Their data, in the top right panel, also show parallelism.

Similar mother-son correspondence is visible in the two factorial graphs of the middle panel. In the mothers' data, at the middle left, the flatness of the lowest curve means that constant blame was assigned when damage was accidental, regardless of amount of damage. Nonaccidental damage, in

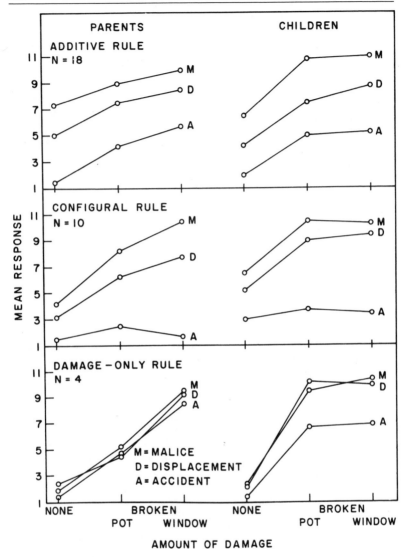

Figure 10.3.   Mothers and sons use same schemas for integrating intent and damage information in judging blame. Accident and Malice refer to accidental and purposive damage; Displacement refers to displaced anger. The response was a judgment of deserved punishment, here interpreted as blame, although the two would not generally be equivalent. From Manuel Leon, "Rules Mothers and Sons Use to Integrate Intent and Damage Information in Their Moral Judgments," *Child Development*, 1984, 55, p. 2109. Reprinted by permission.

contrast, was averaged with the intent, as shown by the parallelism of the two upper curves. This pattern is called the *accident-configural schema*; it was found in the individual analyses for 10 mothers. What is notable is that the factorial graph for their 10 sons also shows the same accident-configural schema.

The final group of 4 mothers followed a damage-only schema, ignoring intent and judging on damage alone. This schema is clear in the nearly identical intent curves in the bottom left. Their 4 sons followed the same schema, although the graphic correspondence in the bottom right is marred by a non-significant effect of intent.

This integration analysis reveals the mother-son similarity despite differences in values. All three groups of mothers considered a broken window more serious than a broken pot, as Figure 10.3 shows, whereas all three groups of sons considered the two about equally serious. Functional measurement could assess the similarity in integration process because it allowed for differences in personal values.

Personal design. Leon's design is personalized in terms of values, design, and data analysis. Each mother served in three replications of the 3×3 design and a separate analysis of variance was done for each mother, with a personal error term based on 18 *df*. The Intent × Damage interaction tests deviations from parallelism, and so constitutes a test of the addition schema. Thus each of the 18 mothers in the main subgroup had significant main effects of Intent and Damage and a nonsignificant interaction (see the section on individual analysis, below).

This schema analysis automatically allows for personal values of each mother. They may all have different values for the intent information. Such value differences would appear as differences in the vertical spacing among the three curves in their personal factorial graphs, but would not affect parallelism. Similarly, differences in values for the damage information would affect the shape of the curves, but not the property of parallelism. This follows the logic already illustrated with Figure 10.2.

Socialization interpretation. The mother-son similarity is considered to originate in family socialization. The mother-son similarity is only correlational, of course, but the patterning in the schema structure points to a causal relation. Although it is possible that mother and son both derived their schemas from some environmental influence, the causal interpretation seems solid enough to warrant more extensive study of schema similarity and how it might be transmitted from parent to child.

Family socialization is hard to study because its effects accumulate gradually over long periods. Personal design, as Leon's experiment illustrates, may be able to provide revealing assessments of long-term socialization processes with short-term experiments. This represents a novel conjunction of correlational and experimental method. For further work, it would seem desirable to construct batteries of judgment tasks to study social development across a spectrum of moral-social judgments. Such batteries would facilitate study of single families with personal design.

Wife-Husband Similarity with Factorial Design

This example, part of work on attitudinal influence within the family (Anderson & Armstrong, 1989), illustrates functional measurement of value similarity between wife and husband. A 3×4, Intent $\times$ Damage design was used, similar to that already discussed in Figures 10.2 and 10.3, with situations selected to reflect realistic child-rearing problems. Wife and husband made separate judgments of how much discipline should be given the story child.

Individual analyses showed that nearly every person used the addition schema. This simplified the analysis of value similarity, which was assessed in two ways. In the first assessment the husbands were dichotomized according to whether intent or damage had the greater main effect. The factorial graphs for these two subgroups are shown in the two left panels of Figure 10.4. Both graphs show the parallelism pattern, but with different values. In the top left panel, the curves are steep, signifying large effects of damage, and close together, signifying small effects of intent. The opposite effects appear in the bottom left panel, where the curves are flat and far apart. These differences represent stable individual differences in personal values among the 20 husbands.

The key question concerns the two corresponding subgroups of wives. If their moral values are similar to those of their husbands, their factorial graphs will show similar patterns. This is indeed the case, as shown at the right of Figure 10.4. The top three curves are steep and close together; the bottom curves are flat and far apart. That the differences seem less pronounced for wives than for husbands merely represents a statistical regression effect. The moral values are visible in the factorial graph, in terms of the steepness of the curves and the spread between them; this is a graphic portrayal of value similarity and difference.

The success of the parallelism property justifies calculation of a moral ratio, defined as Intent/(Intent + Damage), based on the main effects of the two variables. In terms of Figure 10.4, Intent was measured as the vertical distance between the *harm* and *careless* curves in each person's data; Dam-

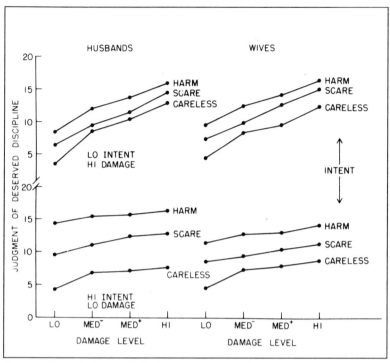

Figure 10.4. Attitude similarity between husband and wife. Husbands dichotomized on moral ratio; upper and lower left panels plot mean factorial graphs for 7 and 13 husbands with moral ratios less than and greater than 0.5, respectively. Right panels for corresponding groups of wives. Lo damage is actually no damage. From N. H. Anderson & M. A. Armstrong, "Cognitive Theory and Methodology for Studying Marital Interaction," in D. Brinberg & J. Jaccard (Eds.), *Dyadic decision making*. New York: Springer-Verlag. Reprinted by permission.

age was measured similarly by the net vertical rise of a single curve. These moral ratios ranged from .00 to .97 and were highly reliable. The wife-husband similarity of Figure 10.4 is reflected in the correlation between their moral ratios, $r(19) = .56$, $p < .01$. Although this ratio index requires theoretical justification (Anderson, in press-a), it should be useful for studying value similarities and differences within single families and other groups.

Wife-Husband Influence with Multiple-Item Design

A *multiple-item design* that allows assessment of mutual influence within individual couples and that is simpler than the foregoing method of factorial design is illustrated in the following study of wife-husband influence. Also of interest in this study is the technique of information priming, which induced an initial difference between the spouses as a baseline from which their mutual influence could be measured.

Wife and husband each received a list of personality traits about a hypothetical man, whom they rated on desirability as a next-door neighbor. The descriptions were somewhat different for wife and husband, an information priming manipulation that was rationalized in the instructions with the statement that similar differences in available information would be common in everyday life. In one part of the experiment, both wrote paragraphs describing the man in their own words, then exchanged paragraphs and rerated the man (see Anderson, in press-a). In another part, which is of concern here, they simply exchanged their initial ratings and rerated. There were 36 such descriptions, with trait information balanced across spouses.

The response measure was a change score: how much wife and husband changed their initial ratings under the influence of the spouse's rating. For each description, the husband's change score was subtracted from the wife's change score to yield a wife-husband difference. This difference will have zero true mean if wife and husband have equal influence on each other. Hence its sign and size measure relative influence of wife on husband and husband on wife. For each couple, accordingly, a *t*-test was run on the 36 difference scores. Of 11 couples, 3 showed highly significant differences and 3 others approached significance. The wife changed more than the husband in 5 of these 6 cases; in the sixth case, the husband changed more than the wife on 34 of 36 descriptions.

Later work has used multiple-item design with more realistic forms of wife-husband interaction and across different kinds of judgments (Anderson & Armstrong, 1989). These results indicate that relative influence depends on the kind of judgment task, a result that points to a need to develop more extensive task batteries to map out the webs of intracouple influence and negotiation.

RESEARCH CONSIDERATIONS IN PERSONAL DESIGN

Individual analysis has been a central theme in the theory of information integration. Considerable effort has been devoted to methodological problems that arise with individual analysis (see Anderson, 1962, 1981, 1982). Much of this methodological work applies to the practical problems of personal design that are discussed in the following sections. For simplicity, most of the discussion will refer to factorial designs. Alternatives to factorial design include the multiple-item design just discussed and the method considered in the section below on self-estimation. It will also be assumed that the person does not change systematically during the experiment, an assumption discussed below in the section on statistical issues.

Data Analysis and Presentation

Individual analysis. The basic problem for personal design concerns analysis of data for single persons. Standard analysis of variance is widely applicable for this purpose in accord with the following rationale. When more than one replication of the design is presented, as is ordinarily done for individual analysis, each design cell contains several responses, corresponding to the several replications. The responses within each cell are treated as independent scores, so the differences among them represent natural response variability. This variability, pooled over design cells, provides the error term for all main effects and interactions. Formally, this is identical with standard independent groups analysis, as though each response were contributed by a different person. Analysis of variance for each individual may thus be obtained using standard calculations or computer programs.

In Leon's mother-son study, for present illustration, individual analyses of variance were performed for each mother. Each mother in the largest subgroup was characterized by significant main effects for damage and intent and a nonsignificant interaction. By virtue of the parallelism theorem, therefore, these mothers were diagnosed as following the addition schema. The mothers in the smallest, damage-only subgroup were characterized by the solitary significant main effect for damage. The mothers in the "accident-configural" subgroup were characterized partly by significant effects for damage, intent, and their interaction, partly by visual inspection. The significant interaction could result from many different integration rules, of course, and visual inspection was used to classify them into a single subgroup. All three integration rules, it may be noted, had been found in previous work by Leon.

Such individual analysis of variance has been standard procedure in the work on information integration theory. It depends on the assumption that the person does not change systematically over the course of the experiment. This assumption seems appropriate for many experiments on social judgment, although preliminary practice may be important to establish a stable frame of reference (see the section below on instruction and practice).

One aspect of procedure is important in justifying such individual analysis: The design treatments should be presented in different orders on successive replications. The order may be random or partly balanced, as in the use of one random order for the first replication and the reverse order for the second. Ordinarily, this procedure will largely balance out possible order or carryover effects (Anderson, 1982, Section 1.3.2) that might arise from shifts in stimulus valuation, rating scale usage, and so on.

Group analysis. Data may be analyzed at a group level with standard repeated measurements analysis of variance. Persons (= subjects) is treated as a random factor, in order to allow statistical generalization across persons. Each main effect and interaction from the basic design thus has its own error term, namely, its interaction with persons. Only one replication per person is required. This analysis has extensions to include different groups of persons, wives and husbands, for example, as a between-subjects variable.

Such group analysis provides a simple, compact summary of the data. It may be useful for a preliminary overview or as a summary after individual analysis has revealed similarity of response pattern. In the wife-husband study of Figure 10.4, for example, the individual analyses showed near-parallelism for nearly all persons, so a group analysis was performed as a convenient summary statistic.

Subgroups of persons may be treated similarly. In Leon's mother-son study, the classification into the three subgroups of Figure 10.3 was based on individual analyses of the mothers because their data were more reliable than the sons' data. In addition, a group analysis was performed for each subgroup of mothers. In the main subgroup, in particular, the Intent × Damage interaction was nonsignificant when tested against the Intent × Damage × Mother interaction. This group analysis is sensitive to small deviations from parallelism that are systematic across mothers, and so constitutes auxiliary support for the addition schema.

Data presentation. Individual analysis generally produces a plethora of graphs and tables that must usually be condensed for public presentation. The simplest case is when most persons exhibit similar patterns, as with the wife-husband study of Figure 10.4. A group graph might then be presented alone, supplemented by any needed verbal qualification about individual deviations from the mean pattern. At the other extreme, with large individual differences, it may be possible to present graphs for a few individuals, selected to be more or less representative of the group. Examples of both cases are cited next.

In an early application of individual analysis in person cognition (Anderson, 1962), each of 12 persons was run five sessions and their data were analyzed individually to test an averaging rule. All persons showed near-parallelism, although the deviations were statistically significant for two or three. The data presented in Anderson (1981, Sections 1.2.1, 2.2.1) include graphs for two individuals, a group graph, and an analysis of variance table for the 12 individuals.

In a study of date ratings by Shanteau and Nagy (1979), each of 12 women judged male photographs on three dimensions: physical attractiveness, likelihood the male would go out with her, and desirability as a date. The theoretical hypothesis was a multiplication rule: Desirability = Likelihood × Attractiveness, which was well supported at the individual level. But although the women followed the same integration rule, they attached quite different values to the photographs, so their graphs had quite different shapes. A group graph would have been essentially meaningless, therefore, and graphs for three selected individuals were presented (see Anderson, 1981, Figure 1.24), together with some summary group statistics.

A third tactic is to classify individuals into subgroups and present graphs for each subgroup. In Leon's mother-son study of Figure 10.3, for example, the 64 individuals graphs were condensed into 6 graphs for the three subgroups of mothers and sons. In the wife-husband influence study of Figure 10.4, similarly, the 40 individual graphs were condensed into 4 graphs for the two subgroups, of wives and husbands.

Subgrouping. Classifying individuals into subgroups, or *subgrouping*, is often a major concern of personal design. Two primary modes of subgrouping are in terms of integration rule and in terms of value.

Subgrouping in terms of integration was shown in Figure 10.3, in which the 32 mothers fell neatly into three subgroups with distinct, well-defined integration rules. An important feature of this example, as already noted, is that the mother-son similarity could be revealed despite the differences in values. This analysis illustrates the joint nomothetic-idiographic capability of functional measurement.

Subgrouping in terms of value was illustrated in Figure 10.4 on wife-husband similarity, which found large individual differences in the moral ratio. These differences lie on a continuum, of course, but dichotomization allowed a simple graphic display of wife-husband similarity of value — together with the generality of the integration rule.

Subgrouping sometimes has a post hoc element. With a small data base, apparent subgroupings may represent merely chance configurations in the data. The danger decreases with larger designs and with more replications. Even with a 3 × 4 design with two replications, it is unlikely that parallelism would be observed unless the true data were nearly parallel. The main problems come with borderline or nonclassifiable cases, which, unfortunately, have no easy resolution.

Development psychology is a prime area for subgrouping as a means to exhibit developmental trends. The common tactic of grouping by age can mask sometimes substantial differences in development among same-age individuals. Although many fewer data are typically obtainable with children than adults, individual child analysis has yielded good results in a number of studies, as already illustrated in Leon's work. Two instructive examples are Dozier and Butzin (1988) and Mullet and Vidal (1986).

Statistical issues. The statistical assumptions of the analysis of variance seem generally well satisfied in personal design. Nonnormality and heterogeneity of variance mainly stem from individual differences, which are absent in individual analysis. Repeated measurements analysis of group data requires a stronger homogeneity assumption and may be less robust owing to individual differences. For the kinds of studies previously illustrated, however, there seems little reason for concern over statistical assumptions. It should also be recognized that the pattern in the factorial graph, which is often the main concern, is independent of normality and homogeneity conditions.

The foregoing discussion of individual analysis assumed that systematic changes of the individual during the experiment were not a serious problem. Some studies, however, may show substantial systematic changes within or between replications. Over multiple sessions with a snake phobic, for example, fairly rapid adaptation might occur initially in each session, together with systematic changes across sessions. The rapid adaptation could be handled with preliminary warm-up trials, perhaps in a separate small design to study the adaptation itself. Changes across sessions could be handled by including sessions as a regular factor in the design, so its main effect and interactions could be assessed (see also Anderson, 1982, p.64). An error term might be obtained by using more than one replication within each session or by pooling higher-order interactions. There are other ways to handle systematic changes in behavior with personal design, but this issue cannot be pursued here.

The persons should ordinarily be told that the same stimulus items may be presented a number of times; that some variability in response is natural and expected; and that they should not try to remember their previous response, but just give their impressions as they see them at the time. A graphic scale may help avoid possible memory effects from a 1–7 type scale. Memory effects can be tested by comparing variability between successive pairs of replications, as in Anderson (1962; see also Anderson, 1982, Section 1.3.3). There is no evidence of any problem in work to date, but the matter should be considered in any new application.

Most statistical issues that have arisen so far in personal design can be handled with standard methods, as indicated above in the sections on individual analysis and group analysis. A few questions that involve special difficulties or pitfalls may be noted briefly here. First, the simplicity of the parallelism theorem may be misleading; other algebraic rules may require complex analyses (see Anderson, 1982; Zalinski & Anderson, in press). Second, incomplete factorial design can be used, in which some stimulus combinations are omitted (Anderson, 1982, Section 1.3.8). Third, the not uncommon methods of *weak inference* are seriously inadequate to test algebraic rules. Thus a rule may account for an impressively high percentage of the variance or show a high correlation, yet still be seriously incorrect (Anderson, 1981, Section 1.2.8; 1982, chap. 4). Fourth, percentage of variance accounted for by the statistical Person × Situation interaction is generally meaningless as a measure of psychological interaction between person and situation (Anderson, 1982, Sections 7.10, 7.11). Fifth, comparison of values across persons is complicated by the lack of any rigorous way to equate personal units of their feeling scales (Anderson, 1981, Section 1.2.1; 1982, Note 2.1.3a, Section 7.4). Finally, the assumption of a linear response scale can be relaxed to use choice data (Louviere, 1988) or rank order data (Anderson, 1982, chap. 5).

Experimental Procedure

Instruction and practice. For most applications of personal design, it is desirable to have the person in a stable state, without systematic changes during the experimental session. The instructions, accordingly, should aim to establish a stable state before collecting regular experimental data. Guidelines to writing instructions are given in Anderson (1982, Section 1.2.3, Appendix A). Persons should, of course, be run one at a time to allow monitoring of their understanding of the experimental task and postexperimental interrogation. Classroom batch experiments have little value in psychological science (Anderson 1982, Section 1.2.6).

Practice is an important part of the instructions (Anderson, 1982, Section 1.2.2). Practice helps generate a stable frame of reference for the experimental task, thereby reducing response variability. Also, practice is essential for establishing the desired linearity of the response scale. Since most applications of personal design use a rating response, the problem of response measurement is considered separately in the following subsections.

Response measurement. A linear (equal interval) response scale is desirable because the observable response then provides a veridical picture of underlying cognition. This is important in analysis based on response patterns, especially with cognitive algebra.

How to obtain linear response measures has long been a problem in psychology. The difficulty is clear. In terms of the earlier discussion of the integration diagram (Figure 10.1), it is desired that the observable response, R, be a linear function of the unobservable feeling, r. If it is, the pattern in the observed data will exactly mirror the underlying cognition. But since the person's feeling is in fact private and unobservable, how can we test whether the observed response is indeed a true linear measure?

A breakthrough on this long-standing problem of response measurement was provided by cognitive algebra. The measurement logic was outlined in the parallelism theorem. Certain experimental procedures are important in practice, however, and are discussed in the next two subsections.

Rating method. The ordinary rating method can provide a true linear response scale, but two experimental procedures are important. To see the need for these procedures, consider the uncertainty facing the person in rating the very first stimulus: This could be the highest stimulus, or the lowest, or anywhere in between. Hence its rating is completely uncertain. It is essential, therefore, to help the person set up a stable correspondence between the stimulus continuum and the rating scale.

The first procedure concerns *end anchors* (Anderson, 1982, Section 1.1.4). End anchors are stimuli mildly more extreme than the regular experimental stimuli. They are given initially, with instructions that they correspond to the two ends of the rating scale. The two end anchors thus define the stimulus range, for all other stimuli must lie between them. They also begin to place this stimulus range into correspondence with the response range. In addition, they eliminate certain end-effects that can bias the response.

The second procedure is supplement the end anchors with practice on intermediate stimuli. This practice further defines the stimulus-response correspondence and helps develop a stable frame of reference. In most tasks to date, people seem able to set up a stable frame of reference for rating with rather little practice. It is sometimes desirable, however, to present the end anchors at various points throughout the experiment in order to firm up the frame of reference.

Although numerical, 1–20-type rating scales are most convenient, graphic rating scales seem to give best results. They largely eliminate residual number preferences found with the numerical format. Also, graphic scales are readily used by young children.

The rating method has been criticized in psychological measurement theory because it is subject to biases. These biases are real, but they can be largely eliminated with the two procedures already indicated. Other attempts to get true linear scales have used the method of magnitude estimation, which asks for numerical judgments of ratios of stimulus magnitudes (Stevens, 1974), or have relied on choice data, as in Thurstone's method of paired comparisons. Choice data, however, are not strong enough for measurement theory, and the method of magnitude estimation was found to suffer severe bias (see Anderson, 1981, chap. 5; 1982, chap. 1).

The key to this measurement controversy lay in cognitive algebra. The parallelism theorem was an impartial judge between the methods of rating and magnitude estimation; both methods had equal opportunity. In the empirical tests, magnitude estimation failed and the rating method succeeded.

The success of the rating method is a blessing of nature; it need not have been true that rating biases could have been eliminated in any simple way. This blessing depended on a second blessing of nature in the form of cognitive algebra; it was the empirical reality of cognitive algebra that provided the theoretical foundation for development of the rating procedures just described. This is one reason for the emphasis on algebraic rules in the theory of information integration. Once established, of course, the rating method may be used to study configural integration that does not obey algebraic rules with some confidence that the pattern in the observed data will mirror the pattern in the unobservable cognition.

Self-estimation. The method of self-estimation can markedly simplify design and procedure. In self-estimation, people are asked directly for their personal values of various informational stimuli. With the parallelism theorem, self-estimates are not necessary because functional measurement can extract the personal values from the factorial pattern of data. But factorial design is inconvenient in some situations and infeasible in many others. Some of these situations can be studied using self-estimation methodology.

The main problem with self-estimates concerns their validity; biased self-estimates will have limited usefulness. To make valid self-estimates, the person must make a valid introspection and give a veridical overt report.

How to assess these two conditions is a central theoretical problem with self-estimation.

This problem can be solved with functional measurement. With the blame schema, for example, the parallelism theorem implies that the personal values of the two stimulus variables are equivalent to the main effects in the factorial design for the blame response. Self-estimates of the values of the two stimulus variable could also be obtained. The functional scales from the parallelism analysis then constitute a criterion against which to assess the validity of the self-estimates.

With such a validity criterion available, it becomes feasible to develop valid methods of self-estimation. If a given method of self-estimation disagrees with the validity criterion, it may be revised and improved. This is the goal: to develop valid *methods* of self-estimation in situations that allow factorial design, methods that can then be used in situations where factorial design is inconvenient or infeasible. Results to date have been promising, although self-estimation methodology is far from complete (see Anderson, 1982, chap. 6; Anderson & Zalinski, 1988).

A denial of the possibility of self-estimation methodology is given by Nisbett and Wilson (1977), who asserted that people lack ability to report accurately on the effects of stimuli on their responses. They cited studies of self-estimates of such stimulus effects as the only area in which they found even meager accuracy of self-report, but claimed that even this meager accuracy resulted from common theories shared with external observers, not from private, introspective knowledge. If Nisbett and Wilson were correct, self-estimation would have no personal value in personal design. It appears, however, that Nisbett and Wilson were wrong (see, e.g., Anderson, 1982, Section 6.2.6). People can make valid self-estimates in a number of situations (Anderson, 1982, Section 6.2; Anderson & Zalinski, 1988).

Nisbett and Wilson also claim that actors and observers share common theories. This claim seems empty without means to determine what those theories are. Integration theory has provided effective means for determining such theories, as with attribution schemas for blame (see Anderson, 1978, 1989, in press-f). But integration experiments have shown a mixed picture of commonality and noncommonality, well illustrated with Leon's three blame schemas of Figure 10.3.

The severe limitations of conscious report have long been known. The change of meaning hypothesis in person cognition, for example, rested mainly on confident, conscious belief that trait adjectives in a person description interacted to change one another's meanings. Experimental analysis, however, showed this conscious belief to be a cognitive illusion (Anderson, 1981, chap. 3; Hendrick & Costantini, 1970). Similar failure of verbal protocols was found in the study of moral judgment (Anderson, in press-d).

The only novelty in Nisbett and Wilson (1977) was their strong claim that essentially nothing is open to introspection in the sense that external observers could assess the influence of stimuli on an actor's responses as accurately as the actor. An acute review of this issue has been presented by White (1988), who concluded that the Nisbett-Wilson distinction between process and product was circular and not meaningful and that actors can, under certain conditions, make causal reports that are more accurate than the causal judgments of observers. From an integrationist view, the Nisbett-Wilson claim seems inconsistent with their admission (e.g., Wilson & Stone, 1985) that actors have access to privileged information. Such unique phenomenological information can be exploited by development of self-estimation methodology (Anderson, in press-a).

Experimental Design

Three kinds of generality. Personal design tends to be demanding about sample size. Individual analysis requires a substantial number of responses if it is to be reliable. Although rule diagnosis may sometimes be possible with as little as a single replication of a 3 × 4 design (e.g., Leon, 1980), multiple replications are generally desirable for more reliable rule diagnosis and for statistical analysis. In Leon's mother-son study, for example, each person went through three replications of the 3 × 3 design. Each individual analysis of variance thus had 18 *df* for error. Around 20 *df* would ordinarily be minimal for comfort, although individual analyses with children may have to get by with fewer because of difficulties in obtaining larger amounts of data from children.

Most personal design also requires a substantial sample of persons. The social reality of the blame schema, for example, becomes clear only when it is found to have some generality across persons. Subgrouping analysis, moreover, may require a large number of persons in order to get even modest representation of less common subgroups. In Leon's mother-son study, only 4 of 32 mothers followed the damage-only rule, a marginal frequency even with so simple a rule.

This example also raises an important problem of tactics not yet addressed in any study. Although 18 mothers are more than enough for the modal averaging rule, 4 mothers are fewer than enough for the damage-only rule. To increase the frequency of the damage-only rule by increasing sample size thus seems unattractive because most additional persons will be unneeded additions to the two larger subgroups. One tactic would be stratify some population on the basis of a short pretest and select more equal frequencies from each stratum. Pretesting would be practicable and efficient in the case in point by giving the pretest to a group of children in a school class. Such prescreening need not be too reliable to return valuable benefits in efficiency and power (see e.g., Anderson, 1982, Note 1.2.5a). Prescreening should also be considered when individuals are to be run in multiple sessions.

Both foregoing aspects of sample size are concerned with generality, within persons in one case and across persons in the other. A third kind of generality also needs consideration, namely, generality across situations within persons. With only one task or situation, it may be more foolhardy than hazardous to generalize to other tasks or situations. Sample size, in this case, refers to sampling across tasks and situations. Some task sampling has been done in studies of marriage influence (Anderson & Armstrong, 1989), but this problem needs more extensive consideration (see the section on situation sampling, below).

With personal design, therefore, sample size has three aspects, referring to replication within persons, across persons, and across tasks and situations. Decisions about sample size may thus be rather complex for personal design. The study of integration processes, which has been the main goal in previous work, emphasizes replication within persons and across persons. To study social/personality knowledge systems, however, requires more extensive replication across tasks and situations.

Standard group design. In standard group design, persons are randomly assigned to different treatment conditions, and the investigator typically wishes to compare relative effectiveness of the treatments. Standard group design is generally used in experiments oriented toward social action, to study effectiveness of different methods of therapy, for example, to evaluate juvenile offender programs, and so forth (see Saxe & Fine, 1981). In these examples, it is not generally feasible to assign a person to more than one treatment condition. Standard group design thus has an important function, especially when seeking outcome generality as opposed to process generality (Anderson, 1981, p. 91).

Much work on social cognition, however, still relies on standard group design in situations in which personal design might be more effective. The choice between group design and personal design deserves careful consideration, but this topic cannot be pursued here.

Multiple-item design. Multiple-item design can assess reciprocal interpersonal effects within a single group, as illustrated in the foregoing discussion of the study of wife-husband influence (see, similarly, Anderson & Armstrong, 1989, "Marital Attitudes," Study 3). Multiple-item design may also be useful in assessing generality of responses across situations or occasions. In a simple case, the same pool of items would be given across a number of situations, and the variability between items within situations would be the statistical error term to test effects of situations for each individual. In addition, the item pool may be split into subpools for different group members (Anderson & Armstrong, 1989, p. 27) or to cover different aspects of the situation.

Situation sampling. Personal design needs to study a variety of situations from everyday life. The blame schema is considered prototypical, but many other variables also influence attribution of blame, and their mode of operation may vary across situations. Blame, moreover, is only one facet of moral-social cognition. Systematic work is needed to develop representative batteries of tasks for general use.

A first step in situation sampling would be to map the geography of basic social domains. In the domain of moral judgment, all relevant variables vary in strength across social situations of kinship and workplace. In the domain of wife-husband interaction, similarly, different attitudes and roles will be elicited in different social situations. At this stage of investigation, phenomenological analysis and observational investigations can make priceless contributions.

The goal of situation sampling, at least for cognitive theory, is to obtain batteries of tasks that embody primary conceptual variables in ways amenable to cognitive analysis. This is quite different from representative sampling from some natural population of situations. Task batteries are here considered tools for cognitive analysis; they should ordinarily avoid conceptual confoundings that characterize many natural tasks, as with the two components of recompense (Hommers & Anderson, in press). This question of confounding does not have an a priori answer, of course, because it concerns conceptual variables that depend on theory for their elucidation and definition. Development of useful tasks is thus a continuing enterprise that goes hand in hand with development of cognitive theory.

Action sampling. To study everyday action in natural settings, some investigators have used a "beeper technique." In Sjöberg and Magneberg (1987), for example, each person from several diverse Swedish groups carried a beeper that signaled him or her through FM stations anywhere in Sweden at five random times per day on seven consecutive days. Upon hearing the beeper, the individual filled out a questionnaire about the action in which he or she was engaged, including items about frequency and importance of the action as well as items about mood and feeling. One interesting result was that actions performed under control of the situation led to negative affect whereas actions performed for personal goals led to positive affect.

Action sampling could be used with personal design. Questionnaire items could be constructed from a factorial design oriented, for example, around a recent instance of blame or excuse. Alternatively, some form of multiple-item design might be used. Personal computers for each person to handle design construction, stimulus presentation, and response recording would seem feasible in home or workplace.

Personalized stimuli. The foregoing experimental illustrations used the same stimulus materials for all persons, and were personalized only to the extent of individual design, values, and analysis. Personalization may be pushed further by selecting stimulus materials separately for each individual. In one such study (Anderson, 1981, p. 319, Figure 4.21), it was hypothesized that marriage satisfaction would obey the same averaging rule that had been found in other areas of social cognition. To test this hypothesis, it was desirable to personalize the stimulus materials to each person's own marriage. Subjects were divorced women, to avoid perturbing ongoing marriages, and in the first part of the session the women recalled specific incidents, both good and bad, from their marriages along dimensions of appreciation and understanding. The experimenter then selected four incidents graded in value from low to high along each dimension and combined these according to a factorial-type design. Each woman thus had the same design, but with personalized stimuli.

In the experimental task, a pair of incidents was presented and the woman rated how satisfied she would have been had this pair of incidents characterized one week of her marriage. The results supported averaging theory. The judgments were retrospective, of course, and hypothetical in that the given incidents did not actually occur in one week. It seems reasonable to expect, however, that the cognitive processes of valuation and integration in these retrospective judgments provide some worthwhile information about ongoing marriage and also about the pastime of reliving one's past.

The most completely realized personal design to date is the study of attitudes and contraceptive behavior in sexually active students by Jaccard and Becker (1985). With personal design, values and integration rules could be determined for individual students. The results showed large discrepancies from the summation theory of attitudes, but supported the integration theory of attitudes (see also Anderson & Armstrong, 1989, pp. 37–39). Attitudes and behavior were highly related. The ingenious procedures used by Jaccard and Becker will repay study as an innovative case of personal design.

Although personalized task and/or stimuli is one of the four ideal properties for personal design listed initially, most applications to date have been personalized only in terms of the first three properties. Greater task/stimulus personalization is desirable, but it tends to be expensive in time if not money. Less personalized experiments may thus serve a good purpose in developing a preliminary knowledge base for planning cost-effective longer-term work.

PERSONAL DESIGN AND EVERYDAY LIFE

Personal design seeks to study everyday life within a framework of cognitive theory. Among the diverse realities of everyday life are obligation, responsibility, and blame; hope and disappointment; justice and injustice; happiness and depression; winning, losing, and saving face; and affection, friendship, and love. These and other concepts need to be personalized within family and workplace.

Many approaches to social/personality theory have stressed the importance of context and situation and the need to focus on their interaction with the person. A few are listed here to emphasize the diversity of approaches that can contribute to the study of everyday life. Most contemporary action theories have a primary concern with everyday life (see, e.g., Antaki, 1981; Frese & Sabini, 1985). An interactionist position has been advocated by Magnusson through many writings, of which the latest (Magnusson, 1988) gives a good overview, while the psychology of situations is discussed by Argyle, Furnham, and Graham (1981) and by contributors to Magnusson (1981). A more personalist emphasis appears in Sarbin's (1977) discussion of contextualism as a worldview for psychology, which gives special consideration to Kelly's (1955) personal construct theory, whereas a more social emphasis appears in Hogan's (1983) socioanalytic theory of personality. The importance of context may be seen in various chapters on personal relations in Gilmour and Duck (1986). Culture as context is a theme of cross-cultural psychology (Cole & Means, 1981; Curran, 1980). Also in this conceptual cluster are the sociological schools of symbolic interactionism surveyed by Stryker and Statham (1985; see Anderson, in press-a).

Many methodologies can help in studying the social personality. Among these are Rosenberg's (1988) new methods for uncovering individual personal constructs, the repertory grid used by followers of Kelly (1955), Magnusson's (1988) observational analysis of longitudinal development, Sjöberg's (Sjöberg & Magneberg, 1987) action sampling, the case study methods expounded by Yin (1984), and various other methods thoughtfully reviewed by Weick (1985). Personal design can supplement these more observational methodologies with greater emphasis on experimental analysis and cognitive theory.

Three aspects of personal design appear in the theory of information integration. One is the emphasis on experimental control. Experimental control is essential to developing a satisfactory empirical base for theory of social cognition. A second is the discovery of cognitive algebra. Cognitive algebra has provided an empirically grounded foundation for dealing with the two basic problems of multiple determination and personal value. Cognitive algebra also allows incorporation of personal design within more observational approaches. Last is the functional perspective, with its focus on the functioning of knowledge systems in goal-oriented thought and action. These three aspects make possible a modest but effective approach to a cognitive theory of everyday life.

REFERENCES

Anderson, N. H. (1962). Application of an additive model to impression formation. *Science, 138*, 817–818.

Anderson, N. H. (1978). Progress in cognitive algebra. In L. Berkowitz (Ed.), *Cognitive theories in social psychology* (pp.1–126). New York: Academic Press.

Anderson, N. H. (1981). *Foundations of information integration theory.* New York: Academic Press.

Anderson, N. H. (1982). *Methods of information integration theory.* New York: Academic Press.

Anderson, N. H. (1988). A functional approach to person cognition. In T. K. Srull & R. S. Wyer, Jr (Eds.), *Advances in social cognition* (Vol. 1, pp. 37–51). Hillsdale, NJ: Erlbaum.

Anderson, N. H. (1989). Functional memory and on-line attribution. In J.N. Bassili (Ed.), *On-line cognition in person perception.* Hillsdale, NJ: Erlbaum.

Anderson, N. H. (in press-a). Family life and personal design. In N. H. Anderson (Ed), *Contributions to information integration theory.*

Anderson, N. H. (in press-b). Functional memory in person cognition. In N. H. Anderson (Ed), *Contributions to information integration theory.*

Anderson, N. H. (in press-c). Information integration approach to emotions and their measurement. In R. Plutchik & H. Kellerman (Eds.), *Emotion: Theory, research, and experience* (Vol.4). New York: Academic Press.

Anderson, N. H. (in press-d). Moral-social development. In N. H. Anderson (Ed.), *Contributions to information integration theory*.

Anderson, N. H. (in press-e). Psychodynamics of everyday life: Blaming and avoiding blame. In N. H. Anderson (Ed.), *Contributions to information integration theory*.

Anderson, N. H. (in press-f). Schemas in person cognition. In N. H. Anderson (Ed.), *Contributions to information integration theory*.

Anderson, N. H., & Armstrong, M. A. (1989). Cognitive theory and methodology for studying marital interaction. In D. Brinberg & J. Jaccard (Eds.), *Dyadic decision making* (pp. 3–50). New York: Springer-Verlag.

Anderson, N. H., & Zalinski, J. (1988). Functional measurement approach to self-estimation in multiattribute evaluation. *Journal of Behavioral Decision Making, 1,* 191–221.

Antaki, C. (Ed.). (1981). *The psychology of ordinary explanations of social behaviour.* London: Academic Press.

Argyle, M., Furnham, A., & Graham, J. A. (1981). *Social situations.* Cambridge: Cambridge University Press.

Berscheid, E. (1986). Mea culpas and lamentations: Sir Francis, Sir Isaac, and "The slow progress of soft psychology." In R. Gilmour & S. Duck (Eds.), *The emerging field of personal relationships* (pp. 267–286). Hillsdale, NJ: Erlbaum.

Cole, M., & Means, B. (1981). *Comparative studies of how people think: An introduction.* Cambridge, MA: Harvard University Press.

Curran, H. V. (1980). Cross-cultural perspectives on cognition. In G. Claxton (Ed.), *Cognitive psychology: New directions* (pp. 300–334). London: Routledge & Kegan Paul.

Dozier, M., & Butzin, C. (1988). Cognitive requirements of ulterior motive information usage: Individual child analyses. *Journal of Experimental Child Psychology, 46,* 88–99.

Frese, M., & Sabini, J. (Eds.). (1985). *Goal-directed behavior.* Hillsdale, NJ: Erlbaum.

Gilmour, R., & Duck, S. (Eds). (1986). *The emerging field of personal relationships.* Hillsdale, NJ: Erlbaum.

Hendrick, C., & Costantini, A.F. (1970). Effects of varying trait inconsistency and response requirements on the primacy effect in impression formation. *Journal of Personality and Social Psychology, 15,* 158–164.

Hogan, R. (1983). A socioanalytic theory of personality. In M. M. Page & R. A. Dienstbier (Eds.), *Nebraska Symposium on Motivation 1982* (pp. 55–89). Lincoln: University of Nebraska Press.

Hommers, W., & Anderson, N. H. (1988). Algebraic schemes in legal thought and in everyday morality. In H. Wegener, F. Lösel, & H. J. Haisch (Eds.), *Criminal behavior and the justice system* (pp. 136–150). Heidelberg: Springer-Verlag.

Hommers, W., & Anderson, N. H. (in press). Moral algebra of harm and recompense. In N. H. Anderson (Ed.), *Contributions to information integration theory*.

Jaccard, J., & Becker, M. A. (1985). Attitudes and behavior: An information integration perspective. *Journal of Experimental Social Psychology, 21,* 440–465.

Kelly, G. A. (1955). *The psychology of personal constructs.* New York: Norton.

Leon, M. (1980). Integration of intent and consequence information in children's moral judgments. In F. Wilkening, J. Becker, & T. Trabasso (Eds.), *Information integration by children* (pp. 71–97). Hillsdale, NJ: Erlbaum.

Leon, M. (1984). Rules mothers and sons use to integrate intent and damage information in their moral judgments. *Child Development, 55,* 2106–2113.

Louviere, J. J. (1988). *Analyzing decision making: Metric conjoint analysis.* Newbury Park, CA: Sage.

Magnusson, D. (Ed.), (1981). *Toward a psychology of situations.* Hillsdale, NJ: Erlbaum.

Magnusson, D. (1988). *Individual development from an interactional perspective.* Hillsdale, NJ: Erlbaum.

Mullet, E., & Vidal, E. (1986). La maîtrise intuitive des relations entre masse, volume et mass volumique chez des élèves du premier cycle. *European Journal of Psychology of Education, 1,* 47–65.

Nisbett, R. E., & Wilson, T. D. (1977). Telling more than we can know: Verbal reports on mental processes. *Psychological Review, 84,* 231–259.

Rosenberg, S. (1988). Self and others: Studies in social personality and autobiography. In L. Berkowitz (Ed.), *Advances in experimental social psychology* (Vol. 21, pp. 57–95). New York: Academic Press.

Sarbin, T. R. (1977). Contextualism: A world view for modern psychology. In J. K. Cole & A. W. Landfield (Eds.), *Nebraska Symposium on Motivation 1976* (pp. 1–41). Lincoln: University of Nebraska Press.

Saxe, L., & Fine, M. (1981). *Social experiments.* Beverly Hills, CA: Sage.

Shanteau, J., & Nagy, G. F. (1979). Probability of acceptance in dating choice. *Journal of Personality and Social Psychology, 37,* 522–533.

Sjöberg, L., & Magneberg, R, (1987). *A study of randomly selected action samples.* Göteborg, Sweden: University of Göteborg Psychological Reports.

Stevens, S. S. (1974). Perceptual magnitude and its measurement. In E. C. Carterrette & M. P. Friedman (Eds.), *Handbook of perception* (Vol. 2, pp. 361–389). New York: Academic Press.

Stryker, S., & Statham, A. (1985). Symbolic interaction and role theory. In G. Lindzey & E. Aronson (Eds.), *Handbook of social psychology* (3rd ed., Vol. 1, pp.311–378). New York: Random House.

Weick, K. E. (1985). Systematic observational methods. In G. Lindzey & E. Aronson (Eds.), *Handbook of social psychology* (3rd ed., Vol. 1, pp. 567–634). New York: Random House.

White, P. A. (1988). Knowing more about what we can tell: "Introspective access" and causal report accuracy 10 years later. *British Journal of Psychology, 79,* 13–45.

Wilson, T. D., & Stone, J. I. (1985). Limitations of self-knowledge: More on telling more than we can know, In P. Shaver (Ed.), *Review of personality and social psychology* (Vol. 6): *Self, situations, and social behavior* (pp. 167–183). Beverly Hills, CA: Sage.

Yin, R. K. (1984). *Case study research: Design and methods.* Beverly Hills, CA: Sage.

Zalinski, J., & Anderson, N. H. (in press). Parameter estimation for averaging theory. In N. H. Anderson (Ed.), *Contributions to information integration theory.*

Within-Person Correlational Design and Analysis

11

JOHN L. MICHELA

John L. Michela is an Associate Professor in the Industrial/Organizational Psychology Program at the University of Waterloo, Ontario. His interest in within-person correlational design developed from an interdisciplinary program of research on food choices by children and adolescents. His other research focuses on problems in health and organizational life for which theories and methods from personality and social psychology are useful, including coping with stress from unpleasant life events, organizational climate, and work stress.

Scientists develop theories or other forms of explanation and description through systematic observation of phenomena. In personality and social psychology, systematic observations often are carried out in laboratory experiments, which allow relatively confident attributions of causality to factors manipulated by the experimenter. Correlational studies also provide a context for systematic observation, usually with somewhat less confidence about causal direction but with greater connection to the natural world. Because the phenomena that scientists seek ultimately to explain are those of the natural world, correlational studies are essential. Perhaps because the applied fields within psychology have a particularly close connection to the natural world, some useful elaborations of correlational design recently have appeared in health psychology, consumer psychology, industrial/organizational psychology, and at the interfaces of clinical psychology and counseling psychology with personality and social psychology.

This chapter is concerned with studies in which two or more variables are measured repeatedly for every person in the sample, for the purpose of calculating correlations between the variables for each person separately. These are within-person correlational studies.

Various topics relevant to personality and social psychology increasingly have been investigated by within-person correlational design. A partial list

AUTHOR'S NOTE: I sincerely thank the following persons for suggestions about the content or writing of this chapter: Isobel Contento, Jean Endicott, Madeline Gladis, James Jaccard, David Kenny, Roger Myers, James Pennebaker, Clyde Schechter, Joe Schwartz, Art Stone, Joanne Wood, Pat Zybert, and several anonymous reviewers.

of these topics includes blood pressure estimation (Pennebaker & Watson, 1988); close relationships (Tiggle, Peters, Kelley, & Vincent, 1982); contraceptive choice (e.g., Davidson & Morrison, 1983); emotions and moods in relation to the menstrual cycle (Endicott, Nee, Cohen, & Halbreich, 1986), to personality processes (Epstein, 1983) to self-focused attention (Wood, Saltzberg, Neale, Stone, & Rachmiel, 1988), and to stress (Watson, 1988); motivation in food choices (e.g., Michela & Contento, 1986) and in work behavior (Mitchell, 1982); schemas (e.g., Judd & Kulik, 1980); and social support (Cutrona, 1986). However, the total number of studies in which within-person correlational design predominates is not large. Evidently, things have not changed much since Allport (1940) called for greater attention to how psychological content and process may differ among individuals. Allport distinguished idiographic research, which is sensitive to the particulars of individuals, from nomothetic research, which strives toward broad generalizations about people (see Jaccard & Dittus, this volume). As Runyan (1983) noted, one of the uses of within-person correlational design is to examine psychological processes idiographically.

The extreme predominance of nomothetic work could change in the 1990s. In the 1970s and 1980s there were several important statements and dialogues concerning the idiographic approach (e.g., see West, 1983), and an awareness has developed that the idiographic and nomothetic traditions can be brought together. For example, within-person correlational findings may be treated as variables measured on individuals in nomothetic analyses. One historically important component of the idiographic approach, Q-methodology, has also seen some resurgence in both its traditional form (see Brown, 1986; McKeown & Thomas, 1988) and adaptations of it (e.g., Bem, 1979). Along with the increased visibility of within-person correlational approaches, very recently these approaches have become much more practical to use due to new features in commonly used statistical programming packages. Analyses that previously required "from scratch" programming by skilled programmers now may be done by computer-literate graduate students.

However, these computer programming techniques and their relation to the substantive issues in within-person correlational design and analysis are not widely known. Different studies illustrate different issues and different approaches; in this sense the field is methodologically fragmented at present. There are at least two ways that this chapter could have addressed this state of affairs. One would have been to develop a logical scheme of relevant issues and corresponding elements of design and data-analytic technique. This approach was rejected, in part because the existing literature provides fine material of this kind in relation to particular issues (e.g., Runyan, 1983).

Moreover, this chapter's primary aim is to provide an introduction to within-person correlational techniques – an objective that seems better met by concentrating on concrete examples as they exist in the literature. Unfortunately, this approach will permit coverage of only a few of the relevant studies. Nevertheless, by using this approach, I hope that many more researchers will be encouraged to try within-person correlational design, and that more methodologists will address themselves to the special issues involved.

The chapter begins with an orientation to within-person correlational design for the novice. Next, some technical issues and practical suggestions for computer programming are discussed. Finally, several additional studies are described that illustrate the many kinds of information that within-person correlational designs may provide.

ORIENTATION TO
WITHIN-PERSON CORRELATIONAL DESIGN

The scheme that appears in Figure 11.1 describes the design of the traditional correlational study in psychology. Persons, represented in the rows of Figure 11.1, are sampled from a population, and variables, corresponding to columns, are selected for measurement in accordance with the aims of the research. Data organized in this fashion permit calculation of Pearson correlations or other statistics to describe the associations among the variables. When these correlations are calculated by working down the columns of Figure 11.1, the correlations tell the extent to which any person's score on one of the variables is associated with his or her score on another variable. Because the correlations are calculated by working from one person to the next, we may call this an across-persons correlational design. Nomothetic studies have this design, as when researchers examine correlations of personality inventories or other personal characteristics with behavior or other "outcome" variables.

A Cube Model of Within-Persons Correlational Design

Figure 11.2 depicts the structure of the data obtained from a single person in a within-persons correlational study. Several variables (columns) are measured repeatedly either across multiple occasions or in relation to multiple stimuli (rows). A study by Pennebaker and Watson (1988) provides an illustration. These researchers obtained measures of systolic blood pressure

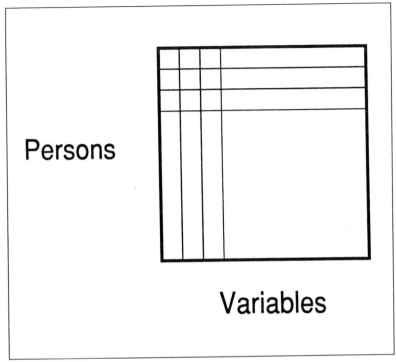

Figure 11.1   Traditional, across-person correlational design

(SBP) along with participants' estimates of SBP at 45 points in time during a 2-hour laboratory session. In terms of Figure 11.2, the 45 occasions form 45 rows and the actual and perceived SBP values form 2 columns. A within-person correlation was calculated for each of the 81 persons in the sample, and the mean of these correlations, calculated across persons, was found to be significant in relation to the N of occasions (mean $r = .25$). These results suggest that some people have at least an inkling of when their blood pressure levels change, which contradicts conventional wisdom among many health care professionals (see Baumann & Leventhal, 1985). The data are relevant to changes in blood pressure in the following sense. By definition, to obtain a positive within-person correlation here, blood pressure and BP estimates must vary (change) across trials, and they must covary (change together) in the same direction. Pennebaker and Watson sought to assure BP changes by interspersing 22 tasks and 23 rest periods across trials. The tasks included mental arithmetic, hyperventilation, and relaxation.

As with other correlations, within-person rs may be conceived as covariances of z-scored transformations of the original variables (in this instance, z-scored within-persons across occasions). Thus Pennebaker and Watson's r of .25 assessed only relative agreement in the sense that the variables tended to change together; the absolute difference between actual and estimated blood pressure could have been large or small. A separate analysis of absolute agreement found that subjects overestimated SBP by an average of 3.91 mm Hg. Although this average was significantly greater than zero, the researchers judged SBP estimates to be "moderately" accurate in light of the relative and absolute agreement.

Research by Michela and Contento (1986) illustrates the use of multiple stimuli in a within-person design. A sample of 107 elementary school students provided ratings of 15 foods (stimuli) in terms of possible choice criteria and social or environmental influences (variables). More specifically, 4 of these foods were chicken, milk, snack cakes, and pizza, and two of the rating scales for choice criteria concerned how good each food tasted (1 = tastes very bad, 5 = tastes very good) and how healthful each food was believed to be. Within-person correlations were calculated between each of these measures and a corresponding, food-specific measure of how frequently these foods were eaten. Cluster analyses that will be described below indicated that an individual's consumption of particular foods usually was associated with either tastiness or healthfulness but not with both of these food attributes. These results challenged conventional wisdom by suggesting that a sizable percentage of children are concerned about the health consequences of their food choices.

Figure 11.3 depicts the data from all occasions or stimuli from all the persons. (Figure 11.3 incorporates Figure 11.2 as one of the slices of the cube from front to back.) This cube model provides a framework for discussing these studies in more general terms. For example, to determine whether any two variables are correlated in the same way for all the persons, data from the front face of the cube, corresponding to the first person, are selected and used in a correlation procedure, then the next slice toward the back of the cube is selected, and so forth. After computation of a correlation coefficient for each person, the distribution of correlations may be examined. For example, Pennebaker and Watson were interested in the overall mean of the rs, which is a parameter of the distribution of rs. Pennebaker and Watson also examined whether accuracy of blood pressure estimation differed among four groups in their sample defined a priori by hypertension diagnosis

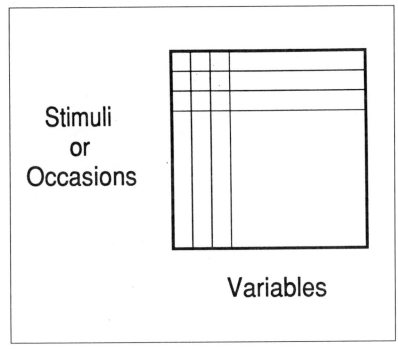

Figure 11.2   A single person's data in a within-person correlational design.

and treatment status. In a one-way ANOVA with within-person rs as the dependent variable, no significant differences emerged. In studies of this kind the relation of the within-person rs to other variables measured on the persons is commonly of interest, because this relation provides a link between the idiographic and nomothetic modes of research.

Criticisms of Across-Persons Designs

Researchers of a variety of topics have questioned whether the persons × variables design of Figure 11.1 provides a logical basis for the inferences its users typically want to make. For example, Davidson and Morrison (1983) raised this question about previous studies of choice among methods of contraception. In an across-persons approach to this problem, correlations might be calculated between women's reports of use of a particular

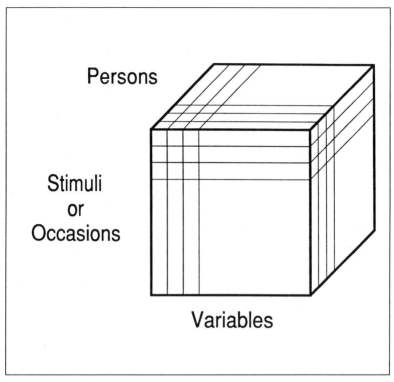

Figure 11.3 A cube model of within-person correlational design.

contraceptive method, such as the pill, and their attitudes toward the pill.
The rational decision-making theory that underlies such a study portrays the
individual as having in mind various behavioral alternatives and various
consequences of each alternative. Thus a more theoretically appropriate test
of the theory would examine whether any given person tends to choose the
behavioral alternative that he or she expects to have the most favorable consequences. (See also Mitchell, 1982, for a similar analysis of studies of
expectancy-value motivation in the workplace.) Davidson and Morrison
interviewed 698 married persons about four birth control methods: condom, diaphragm, IUD, and pill. In terms of the cube model of Figure 11.3,
these methods correspond to rows. One set of analyses examined associations between attitude toward each birth control method, rated on a 7-point,

good-bad scale, and behavior measured one year later (columns in Figure 11.3). These analyses provided evidence of highly significant prediction of behavior on a within-persons basis. Moreover, a comparison of within- and across-persons prediction of behavior, designed to provide equal opportunity (from a design point of view) for within- or across-persons prediction, yielded the strongest associations for within-persons prediction. Specifically, in across-persons analyses done separately for men and women and for each birth control method, phi-square coefficients of association ranged from .41 to .83 with a median of .545; in within-persons analyses, the corresponding coefficients ranged from .60 to .84 with a median of .715.

Some measurement and statistical arguments also favor within-person design. First, the across-persons design requires a particular kind of calibration of persons and variables. For example, researchers generally assume that people whose attitudes are truly more favorable than others will have the highest scores on the attitude measure, even though different use of the response scale by different persons can occur. This assumption about calibration may pose problems, especially with children or others whose use of language does not match the researchers' and, more critically, one another's. In these situations it still would be possible to detect within-person associations of attitude and behavior, provided that the differences in people's use of the response scale does not affect the within-person ordering of objects on the attitude and behavior dimensions. Another potential problem arises when, for example, a given person has highly favorable attitudes toward several contraceptive methods (e.g., IUD and diaphragm) relative to other persons' attitudes, yet the person uses only one method (IUD). Such a person will lower the across-person prediction of behavior from attitude because of the false prediction of diaphragm use produced by the relatively favorable attitude toward diaphragm use. In contrast, the within-person association could still be quite high if the person's attitudes toward IUD use were more favorable than the same person's attitudes toward any other method.[1]

In principle and in fact, differences between across- and within-person results can be striking. Epstein (1983) provides an example of how across- and within-person analysis may produce opposite findings. Epstein obtained daily reports of positive and negative emotions from a sample of persons. Within-person analysis yielded, on average, a negative correlation of anger and sadness, indicating that people tend not to have both of these emotions on the same day. Across-person analysis yielded a positive correlation of these same emotions, which evidently reflects a tendency for people who become angry more often than others also to become sad more often than others. Epstein notes, "Given such findings, it is important that future research examine intrasubject relationships to a greater extent than has been the practice in the past and that findings derived from intersubject data not be applied to processes within individuals" (p.94).

In summary, it should be emphasized that the point is not whether the within-person or the across-person view of the data is more correct; it is that each view answers a somewhat different question. These questions are, at root, about two possible data patterns. Across-person analysis tells whether persons with relatively high scores on one variable also tend to have high (or low) scores on the other variable in the correlation. Within-person analysis tells whether the two variables in the correlation tend to have high (or low) scores on the same occasions or for the same stimuli. The meanings of these data patterns obviously depend on the theoretical and substantive context of the research. The problem of arriving at within-person rs or other indices of these data patterns is the topic of the next section.

TECHNICAL ISSUES AND PRACTICAL TECHNIQUES

Concatenation of Data

In the studies discussed so far, overall assessments of within-person correlations were obtained by calculating the mean of individuals' within-person rs. Another approach to analysis of the three-way data of the cube of Figure 11.3 is to calculate a single r, where the number of cases in the analysis is the number of persons multiplied by the number of occasions or stimuli. This approach was used in a study by Contento et al. (1989) examining mothers' and children's liking for particular foods (food preferences) and their reports about frequencies of eating those foods (consumption). Participants in the study were 152 mother-child pairs, so a data cube for this study would have 152 "slices" from front to back. Three columns in the Figure 11.3 cube correspond to the preference question asked of the child, the consumption question asked of the child, and a question asked of the mother about the child's preferences. These questions were asked about 12 foods, corresponding to rows of the cube. For one set of analyses, data were arranged as shown in Figure 11.4. Here each slice of the cube from front to back has been placed below the previous slice, thus multiplying the original number of cases (which had been the number of stimuli, 12) by the number of mother-child pairs (152), yielding a maximum N of 1,824. This arrangement of data allowed a single r to be calculated across all rows of Figure 11.4. Even though the ages of children in this study were between only 4 and

5 years, a definite though weak relationship was seen between self-reported preferences and food consumption. The obtained r was .20, which was highly significant given the 1,810 nonmissing cases in the correlation. In addition, the corresponding correlation of mothers' ratings of the children's preferences with children's own reported preferences was .39.

Data like those in Figure 11.4 must receive special handling if a single correlation calculated across all cases is to be interpretable. The threat to interpretability arises from the two sources of variance present, between-person (or across-person, intersubject variance) and within-person (intrasubject variance). Between-person variance corresponds with the different means that different persons may have, averaging across stimuli or occasions. Thus a high positive correlation might be seen between variables solely because some people's responses on 7-point scales vary only through the range of 1 to 5 across foods, while other people's responses vary from 3 to 7. Within-person variance logically is residual or orthogonal to between-person variance, and thus corresponds to differences in scores of foods when between-person variance is controlled. In the Contento et al. study described above, this control was achieved by calculating, separately for each person and each variable, z-scores across the 12 foods (see the chapter Appendix for a parallel computational example). These z-scored variables then were arrayed as in Figure 11.4 for use in calculating the correlations reported earlier.

Confounding of between- and within-person variance also is avoided when the mean of individuals' within-person rs is used to provide an overall assessment of within-person correlation. Epstein (1983) noted that this and the preceding approach yield the same result (though this assumes equal Ns per person, i.e., Ms). This correspondence follows logically from the earlier observation that within-person rs are equivalent to covariances of variables previously z-scored on a within-person basis. In comparing the single r and averaged r approaches, it seems preferable to take the mean of within-person rs calculated separately if (a) the range or other parameters of the distribution besides the mean are of interest, or (b) the within-person rs will be used as independent or dependent variables in some further across-persons data analyses. Use of a separate r for each person has the important further advantage that statistical inferences (e.g., about the *population* mean of within-person rs) become possible when these rs are converted to Fisher's z's and the z's are analyzed. This matter will receive greater attention in a later section on r-to-z' transformation.

An additional approach for avoiding confounding of sources of variance is to obtain across-person correlations separately for each stimulus and then

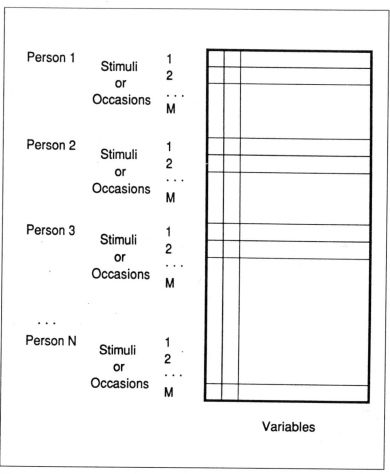

Figure 11.4   Concatenated within-person correlational design.

average across results from the various stimuli. In effect this was the approach of Weidner, Archer, Healy, and Matarazzo (1985), who collected data on 5 foods and 30 families (mothers and 8-year-old children). Correlation coefficients were calculated across persons separately for each food. Thus, in terms of Figure 11.3, the first calculation involved the top slice of the cube, working from the front to the back of the cube, the second calculation involved the next lower slice, and so forth. In examining correlations between preference and consumption in children's data, Weidner et al. found that only 1 of the 5 rs was significant ($r = .40$) based on the N of 30 families. The 5 correlations between mothers' and children's ratings of the children's food preferences varied considerably, ranging from .12 to .69. These results are actually quite similar to those of Contento et al., despite the different cut taken on the data and the differences in the populations studied. When, in a single study on the topic of schemas, Judd and Kulik (1980) compared their average across-person results (b-weights from multiple regression analyses) for various stimuli with within-person results averaged across persons, these two approaches also yielded very similar results. However, as the studies by Davidson and Morrison (1983) and Epstein (1983) illustrate, this similarity is not assured. The two kinds of information, based on across-person and within-person analyses, are complementary in some ways, and the different results for each stimulus obtained with across-person analysis may be quite meaningful for some research problems. Finally, it should be noted that the across-persons approach may not be sensible for designs with multiple occasions in place of stimuli if each occasion is not equivalent from one person to the next.

Computer Programming Techniques

Arrangement of data. Figure 11.4 shows how data should be arranged physically for computer processing of within-person data conceptualized in terms of Figure 11.3 (see Pedhazur, 1982). The leftmost variable on each data record should be a person identifier. Moving down Figure 11.4, this variable should take the same value for as many successive cases in the file as there are stimuli or occasions per person. In other words, if there are N persons and M stimuli, N different values of the person identifier will appear, each of the N values will appear M times, and all M instances of any of the N values will be adjacent to one another. The second variable on the record should identify the stimulus or occasion number. Moving down Figure 11.4, these values should run in a repeating pattern from 1 to M. The remaining variables are those of substantive interest in the study, such as, perceived and actual blood pressure.

The DATA LIST, in SPSS-X terms, or the defined variables, in generic terms, thus should include variable names and formats for the person identifier, the stimulus or occasion identifier, and the substantive variables. From the point of view of the statistical package, the number of cases is the product of persons and stimuli or occasions, so all of the variables should appear on the list of variables only once, not M times.

Calculation of within-person correlations. The analysis depicted in Figure 11.2, which concerns data from a single person, may be accomplished by requesting Pearson correlations after selecting on that person's value of the person identifier. For example, in SPSS-X code (SPSS Inc.,1988):

```
SELECT IF            (ID EQ 24)
PEARSON CORR         BPTHINK BPREALLY
```

In accordance with Figure 11.3, the researcher may want within-person correlations for every person. Again assuming that the person identifier described earlier is called ID, the sequence would be as follows:

```
SPLIT FILES BY ID
PEARSON CORR         BPTHINK BPREALLY
```

which would produce a separate, two-variable correlation matrix for each person.

Use of the within-person correlations as values of variables. To analyze the distribution of these correlations, the printout could be examined and transcribed into the persons × variables matrix form given in Figure 11.1. Indeed, the investigator might already have on hand a matrix of data in the form of Figure 11.1, perhaps providing demographic and psychological information about the persons such as their self-esteem or locus-of-control scores. If so, this file could be edited to include as another column the information from the printout of within-person correlations. Then the within-person correlations could be analyzed in relation to the demographic and psychological variables by ANOVA, multiple regression, or other techniques.

r-to-z' transformation. However, it is advisable to convert within-person *r*s to Fisher's *z'*s when these scores are to be used in statistical procedures for which normality is assumed or when individuals' results are to be averaged or otherwise combined. Unconverted *r*s have a complex sampling distribution that does not justify typical handling of these data (e.g., the sample mean does not provide an unbiased estimate of the population mean). Fortunately, this transformation is easily accomplished either by reference to tables in statistical texts or by computation. Continuing the example in the preceding paragraphs, the computer code for *r-to-z'* transformation would be

```
COMPUTE  BPTHINKZ = (.5) * LN((1+BPTHINK)/(1-BPTHINK)).
```

An investigator might compute the mean of the resulting distribution of

BPTHINKZ scores, and then express the mean in terms of the r corresponding to this mean z'. The computer code for z'-to-r transformation would be

```
COMPUTE  BPTHINKR =(EXP(2 * BPTHINKZ)-1)/
  (EXP(2 * BPTHINKZ)+1)
```

(appearing on a single line of programming code).

Collapsing the cube. Usually, collection of data in the cube design of Figure 11.3 reflects the investigator's interest in establishing within-person associations. However, this design may be used to enhance across-person associations of variables as well. Epstein (1980) has argued that the fundamental issue of measurement reliability was handled insufficiently in many previous studies of prediction of behavior from personality variables. Epstein demonstrated enhancements of measurement reliability by first taking measures of several behaviors (i.e., several variables in Figure 11.3) from several persons on several occasions, and then aggregating each of the behavior scores across occasions. The aggregation effectively collapses the cube onto the "floor" of Figure 11.3, allowing across-persons correlations to be calculated, from front to back, between these more reliable behavioral indicators and personality variables measured on the same persons. If we assume that Epstein's data are arranged physically in terms of Figure 11.4, an aggregation procedure such as AGGREGATE in SPSS-X can accomplish the desired calculations. A separate calculation for each person is achieved by including /BREAK = ID in SPSS-X's AGGREGATE procedure.

Manipulations of data cube may be used to assess the levels of reliability achieved by these kinds of aggregations. For example, instead of collapsing the whole cube of Figure 11.3, the top and bottom halves of the cube each could be collapsed. Then the data from the earlier and later sets of occasions would form pairs of variables to correlate across persons. For example, Watson (1988) measured mood and other variables on a daily basis. Watson performed aggregations corresponding to the top and bottom of the data cube, for the purpose of examining "whether the mean daily variables may, in fact, be validly used as trait measures; that is, do they reliably assess individual differences in mood, personality, and behavior?" (p. 1025). Reliabilities using an average of just over 22 days per aggregate (2 aggregates per person) were quite high; for example, positive affect yielded $r = .87$ across the 80 persons, negative affect yielded $r = .78$, and social activity yielded $r = .92$.[2]

To calculate Watson's earlier- versus later-time split-half reliabilities, one approach is to read the data from each of the days as a distinct variable. This requires redefining what is considered a case to be persons instead of person-day combinations, and reading data from as many data records for each case as there are days. With 4 earlier and 4 later days, the code might then read as follows:

```
COMPUTE        EARLY = MEAN (MOOD1,MOOD2,MOOD3,MOOD4)
COMPUTE        LATE = MEAN (MOOD5,MOOD6,MOOD7,MOOD8)
PEARSON CORR   EARLY LATE
```

This approach assumes that exactly the same number of occasions appears in the data set for every person; this assumption is not required in an alternative approach, using the AGGREGATE procedure in the manner described in the Appendix.

Significance Testing and Hierarchical Partitioning of Sources of Variance

Many investigators have tested the significance of their within-person rs against the N of occasions or stimuli. For example, an investigator might convert within-person rs to Fisher's z', average the z's, and look up the statistical significance level of the corresponding r, given an N of the design's number of occasions or stimuli (M). Although seemingly conservative, this approach fails to take proper account of the number of persons. Consider an instance in which most individuals in a sample do not yield a significant correlation between two variables (by the conventional criterion), yet most persons individually yield a positive relationship between the variables. The null hypothesis (overall within-person $r = 0$) could be tested by a t-test of the significance of the difference of the mean z' from zero, and the null hypothesis might well be rejected (see Judd & Kulik, 1980).[3] It seems reasonable in such instances to consider the mean correlation to be nonzero even if the strength of association is trivial in practical terms; statistical significance and practical significance are two different issues.

At the other extreme, the total N of cases based on the concatenated design of Figure 11.4 makes some sense as the basis for significance testing, because the power of the test increases with increases in both the number of stimuli or occasions and the number of persons. With this approach, however, some account must be taken of the confounding of across-person and within-person variance. In introducing Figure 11.4, a technique was described for removing across-person variance by standardizing each variable on a within-person basis. In the corresponding example (Contento et al., 1989), the statistical significance of the r subsequently computed was tested against the total N of persons × stimuli. However, this N seems too large, in that one might say that degrees of freedom were "used up" in standardizing the variables. This approach has the further statistical problem that homogeneity among the within-person rs is, in effect, assumed but not verified.

An integrated approach for simultaneous handling of across- and within-person variance, significance testing, and other special problems in within-person correlational design may be possible by adapting multiple regression (MR) techniques to these problems, provided that a reasonable causal or predictive ordering of variables exists. Unfortunately, very few investigators have used MR to address the kinds of questions that arise in within-person correlational studies as defined in this chapter, so the following suggestions are rather sketchy. Monte Carlo simulations and other kinds of methodological work on MR as applied to these problems are needed.

Multiple regression procedures. The overall sequence of steps in applying MR to this kind of problem is as follows: (a) Create variables that will encode sources of variance such as *persons* or substantive variables such as *perceived blood pressure*, (b) enter these variables into MR analysis carried out in several hierarchical steps, and (c) arrange information from the various steps into an analysis of variance table. These procedures should parallel those described in Pedhazur (1982) for use of MR to implement analysis of variance having both between- and within-subjects factors.

For example, an MR test of the association of perceived and actual blood pressure could begin with a hierarchical step entering dummy variables for each of the persons (− 1) contributing to the data structure of Figure 11.4. This would remove the variance in actual blood pressure due to persons, so subsequent entry of perceived blood pressure would allow a test of whether perceived and actual blood pressure are associated beyond any association attributable to persons' overall response tendencies. By following Pedhazur's (1982) instructions for constructing an ANOVA table from these analyses, issues concerning proper accounting for degrees of freedom and partitioning of variance in significance testing would be handled. Cutrona's (1986) study of social support provides a further example of this approach.

The special appeal of the MR approach stems from its ability to address many relevant questions. (a) The variance due to persons may be partitioned more finely by including a step in the regression sequence prior to entering the dummy variables for persons. For example, it might be of interest to determine how much of the total variance in actual blood pressure due to persons (captured by the $N - 1$ dummy variables) is attributable to each person's average perceived blood pressure (or to some single report of perceived typical blood pressure), encoded as a single *df* predictor and entered before the dummy variables. (b) A formal test becomes possible for whether different people have the same or significantly different within-person associations. If, for example, perceived and actual blood pressure vary from person to person in their association with one another to an extent beyond that expected by chance (sampling error, etc.), then a test of the statistical interaction of persons and perceived blood pressure should yield statistical significance. This test requires calculating a set of coding vectors that are products of the person dummy variables with the continuous independent variable, perceived blood pressure. When these vectors are entered as a set in a hierarchical step following entry of the main effects for persons and perceived blood pressure, an *F*-ratio may be constructed to test the significance of the variance explained by the interaction. While this test compares the regression slopes of persons in the sample, a direct test of whether *correlations* vary significantly among persons can be derived on the basis of the χ^2 distribution. The idea is that the variance among z's of persons' rs is known, mathematically, to be $1/(M - 3)$ if across-persons variance in correlations is truly zero. It follows that the test statistic

$$(M - 3) \; \Sigma \; (z_i - \bar{z}')^2$$

is distributed as χ^2 with $df = N - 1$, where terms are summed from $i = 1$ to N, and $\bar{z}'$ *denotes the mean of z's across subjects.* Schechter (1989) provides further information about this test. (c) Coding and MR analysis of stimulus effects may be meaningful for some research problems. Given the data structure of Figure 11.4, these effects would be encoded in $M - 1$ dummy variables corresponding to stimuli. Entry of these variables in their own hierarchical step controls for stimulus effects. Thus it would be possible, for example, to rule out stereotypic or culturally shared responses to stimuli as explanations for findings such as parent-child agreement in food consumption reports. (d) Other confoundings or dependencies in the data also may be modeled by use of MR. In particular, there may be autocorrelation or other effects produced by the sequential nature of the data in multiple occasion designs. However, this complex topic goes far beyond the scope of this chapter. An introduction to time-series analyses may be found in McCain and McCleary (1979). (See also Kessler, 1987; Larsen, 1987.)

Empirical illustration. A multiple regression analysis used by Wood et al. (1988) illustrates several of these procedures. Wood et al. analyzed the data from a study of daily life experiences and moods (Stone & Neale, 1982). In terms of Figure 11.4, there were 40 persons and 30 days for each person, yielding a maximum total of 1,200 cases (missing data reduced this N by 76). Initially two kinds of variables were available, a measure of negative mood, based on daily questionnaires, and a self-focus score, based on content coding of written problem descriptions obtained each day. In order to analyze between- and within-person variation in mood as it explains self-focus, two additional kinds of variables were created. First, each person's average of mood scores across the 30 days was calculated and added as an additional variable to the Figure 11.4 data structure; in effect, each person's mean value appeared beside each of the daily mood scores. Second, dummy variables were created for persons (e.g., the first dummy variable had a value of 1 for the first 30 records in the data file, and 0 otherwise).

These variables were analyzed in a hierarchical regression with three steps established a priori. The first step identified the variance in self-focus attributable to persons' averages across the 30 days. The second step identified the remaining variance due to persons, encoded in the dummy variables for persons, thus allowing formation of the error term for the between-subjects portion of the analysis of variance constructed from the hierarchical MR analysis. The final step identified the variance attributable to daily, within-person variance in mood; this step also provided information for constructing the error term for the within-subjects portion of the ANOVA.

Wood et al. found that a small but significant proportion of the variance in self-focus was explained by between-person variance in mood ($F[1, 38] = 5.46$, $p = .024$), but no additional variance in self-focus was explained by daily, within-person variance in mood ($F[1, 1083] = 0.17$). It should be noted that Wood et al.'s use of the full N of 1,124 to test significance of the within–persons association of daily mood with daily self-focus did not spuriously produce statistical significance as might be feared with such a large N; evidently there simply was no daily association residual to the variance explained by person means in these data.

Summary. Analysis of data conceptualized in terms of the cube of Figure 11.3 is carried out by concatenating various people's data to form the matrix in Figure 11.4. This data structure facilitates various aggregations of data as well as computations of correlations within and across persons. A variety of approaches have been used for significance testing and estimation of within-person associations among variables. Because these approaches have not been fully considered by methodologists, researchers must give especially careful attention to these matters when they design and conduct within-person correlational studies.

ADDITIONAL ISSUES AND APPLICATIONS OF WITHIN-PERSON CORRELATIONS

Within-Person Factor Analysis

Researchers have analyzed within-person correlation matrices by factor analysis (P-factor analysis, after Cattell, 1952) for a variety of purposes. As with individual correlation coefficients, it may be desirable to compute an average of individuals' correlation matrices (perhaps with r-to-z' transformations before averaging, as in Endicott et al., 1986) before doing a factor analysis to summarize all persons' within-person results. Zevon and Tellegen (1982) were interested in whether each of the 23 persons in their sample yielded the two factors of Positive Affect and Negative Affect as had been found in across-persons analyses (R-Factor analysis). Data collected on mood adjective checklists across 90 days were analyzed for each individual. The researchers concluded that 21 of the 23 persons evidenced the hypothesized mood structure.

Differences among persons' factor analysis results were of special interest to Epstein (1983), who described in some detail the results of a particular person, "Lara," as compared with the average person in the sample. The structure obtained from a factor analysis of positive feeling states, which had been correlated across 28 days, was essentially the same for Lara as for the average person. However, Lara's negative feeling states factored somewhat differently, for example, her Negative Affect factor included angry, incompetent, and disliked. By Epstein's interpretation, "For the others, anger is frequently experienced as an emotion that protects, and even enhances, self-esteem. . . . For Lara, on the other hand, anger, rather than bolster her self-esteem, produces feelings of fear, disorganization, and lowered self-esteem" (p.148). Epstein provided further support for his conclusions from correlations of Lara's negative feeling states with situational variables and behavioral impulses, which also were measured on each of the 28 days.

Empirical Generation of Taxonomic Schemes

Corresponding to P-factor analysis and conventional R-factor analysis, which tell how variables relate to one another, Q-factor analysis tells how cases relate to one another. There are potential theoretical and practical payoffs in knowing, for example, that persons in a sample tend to have one of three patterns or profiles of scores across variables. Although Q-factor analysis has been supplanted by other methods (Filsinger & Karoly, 1985), acquaintance with the issues in its use is helpful when designing within-person studies.

To perform Q-factor analysis, correlations are computed across variables, so the variables serve as cases and the persons serve as variables in the computations. Because different variances of the original variables would distort the correlations, variables should be converted to z-scores before calculating correlations when their variances differ. Thus, in relation to Figure 11.1, the steps for Q-factor analysis are (a) convert scores of variables to z-scores; (b) transpose the matrix so that persons form columns and variables form rows; (c) calculate a correlation matrix by working down the transposed Figure 11.1, so that in the resulting matrix each row and its corresponding column contain correlations of a given person's profile of z-scores with the other persons' profiles; (d) extract factors; (e) rotate the factors; (f) interpret the solution. If data initially are in the form of Figure 11.3 instead of Figure 11.1, a transformation into the form of Figure 11.1 must be done. For example, an aggregation across occasions might be done ("collapsing" the cube), or correlations might be calculated across occasions or stimuli between a single outcome variable and several potential predictors or correlates.

Q-factor analysis will locate persons together in a space (i.e., where dimensions of the space correspond with factors) when their profiles of scores across variables are similar (thus yielding high correlations among persons). Correspondingly, persons with different profiles will be located apart from one another in the space. It is important to note that only the shapes of profiles and not their elevations will affect the correlations among persons, so only this information will be encoded in the Q-factor analysis. This is probably one reason for the unpopularity of this method; other likely reasons are the apparent fuzziness of the classification of persons based on their positions in the somewhat fluid-appearing space, and the hassle of transforming and transposing the original data.

Among cluster-analytic methods for taxonomic classification, K-means cluster analysis may be the most widely used. In effect, persons again are handled as points in a space, but the distances between points typically are calculated by the Euclidean (or Mahalanobis) formula. In the comparison of any given person with another, distance increases as the scores on each variable are more different from one another. Thus elevation of score profiles as well as shape may affect results. In practice, data in the person × variables form (Figure 11.1) are input directly, and specifications are given concerning the number of clusters to obtain, whether variables are to be standardized before calculating distances, and so forth. The obtained clusters identify homogeneous groups of persons within the sample.

When within-person correlations provide the data in a persons × variables matrix to be analyzed in this way, these data are likely to be highly reliable because they are based on many stimuli or occasions (Epstein, 1983). The study by Michela and Contento (1986) described at the beginning of this chapter provides an illustration. Data entered into K-means cluster analysis were within-person correlations between students' self-reported consumption of each of 15 foods and their ratings of 6 food attributes. (The 6 attributes were selected from a total of 11; each of the nonselected attributes was highly correlated with one of those selected.) Clustering solutions were obtained for various numbers of groups, and the 5 group solution was used. Solutions with more groups yielded group sizes too small for confidence in results, and solutions with fewer groups seemed to obscure some meaningful results. For the present discussion, the major points about the results were as follows. (a) Distinctive group profiles emerged. One group's profile indicated particularly high associations of food consumption with taste of foods (mean $r = .58$); another group's profile showed particularly high associations with healthfulness of foods (mean $r = .64$); a third group had particularly high associations with convenience (mean $r = .65$). (b) Two groups' profiles were nondistinctive in the sense that their within-person rs tended to be either all near zero or all among the highest rs in the sample. (c) Among groups with distinctive profiles, a separate classification of persons for their dietary quality, as judged from a dietary intake interview with a nutritionist, was significantly associated with the classification into the taste-oriented, health-oriented, or convenience-oriented group based on within-person rs. Taste-oriented children had especially poor diets. This finding provided a cross-check on the validity of the correlation-based classification into groups. It also illustrates more generally the potential for using group membership, given by the clustering results, as a nominal variable for use as an independent variable in ANOVA or to cross-tabulate with other variables.

Issues in Interpreting Within-Person Values of *r*

Like any other products of research, within-person correlations have the potential to mislead. Three interpretational hazards are discussed below.

Misleading effects of lack of within-person variance. Within-person correlations are wooden-headed; the data must have particular properties for meaningful use of Pearson r. One key property is the variance of each of the variables, and Tiggle et al., (1982) discovered a situation where lack of within-person variance may produce misleading within-person rs. Tiggle et al. calculated a "correlational index" of accuracy in perceiving the areas of change desired by one's spouse in the marital relationship. Correlations were calculated across questionnaire items concerning behaviors such as "start interesting conversations with me; show appreciation for things I do well; have sexual relations with me; give me attention when I need it" (p. 211). The husband and wife each indicated whether an increase, no change, or decrease in each behavior was desired by the self and by the spouse. High scores on the husband's correlational index indicated that he said the wife wanted the changes that she did, in fact, say she wanted; a corresponding wife's score also was calculated. From the notion that marital satisfaction is promoted by understanding of the spouse's needs, Tiggle et al. expected positive associations between a separate measure of marital satisfaction and the husbands' and wives' correlational indices. Instead, a negative association was obtained initially. Tiggle et al. suggested that this finding might reflect a heightened difficulty, in more happily married couples, of predicting areas of desired change, due to the small number of changes desired. This suggestion was supported when positive associations were found between the correlational indices and indices of within-person variance across areas of desired change. Moreover, marital satisfaction was negatively associated with these indices of variance in ratings of desired change. Consequently, Tiggle et al. recomputed the associations between marital satisfaction and the correlational indices of accuracy in perceiving the spouse's desires for change—partialling out the confounding within-person variance across areas of desired change. This procedure reduced nearly all of the initial correlations effectively to zero, thus solving the initial puzzle. This study also investigated a "discrepancy index" of marital understanding, based on sums of absolute differences between spouses' predicted and actual ratings, and the expected direction of association with marital satisfaction was maintained even when statistical controls for within-person variance were used.

Sometimes undesired properties of r may be overcome by using a different index of association. Boni (1988) demonstrated within-person use of the covariance calculated across areas assessed on questionnaires. (A covariance may be described as a more primitive index of association, which is sensitive to the scaling of the variables involved. Correlations, being covariances of standardized variables, are invariant across scaling.) Boni sought to index person-environment (P-E) fit, where measures of personal motivation were drawn from the field of vocational psychology and measures of the environment were drawn from organizational psychology. Boni obtained data about the perceived environment in a way commensurate with six person types identified by Holland (1985), including investigative, social, and enterprising. Covariances calculated across these six types yielded especially high scores of fit for persons who were highly "differentiated," in theoretical terms, or who had high variance across types, in operational terms. By deviating from the field's usual use of a discrepancy index of P-E fit, Boni was able to analyze P-E fit simultaneously with the main effects of person and environment, and thus obtain more convincing evidence of the effect of P-E fit on work stress.

Personal specificity of covariation. Within-person correlations are seductive; if an *r* is calculated with a particular meaning in mind, other sources of the correlation may not be taken into account. For example, as a validity check, Michela and Contento (1986) computed correlations between children's reports and their mothers' reports about the children's consumption of each of 15 foods. The mean within-person *r* was .55, which exceeded the one-tailed, .05 alpha cutoff value of .44 with 15 cases used in correlations, thus suggesting that the children's reports were valid. Then these researchers considered the troubling possibility that no special knowledge by parents of their children's eating was necessary to achieve the average .55 correlation; instead, a general knowledge of what children eat might have been sufficient. For example, "low ratings for spinach and high ratings for milk might be given by nearly all children and all parents, leading to positive correlations regardless of which parent is correlated with any child" (p. 217). This possibility was tested by deliberately mismatching parents and children in four arbitrary combinations, and obtaining mean within-person *r*s for each of these combinations. The resulting values ranged from .23 to .28, with a mean standard error of .033. These values were judged as too low for concluding that the only source of parent-child agreement was the culturally consensual pattern of food consumption.

Reexamination of the Pennebaker and Watson (1988) study of blood pressure estimation provides a further illustration of how person-specific knowledge may not be the only source of within-person correlations that assess accuracy. As described above, participants performed a series of relaxing or arousing tasks. The presumption is that relatively accurate estimates of BP reflect personal access to information about one's bodily state. However, our culture provides somewhat accurate information about effects of relaxing and arousing tasks on BP, and this information might be responsible for a major portion of the correlation between estimated and actual BP. From the findings reported in Pennebaker and Watson it is not possible to support this possibility with any certainty, yet one of findings is intriguing. Within each of the four a priori groups in the study, data were transposed so that correlations could be calculated among the different persons' blood pressure readings across the 45 trials. Thus these correlations captured profile similarity among persons (as described in the section above on Q-factor analysis). Pennebaker and Watson reported group mean Q-correlations of actual BP ranging from .21 to .34. Because these correlations were quite similar to the mean *r* of .25 between one's own estimated and actual BP, it may be said that changes in a given person's blood pressure across trials are predicted as well by other people's blood pressure changes as by changes in the person's own estimates. However, even if culturally provided information contributed substantially to estimation accuracy, Pennebaker and Watson also provided evidence of a contribution by person-specific knowledge. A statistically significant across-persons correlation of two within-person correlations indicated "that the more accurate one's beliefs [are] about symptom-BP and emotion-BP relationships, the better one is able to estimate SBP within the lab" (p. 325).

These issues are reminiscent of the classic issues in assessing accuracy of person perception (Cronbach, 1955). Perhaps a corresponding analysis could be made of issues for the universe of within-person correlational studies, and correlational solutions to the identified problems could be demonstrated much as Harackiewicz and DePaulo (1982) demonstrated some solutions in the person perception domain.

Issues in sampling of stimuli or occasions. Within-person correlations are fragile; changes in the particular stimuli or occasions across which they are computed are likely to produce changes in obtained *r*s. For example, Pennebaker and Watson sought to show that inclusion of strenuous tasks in the sample of occasions was not necessary for demonstrating a significant correlation of actual and estimated SBP. In fact, this correlation was still significant with removal of the exercise trials, although it dropped from .25 to .14. Michela and Contento (1986) also were concerned about sampling, in this case of the 15 foods used as stimuli. Foods were selected to promote variance on several key variables, such as their popularity with children according to national survey data, their membership in food groups defined by nutritionists, and their positions in a perceptual space obtained in previous research (Michela & Contento, 1984). Despite the resulting heterogeneity, Michela and Contento cautioned that the within-person *r* of any particular food attribute with food consumption may not be directly comparable with that of another food attribute, because the sample of foods may favor detection of an association of one or the other food attribute with food consumption. The safest comparisons are those made for a particular within-person r between various persons or groups, because the basis for every person's r is equivalent.

An innovative way of sampling occasions is the experience sampling method (ESM). Participants are signaled by a pager, portable computer, or other device at random intervals, such as 8 times per day for 7 days. When signaled, participants answer questionnaires. This method has been used to study various aspects of cognitive and emotional experience in relation to behavior and situation (for a review, see Hormuth, 1986). Although these studies have within-person designs, frequently the statistical treatment has involved across-person analysis (e.g., paired t-tests as in Csikszentmihalyi & Figurski, 1982) after aggregations of within-person data appropriate to the research question. These analyses ensure that no differential weight is given to persons with different numbers of occasions. Inspection of graphs and other representations of raw data also have used to analyze ESM data.

Uses of Within-Person Correlations as Measures

Within-person correlations often are conceived as measures—of marital understanding, blood pressure estimation accuracy, and so forth. This is apparent when within-person rs are treated as dependent variables. When conceived as measures, the reliability and validity of within-person rs should be considered carefully. Given enough trials, for example, reliability might be assessed by the split-half procedure described above, to determine whether the same persons tend to obtain high or low within-person correlations regardless of which subset of trials is sampled. Validity is likely to pose greater challenges. Two validity checks in Michela and Contento (1986) were described above, one concerning the raw scores involved in all within-person rs (food consumption report validity, assessed by parent-child rs), and the other concerning the correspondence of the classifications of persons, based on within-person r profiles, with a nutritionist's classification of dietary quality. A further analysis in Contento, Michela, and Goldberg (1988) bears on whether the within-person correlations between food consumption and food attributes properly may be called "correlational indices" of influences of food attributes on food choice. Underlying the analysis was the theoretical assumption that food choices are determined partially by rational choice processes, in which people choose foods that provide what

they want from those foods. The investigators reasoned that if positive correlations involving food attributes reflect rational choice, then a person with a
high within-person correlation should also rate the food attribute involved in
the correlation as highly desirable. Ratings of the food attributes on a 7-point
scale with endpoints of "good" and "bad" differed significantly in predicted
ways across groups defined by profiles of within-person rs. Nevertheless, the
essential findings here are still correlational, so it would be desirable to
bring additional findings to bear on the casual origins of these within-person
correlations.

Useful measures may be generated by calculating within-person correlations between each person's response across a set of stimuli and a template
of responses applied to each person's data. For example, Contento et al.
(1988) made a template for scoring dietary quality by obtaining ratings of 20
foods from 10 nutritionists in terms of the attribute "healthful." The nutritionists' ratings were averaged to produce a single set of 20 ratings, which
then were correlated with each person's self-report of consumption of the
same 20 foods. Persons who had been classified in other analyses as being
motivated to choose healthful foods obtained positive correlations with
nutritionists' ratings, and negative correlations were seen in the group
oriented toward eating foods that taste good. Contento et al. used the same
procedure with other food attributes (fattening, sugar-laden, and so on) to
assess the food consumption patterns of participants in these further
respects. Michela, McDonald, and Contento (1988) correlated nutritionists'
ratings of these food attributes with participants' ratings of the same attributes, for use as measures of nutrition knowledge. Michela et al. argued that
these within-person correlations provide an appropriate measure of knowledge in view of the practical task in health-oriented food choice, which is to
choose foods that are most healthful relative to other foods. With this measure, each person's score for any given attribute of foods, such as healthfulness, tells whether he or she knows the relative standing of foods on that
attribute. There is additional meaning in within-person rs used as measures
of behavioral patterns or knowledge relative to a template, through their
scaling from -1 to $+1$. Scores are immediately interpretable in terms of
extent of match to the template provided by the experts, and thus these measures may be considered criterion-referenced as opposed to norm-
referenced.

This idea of using a fixed template to apply to various persons' responses
was suggested by the "template matching technique" developed by Bem
(1979) and his colleagues. These investigators' objective was to describe

persons and situations in commensurate terms, then show distinctive responses to particular situation types by particular person types. To use this technique, persons are characterized by their responses on the California Q-sort, a set of 100 statements descriptive of personality (e.g., "is critical, skeptical, not easily impressed"). These statements are sorted into 9 categories, ranging from most to least descriptive, to form a forced distribution with a mean of 5 and an approximate standard deviation of 2. In one study, experts (social psychologists) made judgments about the characteristics of persons most likely to respond with attitude change to the classical forced-compliance situation, given one of three theoretical bases for attitude change: dissonance theory, self-perception theory, or self-presentation theory. That is, for each theory a template was devised of how the attitude changer is likely to be described on the Q-sort. Next in this study, Q-sort information on each of 32 college students was obtained from two acquaintances, and within-person correlations were calculated between each person's Q-sort and each of the three templates. Finally, across-person correlations were calculated between these three within-person rs and a score representing amount of attitude change. The largest across-person correlation was with the template for self-presentation theory ($r = .53$). As Bem (1979) explains, although too much could be read into this finding, it illustrates a potential for within-person correlational procedures to help identify underlying processes of observed phenomena.

CONCLUSION

Within-person correlational design has been put to many important uses in research relevant to personality and social psychology. For many of these investigations it is difficult to imagine how any other design could provide the kind of information obtained. Naturally this gain in information over simpler, across-person designs is attainable only by those who pay the price of more elaborate data collection and analysis procedures. Perhaps more widespread awareness and use of these procedures will lead to their becoming better defined, more accessible, and ultimately more meaningful.

Although there are many complexities in within-person correlational design, it is fundamentally like other designs in the demands it makes on researchers. It requires (a) care in sampling and measurement, (b) attention to the possibility of confounding factors, (c) data analysis appropriate to the research question and data, and (d) all the ingenuity the investigator can muster.

APPENDIX:
ADDITIONAL PROGRAMMING TECHNIQUES

Transcribing within-person correlations by computer. In place of the manual transcription method described in the text, the investigator may instruct SPSS-X to save the set of within-person correlation matrices to a file, so that selected contents of this file may later be read as variables to analyze. In the Version 3 release of SPSS-X (SPSS Inc., 1988), the PEARSON CORR (alias CORRELATIONS) line would be followed by:

```
/MATRIX OUT ( * )
```

after which the correlation values for each person would be accessible by referring to the appropriate ID value and referring, by name, to the appropriate rows and columns of the correlation matrix. The naming scheme of rows and columns is described in the SPSS-X documentation. This documentation may be easier to understand by keeping in mind that the file of within-person correlation matrices produced by the MATRIX OUT (*) command is like other SPSS-X system files. That is, rows of the correlation matrices correspond with cases, and columns correspond with variables. One complication is that SPSS-X produces additional cases giving other information besides correlation values, for example, the N on which a given person's correlations are based. A variable created by SPSS-X, called ROWTYPE_, takes string values such as 'CORR   ' for each case to designate the kind of information available from the case; CORR designates correlation information. One additional complication is that the split file structure that enables calculation of within-person correlations must be allowed to revert to a single file structure thereafter, which is accomplished by the keyword TEMPORARY before the SPLIT FILE specification. Thus to obtain a mean of within-person *r*s, the following sequence would be used:

```
TEMPORARY
SPLIT FILES BY ID
PEARSON CORR          BPTHINK BPREALLY
    /MATRIX OUT( * )
SELECT IF (ROWTYPE_ EQ 'CORR  ') AND
    (VARNAME_ EQ 'BPREALLY'))
DESCRIPTIVES BPTHINK.
```

The asterisk in the MATRIX OUT switch instructs SPSS-X to replace its active file, containing the data structure of Figure 11.4, with a new file of within-person correlations and associated parameters such as Ns. Consequently, other information about the persons that might have been available, such as their demographic or psychological characteristics, is no longer available for analysis in relation to the within-person *r*s. It may be made available by use of the MATCH FILES procedure, documented in the SPSS-X manual, after the SELECT IF statement shown above. The file matched to the file containing the correlations must have the structure of Figure 11.1 (as many cases as persons) instead of Figure 11.4 (persons × stimuli or occasions).

Obtaining a single correlation across persons and stimuli or occasions. It was explained above that a correlation calculated simultaneously across persons and stimuli or occasions as Figure 11.4 confounds two sources of variance. To remove the person variance, within-person *z*-scores may be calculated before computing the desired correlation, as follows:

```
TEMPORARY
SPLIT FILE BY ID
CONDESCRIPTIVE      PREFERE CONSUMP
    /SAVE
PEARSON CORR        ZPREFERE ZCONSUMP
```

where ZPREFERE and ZCONSUMP are within-person *z*-scored versions of PREFERE and CONSUMP brought into existence by CONDESCRIPTIVE as directed by the /SAVE specification.

Cutting the cube other ways. The arrangement of data represented by Figure 11.4 facilitates other analyses, such as across-person correlations computed on each stimulus separately, as in Weidner et al. (1985). This is accomplished by the following code:

```
SELECT IF        (STIM EQ 1)
PEARSON CORR     PREFERE CONSUMP
SELECT IF        (STIM EQ 2)
PEARSON CORR     PREFERE CONSUMP
```

and so forth for all the stimuli.

Aggregating across unequal numbers of occasions or stimuli. The text describes a way of aggregating across occasions or stimuli, using COMPUTE statements, that requires equal numbers of these observations for all persons. Use of an aggregation procedure such as AGGREGATE in SPSS-X will get around this limitation in many situations. For example, EARLY and LATE aggregates could be calculated for each person by first using IF statements to create a variable with the value 1 for the cases to be aggregated into EARLY for the first person, 2 for the cases of first person's LATE aggregate, 3 for the second persons's EARLY aggregate, and so forth. Then this created variable would be used in the BREAK specification of AGGREGATE. However, to use this technique, the investigator must write the aggregates to a file as a step between forming the aggregates and correlating them with one another. This intermediate step is necessary so that the early and late aggregates may be treated as variables of a single case (as they may be by reading two records per case when this file is read in the third step); when initially formed by AGGREGATE, the aggregates effectively would be the same variable but for different (successive) cases.

Aggregating across persons. Front-to-back collapsing of the cube in Figure 11.3 seems most difficult with Figure 11.4's data structure as the starting point. However, this is as easy as top-to-bottom collapsing provided that the data are rearranged so that all responses about any given stimulus or occasion are adjacent in the file (instead of all responses by a given respondent being adjacent). This rearrangement is accomplished in SPSS-X with

```
SORT CASES    BY STIM, ID
```

(or BY OCC, ID) and would be followed by the AGGREGATE specifications.

NOTES

1. As Davidson and Morrison (1983) explain, it may be possible to design adjustments of scores that take account of some kinds of within-person data patterns, thus allowing more meaningful across-person correlations to be calculated. Even when such adjustments make it unnecessary to calculate within-person correlations per se, the point remains that consideration of within-person variance, by some method, is crucial for some problems. This chapter emphasizes the cube model because the model is useful for either calculating within-person correlations directly or making within-person adjustments to data prior to other calculations.

2. A potential problem with the approach taken by Watson in this study arises from the possibility that people's moods, personality characteristics, or behavior may vary across time in a cyclical or otherwise systematic fashion. If they do, the within-person variance relative to between-person variance could be overstated using an earlier- versus later-time split-half correlation, thus reducing the apparent reliability. A better correspondence to the final total aggregate might be given by a split half using the mean of even days versus odd days. A combination of programming techniques described in the text and the Appendix, involving SORT CASES followed by AGGREGATE, may be used to obtain separate aggregates for odd and even days. It should also be noted that patterns of response can be imagined for which the even versus odd aggregate would magnify within-person variance spuriously. A more comprehensive approach to this class of threats might be obtained by adapting intraclass correlation statistics to this problem, and, with more conventional methods, use of random samples of days as the basis for aggregation may be the least vulnerable to systematic biases.

3. Schechter (1989) discusses assumptions required for use of this test, including complications produced when different numbers of observations are used in computing different persons' *r*s.

REFERENCES

Allport, G. W. (1940). The psychologist's frame of reference. *Psychological Bulletin, 37,* 1–28.

Baumann, L. J., & Leventhal, H. (1985). "I can tell when my blood pressure is up, can't I?" *Health Psychology, 4,* 203–218.

Bem, D. J. (1979). Assessing persons and situations with the template matching technique. In L. R. Kahle (Ed.), *Methods for studying person-situation interactions* (pp. 1–16). San Francisco: Jossey-Bass.

Boni, S. M. (1988). *Person-environment fit in the workplace and its effect on workers' stress experience.* Unpublished doctoral dissertation, Columbia University Teachers College.

Brown, S. R. (1986). Q technique and method: Principles and procedures. In W. D. Berry & M. S. Lewis-Beck (Eds.), *New tools for social scientists* (pp. 57–76). Beverly Hills, CA: Sage.

Cattell, R. B. (1952). P-technique factorization and the determination of individual dynamic structure. *Journal of Clinical Psychology, 8,* 5–10.

Contento, I. R., Michela, J. L., Basch, C., Gutin, B., Rips, J., Zybert, P., Shea, S. & Irigoyen, M. (1989, March). *Influence of parental food beliefs on the food choices of preschool children.* Paper presented at the annual meeting of the Society for Behavioral Medicine, San Francisco.

Contento, I. R., Michela, J. L., & Goldberg, C. J. (1988). Food choice among adolescents: Population segmentation by motivations. *Journal of Nutrition Education, 20,* 289–298.

Cronbach, L. J. (1955). Processes affecting scores on "understanding of others" and "assumed similarity." *Psychological Bulletin, 52,* 177–193.

Csikszentmihalyi, M., & Figurski, T. J. (1982). Self-awareness and aversive experience in everyday life. *Journal of Personality, 50,* 15–28.

Cutrona, C. E. (1986). Behavioral manifestations of social support: A microanalytic investigation. *Journal of Personality and Social Psychology, 51,* 201–208.

Davidson, A. R., & Morrison, D. M. (1983). Predicting contraceptive behavior from attitudes: A comparison of within- versus across-subjects procedures. *Journal of Personality and Social Psychology, 45,* 997–1009.

Endicott, J., Nee, J., Cohen, J., & Halbreich, U. (1986). Premenstrual changes: Patterns and correlates of daily ratings. *Journal of Affective Disorders, 10,* 127–135.

Epstein, S. (1980). The stability of behavior II: Implications for psychological research. *American Psychologist, 35,* 790–806.

Epstein, S. (1983). A research paradigm for the study of personality and emotions. In M. M. Page (Ed.), *Nebraska Symposium on Motivation 1982* (pp. 91–154). Lincoln: University of Nebraska Press.

Filsinger, E. E., & Karoly, P. (1985). Taxonomic methods in health psychology. In P. Karoly (Ed.), *Measurement strategies in health psychology* (pp. 373–400). New York: John Wiley.

Harackiewicz, J. M., & DePaulo, B. M. (1982). Accuracy of person perception: A component analysis according to Cronbach. *Personality and Social Psychology Bulletin, 8,* 247–256.

Holland, J. L. (1985). *Making vocational choices: A theory of vocational personalities and work environments* (2nd ed.). Englewood Cliffs, NJ: Prentice-Hall.

Hormuth, S. E. (1986). The sampling of experiences in situ. *Journal of Personality, 54,* 262–293.

Judd, C. M., & Kulik, J. A. (1980). Schematic effects of social attitudes on information processing and recall. *Journal of Personality and Social Psychology, 38,* 569–578.

Kessler, R. C. (1987). The interplay of research design strategies and data analysis procedures in evaluating the effects of stress on health. In S. V. Kasl & C. L. Cooper (Eds.), *Stress and health: Issues in research methodology* (pp. 113–140). New York: John Wiley.

Larsen, R. J. (1987). The stability of mood variability: A spectral analytic approach to daily mood assessments. *Journal of Personality and Social Psychology, 52,* 1195–1204.

McCain, L. J., & McCleary, R. (1979). The statistical analysis of the simple interrupted time-series quasi-experiment. In T. D. Cook & D. T. Campbell (Eds.), *Quasi-experimentation: Design and analysis for field settings* (pp. 233–293). Chicago: Rand McNally.

McKeown, B., & Thomas, D. (1988). *Q-methodology.* Newbury Park, CA: Sage.

Michela, J. L., & Contento, I. R. (1984). Spontaneous classification of foods by elementary school-aged children. *Health Education Quarterly, 11,* 57–76.

Michela, J. L., & Contento, I. R. (1986). Cognitive, motivational, social, and environmental influences on children's food choices. *Health Psychology, 5,* 209–230.

Michela, J. L., McDonald, D. D., & Contento, I. R. (1988). *A criterion-referenced measure of nutrition knowledge.* Unpublished manuscript, Columbia University Teachers College, Department of Social, Organizational, and Counseling Psychology,

Mitchell, T. R. (1982), Expectancy-value models in organizational psychology. In N. T. Feather (Ed.), *Expectations and actions: Expectancy-value models in psychology* (pp. 293–312). Hillsdale, NJ: Erlbaum.

Pedhazur, E. J. (1982). *Multiple regression in behavioral research* (2nd ed.). New York: Holt, Rinehart & Winston.

Pennebaker, J. W., & Watson, D. (1988). Blood pressure estimation and beliefs among normotensives and hypertensives. *Health Psychology, 7,* 309–328.

Runyan, W. M. (1983). Idiographic goals and methods in the study of lives. *Journal of Personality, 51,* 413–437.

Schechter, C. B. (1989). *A note on inferences about within-subject correlations.* Unpublished manuscript, Mount Sinai School of Medicine, Department of Community Medicine, New York.

SPSS, Inc. (1988). *SPSS-X user's guide* (3rd ed.). Chicago: Author.

Stone, A. A., & Neale, J. M. (1982). Development of a methodology for assessing daily experiences. In A. Baum & J. E. Singer (Eds.), *Advances in environmental psychology: Environment and health* (Vol. 4, pp. 49–83). Hillsdale, NJ: Erlbaum.

Tiggle, R. B., Peters, M. D., Kelly, H. H., & Vincent, J. (1982). Correlational and discrepancy indices of understanding and their relations to marital satisfaction. *Journal of Marriage and the Family, 44,* 209–215.

Watson, D. (1988). Intraindividual and interindividual analyses of positive and negative affect: Their relation to health complaints, perceived stress, and daily activities. *Journal of Personality and Social Psychology, 54,* 1020–1030.

Weidner, G., Archer, S., Healy, B., & Matarazzo, J. D. (1985). Family consumption of low fat foods: Stated preference versus actual consumption. *Journal of Applied Social Psychology, 15*, 773–779.

West, S. G. (Ed.). (1983). Personality and prediction: Nomothetic and idiographic approaches. Special issue of *Journal of Personality, 51*, 275–604.

Wood, J. V., Saltzberg, J. A., Neale, J. M., Stone, A. A., & Rachmiel, T. B. (1988). *Self-focused attention, coping responses, and distressed mood in everyday life.* Unpublished manuscript, State University of New York, Stony Brook, Department of Psychology,

Zevon, M. A., & Tellegen, A. (1982). The structure of mood change: An idiographic/nomothetic analysis. *Journal of Personality and Social Psychology, 43*, 111–122.

12

Idiographic and Nomothetic Perspectives on Research Methods and Data Analysis

JAMES JACCARD
PATRICIA DITTUS

James Jaccard is Professor of Psychology and Director of the Center for Applied Psychological Research at the University at Albany, State University of New York. His research focuses on the integration of traditional attitude theory with theories of behavioral decision making. This research is conducted in the context of several applied areas, including (a) drinking and driving decisions and (b) population-related issues (e.g., prevention of unintended pregnancies in teenagers, reactions to infertility in married couples, choice of birth control). In addition, he has published several books and articles about statistical analysis in the social sciences.

Patricia Dittus is a doctoral student in psychology at the University at Albany, State University of New York. She is currently conducting research on parent-teenager communication, with a focus on exploring the role of parents in motivating teenagers to avoid premarital pregnancy. In addition, she is studying factors that determine belief salience in decision making.

More than fifty years after Allport (1937) introduced the idiographic and nomothetic distinction into psychology, controversy remains over the most appropriate approach for the study of behavior. Many social scientists argue that idiographic analyses do not belong in the realm of science because the focus of science is on the development of universal, nomothetic laws of behavior. Others maintain that a science of behavior cannot make substantial advances in understanding individual behavior without adopting an idiographic approach. Although several notable proponents of an idiographic approach have defined their positions over the years, little has been done to develop specific methodologies for studying the elusive individual. The vast majority of research in the social sciences continues to focus on aggregate, across-individual analyses, despite the fact that inferences drawn from group behavior do not necessarily lead to an understanding of specific individuals.

The terms *idiographic* and *nomothetic* were introduced by the philosopher Windelband around the turn of the century to distinguish between the sciences seeking general laws (nomothetic, from the Greek *nomos*, meaning "custom or law") and those dealing with structural patterns (idiographic, from the Greek *idios*, meaning "proper to one"). Allport (1937) began using the terms formally within psychology. He disagreed with Windelband, who had believed that science should be concerned only with universal laws and could not be approached idiographically. Allport insisted that the study of the individual was imperative. According to Allport (1960), "As long as psychology deals only with universals and not with particulars, it won't deal with much – least of all human personality" (p. 146). Allport's position was welcomed by the humanists and existential psychologists, but was rejected by the majority of researchers at the time, logical positivists and behaviorists whose main goal was to develop the universal laws that Allport disdained. Critics of an idiographic approach claimed that it would be impossible to generalize results, that the single-case design was too difficult to work with, and that there existed no methodologies with which to implement such an approach (for review of such critiques, see Runyan, 1983). Despite the criticism, Allport's motivation for suggesting new, idiographic methodologies remained: Explanations of behavior based on aggregate or nomothetic methods of analysis were not adequate in determining why a given individual performed a particular behavior in response to a particular stimulus in a given context.

More recently, the idiographic cause has been taken up by personality researchers who stress the need for research in personality from an individual perspective (for example, Bem, 1983; Lamiell, Foss, Larsen & Hempel, 1983). Prominent among these, Lamiell (1981) argues that so-called individual differences research has not, over the years, come any closer to describing an individual's personality. He calls for a new approach, namely, an *idiothetic* one. According to Lamiell (1981):

> All of the so-called personality coefficients index . . . the degree of consistency with which selected attributes are manifested by *groups* of individuals. In the last analysis, it is the simple fact that all of those coefficients are *aggregate* indices, computed on the basis of data summed *across* individuals, that virtually precludes their appropriateness as grounds on which to infer anything about the consistency or inconsistency of any *one* individual. (p. 279; emphasis in original).

Lamiell (1981) introduced a formal rationale for individual measurement, in which a given individual's standing on a given attribute does not depend on the standings of other individuals on that attribute. The rationale was based on the idea that characterizations of individuals can be achieved by contrasting information about what a person *has* done with a conception of what she or he *has not but might have* done. This rationale is distinct from the traditional individual differences conception of personality, where characterizations of individuals are derived by contrasting information about what a person has done with information about what others have done. Lamiell's position has faced opposition from other personality researchers. Paunonen and Jackson (1986), for example, pointed out problems with Lamiell's approach and have argued that nomothetic methods are adequate for explaining personality. They suggested that the abandonment of group norms is not valid and may lead to ambiguities and misinterpretations of personality characteristics. As can be observed from even a cursory glance at the current literature, the idiographic/nomothetic argument is far from being resolved.

In this chapter, we describe three broad approaches used in psychology to study the behavior of individuals: a strictly idiographic approach, an aggregate-nomothetic approach, and a normative-nomothetic approach. Examples of methodological and analytic practices currently used in social/personality research are provided that highlight the potential dangers of using nomothetic-level analyses to make inferences about individuals. We then describe an example of a theoretical/empirical system that incorporates both idiographic and nomothetic perspectives in the analysis of the relationships among beliefs, attitudes, decisions, and behavior.

THREE APPROACHES TO
EMPIRICAL TESTS OF PSYCHOLOGICAL THEORY

A strictly idiographic approach is concerned with making statements about the relationships among variables for a single individual. Examples of the types of questions that an idiographic scientist might ask include the following: Is the behavior of an individual influenced by his or her behavioral intention? Do attitudes influence the behavior of an individual? Does the trait of dominance influence an individual's behavior? What criteria does an individual use to make judgments of drunkenness? Did a treatment have an impact on an individual? Does an individual exhibit more attitude change when exposed to a message under condition A as opposed to condition B? An obvious strength of such an approach is that the behavior of a single individual can be predicted. This makes an idiographic approach most useful in clinical psychology, counseling psychology, and other applied domains where an individual's response to a particular treatment is of interest. A major weakness with this approach is the difficulty associated with using single-subject experimental designs. Methodologies for conducting single-case research in clinical settings are discussed at length in Barlow and Hersen (1984). Kazdin (1982) has edited a volume on a single-case design in the context of clinical research, comparative psychology (Denenberg, 1982), operant conditioning (Johnston, 1982), and psychopharmacology (Connors & Wells, 1982).

Strictly idiographic approaches frequently are characterized as antithetical to the identification and development of universal laws that govern human behavior. This assertion is untrue. The idiographic researcher is interested in explaining the behavior of a given individual and, to do so, seeks a general theoretical framework that specifies the constructs that he or she should focus on and the types of relationships expected among these concepts. This search for guiding framework is no different from that of the scientist who adopts nomothetic perspectives. The major difference is that the idiographic theorist desires to apply the framework to a single person in order to understand the factors guiding that person's behavior.

The basic strategy of the idiographic scientist is analogous to the etic-emic strategy in cross-cultural psychology (see, for example, Jaccard & Wan, 1986). Cross-cultural psychologists attempt to identify constructs that are etic in character—that is, that are (nearly) universal across cultures, such as happiness, attitudes, beliefs, and norms. Although these constructs and, in some cases, the relationships among them are relevant to all cultures, the ways in which they manifest themselves within a given culture are emic in character, that is, culture specific. To construct and empirically evaluate a valid and useful etic theory, one must conduct research on an emic basis, using manifestations of variables that are relevant to the cultures involved. By analogy, idiographic scientists are also interested in developing etic-level theories, that is, theories involving constructs and possible relationships that apply across a wide range of individuals. At the same time, however, these scientists are sensitive to the potential need for emic-level operationalization of constructs and emic-level assessment of the functional forms of relationships among variables when considering a given individual.[1] In the pages that follow, we refer to theoretical frameworks that describe concepts, relationships among concepts, and the "causes" of behavior as applied to a wide range of individuals on an individual-by-individual basis. To avoid confusion with the term used in cross-cultural psychology, we refer to such theories as *idio-etic* frameworks.

Once an idio-etic theoretical framework has been developed, a researcher will want to evaluate the validity of the framework on a large number of individuals and summarize the results of the research accordingly. This approach requires a form of aggregation of data that we refer to as an *aggregate-nomothetic* approach. This approach to characterizing human behavior is strongly tied to idiographic analysis and retains the individual as the focal unit of analysis. However, it goes beyond strict idiography by summarizing across individual analyses, making generalizations regarding groups of individuals. Hence it is nomothetic as well. For example, a theorist might study the relationship between attitudes and behavior in the context of a conceptual system/methodology that permits the analysis of this relationship on an individual-by-individual basis. The results of a study of 1,000 individuals might be summarized by stating that 87% of the individuals exhibited correspondence between their attitudes and their behavior, whereas 13% of the individuals did not. In this case, the attitude construct is useful for explaining the behavior of the vast majority of the individuals, and it is a potentially useful idio-etic construct. Of course, the idiographic researcher would want to identify the relevant constructs to explain the behavior of the remaining 13% of the individuals. The aggregate-nomothetic approach has the benefits of idiographic analyses coupled with the added strength of making possible general statements about groups of individuals. Aggregate-nomothetic analysis is closely tied to idiographic analysis and, in some senses, represents a different facet of the approach, namely, an aggregation facet.

In contrast, a *normative-nomothetic* approach focuses, by definition, on multiple individuals or groups of individuals. The goal is to develop theories that describe and explain the behavior of individuals within the context of a group of individuals. Essential to this approach is the fact that inferences are made regarding the behavior of an individual *relative* to other individuals, that is, within a relative frame of reference. This approach is characterized by the following types of theoretical questions: are people who have positive behavioral intentions relative to people who have negative behavioral intentions more likely to exhibit a given behavior? Are people who have positive attitudes relative to people who have negative attitudes more likely to exhibit a given behavior? Are people who score high on dominance relative to people who score low on dominance more likely to exhibit a given behavior? Are people who are exposed to X more likely to exhibit attitude change than people who are exposed to Y? Answers to such questions enable scientists to derive general laws or rules about the behavior of some individuals relative to other individuals. For example, based upon nomothetic analyses, one might conclude that people who are relatively high in need for achievement tend to be motivated by a middle-level challenge accompanied by feedback, whereas those relatively low in need for achievement are motivated less by challenges than by rewards.

The normative-nomothetic approach dominates current social and personality research. This statement is true even of the majority of personality research that claims to be idiographic in character (e.g., Kenrick & Stringfield, 1980). For example, correlation coefficients that are calculated across individuals are normative-nomothetic by definition. Under certain circumstances, such correlations will reflect processes that are operating for a given individual (e.g., when the individuals are homogeneous in terms of the causal relations between variables). But the inherent assumptions of the analysis are clearly normative-nomothetic.

It is our contention that the development of formal theories of social behavior ultimately must resort to some form of nomothetic analysis. For the most part, social scientists will find a given theoretical framework useful to the extent that it provides perspectives on a wide range of individuals. Scientists typically are interested in developing idio-etic theories. Nomothetic analysis helps to yield perspectives on the applicability of idio-etic theories. However, the two forms of nomothetic analysis, aggregate-nomothetic and normative-nomothetic, represent fundamentally different approaches to theory development and evaluation, each incorporating a different set of methodological assumptions. We do not argue that one approach is necessarily better than the other. They simply are different. Some research questions will be answered better by an aggregate-nomothetic approach, whereas other research questions will be answered better by a normative-nomothetic approach. Each approach represents a potentially useful way to construe, explain, and organize the behavior of individuals who are the subject of scientific study. However, we believe that the normative-nomothetic approach has been too dominant in the development of social/personality theory, and that it may be useful for some of us to refocus our orientations toward an aggregate-nomothetic perspective. Serious obstacles await researchers who do so. Nevertheless, if these researchers approach the task with the same ingenuity as normative-nomothetic researchers, then we are confident that benefits will be forthcoming.

A large number of social scientists strive to develop theories of behavior that involve the concept of causality, that is, they want to know if variable A "causes" or "influences" variable B. Although the precise nature of the concept of causality is somewhat problematic, most social scientists argue that one variable influences another if *changes* in that variable are followed by *changes* in the other variable. Thus if one changes variable A and then observes a change in variable B, A may be said to influence B. In the next section, we illustrate a wide range of methodological and statistical scenarios in which the normative-nomothetic approach leads to radically different conclusions about causal relationships when compared with an idiographic or aggregate-nomothetic approach. The discussion makes explicit some of the assumptions of normative-nomothetic research. When developing the illustrations, we sometimes use subgroups of the population rather than individual cases to show the effects of aggregation. Each subgroup is assumed to be homogeneous in that the causal links and weights between variables are the same for all members of the subgroup. In such instances, the subgroup data accurately characterize the processes operating at an individual level within the subgroup, and vice versa. Reference to homogeneous segments of the population is made primarily for pedagogical reasons, but the operative principles are the same in both cases.

MEASUREMENT ASSUMPTIONS OF
THE NORMATIVE-NOMOTHETIC APPROACH

When analyses are conducted across individuals, it is necessary to make certain assumptions about the nature of the measures. These assumptions may be problematic, especially for rating scales, such as the semantic differential. Consider the following example: A researcher is interested in whether social class is related to attitudes toward a given product and whether this attitude is differentially influenced by perceptions of the cost of the product in upper-class as opposed to lower-class individuals. The researcher begins by developing a set of questions that measure attitudes toward the product. He or she does so by consulting Osgood's tables of adjective descriptors (Osgood, Suci, & Tannenbaum, 1957) that load on an evaluative factor via the semantic differential technique (e.g., good-bad, beautiful-ugly, clean-dirty, tasteful-distasteful). A group of upper- and lower-class individuals is then asked to rate the product on the scales, and an overall attitude score is derived by summing the responses across items. In addition, the product is rated on an inexpensive-expensive dimension.

The researcher analyzes the data by comparing the mean attitude scores for the two groups by a *t*-test, and finds a statistically significant difference: Lower-class individuals reveal a higher (more positive) mean score than upper-class individuals. A correlation between the attitude score and the inexpensive-expensive rating also is calculated for each group, separately. For lower-class individuals there is a moderate negative correlation between the two variables, whereas for upper-class individuals there is a moderate positive correlation. The difference in correlations is statistically significant. The investigator concludes that social class is related to product attitudes, such that lower-class individuals evaluate the product more positively than upper-class individuals. In addition, the researcher concludes that the data support the proposition that perceptions of expense affect attitudes differentially in the two groups. Upper-class individuals' attitudes are favorably influenced by cost, whereas lower-class individuals' attitudes are unfavorably influenced by cost.

A number of measurement assumptions are required for the above analyses. First, one must assume that the rating scales are valid for both groups of individuals. To the extent that the scales are valid for one group but not the other, the conclusions are called into question. Assuming valid within-group measures (in a traditional psychometric sense), a second measurement issue becomes relevant. When an individual is asked to make a judgment about an object on a dimension, he or she must first make the judgment cognitively and then translate that judgment onto the rating scale provided by the investigator. Two individuals might make the same cognitive judgment but differ in their observed ratings if they translate that judgment differently onto the rating scale. At issue is whether the observed differences reflect differences in the true attitudes of the individuals or differences in the ways the individuals use and experience the rating scale.

How might an individual translate a judgment onto a numerical rating scale? There are many possibilities. One strategy suggested by psychophysicists is that the individual will position the center of the scale to correspond to the average subjective value of the stimuli he or she expects to judge. In this case, individuals who expect to evaluate stimuli with generally high values will make lower ratings than individuals who expect to rate stimuli with generally low values on the dimension in question. A second strategy, suggested by Parducci (1965), is that the individual will position the scale so that the two most extreme categories correspond to the most extreme values he or she would assign to the type of stimuli being studied. The individual then equates the intermediate categories with a range of judgments between these extremes. Parducci discussed several situations in which this strategy would produce different ratings for two individuals, even though their cognitive judgment is the same. In fact, Parducci has used such an interpretation as an alternative explanation for several "established" psychological phenomena. Although other plausible strategies could be elaborated, the point is that observed mean differences may reflect systematic differences in the response-translation process. The normative-nomothetic approach makes the assumption that all individuals use the rating scales in the same fashion, with similar experiences in mind.

In the above example, suppose that the product being rated is an appliance. One might reasonably assume that upper-class individuals have had experiences with, on the average, better appliances than lower-class individuals. If individuals use the first strategy identified above for response translation, then one would predict a lower mean attitude score for upper-class individuals as opposed to lower-class individuals. Note that this outcome was observed.

The same measurement assumptions apply with equal force to the analysis of correlations: One must assume that all individuals within a group (but not necessarily between groups) use the response scale in the same fashion and with the same experiences as a referent. For example, consider the negative correlation between attitudes and perceived expense for the lower-class individuals. Suppose individuals with more positive attitudes tend to encounter more expensive appliances in their experiences. If all individuals within this group adopt the first response-translation strategy mentioned above, then individuals with more positive attitudes would tend to rate the appliance as being less expensive than individuals with more negative attitudes (even though true differences in expense judgments might be minimal). This would yield the observed negative correlation where possibly none exists. Thus violations of the assumption of a common response language across individuals can affect either means or correlations.

The normative-nomothetic approach makes a strong measurement assumption about a common response language across individuals. Few social scientists would deny that the assumption is rarely met in practice. Rather, attempts are made to eliminate potential confounding effects that undermine the theory test, and the remaining differences are relegated to error variance that the social scientist must live with. As we will see in later sections, the aggregate-nomothetic approach, in many instances, makes less stringent measurement assumptions.

CORRELATIONAL ANALYSIS AND
THE NORMATIVE-NOMOTHETIC PERSPECTIVE

In this section, we present four correlational examples contrasting the operation of constructs at the idiographic level versus the normative-nomothetic level. The first example focuses on the use of multiple regression analysis to identify the determinants of behavior. Because this approach is used extensively in social/personality research, our comments will be more detailed for this example than others. In addition, our discussion will focus on a specific area of application, namely, the analysis of the attitude-behavior relationship. Nevertheless, the principles are quite general and apply to a wide range of applications of multiple regression, path analysis, and structural equation analysis.

Multiple regression/structural equation analysis. Research on the attitude-behavior relationship has been heavily influenced by multiple regression models, path analysis, and confirmatory factor analysis (CFA). The approach, typified by Fishbein and Ajzen's (1975) theory of reasoned action, has used the attitude construct in the context of linear, additive equations to predict behavior from attitudes and to explain attitude-behavior discrepancies. It treats the attitude construct as one of several predictors of behavior, such that

$$B = w1 \text{ Att} + w2 \text{ } X2 + w3 \text{ } X3 + \ldots + wp \text{ } Xp \qquad [1]$$

where B represents behavior, Att represents the attitude concept, X2 to Xp represent additional predictors of behavior, and w1 to wp represent weights that reflect the "importance" of a predictor in determining the criterion. The typical investigation obtains measures of the criterion and each predictor of behavior for one or more groups of individuals. In the case of multiple regression, the B measures are regressed onto the predictors, and model fit is evaluated by examination of the multiple R. Standardized regression coefficients are interpreted in terms of the "importance" of a predictor in influencing behavior and represent the w in equation 1. Typically, the standardized regression coefficient for a given variable is interpreted in causal terms: A zero or near-zero coefficient implies that the variable has little influence on the dependent variable, whereas large coefficients imply that the variable has an impact on the dependent variable. In the case of confirmatory factor analysis, multiple measures of constructs are obtained, and models dictated by one or more sets of linear equations are evaluated in terms of overall model fit and the magnitude and statistical significance of parameter estimates. Path coefficients are typically interpreted in causal terms, as noted above.

Application of the regression strategy is quite popular in the attitude area. A review of the literature over the past 10 years revealed over 100 studies that have used multiple regression, path analysis, or CFA to explore issues in the attitude-behavior relationship (e.g., Bagozzi, 1981; Brinberg & Durand, 1983; Fredericks & Dossett, 1983; Gorsuch & Ortberg, 1983). In fact, the number of studies using regression-based models outnumbered alternative approaches by a ratio of almost 10 to 1.

Attitude-behavior models that use equation 1 as a format conceptualize weights as theoretical parameters that reflect the importance of each predictor in determining the criterion. Multiple regression analysis (or path analysis) can be viewed as a method for estimating these conceptually meaningful parameters. Consider the case of the 12 individuals in Part A of Table 12.1, using a two-predictor regression model predicting behavioral intent (BI) from attitudes (A) and norms (N). The 12 individuals differ in the weights of attitudes and norms in influencing BI. The weights (and, for technical accuracy, a scaling constant) are presented in the last 3 columns of Table 12.1. Each weight indicates how much BI would change, given a one-unit change in the attitude or norm, respectively. For example, for the first individual, a one-unit change in attitude would result in a one-unit change in BI, whereas a one-unit change in norms would have no impact on BI. For individual 11, a one-unit change in attitude would result in a half-unit change in BI, and the same is true for a one-unit change in norms. The BIs of the first six individuals are determined solely by attitudes, whereas the BIs of individuals 6 through 9 are determined solely by norms. For the last three individuals, both attitudes and norms are influential. A given individual's BI score is a simple, weighted additive function of A and N. Computation of the customary regression statistics would, in this case, yield a multiple correlation of *zero*. In addition, the correlations between A-BI and N-BI are zero (as is the correlation between A and N). Even though all relevant determinants have been included in the equation, and BI is an additive function of attitude and norms for any given individual, the correlations with the criterion are all zero. The traditional interpretation (by attitude theorists) of the standardized regression coefficients would be that, across individuals, changes in either attitudes or norms should not produce changes in BI. However, such a statement is incorrect. For example, a change in the attitude variable of 1.0 units across each of the individuals would yield an overall net change in BI across individuals. Similarly, because of the zero multiple correlation, the attitude theorist might reject the predictors as being irrelevant when, in fact, they are theoretically appropriate from a causal perspective. This point is particularly important because numerous studies in the attitude literature focus on identifying relevant determinants of behavior (over and above attitude), and reject variables that exhibit low correlations with the behavior (e.g., Crosby & Muehling, 1983; Fisher, 1984; Manstead, Proffitt, & Smart, 1983; Wittenbraker, Gibbs, & Kahle, 1983). The above analysis suggests that variables with low correlations could indeed be relevant.

The source of the problem is that the individuals were not homogeneous in the weights given the two variables. By contrast, multiple regression analysis as used in the attitude literature assumes that all individuals have identi-

TABLE 12.1 Homogeneity of Weights Example

Part A

Individual	BI	Attitude	Norm	Weight for Attitude	Weight for Norm	Constant
1	7	7	7	1	0	0
2	6	6	6	1	0	0
3	5	5	5	1	0	0
4	7	7	5	1	0	0
5	6	6	6	1	0	0
6	5	5	7	1	0	0
7	7	5	7	0	1	0
8	6	6	6	0	1	0
9	5	7	5	0	1	0
10	7	5	5	1	.4	0
11	6	6	6	.5	.5	0
12	5	7	7	.5	.21	0

Part B

Individual	BI	Attitude	Norm	X	Weight for Attitude	Weight for Norm	Weight for X	Constant
1	7	7	7	5	0	1	0	0
2	6	6	6	6	0	1	0	0
3	5	5	5	7	0	1	0	0
4	7	7	5	7	0	0	1	0
5	6	6	6	6	0	0	1	0
6	5	5	7	5	0	0	1	0
7	7	7	7	7	0	0	1	0
8	6	5	6	6	0	0	1	0
9	5	6	5	5	0	0	1	0

cal weights. Although the above example illustrates a case that yields zero correlations, nonhomogeneous weights could be introduced to produce virtually any size correlation between the predictors and the criterion, with a sufficiently large sample size.[2] Consider, for example, the data in Part B of Table 12.1. These data map onto a typical regression analysis and a typical result observed with regression models of the attitude-behavior relationship. Behavioral intent is regressed onto two predictors, an attitude and a norm. The theorist is interested in whether a third variable, X, is a possible determinant of BI over and above A and N. Suppose that the BI for each individual is determined by either N or X and that the attitude is irrelevant in all cases. Nonhomogeneous weights exist, as reflected by the ws in the table: For the first three individuals, N is the sole determinant of BI, whereas for the next six individuals, X is the sole determinant of BI. For any given individual, BI is a simple additive function of the three predictor variables.

Multiple regression analyses of these data yield a pattern of results typically observed in tests of regression-based attitude models. Focus first on the two-predictor (attitude and norm) equation. Attitudes and norms are slightly positively correlated ($r = 0.167$). The multiple correlation predicting BI from A and N across the 9 individuals is 0.86. The standardized regression coefficient for the attitude variable is 0.80, and for the norm variable it is 0.20. The traditional interpretation would be that attitudes are more important than norms, when, in fact, attitudes are irrelevant. Attitude theorists might also conclude that changing attitudes will lead to changes in BI when, in fact, this is not the case. The analysis further suggests that the two predictors account quite well for the data (as indicated by the large multiple R), when, in fact, the two predictors are irrelevant (in a causal sense) for two-thirds of the sample.

Now consider the case where the investigator evaluates the potential utility of the third variable, X, over and above A and N by performing a hierarchical analysis (or some form of partial correlation analysis). In this example, A and X are correlated 0.17 with each other and N and X are correlated -0.33 with each other. The three-variable equation yields a multiple R of 0.90. This represents a rather small increment in R relative to the original multiple R of 0.86 for the two-predictor analysis. The attitude theorist might be tempted to conclude that the third variable is of little conceptual/empirical utility because of the small increment in R. The standardized regression coefficients for A, N, and X are 0.73, 0.32, and 0.32, respectively. Again, the interpretation of most theorists would be that attitudes are the most important determinant of BI, when, in fact, they are irrelevant. Furthermore, N and X are of "equal importance" when it is evident from the generating data that X is more important than N (in that X determines the behavioral intention of twice as many individuals as N). Finally, the analysis predicting BI from N and X yielded a multiple R of 0.40. Although this analysis includes both variables that are the sole determinants of BI (in an additive sense, for any given individual), the multiple R is rather weak, accounting for only 16% of the variance in BI.

The major point is that for casual inferences to be accurate, one must assume homogeneous (or nearly homogeneous) weights across individuals. The assumption of homogeneous weights in most applications of regression models in the attitude area seems dubious. In fact, theorists who use this approach emphasize the fact that weights are expected to differ across individuals. Fishbein and Ajzen (1975) stated that "the weights are expected to vary with the kind of behavior that is predicted, with the conditions under which the behavior is to be performed, and with the person who is to perform the behavior" (p. 303; see also Triandis, 1977). The researcher who uses regression approaches is incapable of assessing the weights of predictors for a single individual. Rather, he or she implicitly assumes equal weights across individuals included in the regression analysis. This assumption is troubling in light of the above analysis and the fact that very few evaluations of regression-based models go beyond simple correlational tests. For example, a review of five major social psychology journals in the past five years revealed 36 correlational tests of models like equation 1 and only two experimental tests. Change studies are important in the evaluation of regression models of attitude change, because they can reveal the inadequacies of regression coefficients for making causal inferences given the presence of heterogeneous weights. For example, if the 9 individuals in Part B of Table 12.1 participated in a study that produced a two-unit change in attitude, there would be no resulting change in BI for any of the individuals, in direct contradiction to what would be predicted from the regression coefficients in the normative-nomothetic analysis.

Part B of Table 12.1 also illustrates an important point for the analysis of spurious relationships in general. A spurious correlation exists between two variables, X and Y, when the variables are correlated but in a noncausal sense (i.e., X does not cause Y). Spurious correlations are said to occur when the variables have a common cause (e.g., Z influences both X and Y) or when one of the variables happens to be correlated with the true cause of the other variable. Tests for spuriousness typically use some form of partial correlation analysis: If Z is partialled from X and Y, then the correlation between X and Y should reduce to zero or near zero. Part B of Table 12.1 illustrates a different source of spuriousness (i.e., nonhomogeneous weights) that cannot be adequately evaluated in this normative-nomothetic manner. Specifically, A is correlated with BI even though it has no causal influence on BI. However, partialling the determinants of BI, N and X, from A and BI does not result in a near-zero partial correlation (partial $r = 0.76$), and the spurious character of the relationship between A and BI remains undetected.

If one assumes that equation 1 is a useful way to conceptualize attitude-behavior relationships, then there are three approaches to confronting the problem of weight heterogeneity (or model misspecification). First, one can use regression-based statistics to estimate weights, but define one's subject population narrowly so that the assumptions of homogeneous weights is tenable. This approach is problematic in that the analysis of narrowly defined populations reduces the external validity of the model. Also, the theorist is at a loss if the population he or she is interested in studying is a priori determined on substantive grounds (e.g., studying the contraceptive behavior of teenagers in a large urban area) and weight heterogeneity is likely.

Second, one can attempt to identify variables that influence the relative weights of the predictors, and then incorporate such variables into model analysis to define subgroups characterized by homogeneous within-group weights and nonhomogeneous between-group weights. This approach is tantamount to including such (moderator) variables as interaction terms in the regression analysis. Statistical methods for interaction analysis in multiple regression are described by Jaccard, Turrisi, and Wan (1989). Unfortunately, few attitude theorists pursue this course of action.

A third strategy for dealing with weight heterogeneity is to use approaches other than correlational techniques as a method of weight estimation. Instead, one could derive measures of relative weights for each individual separately, using, for example, self-estimation of weighting parameters. This approach has received virtually no attention in the attitude area and seems worthy of exploration. Attempts to use self-estimated weights in the social judgment and cue utilization literatures have met with mixed success (see Anderson, 1982; Wiggins, 1973). Some studies have found good correspondence between self-estimated weights and actual weights used by individuals (e.g., Birnbaum & Stegner, 1981), while other studies have not (see, for example, Wiggins, 1973). This literature would probably be a useful starting point for the development of an idiographic assessment of weighting schemes.

Our own bias in dealing with the problem (and others associated with regression-based techniques) is to abandon the framework implied by equation 1 altogether. Instead, we use an idiographic and aggregate-nomothetic form of analysis to study the relationship among beliefs, attitudes, and behavior, as outlined below.

The issue of homogeneous weights and causal inferences applies not only to multiple regression, but to most standard forms of correlational analysis conducted across individuals, including structural equation and path-analytic models. The issue is relevant in any area of application in which multiple determinants are present and the relative importance of the determinants can vary from one individual to another. Our comments are not intended to discourage the use of multiple regression and structural equation models when evaluating social/personality theories. This could be counterproductive. However, if a theorist has reason to believe that non-homogeneous weights exist, then the theorist should make every effort to come to terms with this fact conceptually and to develop the necessary research program to deal with the problem, given that causal inferences are the theorist's focus. Failure to do so means that the theorist must live with whatever error is introduced by the assumption of homogeneous weights.

Group-level versus individual-level change. Consider the previous example on consumer attitudes that explored the relationship between perceived expense and attitude toward a product. In the example, perceived expense was positively correlated with product attitudes for upper-class individuals, but negatively correlated with product attitudes for lower-class individuals. Suppose that these correlations are psychologically meaningful and reflective of a causal relationship between the two variables. Suppose further that the investigator who conducted the study did not measure social class. For all individuals considered together (i.e., both upper-class and lower-class individuals combined), the correlation between perceived expense and attitude would probably be near zero (assuming common mean centroids), because the investigator has mixed two groups, one exhibiting a positive correlation and the other a negative correlation. The traditional interpretation of the zero correlation would be that perceived expense has no causal role in influencing attitudes and that a change in perceived expense would not result in a change in attitude. On an aggregate level, this latter statement has some validity. Shifting perceived expense downward would cause the lower-class individuals to revise their attitude upward and the upper-class individuals to revise their attitude downward. The net change in attitude would be minimal. But at the individual level, considerable change would occur, contrary to what one might infer from the correlation coefficient. Similarly, at the individual level, a true cause of the dependent variable has been identified, even though the aggregate-level statistic does not so indicate. In this instance, the correlation coefficient calculated across individuals is not descriptive of the state of affairs within segments of the population, because of subject heterogeneity.

We should emphasize that if a theorist used a normative-nomothetic analysis in the above situation and restricted his or her conclusions to statements that incorporate the overall group-level, "relative-to-others" perspective, then there is nothing misleading about the analysis. It is indeed the case that, for all groups combined, individuals who perceive the product as expensive, *relative to other individuals who do not perceive the product as expensive*, are just as likely to have positive (or negative) attitudes toward the product, which is what the correlation implies. Furthermore, from a causal perspective, for the group as a whole, it is true that changes in perceived expense would have no appreciable impact on the overall net attitude. For these types of conclusions, the level of analysis is entirely appropriate. However, one would not be justified in using the aggregate-based correlation to make causal statements about the variables on a non-relative-to-others basis (e.g., "Perceived expense is not a causal determinant of attitudes for these individuals.") The correlation represents a normative-nomothetic level of analysis and conclusions need to be drawn accordingly.

To state matters succinctly, a measure of association (such as a correlation, an omega-squared, a t-value, and so on) provides a description of how a set of scores are patterned. When a correlation of 0.80 is observed between two variables, we can unequivocally state that high scores on one variable tend to co-occur with high scores on the other variable and similarly so for low scores (assuming normal distributions). However, the measure of association may or may not be diagnostic of the causal influence of one variable on another at *either* the normative-nomothetic level or the individual (homogeneous segment) level. The discussion of multiple regression models of attitudes and behavior illustrated a case where the nomothetically derived measures of association (path coefficients and multiple correlations) were nondiagnostic of the causal relationship involved at *both* idiographic and normative-nomothetic levels. The reason for the failure was model misspecification (as reflected in heterogeneous weight across individuals). The scenario described above concerning product attitudes and perceived expense depicts a situation where the nomothetically derived measure of association is diagnostic of the causal relation at the normative-nomothetic level, but not at the idiographic level. We will now describe some additional examples of cases where a measure of association at the normative-nomothetic level is nondiagnostic of causal influences at both idiographic and normative-nomothetic levels. We then will describe general principles of nomothetic-idiographic divergence and formalize these principles mathematically.

Correlation reversals. Assume that there are three subgroups who are homogeneous with respect to the effects of X on Y within groups, but who differ in terms of their mean centroids on the X,Y vector. For each group, the relationship between X and Y is characterized by a strong negative correlation, that is, X has a causal influence on Y and the two variables are related inversely. The situation is depicted in the scatterplot in Figure 12.1. For any subgroup, the within-segment correlation is diagnostic of the causal relationship that exists (i.e., it is strongly negative). If a correlation is computed ignoring segments, however, a strong *positive* correlation between X and Y results. One might infer from the overall analysis that positive changes in X and Y will yield positive changes in Y, when exactly the opposite would occur. In this case, the aggregate correlation is nondiagnostic of the causal impact of a manipulation of X at both the idiographic and the aggregate levels.

This scenario describes a situation in which X and Y are both positively correlated with a third variable, Z. In this example, Z defines group membership in the three subgroups. At this point, it will be useful to make explicit the mechanisms operating in this and the other situations depicted. Specifically, we offer five basic principles that typically will describe nomothetic-idiographic (homogeneous segment) divergence:

- *Principle 1*: Let X and Y be uncorrelated at each level of Z. If X and Y are correlated with Z in the same direction (e.g., X is correlated negatively with Z and Y is correlated negatively with Z *or* X is positively correlated with Z and Y also is positively correlated with Z), then the correlation between X and Y ignoring levels of Z will be positive.

- *Principle 2*: Let X and Y be uncorrelated at each level of Z. If X and Y are correlated with Z in the opposite direction (e.g., X is correlated negatively with Z and Y is correlated positively with Z *or* X is positively correlated with Z and Y is negatively correlated with Z), then the correlation between X and Y ignoring levels of Z will be negative.

- *Principle 3*: Let X and Y be positively correlated at each level of Z. If both X and Y are correlated in the *same* direction with Z, then the overall analysis ignoring levels of Z will tend to yield a stronger positive correlation in the overall analysis than would be observed for any correlation calculated at a single level of Z.

- *Principle 4*: Let X and Y be positively correlated at each level of Z. If both X and Y are correlated in the *opposite* direction with Z, then the overall analysis ignoring levels of Z will tend to yield a stronger negative correlation in the overall analysis than would be observed for any correlation calculated at a single level of Z.

- *Principle 5*: Let X and Y be negatively correlated at each level of Z. If X and

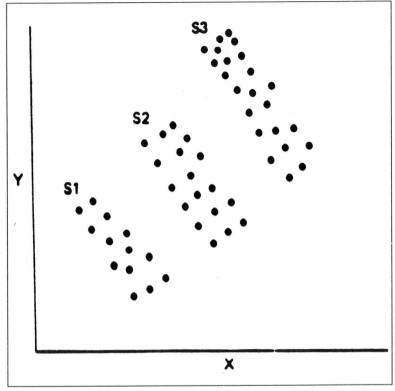

Figure 12.1   Scatterplot for X and Y for each of three subgroups

Y are correlated in the same direction with Z, then the overall analysis
ignoring Z will yield either a reduced negative correlation, a zero correlation, or a correlation reversal, depending on the strength of the correlations between X and Z and Y and Z. This situation was illustrated in
Figure 12.1.

These principles can be formalized by defining the mathematical relationship between correlations of X and Y at each level of Z and the (combined) correlation between X and Y across (i.e., ignoring) levels of Z. Let
us refer to the group of individuals who all have the same score on Z as a *segment*. For any given segment i, let MX = the mean for X, MY = the

mean for Y, SX = the standard deviation for X, SY = the standard deviation for Y, N = the sample size, and r = the correlation between X and Y. The mean on X for the combined segments will be

$$MXT = (\Sigma N_i MX_i) / NT \qquad [2]$$

where the summation is across the segments and NT is the total sample size (i.e., the sum of the sample sizes across segments). The standard deviation on X for the combined segments will be

$$SXT = ([\Sigma N_i SX_i^2] + [\Sigma N_i(MX_i - MXT)^2] / NT)^{\frac{1}{2}} \qquad [3]$$

where, again, the summation is across segments. Comparable terms (MYT and SYT) can be computed for the Y variable by simple substitution. The correlation between X and Y when the segments are combined will equal

$$rT = [(\Sigma N_i r_i SX_i SY_i) + (\Sigma N_i MX_i MY_i) - (NT)(MXT)(MYT)] / [(NT)(SXT)(SYT)] \qquad [4]$$

where the summation is across segments.

Table 12.2 illustrates each of the principles with numerical examples. The sample size is 50 and SX and SY = 2 in each segment. There are three segments, and each can be thought of as a level of Z. Segment 1 represents a low score on Z, Segment 2 represents a moderate score on Z, and Segment 3 represents a high score on Z. The mean X and mean Y scores are presented for each segment. Note in the scenario for Principle 1 that as the value of Z increases, the mean X score increases. This indicates that X and Z are positively correlated across segments. Similarly, in the scenario for principle 2, as the value of Z increases, the mean Y score decreases. This indicates that Y and Z are negatively correlated across segments. X, Y, and Z need not be quantitative variables. The problem of aggregation bias applies to qualitative variables as well as to mixtures of qualitative and quantitative variables. Only the statistic used to index association will differ (e.g., omega squared instead of Pearson's r). Inspection of Table 12.2 clearly illustrates each principle. Equation 4 can be used to explore other scenarios of aggregation bias not detailed in the five principles, including the different forms of aggregation described in Michela's chapter in this volume.

In any given research setting, the presence of a psychologically meaning-

TABLE 12.2 Illustration of Aggregation Biases

Principle 1	Seg 1	Seg 2	Seg 3	**Principle 2**	Seg 1	Seg 2	Seg 3
MX	5	10	15	MX	5	10	15
MY	5	10	15	MY	15	10	5
r	0	0	0	r	0	0	0
	Combined r	= 0.81			Combined r	= −0.81	

Principle 3	Seg 1	Seg 2	Seg 3	**Principle 4**	Seg 1	Seg 2	Seg 3
MX	5	10	15	MX	5	10	15
MY	5	10	15	MY	15	10	5
r	.3	.3	.3	r	−.3	−.3	−.3
	Combined r	= 0.86			Combined r	= −0.86	

Principle 5	Seg 1	Seg 2	Seg 3
MX	5	10	15
MY	5	10	15
r	−.3	−.3	−.3
	Combined r	= 0.75	

ful third variable, Z, that is related to X and Y in the manner described by the above principles can yield different interpretations depending on whether aggregation occurs across Z (i.e., Z is ignored) or analyses are conducted within the homogeneous segments defined by Z. This point has obvious implications for how the theorist draws conclusions relative to his or her data. Hintzman (1980) illustrates some of the difficulties that result from the presence of meaningful Z in the context of research on memory processes (see also Flexser, 1981; and Martin, 1981). For example, in memory research, data are frequently aggregated across items as well as individuals, yielding at least two potential levels of aggregation bias. Consider the following case involving aggregation across items: Tulving and Watkins (1975) describe an experimental paradigm for studying memory traces using successive cueing procedures. The method involves two attempts to retrieve the same memory trace, using a different retrieval cue in each attempt. Independence or dependence between success of retrieval for the two types of cues has implications for the retrieval processes that are operative. For example, if the two cues reach the trace through separate pathways in memory, then one might predict a lack of correlation between retrieval success for the two cues. Retrieval success, however, is likely to be related to the overall strength of the memory trace: The stronger the trace, the higher the probability of retrieval. The strength of the trace represents a meaningful Z variable that is positively correlated to the retrieval of a memory trace by the presence/absence of cue 1 (X) and the presence/absence of cue 2 (Y). If the separate pathway theory is true, and the retrieval processes are indeed independent at any given level of Z, then via Principle 1 above, the aggregate-correlation analysis will lead to rejection of the separate pathway theory, even though it is viable.

Principles 1 and 2 are a formal statement of a traditional spurious relationship between two variables as a function of a third variable. Principles 3, 4, and 5 make explicit other forms of spuriousness that may occur as a result of different functional forms of the relationships between the variables involved. Statistical partialling techniques can be used to deal with some of these aggregation biases (e.g., Principles 1 and 2), if one assumes homogeneous weights in the structural models across individuals or whatever unit is being aggregated across (see the previous discussion on homogeneous weights). These techniques also require that a valid measure of Z be obtained (a task that could prove difficult in the memory examples noted above, because the trace strength of any given stimulus is likely to differ across individuals; see Hintzman, 1980). Other types of aggregation biases (e.g., Principle 5) cannot be detected easily through standard partialling techniques.

Correlating means versus individual scores. As a final illustration for correlational analyses, consider a case we observed in our research investigating a probabilistic model of the relationship between beliefs (Wyer, 1975). According to the model, an individual's belief in a proposition A is predictable from his or her belief in another proposition, B, by means of the following probability equation:

$$p(A) = p(B)p(A|B) + (1 - p[B]) \, p(A|B') \qquad [5]$$

where $p(A)$ is the perceived probability that proposition A is true, $p(B)$ is the perceived probability that proposition B is true, $p(A|B)$ is the perceived probability that proposition A is true given that proposition B is true, and

$p(A|B')$ is the perceived probability that proposition A is true given that proposition B is not true. We obtained measures of the relevant perceived probabilities for 100 subjects for each of 30 pairs of belief propositions. When the fit of the model was evaluated for a given pair of propositions for each subject individually, the fit was relatively poor. However, if the mean probability rating across subjects for each component was computed, and then the mean scores combined in accord with equation 5, the difference between the mean $p(A)$ and the mean predicted $p(A)$ was trivial, suggesting a good model fit. The utility of the model varies, depending on the level of analysis.

ANALYSIS OF MEANS AND
THE NORMATIVE-NOMOTHETIC PERSPECTIVE

Normative-nomothetic analyses can also yield different perspectives from idiographic analysis when analyzing mean scores. We will illustrate this with three examples.

Suppose a population consists of four distinct segments. Each member of the population is asked to rate each of three brands of a product (A, B, and C) on a 10-point "strongly dislike" to "strongly like" rating scale. Assume that each segment is homogeneous in terms of their ratings and that individuals purchase the brands that they like most. The data in Table 12.3 illustrate one pattern of means that might be observed. For these data, nobody would purchase brand B, because it is never the favorite brand within a given segment. Yet, if the ratings are averaged across segments, brand B is the most liked. Examination of the aggregated means might lead to the conclusion that preferences are unrelated to purchase behavior (since the most liked product has the poorest market share), and this is indeed the case at the aggregate level. However, a different conclusion results at the more "idiographic-based," segment level.

Wainer (1986) described a set of data that also exhibited a divergence in conclusions as a function of level of analysis. In 1980 and 1984, mean SAT scores in the United States were calculated for both Whites and non-Whites. Overall, the mean SAT score for Whites increased, on the average, 8 points over the course of the four years. For non-Whites, the corresponding increase was 15 points. Based on this outcome, one would expect the mean increase for the total sample of Whites and non-Whites combined to be somewhere between 8 and 15 points. However, the mean increase for the combined sample from 1980 to 1984 was 7 points. As it turns out, the number of non-Whites who took the SAT increased by almost 26,000 from 1980

TABLE 12.3　Mean Liking Ratings for Three Brands

Segment	A	Brand B	C
1	10[a]	9	1
2	9[a]	7	3
3	1	7	8[a]
4	2	9	10[a]
Mean	5.5	8.0	5.5

a. Chosen alternative.

to 1984, whereas the number of Whites decreased by approximately 34,000. This increase in the relative proportion of non-Whites taking the test, coupled with the tendency of this group to score, on the average, lower than Whites, yielded the state of affairs described above. An aggregate analysis of all individuals would lead to a different conclusion from that found if segments of the aggregate are analyzed separately.

A final example concerns the relationship between intended family size and actual family size as documented in the sociological literature. A group of newly married couples are asked how many children they would like to have in their completed family. Twenty years later, the same group of married couples is investigated in order to determine how many children they actually had. The mean intended family size when the couples married was 2.3 and the mean number of children that they actually had was also 2.3. At the aggregate level, there is close correspondence between how many children people said they intended to have and the number of children they in fact had. However, if the family size intentions are examined relative to actual family size on a couple-by-couple basis, then the correspondence between the two variables is weak. This is due to the fact that some couples had fewer children than they initially predicted, whereas other couples had more children than they initially predicted; the underestimates cancel the overestimates, yielding comparable aggregate-level means.

This same principle applies to the analysis of the stability of attitudes over time. At an aggregate level, the mean attitude score for a group of individuals may change relatively little over time. However, group stability does not imply that attitudes are stable at the individual level. Considerable change can occur, with some individuals shifting their attitudes toward the more positive side and other individuals shifting their attitudes toward the more negative side. At the aggregate level, these changes will tend to offset each other when averaged across individuals.

ANALYSIS OF FREQUENCIES AND
THE NORMATIVE-NOMOTHETIC PERSPECTIVE

As a final illustration, consider an analysis involving a contingency table. Simpson (1951) describes a "paradox" when analyzing contingency tables that represents yet another manifestation of the principles highlighted above. Simpson's paradox refers to the fact that if two or more contingency tables are collapsed into one, the resulting table may show a relationship between variables different from those shown by any of the original tables (Hintzman, 1980). Assume we are studying the effects of an interviewing training course on success in getting a job. Table 12.4 shows the contingency tables for males and females considered separately as well as the aggregate table collapsed across gender. The aggregate table suggests that there is no effect of the training on hiring decision. That is, out of the people who received the training, 50% were hired and 50% were not hired. The same is true for those who did not receive the training. However, if we now examine the separate contingency tables, we find that, in general, training had a positive impact on hiring for males and a negative impact on hiring for females. By collapsing across gender, the differential effect of training on males as opposed to females is masked.

Previously, we stated five principles of nomothetic-idiographic divergence with respect to the correlation between two variables, X and Y, in the presence of a third variable, Z. We can now state an additional principle concerning the independence (or lack of correlation) of X and Y:

- *Principle 6:* Suppose that X and Y are correlated with Z. If X and Y are found to be uncorrelated when analyzed across (i.e., ignoring) Z, then X and Y, by definition, are correlated at levels of Z.

A REPRISE

It should be obvious from the above discussion that the conclusions about the (causal) relationships between variables will differ depending on the level of analysis. The normative-nomothetic approach permits statements about the behavior of an individual relative to other individuals and always in the context of group-level descriptors. Under certain circumstances,

TABLE 12.4 Analysis of Contingency Tables

Male

	No Training	*Training*	*Total*
Hired	.08	.15	.23
Not hired	.06	.09	.15
Total	.14	.24	

Female

	No Training	*Training*	*Total*
Hired	.04	.23	.27
Not hired	.06	.29	.35
Total	.10	.52	

Aggregate

	No Training	*Training*	*Total*
Hired	.12	.38	.50
Not hired	.12	.38	.50
Total	.24	.76	

conclusions made at the normative-nomothetic level will generalize to the idiographic level. But these circumstances may be the exception rather than the rule. The above examples demonstrate the divergence that can occur between the two approaches. The above examples show that the types of conclusions one makes depends on the level of analysis that is being performed. Labels in the literature, such as "Simpson's paradox" or "Lamp's paradox," can be misleading because, in certain ways, there really is no paradox. There are just different levels of analysis. Normative-nomothetic analyses are appropriate given that conclusions are made in the relative-to-others, group-level context in which they are performed (although, as illustrated by some of our examples, causal inferences can be problematic even when interpretation is restricted to the appropriate level of analysis). It is our belief that many social/personality psychologists desire to build causal models that go beyond the normative-nomothetic level of analysis and that reflect causal relations that are operating in a wide range of individuals, considered separately. When a theorist states that "attitudes influence behavior," the theorist might want to know that this is true for at least *some* people considered individually. Normative-nomothetic analysis can be problematic for making such statements and, in this regard, aggregate-nomothetic analysis is worthy of development.

Some critics might be tempted to conclude from the preceding discussion that our current statistical methods are inadequate for making valid inferences about individuals from group-level data. After all, four major forms of data analysis were found to be wanting in this regard. The issue, however, is not a statistical one. Rather, it concerns the data to which the statistics are applied. More specifically, statistics are applied to a set of numbers, and it is only when these numbers are generated on an across-subject, normative-nomothetic basis and interpreted without sensitivity to the level of analysis that the problems described above come into play.

The challenge for the idiographic scientist is to develop methods and analytic procedures that permit the exploration of relationships between variables on a single-subject basis. In order to do so, variability on the constructs in question often (but not always) must be within-subjects in nature. This means that certain relationships, by definition, cannot be studied on an idiographic basis. For example, the relationship between gender and attitudes toward abortion must be studied from a normative-nomothetic perspective, because it is impossible to vary gender on a within-subjects basis. By the same token, traditional uses of within-subjects analyses do *not*, by fiat, represent a form of idiographic analysis. For example, a typical within-subjects experiment might compare mean scores of the same group of subjects under two different conditions, A and B, in which the relationship between the independent variable (condition A versus condition B) and the dependent variable (Y) is evaluated by means of a correlated-groups t-test. Each mean score is calculated across individuals and, because the relationship is inferred based on differences of across-individual means, the analysis is normative-nomothetic. It is true that error variance due to individual background is removed by virtue of the within-subjects design. But this does not alter the normative-nomothetic nature of the analysis and the necessity to make conclusions accordingly. A truly idiographic analysis assesses the relationship between two or more variables for each individual separately. Aggregate-nomothetic statistics are then used to convey the generalizability of the relationship across a large number of individuals.

AN EXAMPLE OF AN
IDIOGRAPHIC/AGGREGATE-NOMOTHETIC PARADIGM

As stated above, we do not argue for the superiority of one approach or another for purposes of building theories of social behavior. All of the approaches have their rightful place in the development of theory, as long as the assumptions and limitations of each are clearly understood. In this section, we describe an idiographic approach that we have been developing for purposes of studying the relationships among beliefs, attitudes, and behavior. The framework is still incomplete and numerous issues remain to be resolved. However, we believe that we have established a potentially useful starting point that stands in contrast to current attitude theories. The approach is described only briefly here. More elaborate descriptions can be found in Jaccard and Wood (1986) and Jaccard, Wan, and Wood (1988).

The framework conceptualizes the belief-attitude-behavior relationship from a decision-making perspective. In general, behavioral decisions can be classified into three types. *Impulsive* decisions are those determined by impulsive or emotional reactions, without reflection. *Routine* decisions concern familiar situations in which decisions are made with little reflection and in accordance with habits, customs, or moral/social rules. *Thoughtful* decisions are made after thought is given to such factors as the problem situation, the alternative courses of action, and the probable consequences of each course of action. When making a decision in a familiar situation, the individual typically accepts the suggestion of impulse, habit, custom, or rule, without serious reflection. Most behavioral decisions in everyday life are of this character. However, when the decision is perceived as being important or when impulse, habit, or custom is questioned, then the individual will reflect on the matter, considering one or more courses of action. Our framework is concerned with thoughtful behavioral decisions.

There are at least eight activities that an individual can engage in during decision making. First is problem recognition, in which an individual determines that a problem exists and that a decision must be considered. Second is goal identification, in which the individual specifies, a priori, the purpose of the decision; that is, the ideal outcome of the decision. Third is option generation/identification, in which the individual thinks of potential alternative solutions to the problem at hand. Fourth is information search, in which the individual seeks information, either about what additional options might be available or about the properties of one or more of the options under consideration. Fifth is the assessment of option information, in which the individual considers the information he or she has about different decision options. The term *information* is used in a general sense and refers to any consequence or concept subjectively associated with a given decision option. It is similar to the concept of "belief" in the attitude literature. When considering the information about the options, the individual forms a preference structure. Specifically, the individual forms an attitude toward performing each option. Given *p* decision options, the *preference structure* is the set of *p* attitudes. Consistent with Fishbein and Ajzen (1975) and most contemporary attitudes theories, an attitude is defined as a general feeling of favorableness or unfavorableness with respect to the attitude object (in this case, the decision option). Sixth is the choice process, in which one of the decision options is chosen for purposes of future behavioral enactment. The choice usually will be some function of the individual's preference structure. Seventh is behavioral translation, in which the individual translates the decision into overt behavior. Eighth is postdecision evaluation, in which the individual reflects on the decision after the chosen option has been enacted and evaluates the decision process in light of the outcomes that have resulted.

Not all of the activities will necessarily be performed by the individual, nor must they be performed in the sequence described. Space limitations do not permit consideration of each activity here. Our primary focus will be on characterizing the information that an individual possesses about a set of decision options, and how this information is integrated to form a preferences structure and choice.

Preferences structures. Many behaviors of interest to attitude theorists can be conceptualized as a choice between behavioral alternatives (e.g., choice of a birth control method, choice of a career). As noted above, the individual may be said to have an attitude toward each of the behavioral alternatives. Consistent with subjective-expected-utility theory, it can be argued that an individual will choose to perform that option toward which the most positive attitude is held. Empirical support for this proposition is presented in four studies reported in Jaccard (1981) and Jaccard and Becker (1985). (However, see Jaccard & Wood, 1986, for a discussion of instances in which this principle does not hold.)

This rather simple formulation of the relationship between attitudes and behavior can be applied to a single individual. A measure of the individual's attitude toward each decision option is obtained, using standard semantic differential scales (see Jaccard & Wood, 1986). The predicted behavior is the behavioral option that has the most positive attitude. The consistency between attitudes and behavior can thus be assessed for any given individual (i.e., does the individual perform the behavior toward which the most positive attitude is held). Measurement assumptions about response metrics are minimal (in contrast to normative-nomothetic analysis). The only assumption is that an individual interprets the scale the same way when rating different behavioral alternatives. There are no weights to be estimated, as in the regression approaches characterized by equation 1. Other variables, such as norms, are assumed to influence behavior through attitudes, as will be elaborated shortly. The results of attitude-behavior analysis can be reported in terms of aggregate-nomothetic statistics, namely, the proportion of individuals exhibiting attitude-behavior consistency and how this varies for different subject populations. Jaccard and Wood (1986) provide a formal comparison of this approach with the more traditional regression approaches based on normative-nomothetic methods.

One of the major determinants of the preference structure is the individual's beliefs about the various decision options. These beliefs are represented in the form of a *perceptual structure matrix*. We will now describe the nature of this matrix and the types of idiographic analyses that can be performed to gain insights into its fundamental character. We then describe procedures for identifying relationships between the perceptual structure matrix and preference structures.

Perceptual structure analysis. For a given decision topic (e.g., choice of a birth control method), the individual will be aware of a set of options from which to choose (e.g., birth control pills, condoms, diaphragm). These options are typically elicited by asking the individual to list all of the options he or she can think of (e.g., "Name all of the methods of birth control that you can think of."). Each option varies on one or more informational dimensions (e.g., effectiveness in preventing pregnancy, health risks, cost, convenience in using). The content of these dimensions is determined by asking the individual to name all of the factors he or she would consider when evaluating the different options. The dimensions vary in their importance to the individual (e.g., effectiveness in preventing pregnancy may be more important to the individual than the cost of the method). Measures of the subjective importance of each dimension in evaluating options also are obtained. The perceptual structure matrix characterizes the individual's perceptions of each option on each dimension, as illustrated in Table 12.5. The cell entries refer to the extent to which the individual believes the option is "good" or "bad" (typically measured on a -5 to $+5$ rating scale) on the dimension in question. For example, the pill might be perceived as being "very good" in terms of its effectiveness in preventing pregnancy, but "bad" in terms of the health risks associated with it.[3]

Given an individual's data for a perceptual structure matrix, numerous insights into beliefs about the decision topic can be gained. For example, for any given pair of options (e.g., the diaphragm and the condom), the degree to which the individual perceives the options as being similar across the dimensions can be calculated. This would take the form of a Euclidean distance score in which the difference between ratings of the options on

TABLE 12.5 Perceptual Structure Matrix

	Option 1	*Option 2*	*Option 3*	. . .	*Option p*
Dimension 1	R_{11}	R_{12}	R_{13}	. . .	R_{1p}
Dimension 2	R_{21}	R_{22}	R_{23}	. . .	R_{2p}
Dimension 3	R_{31}	R_{32}	R_{33}	. . .	R_{3p}
.					
.					
Dimension m	R_{m1}	R_{m2}	R_{m3}	. . .	R_{mp}

NOTE: Cell entries represent ratings of each option on a given dimension in terms of how good or bad the option is on the dimension.

each dimension is computed (e.g., the rating for the diaphragm on the dimension of effectiveness is subtracted from the rating for condoms on the dimension of effectiveness). The differences are squared and summed across all dimensions, yielding a distance score. A score of zero indicates that the ratings of the two options are identical. Larger scores imply greater differences in the ratings. Given p options, a $p \times p$ matrix of dissimilarity scores can be computed and subjected to cluster analysis (or multidimensional scaling [MDS] analysis). The cluster analysis will identify groups of options that are perceived as similar yet distinct from the other clusters of options. In our research, we have found considerable individual differences in the number of clusters of options that result from a cluster analysis. Some individuals exhibit a small number of clusters, indicating that they do not perceive many differences among the various options. Other individuals exhibit a large number of clusters, indicating that the different options are viewed as distinct.

A similar analysis can be conducted for dimensions. A distance score between any given pair of dimensions can be computed by calculating the difference between ratings of the two dimensions on each option (e.g., the rating for the diaphragm on the dimension of effectiveness is subtracted from the rating for the diaphragm on cost). The differences are then squared and summed across all options, yielding a distance score. A score of zero indicates that the ratings of the two dimensions across the options are identical (for example, when effectiveness was perceived as "good," cost also was seen as being "good"; when effectiveness was perceived as "bad," cost also was seen as "bad"). Larger distance scores imply great differences in the ratings, indicating that the dimensions are distinct. Given m dimensions, an $m \times m$ matrix of dissimilarity scores can be computed and subjected to a cluster (or MDS) analysis. This analysis reveals clusters of dimensions that tend to covary in the same fashion and at the same level as one shifts from one option to another. In this way, the extent to which an individual perceives certain dimensions as being related can be isolated. Again, we have observed considerable individual differences in the number of clusters of dimensions. Some individuals exhibit a relatively small number of clusters, indicating that variations in any one dimension are tied to variations in other dimensions. Other individuals exhibit a relatively large number of clusters, indicating perceptions of dimension independence.

For a given individual, the perceptual structure matrix can be transformed to a *relative score matrix*, which involves calculating the mean rating and standard deviation for each dimension across options (see Table 12.6). The scores within a row are then standardized relative to the mean and standard deviation for that row. The mean score for a given row indicates the tendency for the individual to view the options, on the average, as positive (large scores) or negative (low scores). The standard deviation reflects variability in options across the dimension. A small standard deviation would indicate that options tend to be perceived as being the same on the dimension. In general, dimensions with small standard deviations will be unimportant in determining the choice of one option over another, because all options are perceived as being the same on that dimension. Finally, the within-cell standard scores indicate how "unique" an option is on the dimension (relative to the mean and standard deviation).

It is also possible to compute a correlation (for a given individual) between the ratings on a dimension (across options) and the attitude ratings comprising the preference structure (i.e., the global ratings of favorableness-unfavorableness for each option). A large correlation (or some other index of fit) indicates that the variation of attitudes within the preference structure coincides with variation in the perceptions of the options on the dimension in question. In this fashion, the relationship between beliefs and attitudes can explored on an individual level, albeit in a somewhat crude fashion.

Error Theories. The above analyses are conducted in the context of measurement error. Although our research has generally suggested that measurement error is minimal, it is important that the potential biasing effects of measurement error be recognized. With regard to preference structures, we typically obtain attitude ratings on three separate occasions,

TABLE 12.6 Relative Score Matrix

	Option 1	*Option 2*	*Option 3*	. . .	*Option p*	Mean	sd
Dimension 1	Z_{11}	Z_{12}	Z_{13}	. . .	Z_{1p}	M_1	sd_1
Dimension 2	Z_{21}	Z_{22}	Z_{23}	. . .	Z_{2p}	M_2	sd_2
Dimension 3	Z_{31}	Z_{32}	Z_{33}	. . .	Z_{3p}	M_3	sd_3
.							
.							
.							
Dimension m	Z_{m1}	Z_{m2}	Z_{m3}	. . .	Z_{mp}	M_m	sd_m

NOTE: Cell entries represent standard scores relative to the mean and standard deviation of a given row.

and use the mean attitude score for a given option across the three sessions as an index of the "true" score. Differences between means for any two options are then evaluated relative to an index of the average unreliability. This is accomplished using a one-way analysis of variance model, in which the different options define the levels of the analysis, and replicates are the ratings in the three sessions. The mean square within constitutes the index of unreliability, and all between-option differences are evaluated relative to this mean square (e.g., by means of an *F*-ratio). This strategy is similar to the error theory of functional measurement (Anderson, 1982). The major assumption is that within-cell variation reflects only random measurement error. The approach is problematic if the number of options is small, but the problem can be offset in some circumstances by increasing the number of repeated assessments.

A similar approach can be used for the perceptual structure matrix. If repetition of the entire matrix is impractical, then randomly selected cells of the matrix can be reassessed in the same experimental session, to provide at least some appreciation for the amount of measurement error that is operating. The error indices can also be used in the cluster analyses, to help define cutting values that represent more than just measurement error.

Linking perceptual structures and preference structures. In the preceding section, we described a correlational method for assessing the link between attitudes and beliefs for a given individual. A more sophisticated analysis of this link can be accomplished using functional measurement procedures in the context of Anderson's information integration theory. We will briefly describe the approach that we use. An empirical evaluation of our methodology is presented in Jaccard and Becker (1985).

According to information integration theory, the way in which individuals integrate information to form attitudes can be characterized, in many cases, in terms of cognitive algebra. In general, two broad classes of integration rules can be distinguished. *Compensatory* rules are those in which the negative features of an option can be offset by positive features of the option. In essence, the positive qualities "compensate" for the negative qualities in the formation of a judgment of favorableness/unfavorableness of an option. *Noncompensatory* rules are those in which positive qualities do not offset negative qualities. The occurrence of a negative feature on a given dimension may lead to a negative attitude, independent of the positive features of that option on other dimensions. Within each of these general classes of integration rules, there are submodels of the integration process. For example, included among the different types of compensatory rules are the constant weight averaging rule, the differential weight averaging rule, the constant weight summation rule, the differential weight summation rule, and so on. Functional measurement methodology permits the investigator to gain perspectives on the type of integration rule that is operating, as well as how the individual pieces of information are "valued" by the individual. A powerful feature of the methodology is that it can be applied on an idiographic basis.

Functional measurement usually involves factorially manipulating different types of information and then obtaining measures of attitude toward each of the resulting hypothetical stimuli. For example, eight hypothetical methods of birth control can be described as a result of a $2 \times 2 \times 2$ factorial design manipulating effectiveness, health risks, and convenience. Attitudes toward each of the eight birth control methods would then be obtained and analyzed via functional measurement methods. Our research has suggested that the number of dimensions that are potentially relevant to a decision topic, such as the choice of a birth control method, frequently ranges between 10 and 15. Obviously, it is not feasible to manipulate all dimensions orthogonally, because the number of hypothetical options would be overwhelming. The number of stimuli can be reduced by assuming, for example, additive integration rules and using a fractional factorial design. However, this approach is unsatisfactory because the nature of the integration rule must be assumed and not empirically tested.

One solution is to manipulate only a small number of informational dimensions. In our framework, we typically manipulate three dimensions with three levels per factor. The dimensions can differ for each individual studied and are selected by the individual from a list of relevant informational dimensions. The individual rank orders the importance of the dimensions, and the three highest ranked dimensions are used to construct the 27 (3 × 3 × 3) hypothetical stimuli. Each individual responds to the same stimuli in the sense that the three most subjectively important dimensions are manipulated, although the actual content of the dimensions might differ between individuals.

Given that one has identified the dimensions to be manipulated, the selection of values that will be used to manipulate a dimension is of primary importance. The selection of a particular set of values can influence the outcome of the analysis. To the extent that the values are selected arbitrarily, the results of the analysis will also be arbitrary. When forming an evaluative judgment about a behavioral option, people probably translate specific values on a dimension into three to five general subjective categories on the dimension of interest. For example, a birth control method that is 75% effective might be translated into the category "moderately bad" on a dimension of effectiveness and an attitude formed accordingly. Each category will have a range of values associated with it. For example, any birth control method that has an effectiveness rate between 65% and 75% might be classified as "moderately bad." Our methodology manipulates informational dimensions in terms of three general categories, corresponding to "moderately bad" on the dimension, "neutral," and "moderately good" on the dimension. These verbal descriptors are quite general and can be applied to both qualitative and quantitative informational dimensions. They also are directly tied to the ratings made in the context of the perceptual structure matrix, an important aspect of the methodology.

Given the stimuli, the individual completes the functional measurement task by rating the 27 stimuli on the same attitude scale used to assess the preference structure. The task is completed on three occasions, and functional analysis is then undertaken to isolate the relevant integration rule and the subjective values of the response dimensions (see Anderson, this volume; or Jaccard & Becker, 1985.) An advantage of this approach is that a formal error theory is applicable, thus permitting the researcher to consider the effects of measurement error.

One criticism of functional measurement methodology is that it involves hypothetical stimuli. Analyses in such situations may yield conclusions that do not correspond to how beliefs are related to attitudes in real-world applications. Jaccard and Becker (1985) have described a procedure for evaluating this criticism on an idiographic basis. Consider a choice situation involving 10 existing methods of birth control. Based on the functional measurement analysis, a mathematical model can be specified that describes the relationship between beliefs and attitudes in the context of the hypothetical stimuli. The data from the perceptual structure matrix (that contains ratings of each existing method on each informational dimension) can be substituted into the mathematical model, yielding a predicted attitude for each existing birth control method. The correspondence between this predicted preference structure and the observed preference structure can then be evaluated. A poor fit suggests that the functional measurement conclusions may be limited, while a good fit is consistent with the validity of the conclusions.

Summary. Preference structure analysis, perceptual structure analysis, and functional measurement analysis can all be applied to a single individual. The analyses provide perspectives on the relationship between attitudes and behavior, or the relationships among decision options, the relationships among beliefs, and the relationships between beliefs and attitudes, all within the context of formal error theories. The framework can be applied to multiple individuals and the results of the analysis described in aggregate-nomothetic terms (for elaborations, see Anderson, this volume; Jaccard & Wood, 1986). In some of our nomothetic-level analyses, we have been forced to adopt a normative-nomothetic approach where we would prefer not to, because of the lack of adequate analytic tools to do otherwise. However, we are attempting to develop such tools. The ability to analyze the relationships among beliefs, attitudes, and behavior for a single individual stands in sharp contrast to the more popular attitude theories in the literature. For example, using Fishbein's expectancy-value framework, it is impossible to assess the relationship among these variables without recourse to normative-nomothetic analysis.

CONCLUDING COMMENTS

In this chapter, we have highlighted three approaches toward the development and evaluation of social theory: an idiographic approach, an aggregate-nomothetic approach and a normative-nomothetic approach. The first two are intimately linked and contrast considerably with the latter approach. We have noted numerous situations in which nomothetic analysis of data will yield different perspectives on the relationships among variables relative to what is known to be operating idiographically. Social/personality research is dominated by a normative-nomothetic approach to theory specification and theory testing. Although this is an entirely legitimate enterprise, it does require the researcher to maintain the proper frame of reference when discussing the results of his or her research. Too often, such researchers state implications in terms of individual-based phenomena. We have presented six principles that yield perspectives on nomothetic-idiographic divergence. Although these principles were formulated in correlational terms, they apply to any measure of association, including those within analysis of variance frameworks and contingency tables. Idiographic theories and methods are not, contrary to popular belief, incompatible with the development of general laws of human behavior. It is our belief that increased attention to this method of conducting science will ultimately increase our total appreciation for and understanding of the complexity of human behavior and experience.

We have also described briefly a framework for studying the relationships among beliefs, attitudes, decisions, and behavior that can be applied at the idiographic level. Once the relationships between these variables are established on a per individual basis, the data can be aggregated to form group characterizations of the relationships among variables.

The approach also can be integrated with normative-nomothetic methods. For example, we have conducted analyses to compare the consistency of attitudes and behaviors for males as opposed to females in the domain of birth control. Results have shown that, relative to males, females are more likely to exhibit attitude-behavior consistency. This result was not obtained using traditional multiple regression procedures for analysis, but was revealed only when we combined our idiographic approach with the normative-nomothetic approach of group comparison. We do not view the aggregate-nomothetic and normative-nomothetic approaches as necessarily incompatible or in conflict. Rather, they represent different forms of analysis, each yielding certain types of perspectives on a phenomenon of interest. Examples of other domains that are relevant to social/personality research where idiographic and aggregate-nomothetic perspectives are being utilized are discussed in Mancuso and Shaw (1988).

NOTES

1. It is not always the case that operationalizations of constructs will be unique for every individual. There frequently will be cases in which a construct manifests itself in the same way for a wide range of individuals.

2. Several reviewers of an earlier draft of this chapter felt that the misleading nature of the regression coefficients in the examples was somehow an artifact of the correlations

between the predictor variables. This is not the case. Virtually any size correlation between predictor measures can exist and given a large enough sample size a pattern of nonhomogeneous weights can be introduced that will render causal interpretations ambiguous.

3. Normative beliefs, as represented in equation 1, are treated like any other type of informational dimension that ultimately may influence the preference structure. There exists no evidence within the idiographic framework that suggests norms should be treated differently. Controversy currently exists in nomothetic analyses about whether norms and attitudes need to be treated separately. Detailed consideration of this issue is beyond the scope of this chapter.

REFERENCES

Allport, G. W. (1973). *Personality, a psychological interpretation*. New York: Henry Holt.

Allport, G. W. (1960). *Personality and social encounter*. Boston: Beacon.

Anderson, N. H. (1982). *Methods of information integration*. New York: Academic Press.

Bagozzi, R.P. (1981). Attitudes, intentions, and behavior: A test of some key hypotheses. *Journal of Personality and Social Psychology, 41*, 607–627.

Barlow, D. H., & Hersen, M. (1984). *Single case experimental designs*. New York: Pergamon.

Bem, D. J. (1983). Constructing a theory of the triple typology: Some (second) thoughts on nomothetic and idiographic approaches to personality. *Journal of Personality, 51*, 566–577.

Birnbaum, M., & Stegner, S. (1981). Measuring the importance of cues in judgment for individuals: Subjective theories of IQ as a function of heredity and environment. *Journal of Experimental Social Psychology, 17*, 159–182.

Brinberg, D., & Durand, J. (1983). Eating at fast-food restaurants: An analysis using two behavioral intention models. *Journal of Applied Social Psychology, 13*, 459–472.

Connors, C. K., & Wells, K. C. (1982). Single-case designs in psychopharmacology. In A. E. Kazdin & A. H. Tuma (Eds), *Single-case research designs* (pp. 2–14). San Francisco: Jossey-Bass.

Crosby, L. A., & Muehling, D. D. (1983). External variables and the Fishbein model: Mediation, moderation or direct effects? *Advances in Consumer Research, 9*, 94–97.

Denenberg, V. H. (1982). Comparative psychology and single-subject research. In A. E. Kazdin & A. H. Tuma (Eds.), *Single-case research designs* (pp. 15–22). San Francisco: Jossey-Bass.

Fishbein, M., & Ajzen, I. (1975). *Belief, attitude, intention, and behavior: An introduction to theory and research*. Reading, MA: Addison-Wesley.

Fisher, W. A. (1984). Predicting contraceptive behavior among university men: The role of emotions and behavioral intentions. *Journal of Applied Social Psychology, 14*, 104–123.

Flexer, A. (1981). Homogenizing the 2 × 2 contingency table: A method for removing dependencies due to subject and item differences. *Psychological Review, 88,* 327–339.

Fredericks, A. J., & Dossett, D. L. (1983). Attitude-behavior relations: A comparison of the Fishbein-Ajzen and the Bentler-Speckart models. *Journal of Personality and Social Psychology, 45,* 501–512.

Gorsuch, R. L., & Ortberg, J. (1983). Moral obligation and attitudes: Their relation to behavioral intentions. *Journal of Personality and Social Psychology, 44,* 1025–1028.

Hintzman, D. L. (1980). Simpson's paradox and the analysis of memory retrieval. *Psychological Review, 87,* 398–410.

Jaccard, J. (1981). Attitudes and behavior: Implications of behavioral alternatives. *Journal of Experimental Social Psychology, 17,* 286–307.

Jaccard, J., & Becker, M. (1985). Attitudes and behavior: An information integration perspective. *Journal of Experimental Social Psychology, 21,* 440–465.

Jaccard, J., Turrisi, R., & Wan, C. (1989). *Moderated multiple regression: The analysis of interaction effects with continuous variables.* Newbury Park, CA: Sage.

Jaccard, J., & Wan, C. K. (1986). Cross-cultural methods for the study of behavioral decision making. *Journal of Cross-Cultural Psychology, 17,* 123–149.

Jaccard, J., Wan, C., & Wood, G. (1988). Idiothetic methods for the analysis of behavioral decision making: Computer applications. In J. Mancuso & M. Shaw (Eds.), *Cognition and personal structure: Computer access and analysis* (pp. 134–148). New York: Praeger.

Jaccard, J., & Wood, G. (1986). An idiothetic approach to behavioral decision making. In D. Brinberg & R. Lutz (Eds.), *Perspectives on methodology in consumer behavior* (pp. 64–82). New York: Springer-Verlag.

Johnston, J. M. (1982). The role of individual data in laboratory investigations of operant conditioning. In A. E. Kazdin & A. H. Tuma (Eds.), *Single-case research designs* (pp. 28–36). San Francisco: Jossey-Bass.

Kazdin, A. E. (1982). Single-case experimental designs in clinical research and practice. In A. E. Kazdin & A. H. Tuma (Eds.), *Single-case research designs.* San Francisco: Jossey-Bass.

Kenrick, D. T., & Stringfield, D. O. (1980). Personality traits and the eye of the beholder: Crossing some traditional philosophical boundries in the search for consistency in all of the people. *Psychological Review, 87,* 88–104.

Lamiell, J. T. (1981). Toward an idiothetic psychology of personality. *American Psychologist, 36,* 276–289.

Lamiell, J. T., Foss, M. A., Larsen, R. J., & Hempel, A. M. (1983). Studies in intuitive personology from an idiothetic point of view: Implications for personal theory. *Journal of Personality, 51,* 438–467.

Mancuso, J., & Shaw, M. (1988). *Cognition and personal structures: Computer access and analysis.* New York: Praeger.

Manstead, A.S.R., Proffitt, C., & Smart, J. L. (1983). Predicting and understanding mothers' infant-feeding intentions and behavior: Testing the theory of reasoned action. *Journal of Personality and Social Psychology, 44,* 657–671.

Martin, E. (1981). Simpson's paradox resolved: A reply to Hintzman. *Psychological Review, 88,* 372–374.

Osgood, C., Suci, G., & Tannenbaum, P. (1957). *The measurement of meaning.* Urbana: University of Illinois Press.

Parducci, A. (1965). Category judgment: A range frequency model. *Psychological Review, 66*, 27–44.

Paunonen, S. V., & Jackson, D. N. (1986). Nomothetic and idiothetic measurement in personality. *Journal of Personality, 54*, 447–459.

Runyan, W. M. (1983). Idiographic goals and methods in the study of lives. *Journal of Personality, 51*, 413–437.

Simpson, E. H. (1951). The interpretation of interaction in contingency tables. *Journal of the Royal Statistical Society, Series B, 13*, 238–241.

Triandis, H. C. (1977). *Interpersonal behavior.* Monterey, CA: Brooks/Cole.

Tulving, E., Watkins, M. (1975). Structure of memory traces. *Psychological Review, 80*, 352–373.

Wainer, H. (1986). Minority contributions to the SAT score turnaround: An example of Simpson's paradox. *Journal of Educational Statistics, 11*, 239–244.

Wegener, B. (1982). *Social attitudes and psychophysical measurement.* Hillsdale, NJ: Erlbaum.

Wiggins, J. (1973). *Personality and prediction.* Reading MA.: Addison-Wesley.

Wittenbraker, J., Gibbs, B. L. & Kahle, L. R. (1983). Seat belt attitudes, habits, and behaviors: An adaptive amendment to the Fishbein model. *Journal of Applied Social Psychology, 13*, 406–421.

Wyer, R. (1975). *Cognitive organization and change.* Hillsdale, NJ: Erlbaum.

NOTES